THE POWER OF TIANANMEN

THE POWER OF TIANANMEN

State-Society
Relations and the
1989 Beijing Student
Movement

DINGXIN ZHAO

THE UNIVERSITY OF CHICAGO PRESS
CHICAGO AND LONDON

DINGXIN ZHAO is assistant professor of sociology at the
University of Chicago.

The University of Chicago Press, Chicago 60637
The University of Chicago Press, Ltd., London
© 2001 by The University of Chicago
All rights reserved. Published 2001
Printed in the United States of America

09 08 07 06 05 04 03 02 01   1 2 3 4 5

ISBN: 0-226-98260-2 (CLOTH)

Library of Congress Cataloging-in-Publication Data
Zhao, Dingxin
    The power of Tiananmen : state-society relations and the 1989
  Beijing student movement / Dingxin Zhao
      p.   cm.
    Includes bibliographical references and index.
    ISBN 0-226-98260-2 (cloth : alk. paper)
     1. China—History—Tiananmen Square Incident, 1989.
  I. Title.
DS779.32 .Z49   2001
951.05'8—dc21   00-057685

In memory of

my grandmother Wang Cuidi

(王翠娣),

who raised my brother, sister, and me

in our uneasy childhood

Contents

Foreword

In *Dreamtigers*, Jorge Luis Borges tells of an Argentine boy who disappeared in an Indian raid. Years later, the bereaved parents heard of a young man who might be their lost son. Although the Indian-raised man was averse to towns and unable to speak their tongue, the town-dwellers brought their putative son home. When the man arrived at their house, he hesitated at the entrance, then suddenly raced through the foyer and two patios, entered the kitchen, reached into the hearth, and pulled out a knife he had hidden there as a boy. "His eyes shone with joy," continues Borges,

> and his parents wept because they had found their son. Perhaps this recollection was followed by others, but the Indian could not live within walls, and one day he went in search of his wilderness. I wonder what he felt in that dizzying moment when past and present became one. I wonder whether the lost son was reborn and died in that instant of ecstasy; and whether he ever managed to recognize . . . his parents and his home. ("The Captive")

Can any of us travelers ever really go home again? When Chinese troops ruthlessly cleared protesters from Beijing's Tiananmen Square on June 3 and 4, 1989, Dingxin Zhao was completing an entomology doctoral thesis in Montreal. Three weeks earlier he had returned to Canada from a month in Shanghai, his home. During his visit, Zhao had witnessed early stages of the mobilization that culminated in June's government massacre near the Gate of Heavenly Peace. Focusing the eyes of a passionate witness with the newfound spectacles of a skilled sociologist, he has since then become an expert analyst of the Tiananmen mobilization. He has recognized his home, but as only an insider who has journeyed elsewhere can do.

The Power of Tiananmen concerns power in two different senses of the word: as in power struggles and as in the power of an idea or experience. First comes the exercise of power on both sides of the state-society relation on which Zhao pivots his analysis. The book shows how the activation of power in conflict transforms existing structures of power. Second, we have the power of the events Zhao relates to dramatize China's political problems, galvanize political action within China, and redefine the regime's character after the fact. Despite the students' short-run defeat, we learn how the struggle redefined relations between citizens and regime.

Intersection of the two kinds of power poses profound questions about description and explanation of political processes: Given the demonstrated influence of codes, practices, and relations embedded in previous Chinese history, how can outsiders reconstruct, recognize, comprehend, and explain the Chinese struggles of 1989? Assuming some capacity of explication, empathy, and analogy to clarify what happened on the ground, how can analysts translate that grounded experience effectively into idioms of social science developed elsewhere? How can the events in question simultaneously result from historically formed local conditions and be explicable in terms of broadly applicable principles? Let us call these the problems of *reconstruction, translation,* and *generalization.* The three problems confront all historically grounded social science, but they appear with particular vividness in Dingxin Zhao's account of Tiananmen.

Reconstruction? Despite being a savvy insider, Zhao faced serious problems of reconstruction. For one thing, he conducted his main interviews between December 1992 and May 1993, speaking with participants and observers about events that had occurred three or four years earlier. He was unpacking stories that inevitably selected from his respondents' many actions and sentiments of 1989, built in their own self-representations, and responded to their subsequent experiences. He prudently scrutinized the stories with care, cross-checked accounts with each other, and used documentary evidence to contextualize, amplify, and correct them. Still, he had to reconstruct the whole complex of signals and meanings that had prevailed in 1989 when none of his respondents could themselves do so in retrospect. It is a measure of his subtlety that he plausibly reconstitutes meanings, audience by audience, for such complex events as the so-called Xinhua Gate Bloody Incident (April 20) and the hunger strike assembly of May 13.

Translation? Having performed his own reconstructions, Zhao still faced the difficulty of conveying his descriptions and explanations to readers who had vastly less knowledge of Chinese life than he. He actually undertook a double translation. The first rendered Chinese events in western (and more particularly English-language) idioms. The second translated from the language of participant observation to the abstractions of contemporary western sociology. Thus the sprawling Chinese system of power translates into the State as complex interactions among intellectuals, students, workers, peasants, and entrepreneurs translate into Society.

Zhao makes his translations effective by criticizing, reshaping, and illustrating available analogies topic by topic. He identifies connections between the 1989 mobilization and shifts in state-society relations; good and bad analogies to western social movements; social geography as a base for student activation; prevailing discourses as crystallizations of available meanings; interaction among media, participants, and events on the ground in the construction of shared understandings. Even readers who know little of China can easily recognize these categories through analogies with struggles in their own countries.

Generalization? As Zhao shows us amply, analogies are not identities. Considering the large part played in Tiananmen's crisis by locally grounded memories, symbols, meanings, institutions, practices, and social ties, does it make any sense to subsume the crisis under such general headings as revolution, rebellion, social movement, or protest, then hope to show that it conformed to laws evoked by those headings? When it comes to explanation, how can we reconcile particularity with generality? An extreme historicist response says we can't, because every setting and sequence is unique; in that case, the most we can hope for is insight and empathy. An extreme generalist response says we can, once we learn to distinguish between fundamental regularities in behavior and secondary variation.

Zhao points us to a middle ground. He argues that once we single out crucial features of the episodes at hand for explanation rather than imagining that we can explain everything that happened, we can draw effectively on causal analogies with similar features of other episodes in China and elsewhere. Thus he argues at the broadest level that authoritarian regimes undergoing relaxation of central control are especially vulnerable to radical opposition because the sort of organizational structure generated by authoritarianism provides little middle ground and thereby sharpens dissidents' choices between acquiescence and open challenge. Without producing a general law for revolution or rebellion, that argument helps explain a wide variety of struggles outside of China.

Actually Zhao is making astute choices in a very difficult game. Leaving aside those who think social life is so chaotic, individual, or impenetrable that all explanation is futile, social scientists generally choose among four rather different ideas of explanation: systems, covering laws, mechanisms, and propensities.

System explanations consist of specifying the place of some event, structure, or process within a larger self-maintaining set of interdependent elements, showing how the event, structure, or process in question serves and/or results from interactions among the larger set of elements. Thus other analysts have sometimes explained the rebellions that recurrently racked imperial China as necessary readjustments within a highly centralized system. Although a careless reader might read his state-society model as a system account, Zhao generally avoids this sort of explanation.

Covering law accounts consider explanation to consist of subjecting robust empirical generalizations to higher and higher level generalizations, the most general of all standing as laws. In such accounts, models are invariant—work the same in all conditions. Investigators search for necessary and sufficient conditions of stipulated outcomes, those outcomes often conceived of as "dependent variables." Studies of covariation among presumed causes and presumed effects therefore serve as validity tests for proposed explanations. Other students of Tiananmen, as Zhao remarks, have unsuccessfully assimilated the crisis to general models of revolution. Zhao himself conveys ambivalence about covering law accounts, criticizing all concrete attempts to subordinate the events at hand to general laws, yet displaying a wistful hope that his work will contribute to the discovery of such laws.

Mechanism-based accounts select salient features of episodes, or significant differences among episodes, and explain them by identifying robust mechanisms of relatively general scope within those episodes. In analyses of biological evolution, for example, genetic mutation and sexual selection serve as mechanisms of extremely general scope without in the least producing the same outcomes wherever they operate. Social scientists have not identified any mechanisms so robust and well defined as genetic mutation, but such mechanisms as brokerage and identity shift (which figure by implication in Zhao's account) do recur over a wide variety of political processes.

In chapter 6, for example, Zhao's analysis of spontaneity beautifully illustrates mechanism-based explanation. Precisely because no student organization established central control and because intense rivalry and distrust among shifting groups of leaders continued throughout the crisis, two apparently contradictory clusters of mechanisms intersected. On one side, local groups incessantly responded to encounters with representatives of those they defined as belonging to the enemy by improvising coordinated actions of self-defense, solidarity, and attack. On the other side, connections with authorities, allies, potential participants, and supporters determined which of the improvised, locally coordinated actions survived and became part of larger-scale struggle. These mechanisms, familiar to students of war, industrial conflict, peasant rebellion, revolution, and social movements in their own terms, figure centrally in Zhao's explanation of Tiananmen's actual course.

Propensity accounts consider explanation to consist of reconstructing a given actor's state at the threshold of action, with that state variously stipulated as motivation, consciousness, need, organization, or momentum. Explanatory methods of choice then range from sympathetic interpretation to reductionism, psychological or otherwise. In the case of social movements, analysts commonly seek to reconstruct the motives of participants on the assumption that motivation prior to action explains that action. Zhao sometimes turns to propensity explanations, especially when he is seeking to discern the meanings of symbols and practices that would otherwise remain opaque to his readers.

In chapter 9, for example, Zhao makes two consequential arguments. First, the standard communist legitimations of the Chinese regime had begun to lose their grip as a consequence of economic change and the regime's own self-refashioning during the 1980s. Second, as a consequence, Chinese citizens reached into an older but still available repertoire of legitimations in terms of leaders' moral, economic, and political performance. During the Tiananmen crisis, according to Zhao, that process accelerated. Themes of filial piety ("Grandpa Zhao, uncle Li, come save our big brothers and sisters!") and submission (kneeling on the steps of the Great Hall as a way of calling for Li Peng to receive a student petition) resonated in the setting as they would never resonate in Paris or San Francisco. Zhao remains discreetly silent about the extent to which these themes motivated those who broadcast them. But he leaves no doubt that they affected propensities of observers to join or support the action. We might therefore characterize his analyses as mechanism-based explanations in which activation of propensities plays a significant part.

So what? This strategy allows Zhao to reduce the risks of his daring enterprise. By eschewing any claim to have explained everything that happened in Beijing's turbulent spring of 1989, much less to have subordinated it to some general law of revolution or some recurrent feature of the Chinese social system, Zhao has freed himself to reconstruct, translate, and generalize. He helps readers who have never passed through the Gate of Heavenly Peace to understand why thousands of Beijing residents once risked their well-being there. He shows us a knife hidden in a hearth. At length we learn, with gratitude to Dingxin Zhao, how it got there.

Charles Tilly

Preface

In 1989, facing rising social problems, Beijing students took the sudden death of Hu Yaobang as an opportunity to start perhaps the largest student movement in human history.[1] Between April 15 and early June of that year, Beijing students initiated several demonstrations, in which the majority of students participated. They also occupied Tiananmen Square and staged a massive hunger strike. The movement caught the hearts of millions of Chinese and spread to most of urban China. It also received great attention from the international media; few adults alive today did not hear of and wonder at the excitement and the bloody confrontation in Tiananmen Square. While the movement was eventually suppressed by military forces, considering its duration, scale, and on-going impact on Chinese politics, it was unquestionably one of the most important events in contemporary China. This book explains the rise and development of this great student movement.

Let me start the book by explaining how I decided to conduct research on the 1989 Beijing Student Movement. On April 5, 1989, I, a doctoral candidate in entomology at McGill University in Montreal, Canada, took a trip to visit my family in Shanghai. Like many other Chinese students studying abroad back then, I planned to return to China after finishing up the program. However, as soon as I arrived in Shanghai, I was shocked by the dramatic changes to the political landscape that had occurred while I was away. Only two and a half years earlier, when I had left Shanghai, most people there had been quite content with their life. But now, wherever I went, including on the bus and on street corners, people were talking about inflation, corruption, income disparities, and widespread crime. In those days, "Do not come back," "Stay in

---

1. Hu Yaobang was the former general secretary of the Chinese Communist Party (CCP). He lost this position in part because of his soft attitude toward a student movement in 1986. After his resignation, Hu became a highly respected figure among Chinese students and intellectuals.

Canada," and "China is hopeless now" were the most frequent words of advice that I received. My mentor in Shanghai was a left-wing progovernment intellectual who in the early 1950s had returned to China from the United States to answer the call from the newly established People's Republic. In 1986, before I left for my doctoral study, he was still very confident about China's future and advised me to return home as soon as I finished my studies. This time, however, when I visited him he suggested that I stay in Canada. He also complained: "The situation now is just like in 1948. I saw how the Guomindang [the Nationalist Party] lost power. Now I see it happening again to the Communists." I was shocked by the drastic change in his attitude over such a short period.

Ten days after I arrived at Shanghai, on April 15, 1989, Hu Yaobang died of a heart attack. Big-character posters immediately appeared at major Beijing campuses upon Hu's death. Two days later, students went to the streets claiming to mourn the ousted former CCP general secretary. The 1989 Movement then broke out. I happened to be there. In retrospect, I see now that I was then experiencing the pre-revolutionary public mood.

Although I knew little about the movement then in comparison with what I know today, I was glad to see that students raised many serious social problems publicly. I was also happy to see that by late April students and the government had begun to hold dialogues, and that China's major media had started to cover the movement in either a neutral or positive tone. After ten years of reform, the Chinese had become more open and the Chinese government seemed to be more tolerant of differences. Yet although I was impressed by this political development, I was uninvolved in any of the movement's activities. Even when I was in Beijing applying for a visa to return to Canada during early May, the only activity that I was involved in was watching a student demonstration. I firmly identified myself as a natural scientist, and took my China visit as only a private trip.

I returned to Montreal on May 13, the day when some Beijing students started a hunger strike at Tiananmen Square. At that point, the 1989 Movement had become the single biggest item of international news on all the major North American news networks. Therefore, I was able to follow, day by day, the increase in the number of hunger strikers from a few hundred to over three thousand students, the expansion of the Tiananmen Square occupation, and the mass support and emotion in and around Tiananmen Square. In the process, I, like most Chinese students then studying in North America, became more and more concerned about the health conditions of the hunger strikers and the development of the movement. During that time, while people in Beijing came out in millions to support the hunger strikers, we, the students in Montreal, organized fundraising activities and demonstrations to condemn the government. I also learned through the media that Chinese all around the world had staged demonstrations. The movement had become a focus of worldwide attention.

The Chinese government announced martial law seven days after the start of the hunger strike. On the night of May 19, hundreds of thousands of soldiers entered Beijing. I was very nervous at first, but was surprised to find that most soldiers were unarmed and were easily blocked by the students and the Beijing residents. In the following days, we saw on TV the people's dances and songs in Tiananmen Square, the emotional speeches, the beautiful nylon tents donated from Hong Kong, the famous goddess of democracy, and other activities that captured the attention of Western news reporters.

The failure of the early implementation of martial law boosted the excitement of overseas Chinese students. Many students in Montreal, for example, considered the movement "a final battle between darkness and light" and supported the movement more strongly. Yet my worries were intensifying. I was particularly pessimistic about how the movement would end. My intuition warned me of pending military repression, but this side of me was very repressed. During that time all I did was watch TV, read newspapers, discuss and debate various issues with other Chinese students, and join all the activities supporting the Beijing students. I guess that even the most realistic mind longed for a romantic ending.

Martial law troops entered Beijing once again on June 3. On TV, I saw rolling tanks and fully armed soldiers. I heard nonstop gunfire, and saw fire and live ammunition flashing across the dark sky. I saw street barricades and angry people throwing bricks. I saw burning tanks and military trucks. I saw survivors dragging the wounded and the dead. I saw hospitals filled with wounded people. I saw blood, lots of blood. In those days, rumors were everywhere. The reported deaths skyrocketed from dozens and hundreds to thousands and even tens of thousands. Every new update was like a knife slowly pushed into my heart.

In the following months, I became very depressed. Before the movement, I had completed all the requirements of my doctoral program, except for one chapter of my dissertation, and I was expected to complete the first draft within two months. However, for several months after the crackdown, I was unable to write anything substantial. Every time I sat down, the tragic images that I saw on TV came to me. As a child of the Cultural Revolution, I had witnessed too much senseless fighting and killing. I had developed a deep-seated distrust of ideological zeal, and saw solutions emerging through gradual transitions. I hoped that China could develop a culture that would tolerate differences. I also hoped that the Chinese regime could gradually evolve into a nonideological government with a routine transition of political power. The tragic ending of the movement, however, put all my hopes into question. Countless acts of repression have occurred in twentieth-century China, each time only provoking more radical reactions. In each political struggle, the Chinese believed that they were fighting "the last battle between darkness and light," only to end up with another tyranny. I was worried that the tragic ending of the movement might actually delay China's political modernization and reduce the possibility of a peaceful democratic transition. In those months of painful reflection, I found that my deep concern for China had taken away my interest in insects.

After several months of reflection, I decided to change my major to sociology. The good news was that, after I made the decision, I was able to go back and finish my dissertation on entomology. I submitted the dissertation a few months later and entered a Ph.D. program in sociology in 1990, also at McGill University. Naturally, the first thing I wanted to do in sociology was to study the 1989 Movement. I also decided to devote as much time as was needed to learn sociology, to do solid research, and to overcome the emotions that I experienced immediately after the movement.

In 1989, most people predicted that the Chinese regime would fall within a couple of months or a few years. Yet I was quite sure that the regime was not going to fall in a short period of time. Instead, it would renew itself economically during the 1990s. I theorized this understanding in a 1994 article entitled "Defensive Regime and Modernization."[2] Still, although the regime did not fall immediately, the legacy of the 1989 Movement has not gone away. In early 1999, a new wave of protests was occasioned by the tenth anniversary of the movement. In Beijing, Ding Zilin and four other people published their *Manifesto of Freedom and Citizen Rights* and *Manifesto of Social Equality and Citizen Rights*. In many Chinese provinces, intellectuals tried to establish new parties, such as the Chinese Democratic Party, the Chinese Socialist Party, and the Chinese Labor Party. In New York, former student leader Wang Dan and many other dissidents in exile sought to get a million people across the globe to sign a petition demanding that the government rehabilitate the 1989 Movement on its tenth anniversary. In Europe, over twenty human rights organizations convened an

2. Zhao Dingxin (1994).

"International Committee for the Tenth Anniversary of the June Fourth Incident." They decided to erect five hundred miniature Tiananmen Squares in Europe on June 4. Although the momentum of antigovernment protest in China was later diverted by the surge of nationalism triggered by the NATO bombing of the Chinese Embassy in Yugoslavia, as time goes on the legacy of the movement will again and again enter into Chinese politics and draw the attention of the international community.

Although I am aware that the impact of a serious scholarly work can be limited, I also believe that humans are able to learn from the past. I wish for China to have a successful economic reform and a peaceful transition to democracy. I also hope that the bloody confrontation of the 1989 Movement will be the last of modern China's many political tragedies. To avoid more such tragedies, we must first understand what happened before and during the 1989 Movement. To this end, this book presents a sociological analysis of the causes and development of the 1989 Movement. The book consists of a theoretical introduction, a conclusion, and ten empirical chapters. The empirical chapters come in two parts. The first part discusses the factors that led to the rise of the movement. The second part starts with a history of the movement, which is followed by four analytical chapters explaining the movement's development. The introduction presents the explanatory paradigm that guides the analysis of the empirical chapters. Although I have tried to write the introduction in a way that I hope will be easy to understand, some parts of it might still be heavy going for those who are not so interested in sociological theories. I suggest that those readers skip such parts.

This work would not have been possible without the support of many people. First, I would like to thank all the people whom I have formally or informally interviewed at various stages of the research. I am grateful to those I had interviewed in Montreal and especially in Beijing. Their trust, frankness, and encouragement have inspired me.

While at McGill, I received help and encouragement from many friends. In particular, I would like to mention Marcia Beaulieu and Muriel Mellow for their painstaking editing of earlier chapters of the book. Through their help, I gradually learned how to write in English. Four teachers (and friends) exerted an enormous impact on me while I was studying at McGill. Donald von Eschen's effective teaching on the complexities of historical social changes in different geographical areas transformed me from a natural scientist inclined to find universal laws into a social scientist sensitive to diversities of human experience. John A. Hall introduced me to various state theories and theories of civil society. From Steven Rytina I learned organization theories, game theories, and resource mobilization theories. Finally, I learnt from Maurice Pinard the classic theories of social movements and the importance, in social movements, of motivations other than interests. I want here to take the opportunity to express my deepest appreciation for their guidance and friendship.

At the University of Chicago, my colleagues Andrew Abbott, William Parish, Edward Laumann, Roger Gould, Robert Sampson, Martin Riesebrodt, and Doug Mitchell have read some chapters of the book and provided valuable suggestions for improvement. Mayer N. Zald, John McCarthy, Suzanne Staggenborg, Yuezhi Zhao, and Craig Jenkins have also made suggestions on some chapters. During the revision, Jack A. Goldstone, Neil J. Smelser, Tang Tsou, Dali Yang, Feigon Lee, Harris Kim, Yiqun Zhou, and Yang Su have read the manuscript and provided many valuable suggestions.

During the book's final revision, Charles Tilly, then acting as an anonymous reviewer, read the manuscript three times and provided many highly valuable criticisms and suggestions. Here, I wish to register my deepest appreciation.

Funding for the research was provided by Canadian Social Sciences and Humanities Research Council (SSHRC) doctoral and post-doctoral fellowships, the Thesis Research Grant of McGill University, and the Social Science Divisional Award at the University of Chicago. In my final writing-up of the book, the Franke Humanities Institute at the University of Chicago provided me with a fellowship. I received help from the fellows of the institute, especially Samuel Baker and Pi-yen Chen.

I wish to thank several publishers for permission to use the material that appeared in the following papers: the University of Chicago Press for "Ecologies of Social Movements: Student Mobilization during the 1989 Pro-democracy Movement in Beijing," *American Journal of Sociology*, vol. 103 (1998), and "State-Society Relations and Discourses and Activities during the 1989 Beijing Student Movement," *American Journal of Sociology*, vol. 105 (2000); the Institute for Far Eastern Studies, Kyungnam University, for "State Legitimacy, State Policy, and the Development of the 1989 Beijing Student Movement," *Asian Perspectives*, vol. 23 (1999); JAI Press Inc. for "Decline of Political Control in Chinese Universities and the Rise of the 1989 Chinese Student Movement," *Sociological Perspectives*, vol. 40 (1997); Kluwer Academic Publishers for "Foreign Study as a Safety-Valve: The Experience of China's University Students Going Abroad in the Eighties," *Higher Education*, vol. 31 (1996).

Finally, I also would like to take the opportunity to express my deepest appreciation to my wife, Qin Chen. She showed great understanding and support for my decision to embark on another Ph.D. program. Without her understanding, this could never have been possible. Moreover, she has been a loyal reader and always a sharp critic of the first draft of almost every chapter in this book. She has also, while in her own Ph.D. program, brought into the world our two most adorable daughters, Linda and Lily. Their arrival changed the meaning of my life.

The final stages of this book's production coincided with the publication of *The Tiananmen Papers*, a collection of what has been described as the Chinese government's secret documents on the 1989 Movement. *The Tiananmen Papers* created great controversy as soon as it was published. It has been acclaimed as a milestone in the study of Communist China, but at the same time its authenticity has been seriously challenged. This controversy, however, has little relevance to my book, since *The Tiananmen Papers* does not contain any new information that would compel me to rethink my original arguments.

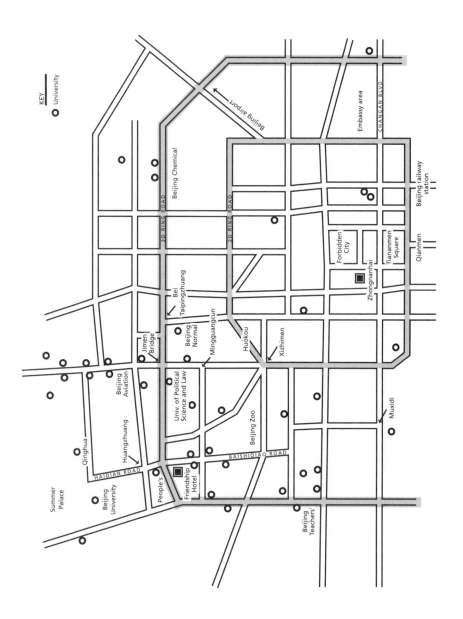

Map of Beijing

Chronology

1980   SEPTEMBER   Third session of the Fifth National People's Congress.
        Hua Guofeng is pushed to abandon the Four Modernizations
        Plan. Zhao Ziyang replaces Hua as China's premier.

1981   The state initiates a criticism of the discussion of socialist alienation
        and Marxist humanism. Bai Hua's film script "Unrequited Love"
        is criticized.
        JUNE   Sixth Plenum of the Eleventh Central Committee. Hua resigns
        as the chairman of the CCP and Hu Yaobang takes the position
        under the title of the CCP general secretary. The meeting ap-
        proves "A Resolution on Certain Questions in the History of
        Our Party Since the Founding of the People's Republic of China,"
        in which Mao is openly criticized.
        DECEMBER 1982   Fifth Session of the Fifth National People's Con-
        gress. The meeting adopts a new constitution in which the right
        to strike and the "Four Great Freedoms" are removed. The *xiang*
        replaces the commune as the lowest level of rural government, the
        private economy is formally accepted, and foreign enterprises are
        allowed in China.

1983   JANUARY   Document No. 1 of the CCP Central Committee endorses
        rural decollectivization.
        OCTOBER   The CCP launches an attack on "spiritual pollution."

1984   OCTOBER   Third Plenum of the Twelfth Central Committee endorses
        urban reforms.

1986   NOVEMBER – DECEMBER   Students in Hefei, Shanghai, Beijing, and
        some other major cities demonstrate in the street.

1987   JANUARY   Enlarged meeting of the CCP Politburo Central Commit-
        tee. Hu Yaobang accepts responsibility for the student movements
        and resigns from the post of CCP general secretary, but he still
        keeps his position as a member of the politburo. Zhao Ziyang be-
        comes the CCP general secretary. The campaign against bourgeois
        liberalization starts.

1988   Corruption and inflation become a threat to normal life. Urban re-
        form is in crisis. Intellectual elites are very active on Beijing cam-

puses and openly push the state for political reforms. Small- to medium-scale student protests become frequent. The state is forced to adopt an economic adjustment policy.

During the 1989 Chinese Student Movement (Events in Beijing Only)

APRIL 15 Hu Yaobang dies of a heart attack.

APRIL 16 Wreaths and elegiac couplets appear in Tiananmen Square and at many Beijing colleges. Hu's family, intellectual elites, and students demand that the government rehabilitate Hu from his 1987 disgrace.

APRIL 17 Several hundred people from the University of Political Science and Law march to Tiananmen Square to lay wreaths. The same evening, around two thousand Beijing University students also march to the Square. Protest activities are continuous from this time up until the final government crackdown on June 3. The movement's focus gradually moves away from mourning Hu's death.

APRIL 20 Minor skirmishes occur between policemen and students at the Xinhua Gate, the south gate of the government compound. Students call it the "Xinhua Gate Bloody Incident." Students in some universities start a class boycott.

APRIL 22 Hu's state funeral is held at the Great Hall of the People, located on the west side of Tiananmen Square. Around 50,000 students march to the Square overnight to participate in the funeral. During the funeral students attempt many courses of action, the most well known being that in which three students kneel on the steps of the Great Hall of the People for about forty minutes to deliver a petition and to demand a meeting with premier Li Peng.

APRIL 23 The Beijing Student Autonomous Union Provisional Committee is founded.

APRIL 26 A *People's Daily* editorial labels the movement "a planned conspiracy" and "turmoil."

APRIL 27 About 100,000 students march to Tiananmen Square to protest the editorial. The State Council expresses willingness to hold a dialogue with students.

APRIL 29 Yuan Mu, a State Council spokesman, and some senior officials hold a dialogue with 45 students from sixteen Beijing universities. Yuan claims that the April 26 editorial is only aimed at a very small number of black hands. Students challenge both the procedures of the dialogue and the representativeness of the participants because some of them are drawn from official student unions.

MAY 4 Students hold a march in commemoration of the May 4th Movement of 1919. Zhao Ziyang speaks to delegates of the 22nd Annual Meeting of the Asian Development Bank. He claims that most students support the government and that China will not experience large-scale turmoil.

MAY 5 The Beijing Student Dialogue Delegation is formed. Most students in Beijing return to class.

MAY 13 About three hundred students start a hunger strike in Tiananmen Square. The number eventually rises to over three thousand. A huge number of students begins to occupy the Square.

MAY 14 A high-level state delegation starts an emergency dialogue with student activists. The meeting goes chaotically because different students have totally different agendas in mind. In the evening students withdraw from the talks. The hunger strike continues.

MAY 15 Gorbachev arrives. The state has to hold the welcome ceremony at the Beijing Airport.

MAY 17 Over a million Beijing residents of all occupations march in Beijing to express their concern for the hunger strikers and to support the students.

MAY 19 Li Peng declares martial law, but the martial law troops are blocked by Beijing residents and students. More and more students from universities outside Beijing arrive in the city.

JUNE 3 Military repression starts. Hundreds of people are killed during the confrontation.

JUNE 4 The remaining 4,000 students leave the Square after they are completely encircled by the troops.

INTRODUCTION

The state is like a vessel and the people are water.
Water can carry or sink the vessel.

Xun Zi (ca. 298−238 B.C.)

Scientific explanation consists not in moving from the complex to
the simple but in the replacement of a less intelligible complexity by
one which is more so.

Claude Lévi-Strauss (1966, 248)

On the morning of April 22, 1989, seven days after the emergence of the 1989 Beijing Student Movement, a state funeral was held for Hu Yaobang inside the Great Hall of the People.[1] The previous night, about 50,000 students had gone to Tiananmen Square, just outside the Great Hall of the People, in order to be part of that funeral. Throughout the morning of

---

1. Chinese personal names in the text, notes, and bibliography follow Chinese practice, in which the surname comes before the given name. Excepted from this rule are the names of people with Western given names. I have used the pinyin system for all Chinese words and names, even for names that are well known in other forms. For example, Chiang Kai-shek and Sun Yat-sen appear in this book as Jiang Jieshi and Sun Zhongshan.

April 22, activists from different universities staged various and often uncoordinated protests, the themes of which were mostly irrelevant to Hu's state funeral. Among these many protest activities, the one that most resonated with the students' emotions was the kneeling of three students in front of the Great Hall of the People. These three students knelt there for over half an hour with a petition in their hands, insisting that premier Li Peng come out to receive the petition and meet with the assembled students. In imperial China, kneeling in front of a government building to present a petition had been a popular way for the Chinese to address their public grievances, and a good official was expected to come out and receive the petition, yet Li Peng did not appear. The students were distraught; some cried like babies, while others shouted antigovernment slogans.

Four days later, on April 26, the Chinese government published a *People's Daily* editorial that departed from the remarkably tolerant stance of the previous eleven days, which labeled the movement antirevolutionary agitation by a small number of conspirators. Chinese would usually have been discouraged by such a message, indicative as it was of impending government repression. Yet to most people's surprise, instead of backing off, the Beijing students defied the editorial with a large-scale demonstration. On the morning of April 27, students from most of Beijing's sixty-seven universities went into the streets. At a few major universities, including Beijing University and Qinghua University, the participation rate reached over 90 percent. Some reports estimated that as many as 100,000 students, or more than half of the students in Beijing, participated in the demonstration.

The kneeling of the three students in front of the Great Hall of the People, the government's drastic policy shift from its early concessions to its repressive April 26 *People's Daily* editorial, and the mass participation in the April 27 demonstration, are all very well known episodes of the 1989 Movement. The April 27 student demonstration marked the first large-scale open defiance of the state by the Chinese people since the Communists took power. In many ways, the success of this demonstration shaped the subsequent dynamics of the movement, leading, finally, to the state crackdown. The same was true of the action of kneeling. This protest so effectively mobilized the emotions of students that no other activities staged on that day could match it. The next day's Beijing-wide class boycott became possible largely because the kneeling, and the fact that Li Peng did not come out to receive the petition and meet with the students, triggered the anger of Beijing students.

The events of April 22 and 26 also reveal three of the major characteristics of the 1989 Movement: frequent government policy changes back and forth from concession to repression, quick and successful participant mobilizations, and the dominance of traditional forms of language and action during the movement. These characteristics shaped the movement's development and contributed to its tragic outcome. They, therefore, have received a great deal of attention in scholarly analyses.

So far, most writings treat the change of government policies and the consequent dynamics of the 1989 Movement as a result of reformer-hardliner *factional struggle* within the government.[2] They also take the eventual imposition of military repression as a signal that hardliners gained the upper hand in the power struggle, bringing an end to China's reform. There are various interpretations of the stunning success of student mobilization during the movement. Some scholars attribute the rise of the 1989 Movement and the massive movement participation to the rise of *civil society* through the process of the economic reform. They argue that while China's economic reform facilitated the formation of numerous interest groups, the slow pace of political reform simply could not cope with the situation. Hence, when China's economy faced problems, these interest groups took action against the state.[3] Others attribute the movement's scale and mode of development to the *lack* of civil society in China. They argue that the totalitarian Chinese state, by eliminating civil society, produced a large number of people with similar experiences, grievances, and unorganized interests. Once collective actions occur in such a society, the argument goes, they will happen on a large scale and with great spontaneity.[4] Finally, scholars who have studied the language and activity of the 1989 Movement have emphasized the importance of *Chinese culture* for the movement.[5] They suggest that while students cried out for democracy, their way of thinking, their rhetoric, and their activities closely followed traditional Chinese cultural scripts. This traditionalism is also identified as one of the most important causes of the tragic outcome of the movement.

Although the above arguments all have their strengths, a number of facts put their premises in question. In regard to elite factionalism: while its existence is a truism, as an explanation for the development of the 1989 Movement it encounters several difficulties. First, the theory does not explain the timing of

---

2. See, for example, Chen Yizi (1990), Cheng Chu-yuan (1990), Dittmer (1990a, 1990b), Kristof (1990a), and Nathan (1990) for analyses that emphasize the impact of factionalism on the rise and development of the 1989 Movement.

3. See Burns (1989), Huan Guocang (1989), Strand (1990, 1993), and Sullivan (1990) for the argument.

4. Zhou Xueguang (1993).

5. See Calhoun (1991, 1994), Chan and Unger (1990), Esherick and Wasserstrom (1990), Macartney (1990), Perry and Fuller (1991), Pye (1990), and Wasserstrom (1991).

some important events. For example, Zhao Ziyang was generally believed to be a reform leader, and the April 26 *People's Daily* editorial was thought to have been made possible because he was in North Korea for a state visit.[6] However, this does not explain why the state shifted back to a concessive strategy on April 27 and held a dialogue with students on April 29—while Zhao was still in North Korea. Secondly, the course of events since the 1989 Movement does not bear out the predictions of models based on factionalism. There was no extensive purge of the so-called reformers in the CCP after the movement, and China's economic reform gathered new momentum after 1992. The elite factionalism theory may have a certain value in analyzing Chinese politics before the 1980s, when the state could make policy choices relatively free from social pressure and when its policies could penetrate society and make a great impact. By the late 1980s, however, most Chinese no longer believed in communism and were concerned about the state's economic performance. The resultant social pressure narrowed the state's policy choices.[7]

As for the rise of civil society argument: while it was true that intermediate associations greatly expanded in China during the 1980s, most of these associations were semi-officially organized. Their relationship with the state was more one of subordinate cooperation than one of confrontation.[8] Moreover, if a so-called civil society did contribute to the movement, the scale of the movement in a region should positively correlate with the extent of the market reform in that region. In fact, the movement was much weaker in Guangzhou and Xiamen, where the market economy was more developed, than in other major cities.[9] One piece of evidence cited by the rise of civil society argument is the

6. Chen Yizi (1990a, 152–53); Chen Xiaoya (1996, 206–7).

7. A typical example is Nathan's prediction. According to Nathan (1990, 46), factional struggle in China should have led to such pernicious outcomes as a reversal or partial reversal of Deng's program, another Cultural Revolution, or a senseless power struggle leading only to immobilism. Nathan's assessment certainly does not fit what actually happened in China in the 1990s. Schram's (1988, 189) assessment of the possible political outcome in China makes more sense: "From a political perspective, I would argue simply that the overall process of reform has almost certainly passed the point of no return. It is extremely doubtful whether even Chen Yun and his supporters, whatever may have been their aspirations prior to the Decision of October 1984, would now seriously seek to return to the methods of the mid-1950s, even in modified and updated form." (Chen Yun was an alleged paramount conservative leader.)

8. White (1993) and Wang, Zhe, and Sun (1993, esp. 34 and 72) show that although intermediate associations mushroomed in Xiaoshan City, Zhejiang province, from only four in 1978 to ninety-nine in 1990, 70 percent of them had a semi-official status. Their leaders were appointed or at least acknowledged by the local state agencies, and their financial resources came partly from the state. These associations did have limited autonomy in guarding the interests of their members, but they also extended state control. For other discussions of Chinese civil society, see Huang (1993), Chamberlain (1993), and Wakeman (1993).

9. For example, in the 1980s Guangdong's reform was far more advanced than most other areas (Vogel 1989). However, Liu Zhongyi (1989) reported that by May 10, 1989, only a small-scale student demonstration

heavy worker participation in the late period of the movement. However, what I found in my study is that most worker participation was coordinated by lower-level government cadres during the hunger strike and was neighborhood-based during the martial law period. Even the major workers' unions formed during the movement were actually established, supervised, and financially supported by the students (chapter 6).

Likewise, the lack of civil society argument also fails to adequately explain the rise and development of the 1989 Movement. During Mao's era, when the Chinese certainly shared more similar life experiences, China had no large-scale social movements except for government-initiated campaigns. It was only many years after reform, when people's life experiences and interests had become greatly differentiated, that large-scale social movements broke out. In addition, thousands of collective actions occurred during the 1980s: in 1988, over 210 student protests and 1,100 wall posters appeared in Beijing alone,[10] although only two of the protests reached a moderate scale. This shows that small- to medium-scale collective actions are possible in China, and that the large-scale 1989 Movement was actually a rare kind of event.

Explaining the pattern of student activities during the movement as a manifestation of Chinese culture is likewise problematic. It is argued that the movement was sustained because during it students were increasingly committed to a culturally embedded student identity.[11] Although I did find in my research that a few student activists had become increasingly committed to the movement, I did not find that this was a general trend. As a matter of fact, by the end of May most Beijing students were very tired and went home, and the Tiananmen Square occupation was sustained by students from other provinces, who were continuously arriving at Beijing after mid-May. Since identity cannot be borrowed from someone else, the prolonged movement must not be due to an internal identity transformation. It is also argued that because Chinese culture censures self-interested behavior, students (and the government) had to attack the other party with lofty, symbolic, and moralistic rhetoric and activities. Since a battle of morality and shame has a positive feedback nature, such interactions have been thought to portend not only the movement's bloody ending but also the likelihood of severe reprisals against students and reformers by the government.[12] Although the argument is a logical one, it neglects the facts

---

(about 1,000 students) occurred in Guangzhou on the evening of May 4. This contrasted sharply with numerous large-scale demonstrations staged in most other cities of a comparable size.

10. Ren Yanshen (1990, 127).

11. Calhoun (1991, 1994).

12. Pye (1990).

that both the students and government made frequent compromises, many of which almost worked, during the 1989 Movement (chapter 6), that subsequent Chinese politics was not governed by a desire for revenge, and that the economic reform continued.

In Search of a General Explanation

Based on materials from an extensive research, I found that the above-listed three features of the 1989 Movement can be better explained as follows. With regard to the government's frequent policy changes toward the movement, I argue that while the existence of power struggles among Chinese top leaders is a truism, the key factor behind the policy changes was the ineffectiveness of previous policies, an ineffectiveness that resulted from different understandings of state legitimation on the part of the top state elites and the general public (chapter 7). During the late 1980s, while the majority of top state elites still hung on to communist ideology, most students and Beijing residents evaluated the state by its economic and moral performance. Thus when the government was challenged ideologically and morally, the challenge resonated widely. However, when the government invoked ideological or legal dimensions of state authority to control the movement, its measures only antagonized people. To adopt a game theory analogy, the whole situation was such as if the state elites treated the game as chess and the people took it as *Chinese* chess. Since the chessmen for the two games are similar, each side remained unaware of the situation. Therefore, each player kept making moves that violated the other player's sense of the rules of the game, as if continuously applying Garfinkel's "breaching experiments" to each other. Both sides became increasingly irritated; eventually, the chessboard was overturned.

With regard to the high rate of student participation, I found that the physical environment of the Beijing campuses played a crucial role (chapter 8). As a result of state policies in the 1950s, most of the sixty-seven universities in Beijing were located in the Haidian District. This environment enclosed a huge number of students in a small area with a unique spatial distribution. The setting had facilitated government control over students during Mao's era, when most students still believed in communism and when mutually checking upon each other's political conduct was not considered immoral behavior. However, after the ideological legitimation of the state declined and other channels of upward mobility opened up, the same setting became fertile ground for student mobilization (chapter 4). During 1989, this campus ecology nurtured many close-knit student networks as well as directly exposed all Beijing students to a collective action environment. The campus ecology also provided some central locations for participant mobilization, induced dormitory-based communication and coercion, facilitated interuniversity competition for activism, and shaped the routes of student demonstrations both on and off campus. Hence it played a crucial role in student mobilization and in the dynamics of the 1989 Movement.

To treat the dominance of traditional Chinese culture during the movement, I compared the language and forms of activity used during the 1989 Movement with those used during the May 4th Movement of 1919 and the December 9th Movement of 1935–36, the two largest student movements of Republican China. I found the rhetoric and forms of activity of the 1989 Movement to actually be more traditional than those of its forerunners. Since Chinese culture has experienced dramatic modernization in the twentieth century, if movement participants simply acted according to cultural scripts, we should expect that traditional Chinese culture would be less manifest in the 1989 Movement than in the two earlier student movements. Therefore, this finding poses a puzzle. I argue that, in comparison with the two earlier student movements, the students during the 1989 Movement faced stronger repression and therefore resorted to culturally accepted forms of collective action in order to reduce the chances of immediate repression. Also, in comparison to the two earlier movements, the 1989 Movement was poorly organized, and composed of participants who tended to judge the government by its moral performance (a major source of state legitimation). I argue that when a movement is poorly organized, the psychology of its audience becomes more important. Traditional rhetoric and forms of activity also shaped the 1989 Movement because the movement participants were more easily moved by morally charged activities, becoming very emotional when the government responded improperly to the morally centered challenges from the people.

Readers may notice some commonality in the explanations provided above. In explaining the forces behind the frequent shift of government policies, I use the concept of state legitimation. Treating the high level of student participation during the movement, I stress how campus ecology offset the weaknesses of movement organizations and otherwise played a crucial role—but campus ecology was in turn a result of past state designs, and it would not have been so effective for student mobilization without a great decline of the student control system in universities. In regard to the dominance of traditional Chinese culture during the 1989 Movement, I stress factors including strong state repression, weak intermediate associations, and a morally based concept of state legitimation. Three sets of embedded structural factors emerge in these analyses. These are the nature of the state (including the state's behavior, its strong repressive capacity, and its weakening student control system in the universities), the nature of society (the weakness of intermediate associations, and the spatial layout of the university campus), and the linkages between the state and society (here mainly the various articulations of the sources of state legitimation). They are all under the domain of *state-society relations*.

I argue that the rise and development of the 1989 Beijing Student Movement, in all of its aspects that I found important, can be explained in terms of state-society relations in China, understood in three impure dimensions: in terms of the nature of the state, of the nature of society, and of the economic, political, and ideational linkages between the state and society. More specifically, I argue that, during the 1980s in China, the state was authoritarian, society was poorly organized, and state legitimation was based on its moral and economic performance. This particular "state-society relationship," in conjunction with the great uncertainties and conflicts brought about by state-led economic reform, led to the rise and shaped the development of the 1989 Movement. The following paragraphs further summarize this book's main arguments.

Due to the disastrous Cultural Revolution, the Chinese economy was on the verge of collapse by the time of Mao's death in 1976. The Chinese government had to start a reform in 1978. During that process, the Chinese state began to transform from an ideology-based revolutionary regime into a performance-based authoritarian regime. The society became increasingly pluralist, but it was still poorly organized (chapter 1). China's reform went well initially. Within a few years, the standard of living of most Chinese had improved greatly. However, by the late 1980s China's economy had run into a crisis. Problems such as high inflation and rampant official corruption mounted in society. The government had to start an economic adjustment.

The 1989 Movement was initiated by a small group of pro-Western intellectual elites and a few students who were influenced by them. It was soon joined by rank-and-file students and intellectuals. The two groups participated in the movement for somewhat different reasons. The pro-Western intellectual elites had emerged in the process of China's reform. People in this group had very painful memories of Maoist rule and saw a lack of democracy as a crucial factor in the rise of Maoist tyranny. There was an uneasy cooperation between the intellectual elites and the state during the early 1980s, when the reform was going well. During the late 1980s, however, as the economic crisis deepened, the intellectual elites diagnosed China's political system as its root cause. Haunted by the memory of the Maoist past, the intellectual elites considered the state's economic adjustment policy as a leftist revival. They, therefore, engaged in a crisis discourse, pressing hard for more economic reform and democratic openings. Their discourses and actions paved the ways for the rise of the movement (chapters 2, 5). Most rank-and-file students and intellectuals also disliked Maoist rule and supported the reform. Yet with little knowledge of a market economy, they tended to believe that a market-oriented reform should bring them more benefits. They became very disappointed by the fact that a few less-educated people or people with government connections became rich first in the reform (chapter 3). During the late 1980s, when the Chinese economy was in a deep crisis, the living standard of intellectuals declined and students had a hard time finding desirable jobs after graduation. Students and intellectuals were demoralized. When this aggrieved population was galvanized by campus crisis discourse after 1986, the result was frequent student protests, which culminated in 1989.[13]

When it comes to the development of the 1989 Movement, I focus on the question of why the movement ended tragically even though the majority of student activists, intellectual elites, and government leaders all struggled for a compromise solution. I first give a historical account of the movement, intended to provide an in-depth narrative of the most important events of the movement and to reveal the role of contingent factors and activities in its development (chapter 6). I then analyze the tragic dynamism of the movement from four different angles (chapters 7 through 10), each of which involved state-society relations. I argue that by the late 1980s China's state-society relationship had crystallized into an authoritarian regime with performance legitimation, a relatively strong capacity for repression, and weakly developed intermediate organizations. This particular set of state-society relations simultaneously shaped the patterns of interaction between the state and the movement (chapter 7), the movement's mobilization structure (chapter 8), the patterns of language and activity used during the movement (chapter 9), and the behavior of the media and public opinion (chapter 10). These factors all contributed to the development of the movement and to the final head-on confrontation between the state and the people.[14]

I chose "state-society relations" to model the 1989 Movement with another consideration in mind. China has the longest uninterrupted state tradition in

13. In the literature of the 1989 Movement, while some claimed that Chinese students had little understanding of democracy, others, such as Calhoun (1994), found that students had an excellent understanding of it. In fact, they may have referred to different student populations.

14. I omit a more detailed description of the chapters related to the dynamics of the 1989 Movement since the arguments made in chapters 7, 8, and 9 have been summarized earlier in this section.

the world. Confucianism, the most important political philosophy in China, is essentially an ingenious design of state-society relations for an agrarian society with a strong patrilineage tradition. Moreover, since the communists took power, the Chinese government has initiated numerous social programs aimed at changing the state, society, and their relationships. Each of these programs has had a profound impact on the population. The Great Leap Forward, the Cultural Revolution, and, to a great extent, the current reform, are only the best-known examples. In fact, for those who know China, it is very hard not to think of Chinese politics in terms of the state and of state-society relations. I imagine that it is for this reason that many China scholars have adopted approaches that either directly use or imply the idea of state-society relations. For example, Tsou Tang has used the concept of state-society relations in his analysis of the 1989 Movement.[15] Zhou Xueguang's "large number" and "unorganized interests" concepts also contain the idea of state-society relations. In other research areas, Tang and Parish's recent study of social changes during Deng's era, Shirk's interpretation of the drives of China's economic reform, Liu's study of China's mass politics, Wong's study of tax resistance in Chinese history, Kate Xiao Zhou's study of Chinese farmers, and Shue's study of the state's capacity before and after the communists came to power, to mention just a few, have all explicitly used or implied a state-society relations perspective.[16]

Theoretically, it is also well known that in the last few hundred years, since modern social movements were born,[17] the state and state-society relations have become increasingly important to the rise and development of social movements—especially to large-scale social movements occurring in authoritarian regimes.[18] First, in the last few centuries, the world has experienced ongoing processes of state building, nation building, and the development of capitalism. As these processes have evolved, the state has continuously changed its

15. Tsou Tang (1991).

16. See Zhou Xueguang (1993), Tang and Parish (2000), Shirk (1993), Alan P. L. Liu (1996), Wong (1997), Kate Xiao Zhou (1996), and Shue (1988).

17. Tilly (1982, 1986) has excellent analyses on the rise of modern social movements in Western Europe.

18. By large-scale social movements I refer to the movements that involve a significant proportion of the population and that aim to achieve fundamental changes in the society. There is no objective dividing line between large-scale social movements and revolutions and other social movements. However, the Solidarity movement in Poland, the student and civil rights movements in the 1960s in the United States, and the 1989 Beijing Student Movement are clear examples of large-scale social movements. Please notice that the state-society relations theory developed in this introduction is intended for large-scale social movements and revolutions rather than small-scale collective actions such as a strike in a factory.

nature and expanded its scope.[19] Tax, judicial, welfare, military, and other powers that formerly belonged to local communities have been taken up by the
state. Since the state has become increasingly relevant to ordinary life, it has
naturally received more attention from society. In a way, many modern social
movements can be seen as people's attempts to harness an increasingly powerful state or to use the state to advance sectorial interests.[20]

Second, following the above logic, the role of the state is more important for
social movements in less developed nations than in developed ones. Historically, many less developed countries have had a weaker state tradition than developed nations. They thus underwent state building within a much shorter
period than the developed nations. Moreover, the state in less developed nations often takes on a much more active role in economic development than in
developed nations.[21] In functional terms, all state initiatives during late development entail the reallocation of resources among social groups whose own interests and identities are also changing rapidly. The dislocations resulting from
state-led modernization are apparently even stronger in the underdeveloped
nations than in the developed ones, as depicted by Huntington, Johnson, and
others in the Durkheimian tradition.[22] On top of that, many initiatives by states
of less developed countries have been corrupt or even parasitic, inducing a sense
of injustice in aggrieved populations.

Third, the importance of the state for the rise of a social movement varies
with different state-society relations. If one views those relations along a total-
itarian-democratic continuum (ideal forms at both extremes), one sees that the
state is the center of attention of any social movement in a totalitarian context,
for since a totalitarian state exercises control over everything, even the most
trivial matter can be political.[23] On the other hand, at the democratic end, the
state becomes only a "referee," while the rules of the game are set by competing

---

19. Mann (1988, 1993), Poggi (1990), and Tilly (1975, 1992).

20. See Bright and Harding (1984), Tilly (1975, 1978, 1986), and Tilly, Tilly, and Tilly (1975).

21. All the modern states are more or less what Migdal (1994, 13) calls transformative states. However,
the states of underdeveloped nations tend to occupy the higher end of a transformative scale. See Evans
(1995), Gershenkron (1952), Haggard (1990), Wade (1990), and Zhao and Hall (1994) for more discussions
on the role of the state in economic development.

22. Huntington (1968); Johnson (1982).

23. For example, food riots were common in eighteenth-century Europe. However, food became a
political issue in France because the Old Regime accepted responsibility for the bread supply (Mann 1993,
ch. 6). Also, in China job security was usually a political issue because the state took responsibility for en-
suring employment. However, during the 1990s, that is, after the labor market reform, job security became
increasingly an economic issue tied with the performance of individual companies.

organizations. Thus, the state becomes irrelevant and "society" becomes the target of social movements.[24]

Finally, after a social movement directly or indirectly challenges a state, there are two actors, the state and society. However, different types of states have different strategies and capacities to deal with the same type of social movements.[25] People's reaction to the same state action also differs according to the ways they are organized and to their perception of state power. Under some state-society relationships, strong grievances can be alleviated and nonconformist ideologies can be marginalized. In other cases, minor grievances may intensify and initially conformist programs can be radicalized. Thus, when a social movement begins, its dynamics are shaped by a state's capacity to contain political conflicts—a capacity that is a function of state-society relations.

Obviously, the 1989 Movement was a large-scale social movement that broke out within an authoritarian regime. It was triggered by economic and political crises brought on by a state-led economic reform. Throughout the movement, students challenged the state by demanding political liberalization. To some extent, the movement can be viewed as a failed revolution. If it had succeeded, as happened in Eastern European countries, it not only would have toppled the government but would also have brought about drastic changes in the social and political structure of Chinese society. Therefore, it is ideal both empirically and theoretically to study the movement by focusing on the state and on state-society relations during and before the movement.

State-Society Relations and Patterns of Social Movements

The phrases "state and society" and "state-society relations" existed only marginally in sociology before the 1970s.[26] Back then, the dominant theories and research agendas in sociology were largely society-centered;[27] "state-society relations" was more a casual phrase than a theoretical framework. The situation gradually changed during the late 1970s and 1980s. One of the pioneering works was Skocpol's classic study on the role of the state in great social revolutions. In that work, Skocpol treats the state "as an autonomous structure—a struc-

24. For instance, gay and lesbian movements in the West, even though they often try to influence the state to increase special rights and protections, can be seen mainly as a challenge to traditional civil society rather than to the state.

25. See Mann (1993, chs. 15–18) for examples of how working-class movements have been treated differently in different Western states.

26. For example, Bendix (1968), Blelloch (1969), and Morley (1949, ch. 5).

27. Skocpol (1975).

ture with a logic and interests of its own not necessarily equivalent to, or fused with, the interests of the dominant class in society or the full set of member groups in the polity."[28] Since then, state-centered research has blossomed not only in the study of social revolutions,[29] but also in studies of other types of contentious politics, such as working-class movements,[30] contemporary social movements,[31] and economic development.[32]

However, as this research has developed, more and more societal factors have been brought back into state-centered analyses. In the area of economic development, instead of arguing for a "strong state," Zhao and Hall as well as Evans try to capture the importance of state-society linkages in economic development with such concepts as "bounded autonomy" or "embedded autonomy."[33] In the study of social revolutions, scholars—in particular Goldstone and Mc-Daniel—emphasize not only the structure and nature of the state but also factors such as population density, economic structure, culture, and ideologies.[34] By far the largest amount of recent research to focus on state-society relations concerns democratic transition and consolidation.[35] Although their approaches vary, most such studies treat democratization as an interactive process between the state and society, by examining the impact of such factors as the nature of the state, the nature and strength of civil society, and socioeconomic structure on democratization. Obviously, the state-society relations perspective is intended to achieve a more balanced understanding of some political processes by apprehending not only the structure and nature of the state but also the interactions between the state and society.

The state-society relations model differs from the currently dominant resource mobilization or political process theory in several aspects. Most importantly, however, while the early models emphasize the importance of structural conditions such as the amount of resources or changes of political opportunities in the rise and development of a social movement,[36] for the state-society

28. Skocpol (1979, 27).

29. Farhi (1990), Foran (1997), Goodwin (1989), Goodwin and Skocpol (1989), McDaniel (1988, 1991), Skocpol (1994), and Wickham-Crowley (1992).

30. Katznelson and Zolberg (1986), Lipset (1983), Mann (1993, chs. 15–18), and Marks (1989).

31. Jenkins and Klandermans (1995), Kitschelt (1986), Kriesi (1996), and Kriesi et al. (1995).

32. Amsden (1989), Deyo (1987), Evans (1995), Tom Gold (1986), Haggard (1990), and Wade (1990).

33. Zhao and Hall (1994); Evans (1995).

34. Goldstone (1991); McDaniel (1991).

35. See Casper and Taylor (1996), Chehabi and Stepan (1995), Diamond, Linz, and Lipset (1988), Diamond and Plattner (1996), Huntington (1991), Linz and Stepan (1996), O'Donnell, Schmitter, and Whitehead (1986), Schmitter (1993), Stepan (1978, 1989), and Weil (1996).

36. See McCarthy and Zald (1973, 1977) for the resource mobilization model, and Tilly (1978) and McAdam (1982) for the foundation of the political process model.

relations model the dynamics of a social movement is also determined at *intersections* of the interactions between the state and movement participants or among the movement participants. Therefore, it can be labeled as an *intersection model*.

Recently, scholars have also begun to agree that large-scale social movements are often contentions between the state and people in society and that the outcomes of such movements (ranging from a total failure to a successful revolution) depend not only on structural factors and on actors' intentions but also on path-dependent interactive processes between the state and movement actors.[37] To focus on just one or the other is to risk missing the essential drama of a complex political process.[38] For such reasons, some recent writings on social movements and revolutions have started to examine social movements in a relational process between the state and society.[39]

Yet although recent writings have placed a greater emphasis on the relational and interactive processes between social movements and authority, they share some weaknesses. First, most treatments of state-society relations in social movements deal either with social movements in democratic countries or with revolutionary movements in authoritarian states.[40] Except for a recent theoretical discussion by Goldstone,[41] few studies examine how interactions between the state and the people as well as among the people might turn a social movement into a revolutionary confrontation, or vice versa. This study is an effort in this direction of research. For while the 1989 Movement was largely reformist in origin and had many characteristics of a social movement as that phenomenon is commonly defined,[42] it took place in what was clearly an authoritarian state, and its relationship with that state molded a course of action that nearly reached a revolutionary outcome.

Second, recent relational studies on social movements tend to treat the interactions among major social movement actors as the "bargaining processes" of rational actors.[43] This approach may have a great validity in studying social movements in a democratic regime, where intermediate organizations are fully developed and social movements become similar to interest group poli-

---

37. Goldstone (1998).

38. Hanagan, Moch, and Brake (1998, ix).

39. Hanagan, Moch, and Brake (1998), Brake (1998), Weil (1996), Giugni, McAdam, and Tilly (1998), and Tilly (1999).

40. McAdam, Tarrow, and Tilly (1996).

41. Goldstone (1998).

42. See Tarrow (1998, 1–9) for a recent definition of social movements.

43. Brake (1998, 7).

tics. However, this approach is difficult to apply to an authoritarian regime and traditional society where civil organizations are sanctioned by the state, social movements tend to develop with great spontaneity, and politics is based on "right or wrong" rather than on "gains or losses." Therefore, by interactions, this book refers not only to a kind of rational-choice-based bargaining process but also to a value- or norm-driven emotional process. (That is why the concept of legitimation is so central in my analysis). I have borrowed extensively from the early symbolic interaction approaches on social movements and from Collins's model of "interaction ritual chains."[44] I will further clarify this position in the conclusion.

Third, most studies of the state or of state-society relations have focused on a narrow range of issues. Questions about patterns of state behavior, movement language and activities, movement-media interactions, and the structure of movement mobilization have either been neglected or have been treated under different theories. Political process scholars are interested in all these questions. However, in their analyses, the role of the state in a social movement is studied through "political opportunity structures." Studies of mobilization structures have been largely conducted within the context of analyses of organizations and networks. The study of the rhetorical and symbolic activities of a social movement has traditionally been the realm of strategy framing and cultural perspectives. The media's role in social movements has been described as a part of cultural hegemony.[45] In such analyses, the "dependent factors" for one research question are often turned into "independent factors" in another research agenda, making the reasoning circular.[46] In this book, I intend to explain the above-mentioned issues in a large-scale social movement within the general framework of a state-society relations theory.

However, the concept of state-society relations is capacious. Although many studies have mentioned "state-society relations,"[47] with the noticeable exception of Linz and his associates' work on democratic transition and consolidation, the concept tends to be casually used, and very few concrete analytical tools have been developed to assist such analysis. For example, in the area of

44. See Blumer (1969) and Turner and Killian (1987) for the symbolic interaction approaches to social movements, and Collins (1981, 1990) for the theory of interaction ritual chains.

45. Gitlin (1980); Gamson and Modigliani (1989).

46. For example, in McAdam, McCarthy, and Zald's (1996) recently edited book, political opportunities and resource mobilization are treated as part of the frame process, and mobilizing structure is constrained by both the frame and political opportunities.

47. For example, Alford and Friedland (1985), Lisa Anderson (1986), Entelis and Naylor (1992), Hildred Geertz (1991), Gellner (1988), Nee and Mozingo (1983), and Rosenbaum (1992).

economic development, where the theory of state-society relations is more developed, scholars have used concepts such as "bounded autonomy," "embedded autonomy," or "the state in society" to capture state-society relations conducive to development.[48] Although these concepts are crucial, they are not very helpful for capturing the path-dependent interactive processes between the state and society, which are vital to the trajectory of a large-scale social movement. Obviously, we need concepts that are less abstract and more capable of catching interactive processes between the state and society. To this end, my strategy is to separate state-society relations into three impure but non-reducible dimensions: the nature of the state, the nature of society, and linkages between the state and society.

In the following, I first define the state and its nature. Then, I discuss state-society linkages. Finally, through a discussion of the nature of society, I bring in a set of propositions that relate the nature of social movement dynamics to state-society relations. Please notice that these propositions are not waiting to be formally tested in empirical chapters, nor are they supposed to exhaust all the possible dimensions of state-society relations. Rather, they outline some major patterns of contentious politics in relation to different state-society relationships that are particularly relevant to this book. They serve as theoretical guidelines for the empirical chapters.

THE STATE AND ITS NATURE

Following Michael Mann, I define the *state* as a complex, territorially centered organization with a differentiated set of institutions, including military organizations.[49] I do not define the state in functional terms because states perform multiple functions that vary over time and across different countries. Historically, states emerged as territory-centered organizations whose functions centered on defense and warfare. But states also acquired class domination, lawmaking, welfare, and other functions. States are often classified in terms of their political nature. Different classification systems have been proposed.[50] In this book, I simply adopt the democracy versus authoritarianism dichotomy. A state is democratic when the government commits to the rule of law, tolerates

48. See Zhao and Hall (1994), Peter Evans (1995), and Migdal (1994) for sources of these concepts.

49. Mann (1986, 1993).

50. Recently, Finer (1997) has classified major regime types based on four institutional sources: palace, forum, church, and nobility. Their combinations yield six hybrid types. In their study of the democratic transition, Linz and Stepan (1996) identify five ideal types of modern states: democratic, authoritarian, totalitarian, post-totalitarian, and sultanist. Different regime types have different paths and tasks in making a transition to democracy.

minorities, and elects leaders by regular and competitive elections in which the majority of the adult population participates. A state is authoritarian when the regime has weak political, social, or even economic pluralism and is led by leaders who are not popularly elected and who are not always subject to the legal codes that they have created.

These are ideal types. Within democracy, there are presidential and parliamentary variations. There have also been many democracies in which minorities were not much tolerated. Variations within authoritarian regimes are even wider. They encompass autocratic regimes ruled by a divine king, totalistic regimes ruled by an ideological party, and authoritarian regimes that coexist with a de facto plural society because of their weak capacity to penetrate society. Some authoritarian regimes are situated in an environment so insecure that the state leaders harvest any gain they can get before being overthrown.[51] In the 1980s, the nature of the Chinese state, which I will discuss in the next chapter, was similar to that which Linz and Stepan call a post-totalitarian regime.[52] However, in most of this book, I have implicitly or explicitly compared the 1989 Movement to social movements under Western democracy. Therefore, a simple democracy versus authoritarian dichotomy is sufficient for my purposes here.[53]

A state's political nature shapes, but does not determine, state behavior. Once state elites sense a real danger, the state can do much more than what a dogmatic structuralist can imagine. The French Revolution was instructive for other European Old Regimes, leading them to act more prudently in order to prevent further revolutions. Similarly, the Great Depression triggered waves of reforms in capitalist states unimaginable to orthodox Marxists. Finally, the economic miracles of East Asian NICs (newly industrializing countries) and the collapse of Eastern European communism have motivated the current Chinese state to reform itself. These reforms have made the Chinese state look much more like a bureaucratic-authoritarian state of the former South Korean and Taiwanese type than like a Stalinist totalitarian regime.[54] Very few social outcomes are inevitable.

51. Bates (1981).

52. Linz and Stepan (1996).

53. Chapter 9 is an exception. In that chapter, I compare the movement languages and activities of the May 4th Movement of 1919, the December 9th Movement of 1935–36, and the 1989 Movement, the three largest student movements in China before the 1990s. Since the states behind these movements were all authoritarian regimes, I thus make a further differentiation among the natures of the states behind the three movements.

54. Kornai (1959, 1989) and Szelenyi (1986), based on their own experiences of Eastern European Communist reforms and their Marxist notion of the state, conclude that economic reform cannot succeed in

A state has autonomy. State autonomy is derived from unique functions that other organizations cannot provide.[55] Over time, a state also gains autonomy from elements of the nature of state organization itself, such as its special access to information, expertise, and resources.[56] State autonomy allows political elites to initiate state-centered programs. Yet although the state has some autonomy, its behavior is not necessarily coherent. Such incoherence derives from the autonomy of different state organizations, from various social pressures, and from the crosscutting identities of state elites. However, this is not to say that a state is not able to make coherent decisions. State cohesion depends on elite unity, or on the ability of a dominant state organization (i.e., the cabinet in many cases) to control and coordinate more peripheral institutions.

Even when a state is able to come up with coherent policies, nothing guarantees that a policy will effectively penetrate society. Thus, another important dimension of the state is its capacity. A state's capacity depends, again, on internal cohesion on the part of the elites. It also depends on what Mann terms the state's "infrastructural power."[57] Mann's original formulation emphasizes the importance of roads, universal coinage, and communication for state capacity (I classify these as infrastructural hardware). Infrastructural power is defined by Mann as the capacity of a state to actually penetrate society to generate revenues or mobilize people for various purposes.[58] By defining infrastructure in this way, Mann predicts a high stability in modern authoritarian regimes, since they have high levels of despotic as well as infrastructural capacity. What Mann neglects is, however, people's voluntary cooperation with the state (I classify it as "infrastructural software"). This aspect of infrastructural power depends, among other things, on the level of legitimation that a state enjoys.[59] Legitimacy is a concept that I will turn to shortly.

---

communist regimes because during the reform the state will always try to save inefficient firms as a result of inseparable interests. Obviously, this is much less true for the reform in communist China.

55. Mann (1988).

56. See Michels (1962) for a classic discussion on the oligarchic tendency of large-scale organizations.

57. Defined this way, the idea of state strength is different from traditional "strong state" ideas (Peter Evans 1979; Migdal 1988).

58. Mann (1988) classifies state power into despotic and infrastructural power. By despotic power, Mann refers to the power that state elites have to act upon their will. Obviously, what is important for a modern state is not only how much autonomy the state has to act upon its will but also the capacity of a state to penetrate and coordinate society.

59. For example, the communist regimes in Eastern Europe collapsed suddenly. However, they collapsed not because there was a lack of despotic power or because their infrastructural hardware deteriorated, but because the state could neither sustain elite cohesion nor receive cooperation from society. In general, a modern authoritarian regime, especially that with a weak tradition of bureaucracy and civil law, regardless of how well it is equipped with infrastructural hardware, faces legitimacy problems in the long run. The

In conclusion, the nature of a state carries two impure meanings in this book: its political nature as well as its strength. State strength is determined by elite cohesion and by the capacity of the state to penetrate society. Both are related to the level of state legitimation.

STATE-SOCIETY LINKAGES

The nature of a regime links the state and society politically, yet state and society are also related through psychological and economic aspects. By psychological relations, I mean the legitimacy of state power as perceived by rank-and-file citizens and by state elites themselves. Needless to say, links between the state and society are multidimensional, and these dimensions are entwined. The importance of economic relations is conventional wisdom and is emphasized in this book. As chapter 3 shows, except for a few ideologically motivated intellectuals and students, the majority of students initially supported the 1989 Movement because some reform measures reduced their economic benefits and blocked their channels of status attainment. However, a large-scale social movement cannot be just a rational-choice-based strategy game; it is also an emotional moral crusade. Therefore, beyond political and economic linkages, what I want to elaborate here is another aspect of state-society linkages—the sources of state legitimacy. But first, let me briefly define ideology and political culture, a set of closely related concepts that will be frequently used.

Culture has been defined most broadly as both a system of symbols and meanings and a pattern of practices.[60] However, culture is useful to sociological analysis when it is considered as autonomous yet influential on patterns of social practice. If culture is already defined as both a meaning and a performative system, what else is there to explain? In this book, like Geertz and Schneider,[61] I define both ideology and culture as systems of meaning, not performance. Ideology is a belief system with various degrees of false (or true) content, while political culture is a repertoire of traditional (and modern) beliefs, values, and symbols. Here, "ideology" is restricted to grand visions such as communism, socialism, liberalism, and nationalism, whereas by "culture" I refer to a relatively stable meaning system that passes down through socialization. Again, the distinction is impure.

---

honeymoon of a revolution that brought the authoritarian regime fades, charismatic leaders die, the economy has downturns, political mistakes are inevitable, and the political system becomes less flexible.

60. See Steinmetz (1999, 4–8) and Sewell (1996) for summaries of various definitions of the concept of culture.

61. Geertz (1973, 1983); Schneider (1976).

To understand the importance of *state legitimacy* to social movements, we need
to understand the close relationships between legitimation, ideology, and political culture. Intuitively, state legitimacy is part of political culture. Indeed, the
form of state legitimacy will change a society's political culture and slowly become an integrated part of that political culture. However, political culture and
state legitimacy have this subtle difference: culture is habit-dependent, while legitimation is state-dependent. Culture is a relatively stable aspect of human life.
We do not expect the political culture of a nation to change overnight. However, legitimacy related political behaviors can change very quickly. Legitimacy
and ideology also share many similarities. A form of legitimacy, for example,
can be justified or opposed in ideological terms. The difference is that state legitimacy itself is just an unwritten social contract. It is a shared understanding
of state-society relations, not an ideology.

State legitimacy certainly depends on social structure. A certain form of social structure (say, a strong civil society) often correlates with a certain form of
state legitimacy (say, legal-electoral legitimacy). However, state legitimacy in
turn confines the behavior of state elites, dominant classes, movement activists,
and people's interpretation of (or sentiment towards) others' behavior. (For example, it determines when the people will think that a state action is an injustice and get upset, and when state elites are demoralized and refuse to repress
the rebels, and so forth). These cannot be explained by simple resort to socioeconomic structures. Therefore, legitimation is not only a "mediating" but also
an independent factor.[62]

Legitimacy has been a very popular concept in political analysis. It has been
used in explaining a wide range of phenomena, from the crisis of capitalism to
the democratization of authoritarian regimes.[63] Unfortunately, legitimacy also
remains a vaguely defined and much abused concept. Until very recently, scholars continuously used "limits of legitimacy," "legitimation crisis," or "lack of
legitimacy" to explain the rise of a movement or the crisis of a regime.[64] When
they do not specify what kind of legitimation crisis a state is facing, and which
population has experienced a legitimation crisis, such analyses remain un-
convincing.[65] Therefore, as a first step, we need to define several dimensions of

---

62. Skocpol (1979), for example, has insisted that state legitimacy is a "mediate" factor.

63. See Habermas (1975) and Offe (1973) for their analyses of the crisis of capitalism. See Chehabi and
Stepan (1995), Linz (1988), and Huntington (1991) for analyses of democratization.

64. See, for example, Wolfe (1977), Habermas (1975), Offe (1973), Johnson (1982), and Oberschall
(1996).

65. For example, Lipset (1981, 64) defines legitimacy as "the capacity of the system to engender and
maintain the belief that the existing political institutions are the most appropriate ones for the society."
Barrow (1993, 25) argues that "the legitimacy of a state is ultimately expressed in people's willingness to

state legitimacy that can be empirically measured, independent of the social movement being studied. In chapter 7, when I analyze the relationships between the Chinese state and the 1989 Movement, I shall specify the major Chinese urban population's perception of state legitimation during the late 1980s.

According to Weber, habit, affection, and rational calculation are three bases of human compliance. Correspondingly, he proposes three ideal types of authority relations: traditional, charismatic, and rational.[66] While the typology has been criticized in different ways,[67] critics still accept it. Weber's classification is certainly illuminating. However, when these ideal types are used to analyze state power, there are two problems. First, as Collins has argued,[68] Weber's typology is static. Authority relations are interactive and dynamic; people's perceptions of a state's legitimacy influence how they interact with the state, but in turn their interactions further shape their judgments of the state's legitimacy. Second, Weber's ideal types separate the emotional and cognitive elements in people's perceptions of state legitimation. In actual situations, people's (especially dominant-class members') sense of state legitimation always involves a mix of sentiment and rationality regardless of the ways that a state tries to legitimize itself. For example, in historical China the emperor was legitimized as "the son of the heaven." Nonetheless, dynasties were frequently challenged and overthrown when heaven's son failed to provide basic services. The same is true when people (especially the dominant classes) support a charismatic leader. They do so out of affection as well as in hope of a promising reward. These two problems, concerning the interactive and dynamic nature of authority relations and the isolation of emotional and cognitive elements in the concept of legitimation, make it difficult to adopt Weber's ideal types as the basis of an empirical analysis.

In this book, legitimation is treated as a relational and interactive concept. My aim is to show empirically and in detail how people's assessments of state legitimacy manifested themselves in the meso- and micro-level interactions among participants in the 1989 Movement and between the participants and the state. Sources of state legitimation are classified not in terms of ideal types of human compliance but by the ways that state power is justified: by a commonly

---

comply with decisions made by the state apparatus." Linz (1988, 65) defines legitimacy as "the belief that in spite of shortcomings and failures, the political institutions are better than others that might be established and therefore can demand obedience." These are all reasonable definitions. Their common weakness, as I have explained in the text, is that they have not specified dimensions of legitimacy, which is essential for an empirical analysis.

66. See Weber (1978, 28) and Bendix (1962, 290–97) for the typology.
67. See Blau (1963) and Eckstein and Gurr (1975) for some of the criticisms.
68. Collins (1995, 1565–66).

accepted procedure, by the service that the state has provided, and by a future promise. Correspondingly, I define three types of state legitimation as perceived by different sections of people in society and by state elites themselves: legal-electoral, ideological, and performance legitimacy.

A state is based on legal-electoral legitimacy when it takes laws as binding principles for all social groups including state elites themselves, and when top leaders are popularly elected on a regular basis. Ideological legitimacy means that a state's right to rule is justified by a grand vision based on a future prom-ise to which a government is committed.[69] Performance legitimacy means that a state's right to rule is justified by its economic and/or ritual performance and by the state's capacity for territorial defense. Finally, when citizens tie their hopes to the ability and personality of one or a few state leaders, the state en-joys charismatic legitimacy. Charismatic legitimacy can be supplementary to any kind of state legitimacy, but it tends to be an extreme form of ideological legitimacy. Again, these are not pure types but impure constructions. A state can never secure its survival with a single source of legitimacy. Nevertheless, in one country at a particular time, one source of legitimacy tends to dominate. The dominant source of state legitimacy defines the nature of a state in addi-tion to the authoritarian and democratic dichotomy.

The above definition allows us to measure the type and level of legitimacy as perceived by different sectors of a population, including state elites. Legal-electoral legitimacy is the easiest to assess. By definition, states under Western democracy are based on legal-electoral legitimation. One of the striking fea-tures of Western democracy is that the state can enjoy a great legitimacy even when people have little trust in some leaders and government institutions.[70]

---

69. People may find similarities between legal-electoral and ideological legitimacy since legal-electoral legitimacy has democracy as its ideological base. However, they are different in two aspects. Democracy promises only a procedure to select leaders, not a utopian future. Most importantly, my definition of legal-electoral legitimacy emphasizes procedure, not ideology. Although legal-electoral legitimacy can be justified by democratic doctrines, over time it is the commonly accepted procedure of leadership selection, not the value system, that legitimizes such a state. I want to stress here that stability is an important feature of legal-electoral legitimation. Since election itself forms the basis of this legitimation, a government can rule such a society without a grand ideology, and policy mistakes and scandals can lead to governmental change with-out a legitimacy crisis. In this system, elite conflicts and electoral changes still systematically provide op-portunities to political outsiders, which lead to a gradual opening of society or democratic consolidation (Rueschemeyer, Stephens, and Stephens 1992). However, this extension of pluralism encourages individu-als to organize themselves on a sectional or sectorial basis in ways that further lower the possibilities of mobilization on the national level. Therefore, if we treat Western electoral democracy as a culture, its "hegemony" is pervasive.

70. Dogan (1995, 65).

This is possible because a democratic state does not base its legitimacy primarily on the quality of leaders and institutions. On the other hand, an authoritarian state like China may not be able to sustain political stability in the long run if a significant proportion of the citizens strongly dislike their leaders or institutions, because China does not have routine electoral channels that could potentially be used to get rid of the leaders and institutions.

While legal-electoral legitimation tends to be the basis of democratic regimes, ideological legitimation is often characteristic of authoritarian regimes. In China during the 1980s, the state still claimed its legitimacy in the ideological terms of the Four Cardinal Principles written into the preamble of the Chinese Constitution.[71] People's perception of the ideological legitimacy of the Chinese state can thus be assessed by their attitude towards these principles.

The principal dimensions of performance legitimation include economic performance, moral conduct, and territorial defense. Without a pending threat from other countries, the economic and moral dimensions of state performance tend to dominate. Economic performance can be measured objectively, by economic growth and tangible benefits to specific populations, or subjectively, by directly asking individuals to evaluate a state's economic performance. Moral performance is embedded in the traditional unwritten form of a "social contract": in terms of the proper behaviors and rituals that good rulers should perform.[72] It is a defensive form, and a cultural dimension, of state legitimation. Its measurement should start with an understanding of a local culture. In the book, I argue that the source of state legitimation in China during the late 1980s was predominantly economic and moral performance, not ideology, and that much of the protestors' behavior during the 1989 Movement was shaped by this form of state legitimation.

THE NATURE OF SOCIETY, STATE-SOCIETY RELATIONS, AND MOVEMENT DYNAMICS

The nature of society primarily depends on its structure. In traditional Marxist literature, social structure is equated with economic and class relations. However, class is a weak identity in comparison with identity categories that have clear territorial and linguistic bases (such as nation or ethnicity). More hurdles need to be overcome before a class is capable of forming an imagined

71. They are the adherence to socialism, adherence to the leadership of the CCP, adherence to Marxism-Leninism and Mao Zedong thought, and adherence to the dictatorship of the proletariat.

72. The concept is in part from Durkheim's (1933) idea of "non-contractual elements of contract."

community.[73] As studies of working-class movements demonstrate, workers do not automatically develop a class-consciousness under capitalism unless they are treated by the state in certain ways.[74] Historically, most large-scale human conflicts have been organized political struggles rather than economically based class struggles. I thus define *social structure* more broadly, in terms of the spatial relations among people as well as in terms of the density, diversity, and relationships of social organizations in a society.[75]

Within the non-Marxist tradition, civil society has been revived as a popular term describing the structure of society.[76] It is defined in a narrow sense as the sum total of autonomous social organizations that counterbalance the state.[77] Recently, civil society has also been defined as an ideal society in which membership in social organizations is "both voluntary and overlapping" so that individuals are free not only from the tyranny of the state but from all forms of social cages.[78] This form of society, according to Gellner, is actually trustworthier than democracy. In most non-Western societies, however, intermediate organizations take forms far from this ideal definition. The usage of "civil society" in this book is therefore closer to its narrow definition, in which a strong civil society implies the existence of strong and heterogeneous intermediate organizations that counterbalance the state.

The density, diversity, and strength of intermediate organizations are important indexes to the nature of a society and of state-society relations.[79] First, strong and diverse intermediate associations not only check state power but also facilitate the state's penetration into society. Without intermediate organizations, state power will be despotic and people's attention will be state-centered. Without cooperation between social organizations and the state, state power cannot penetrate very deeply into society and generate concerted social energy for achieving various state-centered projects such as modernization or warfare.[80] Second, intermediate organizations nurture bonds and contractual

73. The term "imagined community" is borrowed from Anderson (1983).

74. Katznelson (1985), Lipset (1983), Mann (1993, chs. 15–18), and Marks (1989).

75. Here, I define organization as a social group which is constructed to achieve specific goals through coordinated effort. It usually has a nonrandom division of labor, power, and communication responsibilities (Etzioni 1964). Churches, unions, neighborhood associations, student and professional associations, and social movement organizations are some examples.

76. See Gellner (1994), Hall (1995), Keane (1988), Schmitter (1993), and Seligman (1992) for recent developments of the civil society theory.

77. See Kumar (1993), Wank (1995), and Whyte (1992) for similar definitions.

78. See Gellner (1994) and Hall (1995, 15) for this definition of civil society.

79. See Tocqueville (1972) for discussion of the roles that intermediate associations have played in stabilizing American democracy.

80. Hall (1985a); Zhao and Hall (1994).

relations among social groups, creating and sustaining shared identities and traditions. Poorly organized individuals tend to have little mutual understanding and shared sense of reality, and tend to pursue their interests in an uncoordinated fashion. Finally, a high density and a diversity of intermediate organizations in society facilitate sectional and segmental mobilization and prevent national-level uprisings.

Students of resource mobilization theories criticize Kornhauser's mass society theory by emphasizing the importance of organizations for movement mobilization,[81] and indeed organizations do sometimes play a crucial role in how movement participants are mobilized. When society is treated as a whole, however, strong and diverse intermediate organizations actually reduce the chances of a national-level grand mobilization. This is because different organizations tend to have distinctive interests and tend to nurture crosscutting identities among their members. An issue of great interest to one social group may be totally irrelevant to or even at odds with the interests of another group. People are less likely to act radically when intermediate associations in a society are well developed. This discussion can be concluded with a proposition that links the nature of society with the strength of intermediate organizations in that society:[82]

    a. A society with a high density of heterogeneous intermediate organizations independent of the state tends to be conformist, while a society with poorly developed intermediate organizations inclines to be radical.

By "conformist" I refer to a society where radical ideas and activities are kept on the margins and where the mainstream generally sticks to the existing order or pursues reformist changes. By "radical" I mean a society where people are more likely to support anti-establishment ideas and participate in social movements that aim to fundamentally change, or even abolish, the current social-political systems. Thus the proposition says that large-scale social movements and revolutions are more likely to happen in countries with poorly developed intermediate organizations. However, poor development of intermediate organizations is not a sufficient condition for large-scale social movements.

81. See Kornhauser (1959) for the "mass society theory." Also, see Oberschall (1973), Pinard (1975), Tilly (1978), Halebsky (1976), Useem (1980), and von Eschen, Kirk, and Pinard (1971) for criticisms of the mass society theory and for their emphases on the role of organizations in social movement mobilization.

82. I would like to make it clear that, first, all the propositions that I propose in this chapter assume "other things being equal." Second, for those propositions that link the nature of society to the type of regime, the validity of these propositions, when they are applied to other cases, depends on how close that regime is to the ideal regime types that I have defined earlier in this chapter.

Large-scale social movements are always accompanied by some sort of social changes that undermine the state's capacity to control society. Therefore, we need the following two propositions, which relate the rise and nature of social movements to the strength and scale of changes in intermediate organizations:

b. A state will be politically stable under two ideal conditions: either the existence of strong and heterogeneous intermediate organizations, or a complete absence of intermediate organizations. In the case of strong intermediate organizations, political stability does not mean no, or even fewer, social movements, but a lower chance of revolutionary turmoil.

c. Revolutionary turmoil is most likely to occur when intermediate organizations in a society are emerging or in decline, although in neither case is a revolution inevitable.

When intermediate organizations are completely absent, as in a totalitarian regime, a state achieves total domination.[83] No opposition is possible. More explanation needs to be provided for the second part of this proposition: "In the case of the existence of strong intermediate organizations, political stability does not mean no, or even fewer, social movements, but a lower chance of revolutionary turmoil." Since the early 1970s, Kornhauser's mass society theory has been severely criticized by resource mobilization scholars. This proposition gives some credit to Kornhauser. Kornhauser's mass society theory implies that large-scale social or political movements are more likely to occur in societies with weak intermediate organizations,[84] whereas his opponents focus either on social movements that occur in democratic societies with strong intermediate organizations or on micro-level mobilization processes. Preexisting organizations are certainly important to micro-level movement mobilization; therefore, a society with strong intermediate organizations experiences many more social movements than a mass society. Yet it is exactly the nature of a strong civil society—that is, the low cost of initiating a movement, the heterogeneity of intermediate organizations, well-calculated interests, and the crosscutting identities of the people as a consequence of organizational heterogeneity—that helps prevent revolutionary turmoil. Therefore, mass society theory at least correctly

---

83. See Arendt (1951) and Friedrich and Brzezinski (1965), among others, for theories of totalitarianism.

84. In a recent article, McAdam, Tarrow, and Tilly (1996) also argue that authoritarian regimes are more likely to give rise to rare but revolutionary mobilization.

predicts that weak intermediate associations create political niches for national mobilization. How organizations facilitate movement mobilization is an issue at another level.

Proposition "c" is Durkheimian, because it predicts that large-scale social movements are more likely to occur in a process of social change. Empirical cases that fit "the decline of intermediate organizations and revolution" argument are those of failed attempts at state centralization. For example, in Iran the Shah's modernization threatened many segments of society, especially two powerful groups, the ulama and the bazaar merchants, thereby provoking a revolution.[85] For the emergence of intermediate organizations, the examples are the decay of totalitarian regimes and state-led reforms in those regimes during the 1980s.[86] However, revolution is not inevitable during either the emergence or decline of intermediate organizations. Simply put, state centralization can be successful, and an emerging society does not necessarily clash head-on with the state.

In a democratic regime, a state does not prohibit organizations founded and operated under the law. Therefore, a real democracy should be accompanied by numerous intermediate organizations. In contrast, modern authoritarian regimes commonly emerge in countries with weak intermediate organizations, and they implement sanctions against social organizations outside the realm of state control. Since the density and diversity of social organizations is closely related to the character of a regime, the mobilization potential of a society is directly related to the nature of a state:

> d. A society tends to be radical in an authoritarian state and conformist in a democratic state.

This proposition depicts the distinctive nature of state-society relations under different types of state. It implies that opposition movements tend to be radical in authoritarian states and reformist in democratic states[87]—a crucial difference of social movement dynamics. In light of this proposition, many theories of social movements developed in the West can be seen as more suitable to explain social movement dynamics in democratic states than elsewhere. For

85. Arjomand (1988), McDaniel (1991), and Skocpol (1982).

86. For the decay of totalitarian regimes, see Janos (1986), Jowitt (1983), and Rigby and Feher (1982). For the state-led reforms and social movements, see Di Palma (1991) and White (1993).

87. McAdam, Tarrow, and Tilly (1996) express a similar view.

example, Gamson concludes that social movements which fight for less radical issues tend to flourish.[88] However, during the 1989 Movement, activities that fundamentally challenged the regime tended to win popularity (chapters 6, 9, and 10).

During the 1980s, the Chinese state retreated both organizationally and ideologically (chapter 1). Many institutions that once belonged to the state, such as the media, public opinion, and the universities, were freed from the tight control of the state and became increasingly "societal" in nature. Taking this into consideration, the above proposition can be extended into the following corollaries:

d.1. Media and public opinion tend to be conformist institutions in a democratic regime. However, in an authoritarian regime media and public opinion tend to be radical institutions, especially immediately after they free themselves from state control.

d.2. Universities tend to be more radical in an underdeveloped authoritarian regime than in a Western democratic regime.

Here, the first corollary depicts the different nature of media and public opinion under the two types of regime. The nature of mainstream Western media and public opinion is well documented. It is generally agreed in communications literature that the modern Western media tend to follow the dominant culture and the majority view, to rely on government sources for news, and either to neglect a social movement or to produce biased reports on a movement that aims at challenging the establishment.[89] Moreover, the public in the West tends to see the media as an institution independent of the state and to read the media's messages constructively.[90] By contrast, during the 1989 Movement, Chinese media tried to escape from state control by positively reporting on the movement, and public opinion followed rumors most of the time, except when

88. Gamson (1975).

89. However, scholars have attributed this conservatism to different factors, ranging from the functional routine of the media (e.g., Fishman 1980; Gans 1979), market forces (Epstein 1973; Ryan 1991; Tuchman 1972), and cultural hegemony (Gitlin 1980; Herman and Chomsky 1988; Molotch 1979). I will provide a more detailed review of this literature in chapter 10.

90. See Lang and Lang (1981) and Gamson and Modigliani (1989), among others, for the constructive nature of public opinion in the West.

the media reported on the movement positively. In chapter 10, I explain this fundamental difference in the behavior of the media and public opinion.

Although universities have been arguably the most radical institutions in democratic regimes, they were born in the West and maintained largely as a conformist institution. In medieval Europe, the university was controlled by the church, its curriculum was based on indigenous higher culture, and its students were almost exclusively from upper-class families. It was not until the middle class had become a dominant class that its children commonly went to the university. The Western university was gradually converted into a modern institution over a long historical period.[91] By contrast, the university in most underdeveloped authoritarian countries was a foreign institution with few or no indigenous cultural roots. It was founded as a part of the package of forced development, and the subjects taught in it have introduced foreign ideas that undermine the traditional social order.[92] On top of that, in order to develop modern industry, almost all the underdeveloped authoritarian states have tended to greatly emphasize higher education, and thus to "over-produce" students, which also leads to radicalism.[93] In chapter 3, I analyze how a set of state policies encouraged radicalism in Chinese universities.

Scholars generally find organizations and preexisting movement networks to be important for social movement mobilization.[94] In many authoritarian regimes, however, organizations outside the control of the state are poorly developed, and dissident networks are confined to a very small circle. A sudden rise of a large-scale social movement is thus an anomaly.[95] However, while authoritarian regimes may be able to crush intermediate organizations, they have never been able to eliminate everyday human relations. As chapter 8 shows, when a strong authoritarian regime undertakes a large-scale transformative project, it often does so by gathering a large homogenous population into a common physical environment. The spatial layout of the people facilitates active interactions among people as well as passive encounters between them.

91. Ringer (1979); Vaughan and Archer (1971).

92. Lipset (1967); Altbach (1981).

93. Therefore, for example, except for German student movements in 1848, students in the West were not a major force in national politics until the 1960s, whereas students in underdeveloped nations have always been involved in nationalist, communist, and currently, democratic movements (Altbach 1968a, 1989; Chow 1967; Shils 1968).

94. See Fernandez and McAdam (1989), Roger V. Gould (1991), McAdam (1986), McCarthy (1987), McCarthy and Zald (1973), Opp and Gern (1993), and Snow, Zurcher, and Ekland-Olson (1980) for the role of social networks in movement mobilizations.

95. Olson (1990).

In a political crisis, such an ecology often becomes the basis of a social movement mobilization.[96] Thus, we have the following proposition:

e. When intermediate organizations are poorly developed in a society, social movement mobilization tends to be spontaneous and highly dependent upon the ecology of the living and working environments of the individuals to be mobilized.

In chapter 6, I discuss the empirical meaning of the concept of spontaneity during the 1989 Movement. Here, by "spontaneity," I simply mean how movement organizations were frequently incapable of controlling movement participants, and how a significant number of movement activities were voluntarily initiated by individuals or a small groups of people who were not necessarily the leaders of the movement organizations. This proposition states that, when a society is poorly organized, the density, distribution, and spatial routine of the people that movement activists intend to mobilize are crucial in participant recruitment and in shaping the development of the movement. It also claims that social movements breaking out under authoritarian regimes will be more spontaneous in nature. The following corollaries further link a movement's spontaneous nature to its dynamics:

e.1. When intermediate organizations in a society are weak, social movement activities tend to be initiated at an individual level, and the development of a social movement tends to be driven more by emotions than by strategies.

e.2. When intermediate organizations in society are weak, structural conditions become more important in shaping social movement dynamics. In other words, although individuals are "freer" in such situations, their contingent choices have less impact on social movement dynamics.

The first corollary assumes that organizations are better equipped to overcome the influence of individual-level emotions in making strategic decisions. The second corollary implies the principle of the "invisible hand." That is, when many activities occur at the same time and place, what makes a certain action dominate is not so much the minds of actors as the minds of the observers. An action dominates because it is better able to move the audience. It moves the

96. Recently, Goldstone and Useem (1999) have demonstrated the importance of prison ecology to prison riots. In the study of poor people's social movements in Iran, Bayat (1997) also emphasizes the importance of spatial proximity, not formal networks and organizations, in movement participation.

audience more effectively, in turn, because it matches with the existing popular "schemata of interpretation" in society. (In this book, these schemata are the existing popular perceptions of state legitimation.) Several chapters of this book, especially chapters 8 and 9, take the above propositions and corollaries as a starting point.

Since the early 1990s, scholars have regained interest in the role of crowd be-havior and emotion in social movements.[97] Most of the studies, however, tend to emphasize the importance of crowd behavior and emotions in social move-ments without specifying the structural conditions under which the crowd be-havior and emotion become dominant in a social movement. This set of propo-sitions is an effort to redress such tendencies.

The above propositions come together to relate the potential and character-istics of social movement mobilization and dynamics to the structure and na-ture of society. They also link the nature of society (in terms of its mobiliza-tion potential) to the nature of a state. They depict different social movement dynamics under democratic and authoritarian regimes. These propositions do not exhaust the repertoire of possible state-society relationships and their im-pact on social movement dynamics. As chapter 9 demonstrates, state-society relations differ within authoritarian regimes. They need to be empirically de-termined. However, the nature of the state, the nature of society, and link-ages between the state and society are the three aspects that are basic to under-standing the impact of state-society relations on large-scale social movements.

Methodological Remarks

Before moving to the empirical chapters, it will be helpful to make two methodological comments on the book's theoretical arguments and empirical data. I have made various theoretical arguments to which some readers may pose counterexamples (for instance, when I argue that ecology-based mobiliza-tion dominated the 1989 Movement, one may immediately point out the role of organizations in that movement). I make three types of arguments in this book: definitional, comparative, and competitive. Although I will qualify each argument where it appears, it is useful to discuss the problem more generally by explaining specific issues with regard to each type of argument.

97. See Oliver (1989) and McPhail (1991) for the recent crowd behavior literature, and Jasper (1997, 1998), Scheff (1994), and Goodwin (1997) for studies of the role of emotions in collective actions. See also Smelser (1962) for earlier literature.

First, there are definitional arguments. For instance, I define the media in democratic regimes as a conformist institution. Here I am not ignoring the existence of far-right and far-left media, variations in mainstream media contents, and journalists' reformist efforts under Western democracy. Rather, when I lay out this type of definition, I see what is to be defined as following a "statistical distribution," of which my definition captures the "central tendency." Counterexamples do not undermine the definitions unless their existence significantly alters the "central tendency."

The second type of argument is comparative. For example, I argue that universities tend to be more radical in an underdeveloped authoritarian regime than in a Western democratic regime (chapter 3). This should not be taken as suggesting that universities will revolt every day in underdeveloped nations and will never revolt in democratic regimes, that there are no variations in students' political behaviors within underdeveloped (or developed) nations, or that students' political behavior in a nation never changes. Still using the statistical analogy, a comparison of this kind could be considered as a t-test (or ANOVA and other multiple test methods when more than two groups are involved). The argument is valid as long as universities in underdeveloped authoritarian nations as a whole are much more radical than their counterparts in Western democracies. Some counterexamples to my argument, such as the student movement in 1848 Germany and the New Left movements in the 1960s, can be taken as within-group variations when compared with the frequent radical student movements in authoritarian regimes.[98]

The last is the competitive type of argument, to which the major arguments in chapters 7, 8, 9, and 10 belong. This type of argument usually comes together with competing argument(s), and the intention is to show that the argument explains significantly more variations than the competing ones. For example, in chapter 7, I argue that the state behavior and consequently the dynamics of the 1989 Movement were primarily driven by state-society relations rather than by factionalism among the top state elites. There is obviously evidence of power struggles among top state elites during the movement. However, unless one shows empirically that a model emphasizing factionalism does explain larger variations than the state-society relation theory, my arguments remain unfalsified.

Still more important, however, are the issues concerning the methods by which this book's major empirical evidence has been gathered. While a more detailed description of the interviews will be presented at the end in an ap-

98. Lipset (1967); Altbach (1981, 1991).

pendix, it may be useful to discuss the most crucial issue here. My writing is based mainly on data collected from three sources. First, I formally interviewed seventy informants in 1992–93. They ranged from movement activists and students to teachers and student control cadres in universities. Second, I collected materials available at McGill, Princeton, Harvard, the University of Chicago, and the Chinese University of Hong Kong. Third, I went to several major libraries in China, and, with the help of some friends, obtained many materials from Chinese sources. Each of these sources has its own strengths and weaknesses. For example, regarding the interview data, I am concerned about biases in retrospective reporting such as forgetting and recasting particular events according to general opinions or personal views. Even though the interviews were constructed to avoid these shortcomings, they may not be totally eliminated. Therefore, an immediate question is how I selected materials from such voluminous sources—a legitimate concern regarding the reliability and validity of the data used in the book.

As a rule of thumb, I took great caution with all of the data, especially those related to important events. I compared different accounts within the same source or/and across different types of data. Relying on a process that Chinese historians call *kaozheng*, which could be roughly translated into English as cross-validation, I tried to figure out what most likely happened. Admittedly, this did not protect me from various personal biases in making judgments. However, potential biases were minimized when I applied falsifiable logics in rendering judgments. I sometimes followed the account of my informants or of the secondary nongovernmental sources, sometimes followed the Chinese government account or/and semi-official sources from China, and sometimes adopted bits and pieces of accounts from each of the sources. Sometimes, I followed none of them. Instead, by reading between the lines in all the materials, I constructed a picture or captured a social mood that was not clear in any one of the sources. Due to the scope of the research and enormous diversity of the events, it is very difficult to summarize the processes for each event. Let me just give an example of how an event is typically constructed.

On April 19, the police tried to restore order in front of the Xinhua Gate, the south gate of the government compound. By the early morning of April 20, about 200 students still refused to go. Policemen dragged them into a very big bus and sent them back to Beijing University. When some of them arrived at the university, they held bloodstained clothes and shouted slogans angrily. Rumors about police brutality spread out and a class boycott immediately followed in several major universities. The whole event, which is discussed in chapter 6, was labeled the "Xinhua Gate Bloody Incident" (*Xinhuamen canan*). So far, most writings have simply followed what rumor has said. Indeed, the rumor has become a widely shared "historical memory." [99]

However, a government-controlled newspaper claimed that the blood was from some students who were cut by glass while trying to break the bus windows. These students got off the bus and the bus driver saw them stopping a truck, which took them away. The accounts are obviously contradictory. I also saw a big-character poster written at about that time by a student. The student denounced the behavior of a group of his fellow classmates who were discussing how to induce the police to beat them so that they could use the incident to mobilize other students. I cannot, however, simply follow the student's account, since people may argue that the student might be a government agent. Nevertheless, I became alert to the issue.

In my interviews, two students claimed that they had direct knowledge of this incident. One student provided details of how one of his classmates was beaten by police. However, from other sources I found out that the classmate, named Wang Zhixin, was beaten near the Qianmen subway station in a brawl with several policemen when he was alone and on his way to school. It was unrelated to the Xinhua Gate Incident. Another student who was among the last two hundred told me that there were skirmishes that morning, but that the police did not really hit them with full strength. Yet I was still worried that this could have been only his personal experience.

I continuously searched through materials related to the event. Then, I encountered an account by student leader Zhang Boli, who left Xinhua Gate only a little earlier than the last two hundred students did. He recalled:

> As soon as I went back to Beijing University, Peng Rong and other students (they were among the last 200 students) were also back. They were on a big truck. When the truck arrived, I heard them shouting "Police brutality!" I asked Peng Rong what had happened. Peng showed me a big piece of glass with a large spot of bloodstain. He then said: "This is the evidence of a bloody crime. What should we do?" I said: "We should get all the students in our university and go demonstrate." Then I planned the major slogans: "The savage police, beating the students; countrywide class boycott, etc., etc." [100]

I was surprised to find that the account of the broken glass and the truck was nearly identical with the governmental one. The beauty is also that when Zhang

---

99. For the importance of historical memory in contentious politics, see Corney (1998), Polletta (1998), and Tilly (1994).

100. *Huigu yu Fansi* (1993, 52–53).

was making this account, he was only trying to explain how the class boycott in Beijing University was initiated, not provide evidence related to the Xinhua Gate Incident. (Such unintended recall usually has less systematic bias, and I relied heavily on it in constructing the book.) I then visited the Xinhua Gate area and found no glass windows around. It also does not make sense to assume that the police had beaten students with glass or that wounded students went somewhere to find broken glass on which to collect the blood as a specimen.[101] The police brutality accusation also did not fit the larger context of the time. As many observers agreed, the government at this stage was very afraid of antagonizing the students and still hoped to reach a peaceful settlement.[102] Up to that point, I became confident in concluding that skirmishes between the police and students did happen that night and some students were indeed hit by police. However, the so-called Xinhua Gate Bloody Incident was most probably an unfounded rumor. This is how a small section in chapter 6 was constructed. This kind of methodological approach, while painstaking, is actually very rewarding. It has given me not only great confidence in the empirical evidence but also many unanticipated insights into the movement.

101. A remaining question is whether the side windows on the bus were made of safety glass. If so, the glass in the windows could not cut the students because it would break into very small pieces when smashed. However, I consulted a Chinese car expert, who told me that, because safety glass is very expensive in China, all the side windows on buses made in China and used in domestic public transportation are made of ordinary glass.

102. See Feigon (1990, 139) for his observation of the government's tolerance in that period.

PART ONE

THE ORIGIN OF THE
1989 STUDENT MOVEMENT

one

CHINA'S STATE-SOCIETY RELATIONS AND THEIR CHANGES DURING THE 1980S

I have laid out a theoretical framework that argues that state-society relations—understood in terms of the nature of the state, the nature of society, and the linkages between the state and society—are the most important factors underlying the rise and development of a large-scale social movement or revolution. Before moving into empirical analyses of how particular state-society relations contributed to the rise of the 1989 Beijing Student Movement and shaped its development, we need some knowledge of the history of China's historical state-society relations before the rise of the 1989 Movement as well as an overview of Chinese society in the 1980s. This chapter serves both purposes.

The History of State-Society Relations in China

From 221 B.C. to A.D. 1911 China was ruled for the most part by unitary agrarian empires. During that long period, China underwent tremendous changes in its demography, politics, economy, and social structures; but it was in the twentieth century (between

1911 and 1978) that China experienced perhaps the most dramatic changes in its long history. Any short summary will not do justice to the great changes over these long spans. What I present here captures only some of the essential features.

In the seventh century and after, the Chinese agrarian empires were headed by an emperor who inherited his crown from his family and were managed by a bureaucratic administrative system whose members were selected by means of periodic civil service examinations.[1] The emperor was legitimated as "the son of heaven." Such legitimation not only gave the emperor a supernatural and divine quality but also assigned him two mandates: to serve the people and to observe a vast number of normative rites and customs. There are many sayings in Chinese texts regarding the first mandate, including: "people are the heaven of their prince; food is the heaven of the people"; "heaven looks accordingly as the people look and listens accordingly as the people listen"; and "the people first, territory next, and the king last."[2] Obviously, state legitimacy in historical China always had a very important performance dimension. When an emperor failed to deliver public goods that the people had expected, he could lose the mandate of heaven, giving people the right to rebel.

The rites and customs that an emperor had to follow varied to some degree from dynasty to dynasty, but they were largely founded in the works of Confucius and Mencius and interpreted by a body of state bureaucrats whose support was indispensable to the emperor. "Any infringement of the rites and customs always provokes strong reactions and grave disorders."[3] In this sense, a Chinese emperor usually had very limited power.[4] In the Chinese empire, modern "totalistic" pretensions were not only technologically infeasible but also normatively impossible.

The civil service examination system also shaped the nature of Chinese society. Becoming an official was such an important mode of status attainment that the examination encouraged local education and gave rise to a *literati* or gentry class. Yet because of its limited financial resources, a state could only recruit a small proportion of the *literati* into the bureaucracy.[5] Given China's size and population, the number of officials employed by the state was far from sufficient to govern the whole country. Local affairs below the county level were actually managed by the lower-level gentry. The state needed the cooper-

---

1. From time to time eunuchs could also be important in palace politics.
2. See Hsieh (1978, ch. 1).
3. Gernet (1987, xxii).
4. Gernet (1987), Hsieh (1978, ch. 1), and Ray Huang (1981).
5. At the time of the Qing dynasty, the bureaucracy was about 40,000 strong (Skocpol 1978, 69).

ation of local gentry to collect taxes and to maintain order in towns and peasant villages. Such gentry-led and village-based power networks constituted a
dominant structure in society. Horizontal links among the people were sanctioned mainly through various secret societies.[6] In times of social disorder, secret societies were often a major force for rebellion because of their size and
their entrenched organizational networks.

In sum, historically China had a bureaucratic-authoritarian regime with
largely performance-based state legitimation, an emperor whose power was
checked by complicated rites and customs interpreted by the bureaucrats, and
a peasant society that was vertically led by the gentry class and horizontally
linked by secret societies. This light form of norm-centered and maintenance-
oriented government was challenged, in the nineteenth century, by the "goal-
oriented" capitalist nations.[7] Faced with Western imperialism, China tried to
implement different reform measures. Although such reforms brought many
changes, they failed to create a government that could defend China from
Western imperialism (see chapter 2). The failure of less radical reforms provoked more radical attempts, eventually leading to the establishment of the
communist government in 1949.

China's state-society relations underwent a tremendous change after the
communists came to power. China was now led by a goal-oriented Leninist
party. Because many Chinese in the 1950s and 1960s believed that communism
would bring a bright future, and because of the past success in the war with the
nationalist government, the CCP, and especially Mao, enjoyed a high level of
ideological and charismatic legitimacy. Since the 1950s, the CCP under Mao's
leadership conducted many social engineering programs that tremendously
changed the nature of society. The most important among them were the
collectivization of agriculture, the nationalization of industry, and the adoption
of a planned economy. From the 1950s on, the Chinese were organized around
the commune system in the countryside and the work-unit (danwei) system in
the cities.

With the establishment of the commune and work-unit system, the state
was for the first time in history able to penetrate society down to the village and
factory level and to effectively engage in radical transformative programs according to utopian visions. Freed from rites and customs, Mao also placed himself among the very few Chinese "emperors" who could dominate the entire

6. Chesneaux (1972), Eastman (1988, ch. 10), and Esherick (1987).
7. The notion that societies may be either "maintenance oriented" or "goal oriented" is from Schwartz
(1987, 3).

state bureaucracy and determine China's fate according to his personal visions and interests. Even the traditionally weak secret societies were wiped out under Mao's rule. In this period, Chinese society became highly atomized.

Such state-society relations, which have been variously labeled as "totalitarian" or "totalistic," led to disastrous outcomes.[8] Since policy mistakes and personal powers were not checked, state social engineering activities after the mid-1950s brought disasters upon Chinese society. The three-year famine of 1959 through 1961, during which about 30 million people died of hunger, and the Cultural Revolution are only the two most well-known examples. By the time of Mao's death in 1976, the Chinese economy was on the verge of collapse,[9] Chinese people were living in poverty, and grievances were mounting in society. It was largely the widespread crises brought by the Cultural Revolution that pushed China's new leaders to start a reform in 1978. The reform had an initial success. Because of the reform and the new open-door policy, the Chinese acquired a level of political freedom and economic affluence that they could not even have dreamed of during Mao's era. However, reform once again fundamentally changed state-society relations, in a manner which I will now discuss. Please note that the following is again only a brief overview. More systematic discussion and analysis of China's state-society relations in the 1980s and their impact on the 1989 Beijing Student Movement will be given in later chapters.

"Social Fevers" as an Indication of the Change

There are many ways to look at Chinese society during the years of reform.[10] For the purpose of understanding the origin of the 1989 Movement and mass participation during it, I start with the social changes brought about by the largely state-led reform.[11] China experienced a great deal of change after the start of reform: class labeling of citizens was abolished; economic modernization became the principal, if not the only, national goal; a market economy was introduced; and new industrial sectors such as private business, joint ventures, and foreign firms mushroomed—yet so too did corruption and other anti-

8. See Tsou Tang (1991) for the concept of a totalistic regime.

9. Meisner (1986).

10. See, for example, Baum (1994), Nathan (1997), Shirk (1993), and Kate Xiao Zhou (1996).

11. See also Byrd (1992), Byrd and Lin (1990), Fewsmith (1994), White (1993), and Harding (1987) for economic reform, and Barnett and Clough (1986), Baum (1994), Davis and Vogel (1990), Lull (1991), and Schell (1988) on other aspects of Chinese society during the period of reform.

market forces. State control over intellectual activities was loosened, allowing extensive exploration of pro-Western forms of literature and the other arts. State control over public and private life was also relaxed, which led to the resurgence of religion as well as of some old Chinese traditions. The ordinary Chinese person's standard of living skyrocketed during the period from 1978 — when, for instance, a mechanical watch was a luxury—to 1989, when color television sets and refrigerators became common for many rural as well as urban families. The list could go on and on.

The scale and impact of the social changes brought by the economic reform was revealed by waves of "social fevers" *(re-dian)* [12] during the 1980s.[13] Table 1.1 lists the decade's major social fevers.[14] The table also briefly explains the meaning of different social fevers, except where their names are self-explanatory. This is by no means a complete list. It does not include some cases, such as those of "conference fever" and "reportage novel fever," which were more directly related to the 1989 Movement and will therefore be discussed separately in the next chapter. It does however illustrate the scale of social change in the 1980s. Frequent changes of social fevers brought great uncertainties to most people in society. Culture fevers brought values or ways of life that were in conflict with the prevailing orthodoxy. Socioeconomic fevers often turned past winners into losers—yet the force of transition was so irresistible that many joined them willy-nilly. Thus, although social fevers came into being under the impetus for change, they also brought great pain both to the people caught up in them and to the people left on the outside.

The social fevers listed in table 1.1 can be roughly categorized into three types: socioeconomic fevers, high culture fevers, and popular culture fevers.[15] Socioeconomic fevers can be seen as people's reactions to the sudden emergence of new economic and political freedoms as a result of state reform policies.

12. The Chinese word *re* can be translated into English as "hot," "warm," "fever," "fad," or even "wave" or "tide." In this context, I translate *"re"* as "fever," by which I mean a sudden increase of interest in the same subject on the part of a large population. For example, *chuguo-re* (going abroad fever) means the sudden passion of many people for going abroad.

13. Frequent social fevers are the expected outcome when a formerly isolated population is suddenly exposed to an influx of new information and opportunities. In a closed society, opportunities are few and individuals have narrow and homogenous ideas. Its people tend to be simultaneously excited by new opportunities or concepts. When a closed society is just opened, everything is new, and information and opportunities fluctuate rapidly. Social fevers, therefore, are themselves significant signs of the scale and scope of social changes.

14. The data in table 1.1 come mainly from Xiao Qinfu (1989), Wang Jintang (1990), Yang Xiong (1991), and from my interviews.

15. See Wang Jing (1996) for a recent discussion of the high culture fever during the 1980s.

TABLE 1.1   Major Social Fevers in Urban China during the 1980s

Types	Examples	Explanations
Socioeconomic fevers	Study fever and diploma fever	Arose because early reform policies emphasized intellectuals' role in economic reform and greatly elevated the political status of intellectuals.
	Congzheng re (political career fever)	Arose due to massive recruitment of state cadres among university graduates during the early 1980s and diminished after state offices were saturated in the mid-1980s.
	Business fever	Arose with the opportunities created by the market-oriented reform and peaked in 1988, when some intellectuals and students, many in a protesting mood, got involved in commercial activities.
	Going abroad fever	Students and some young urban workers tried any means to study or work abroad in order to have a better life and career and to escape from Chinese realities. Peaked in the late 1980s, when the reform was in crisis and as more and more students became familiar with the procedures for applying to foreign universities.
	Special economic zones (SEZs) fever	Massive numbers of people flooded into the SEZs to look for better opportunities. The most infamous such fever was Hainan fever in the late 1980s, when hundreds of thousands flooded to the newly founded island province and SEZ, seeking better opportunities.
High culture fevers	Western culture fever: Sartre fever, Nietzsche fever, and Freud fever	A series of social fevers affected Chinese intellectuals and students searching for meaning in the wake of the decline of Marxism.
	Western religion fever	In cities, mainly the fever for Christianity. People looked for alternative faiths after Marxism, although many followed just out of pro-Western curiosity.
	Culture criticism: culture fever, *Heshang* fever, world citizenship discussion	Culture criticism started in the mid-1980s and peaked in 1988 with the TV series *Heshang* and the world citizenship discussion. The central idea here was that Chinese culture should be held responsible for the failed development and tragedies of Mao's era.
	Xungenre "searching for roots" fevers: "searching for roots" literature, Neo-Confucianism, I-Ching, and Qi-Gong fevers	Most of these fevers were apolitical. They marked the revival of Chinese culture after the death of Mao, headed by intellectuals absorbed by features of traditional Chinese culture.

TABLE 1.1   Major Social Fevers in Urban China during the 1980s (*continued*)

Types	Examples	Explanations
Popular culture fevers	The Hong Kong/ Taiwan pop song fever	During the early 1980s, Hong Kong and Taiwan pop songs flooded the mainland. The state initially tried to resist but eventually acquiesced.
	Jeans fever, brand name dress fever, make-up fever	Western and Hong Kong–style dress and ideas of beauty dominated Chinese cities and coastal areas after these and other similar fevers.
	Western food and holiday fevers	Eating Western food and celebrating Western holidays such as Christmas became very popular from the mid-1980s, especially among students.
	Pop and movie star fever	Since the late 1980s, fans of movie stars and pop singers acted more and more like their Western counterparts.
	Mah-jongg fever	Mah-jongg fever represented the revival of many traditional recreational activities, rituals, and superstitions.

Both the high culture fevers and the popular culture fevers resulted from a sudden influx of new information from the West and a simultaneous rediscovery of the Chinese past. High culture fevers can be further divided into three subtypes: Western culture fevers, (Chinese) culture criticism fevers, and traditional Chinese culture (or "searching for roots") fevers. The first two subtypes are two sides of the same coin. While the culture criticism fevers treated Chinese culture as a major hurdle to modernization, the Western culture fevers looked to the West for solutions.

Behind these rather bizarre fevers, however, were major transformations of state-society relations: transformations of the state, of the economy, and of society. The state was gradually changing from an ideology-based totalitarian regime into a performance-based authoritarian regime;[16] the economy was moving from a planned to a market basis; and Chinese society in general was reviving, transforming itself from one based on a collectivist ideal into one that was increasingly pluralistic, though still poorly organized (table 1.2). I will now discuss the major changes along the three dimensions and their impact on the urban population.

16. By totalitarian regime I mean the totalitarian intentions of the state during Mao's era, not the reality. As for the realities, see, for example, Walder (1986) and Friedman, Pickowicz, and Selden (1991). Also, see Zhao Dingxin (1994) for more discussion of the nature of the current regime.

TABLE 1.2 Three Major Ongoing Transformations in China during the 1980s

State:	Ideology-based totalitarian regime	→	Performance-based authoritarian regime
Economy:	Planned economy	→	Market economy
Society:	Highly suppressed unitary society	→	Increasingly plural but still poorly organized society

The State in Retreat

Under the enormous pressure of past failure, the Chinese government started along a path of reform in 1978. Although the political dimension of the reform was limited to policy rationalization and a controlled political participation, it still greatly changed the nature of the state. One of the major goals of political reform was to separate the CCP from the government. Before the reform, for example, the party secretary of a work-unit often held the position of general manager of that work-unit. Even when the position of general manager was held by an expert, the real decision-making power rested in the hands of the party boss. The reform introduced various responsibility systems that gave power to presidents in universities, directors in research institutions, editors in newspapers, magazines, and publishing companies, and managers in state-run factories. Under these systems of responsibility, party secretaries could no longer interfere with the decisions made by administrative authorities. Similar reforms were also carried out in rural areas. To accommodate the household responsibility system, for example, communes were dismantled and the traditional *xiang* was restored as the basic unit of rural government. The party's absolute power was weakened in the process.

Another part of political reform was the meritocratic selection of state bureaucrats and the abolition of tenure in leadership positions. Under the new policy, aging bureaucrats or those with less education were typically either forced out of office or stripped of their chances for further promotion. They were replaced by people who had a better education.

Although the nature of Chinese state was in a state of rapid change, this state of change should not be understood as a simple decline of state power. Many political reforms were at least intended to increase the state's capacity to penetrate society.[17] Moreover, because most top state leaders joined the CCP long before the communist victory and had a great faith in the regime (chapter 7),

17. See Shue (1988).

the state still possessed a high degree of unity and a similarly high capacity for repression. Nevertheless, under the open-door policy, the state was no longer able to rule the people as it used to. One of the indications of this change was that the punishment of those who challenged the state's legitimacy softened over time during the reform. When Wei Jingsheng challenged the regime, he was sentenced to fifteen years; when Fang Lizhi, Liu Binyan, and Wang Ruowang did so, however, they lost their CCP membership but still retained such basic freedoms as the ability to do research, to publish, to make public speeches, and even to go abroad. Even the June 4 repression in 1989 was more a matter of the panicking of a desperate state than of the return of old "hardliner policies." After the state recovered from the 1989 crisis, the political atmosphere loosened again. In summary, during reform the Chinese state had gradually converted from an ideology-based revolutionary regime into a performance-based authoritarian regime.

Toward a Market Economy

Reform of the economy was at the core of the Chinese efforts at reform. Although the direction of economic reform was not so clear in the beginning, it later became increasingly clear that it was one of moving away from a planned economy toward a market economy. Economic reform brought great changes in the structure of society, such as an increasing spatial movement of the people, the quick rise of village collective enterprises, and the emergence of private sectors and a business class. It also contributed to a high speed of development and a general increase in the standard of living. Meanwhile, it made most Chinese *shiheng* (lose psychological balance) to varying degrees.[18]

Economic reform widened income disparities and greatly raised expectations.[19] Before the reform, the overall wage differential between the ends of urban population was less than two to three times, and the greatest difference did not exceed ten times. By the end of the 1980s a few famous singers were earning

18. *Shiheng* has been one of the two most often used terms in Chinese scholars' analyses of social problems. The other is *shifan* (to "lose one's moorings"), which translates into Chinese Durkheim's "anomie." During my visit to China in 1993 I found that these had become catchphrases used by Chinese to comment on other people's uneasiness under the impact of economic reform.

19. The absolute income disparities should not be overstated. In 1988, the gini index was 0.18 for urban areas and 0.30 for rural areas. Even the income disparities in rural areas were still considerably lower than in South Korea in 1976 (gini = 0.36), and still much lower than in Latin America, where most countries' gini indexes were around the 0.5 level (Zhou and Yang 1992, 69–74). For other discussions of income distribution during the reform era, see Walder (1990) and Zhu Ling (1991).

several thousand yuan for singing a song, which was equivalent to a year's wage for an average worker. A private entrepreneur could earn in a day an amount equal to one month's wage for a professor.[20] The differential between the highest and lowest incomes had hence reached hundreds of times. As a result, many people began to purchase luxury goods, such as brand-name foreign dresses, cars, and Western-style cottages. Although rich individuals constituted only a very small percentage of the population, their impact was enormous, because they became a comparison group for a population that was not yet accustomed to income inequalities.

The economic reform also brought a great sense of insecurity to urban residents. It gradually became apparent that people could no longer hold their "iron bowl" and take an "iron wage" regardless of their work performance.[21] Factories had to declare bankruptcy if they were unable to find a way to make a profit. Pensioners worried about their future because of inflation.[22] Those who became rich were afraid of unfavorable policy changes. With the speed of economic growth and of changes in policy, virtually everybody felt uncertain.

The market economy encouraged competition, profit making, risk taking, and individualism, initiatives that clashed with the collective and cooperative ethics which had been propagated by the same government before the reform.[23] A market economy needs laws—but most Chinese were not yet accustomed to respecting laws not in line with traditions.[24] The new market economy also

20. According to the Chinese government's method of classifying those who work in the private economy, individual laborers are those who work on their own or who hire less than eight workers in their enterprises, while private entrepreneurs are those who hire eight or more workers.

21. "Iron bowl" and "iron wage" are metaphors for the highly secure state-sector job and wage systems under Mao.

22. In Anhui province in 1988, even retired veterans, who were supposedly among the privileged groups, applied for permission to demonstrate against their declining living standard (Wu Ren 1990a, 15).

23. For example, during the early 1980s commercial activities were often treated as indecent behavior in many northern and inland provinces (Wang and Bai 1986). Commercial activities in many of these regions were actually conducted by people from Wenzhou, a district of Zhejiang province. Until the mid to late 1980s, such people were generally looked down upon by local residents for their humble occupations.

24. The traditions which the Chinese thus followed include many formed after the communists took power. For example, because the communists abolished direct taxes in the 1950s, by the time the reform started people had lost the habit of paying them. State taxation was a major grievance of private businessmen and individual laborers. One might attribute such grievances to the corrupt tax collectors, and there is some truth to this. But in reality, the government's tax rate was not high. For example, for small-scale private enterprises the tax rate was only 5 percent of sales and 2 percent of income (Ma 1987); the real tax paid was even lower because of large-scale tax evasion, which most Chinese never thought of as a crime (He 1993). Tax rebellions were frequent, especially in rural areas. In 1987, there were 2,493 incidents of tax rebellion, on various scales. During these incidents 1,830 tax collectors were beaten, among whom 263 were seriously wounded and 7 killed. In 1988 tax rebellions broke out at an even higher rate (Chen and Yang 1989).

crashed head-on into elitist sentiments, a conflict that constituted a major grievance of Chinese intellectuals and students (chapter 3).

The immaturity of the market economy also brought side effects. For example, the coexistence of planned and market economies became the source of massive official corruption. Without a robust legal system, the commercial world was under the law of the jungle. The dismantling of communes in the countryside released a massive rural labor force which had formerly remained underemployed. Many of these labors migrated to cities looking for better opportunities. Their arrival greatly increased competition and crime rates in cities.[25]

The impact of economic reform on different sectors of the urban populations varied. Based on formal interviews as well as extensive informal interviews, my impression is that virtually everyone's living standard increased to some degree. Nevertheless, at least during the 1980s, almost everyone, including students, intellectuals, and even successful private businessmen, had grievances directed at economic reform, albeit to varying extents and along different dimensions. Some went so far as to say that Mao's era was better. In fact, most Chinese did not really want to live a Maoist style of life. Nevertheless, they had not yet fully adapted to the changes, and they greatly envied those who had benefited from the changes more than they had. They also had grievances because they were not sure where China was heading.

The Revival of Society

Under the Maoist regime, the state almost completely dominated society, and individual desires were constantly assaulted and suppressed. Afterwards, along with political relaxation and economic reform, Chinese society also started to revive. Part of this revival could be characterized as a strong wave of Westernization. Under the influence of this trend, Chinese culture was charged with being responsible for Mao's tyrannical rule and for the poor economic performance of the state. Bo Yang's *The Ugly Chinese* became a best-selling book,[26] and the TV miniseries *River Elegy (Heshang)*, with its critique of Chinese tradition, achieved enormous popularity (see chapter 2). A more visible change, however, was the Westernization of popular culture, which was indicative of a relaxation of the former suppression of human desires. Pop songs and rock and roll replaced revolutionary songs; free-moving disco dancing replaced stiff

25. Wu Ren (1990a).
26. Bo Yang was one of the most famous Chinese culture critics in Taiwan during the 1960s.

revolutionary dances; pop singers popular in Hong Kong or in the United States were soon popular in China; and the "blue ants," the nickname for people who all wore the blue Maoist suit, began dressing in ways that were almost indistinguishable from those of their East Asian neighbors. With Westernization came individualism. The attitude of the post-reform generation changed so rapidly that students with only a two or three year age difference talked about "gaps" among themselves. Lei Feng's spirit was openly challenged.[27] More and more youths started thinking independently and openly took *geren shixian* (personal achievement) as their ultimate goal.[28]

The transitions during the 1980s were not a simple matter of the rise of a civil society, however. During the 1980s, although the state was retreating, it was still able to keep a lid on society, especially on nonconformist activities. As several studies have indicated,[29] although Chinese society became more and more diversified and people's interests increasingly differentiated, most emergent organizations were still controlled by the state. Their relationship with the state was similar to that of local gentries to the state in traditional society. Before the rise of the 1989 Movement, formal independent organizations were still at a very rudimentary stage of development, and the state kept dissident networks on a very short leash. Thus, although people's interests became increasingly diversified, society remained poorly organized.[30]

Nor was this transition a simple Westernization. Parallel with Westernization, there was a strong resurgence of old Chinese traditions. China saw a revival of interests in Confucianism and Neo-Confucianism. It saw "I-Ching fever" and "Qi-Gong fever" appear hand in hand with the anti-traditional *"River Elegy* fever." Many traditional Chinese festivals were once again celebrated in traditional ways, and religions underwent a great revival.[31] Mah-jongg was repopularized, as were gambling, drugs, and prostitution. A disturbing phenomenon

27. Lei Feng, a model soldier in the 1960s, was a major inspiration to Chinese youths during the 1960s and early 1970s. The essence of the Lei Feng spirit was "be a rustless screw of the party and the country." In the late 1980s, however, a survey showed that among soldiers, who are supposedly a relatively conformist population among Chinese youth, only 8 percent treated Lei Feng as their role model, and that most thought Lei Feng a "stupid man" (Wang Guisheng 1989). See Yang and Chen (1984) for a discussion of youths in the 1960s.

28. In 1988, for example, 2,552 youths in nine provinces were questioned as to what things led them to the greatest happiness (Lu 1991). Among several choices offered, the least chosen was joining the Communist Party or the Communist Youth League, which fifteen years earlier most individuals would have selected. On the other hand, choices such as "have a good family," "feel free," "have a successful career," and "be rich" were among the most chosen.

29. See White (1993) and Wang, Zhe, and Sun (1993).

30. Zhou Xueguang (1993).

31. See MacInnis (1989) and Xue (1989) for the revival of religions in China.

was the reemergence of feuding between clan-based villages in rural areas. Such fighting may involve up to several thousand people and result in large numbers of deaths.[32] The development of Chinese society thus showed multiple and contradictory tendencies.

Confusions over this far-from-settled transition were widespread. The transition involved the decay of communist ideology and of collective-based ethics, but the population had not yet adjusted to living under conflicting values and beliefs. As China moved forward as a supposed whole, tensions sprang up between the traditional and the new, and between the young and the old. In cities, when youths started wearing jeans, the older generations found many reasons to discredit the practice, ranging from jeans representing a "capitalist lifestyle" to their being unhygienic. But a few years later jeans became cross-generation casual wear. People's attitudes toward disco dancing were similar. By the late 1980s, the old generation not only accepted but also indulged in the so-called "old people's discos."

In terms of knowledge influx, ways of thinking, value systems, and the mode of economic resource reallocation, the speed and scale of social changes during the 1980s were tremendous. Most Chinese at that time were in different ways and senses "against" the reform, whether they were intellectuals, students, workers, peasants, or state bureaucrats, and regardless of how much an individual thought of himself/herself as a strong supporter of reform. This does not mean that most people wanted to return to Mao's era. Rather, they wanted reform to bring more benefits to themselves, and they universally felt uneasy with some results of this swift transformation of state-society relations. Therefore, people's grievances in this period tended to be not only strong but also state-centered because it was the state that was responsible for changes that a particular population perceived as unfavorable to them.

Conclusion

I have discussed China's historical state-society relations and the most recent developments, arguing in particular that China's state-society relations underwent great changes after the reform started in 1978. During that process, the Chinese state began to transform itself from an ideology-based totalitarian regime into a performance-based authoritarian regime, the economy began to

32. Tan Gengbing (1992) reported fifty-two incidents of clan-based fighting during 1989 and 1990 in one county of Jiangxi province. Each involved one hundred to several thousand people. Some feuding even involved guns and resulted in deaths and many injuries.

move from a planned to a market basis, and society began to convert from one that enforced a highly suppressed uniformity into one that is increasingly pluralistic but still poorly organized. My analysis of the rise and development of the 1989 Movement in the rest of the book starts from this formulation of China's state-society relations.

It may be argued that the scale of change and the uncertainties involved were themselves important to the rise of the 1989 Movement. An explanation at this level, however, is too general. Other urban populations, such as workers and rank-and-file state bureaucrats, also had many grievances and a great sense of uncertainty as a result of the reform, but they did not initiate the 1989 Movement, and they supported the students on a massive scale only after mid-May, when the students started their hunger strike at Tiananmen Square (chapter 6). To understand the rise of the student movement as such, we must examine more specifically the nature of state-intellectual elite relations and state-student relations both before and during the economic reform.

In the rest of part 1, I argue that the way that intellectuals were treated by the state during Mao's era facilitated the rise of the idealistic and radical intellectual elites that prepared the ideologies of the movement (chapter 2). During the 1980s the Chinese state adopted a market-oriented, labor-intensive strategy of economic reform, but because of a so-called Marxist conviction that science and technology were the first forces of production, the state also heavily emphasized higher education, overproducing millions of students. This set of contradictory state policies not only made receiving higher education a poor investment but also provided a huge aggrieved young population ready for social movement participation (chapter 3). When the communists had just taken power in China, they adopted a student control system based on mutual supervision. This control system was highly effective when the state enjoyed a high level of ideological legitimation and when active participation in mutual supervision was economically and politically beneficial to students. It declined, however, during the 1980s, when the state's basis of legitimacy changed from ideology to performance and when other channels of upward mobility opened up. Now, the dense student living environment on campus, which assisted student controls during Mao's era, facilitated the spread of nonconformist ideas (chapter 4). Thus, when in the late 1980s China's economic crisis deepened and major "safety valves" in society diminished, a large-scale student movement broke out (chapter 5).

INTELLECTUAL ELITES AND
THE 1989 MOVEMENT

Alternative ideas and visions of politics are at the core of modern revolutions and large-scale social movements. Nonconformist ideas are usually created by intellectuals who either no longer identify themselves with the existing political system or who want to considerably modify that system. When a significant number of elite intellectuals in a nation participate in anti-establishment discourses, a large-scale social movement or a revolution is pending in that society. The 1989 Movement was framed around issues concerning the economic crisis and pro-democratic political reform. This framing of the issues marked the extension of popular intellectual discourse during the 1980s. While the rank-and-file students provided manpower, it was the intellectual elites who supplied ideologies for the movement. In this chapter, I discuss how state-society relations during and before the reform era gave rise to radical intellectual elites, and how those elites in turn contributed to the rise of the 1989 Beijing Student Movement.

In this book, the term "intellectual elites" refers to groups of intellectuals with high political awareness and great aspirations to change the country through their own political activities. Although by the late 1980s most urban Chinese who considered themselves intellectuals did not really believe in communism and held various grievances toward the regime, only a few of them spent much time and energy in activities that aimed to bring about political change.[1] The core of this group of intellectuals in China was thus rather small, consisting of perhaps no more than a few hundred people. However, because they had occupied strategic positions in China's communication networks, even holding institutional leadership positions and maintaining close ties with the top state elites, the impact of these political intellectuals on politics had been enormous. They, however, by no means made up a cohesive group.[2] The intellectuals who held leadership positions in China's leading research institutions or in the government were much more interested in reforming the system from within than were radicals who did not hold government positions. However, all the intellectual elites, by and large, shared some general characteristics. This chapter focuses on the major characteristics of intellectual elites and on their impact on Chinese politics during the 1980s. Since this chapter is mainly about intellectual elites, I will simply use "intellectuals" to refer to this group. In the next chapter I discuss the larger population of intellectuals.

The role of intellectuals in the rise and development of student movements during the late 1980s has received a great deal of attention.[3] Currently, there are two types of writings in the literature. The first simply construes the whole process as the intellectuals' persistent push for more democratic openings. However, although the intellectuals during the 1980s did consistently push the regime for more democracy, the 1989 Movement was totally out of their control and the outcome of the movement (that is, military repression) was what the intellectuals had least wanted.[4] We need to explain why the outcome that the intellectuals least intended was the one that they in the end encountered.

---

1. "Intellectuals" commonly refers only to cultural creators, such as professors, writers, and researchers. When modern education had just started in China, to encourage students to enter the modern school the Qing court granted those who received a Western education an equivalent gentry title. University graduates were equated to the *Jinshi* rank, high school graduates to the *Juren* rank, and middle school graduates to the *Xiucai* rank (Bastid 1988, 37–40; Fairbank and Reischauer 1978, ch. 12). Hence in China even middle school graduates were once considered intellectuals. Middle school graduates stopped being considered intellectuals after the Cultural Revolution, since by then most youngsters in cities had a middle school education. However, until very recently most Chinese still considered university students as intellectuals. In this book, I put university students in a broad intellectual category.

2. See Ding Xueliang (1994) for a discussion of the different types of intellectuals during reform.

3. Black and Munro (1993), Ding Xueliang (1994), Goldman (1994), and Perry (1991).

4. In chapters 6 and 8, I will show that although many intellectuals tried hard to steer the movement in a direction they desired, their efforts were futile. Eventually the movement crashed head-on into the state; most top intellectuals either fled the country or were silenced after the 1989 Movement, and China's political reform was delayed.

Writings of the second type focus with ambiguous feelings on how traditional Chinese culture contributed to the particular way of understanding democracy and politics that in turn patterned the activities and the development of the 1989 Movement. This perspective helps explain why intellectuals' political activities led to unwanted consequences during the 1989 Movement. However, it cannot explain why Chinese intellectuals in the 1990s became less interested in challenging the state, even though traditional Chinese culture did not change greatly in the same period. In this chapter, therefore, while I accept that both of the above-mentioned analyses are valid to a degree, my focus will be on state-society relations during Mao's era. I argue that the nature of intellectuals during the 1980s and their patterns of political activity were largely shaped by the state-intellectual relations during Mao's era.

In what follows, I first give a brief overview of the characteristics of modern Chinese intellectuals before the communists took power. I then analyze the impact of communism and especially of Mao Zedong's rule on Chinese intellectuals. The picture that I try to draw is one of how, after they had been frightened by state power under Mao, intellectuals persistently fought for democracy during the 1980s. In the meantime, however, their understanding of democracy, as well as of China's problems in general, had been severely limited both by Marxist and populist thinking and practice and by their poor intellectual capacity in the wake of the state's long-time monopoly of information. Both of these conditions were a result of Mao's rule. Finally, I discuss the major activities of intellectuals on the eve of the 1989 Movement, showing how these activities contributed to the rise of the movement.

The Strong State Dilemma

To understand Chinese intellectuals during the 1980s, we have to have a basic knowledge of their past. How far back are we to trace this past? Some scholars have traced the character of modern Chinese intellectuals to Confucianism or to other ancient Chinese cultural traditions.[5] While the distant past certainly matters, I believe that the nature of Chinese intellectuals was mainly shaped by the sociopolitical environment during approximately the last hundred years. This section briefly outlines some major characteristics of Chinese intellectuals in the twentieth century. Before moving on, I want to make it clear that the

5. See, for example, Chang Hao (1987), Schwartz (1964), Tillman (1990), and Wasserstrom and Perry (1992).

following narrative intends only to capture a dominant intellectual trend. I do not assume that all intellectuals thought and acted similarly.

The period between the Sino-Japanese War in 1894 and the May 4th Movement in 1919 was crucial for the formation of modern Chinese intellectuals.[6] For a time in the mid-nineteenth century, Chinese intellectuals had thought Western technologies were a panacea for China's weaknesses. Defeat by the Japanese, however, made it apparent that China could not be saved merely by introducing Western technologies. Equally importantly, the defeat changed the regional geopolitics. China became the immediate target of a new power. The burning question before Chinese intellectuals from then on shifted from "How can we be strong?" to "How can we survive?"[7] To have a strong state to save China became the strongest wish of Chinese intellectuals.

Seeking to save China, tens of thousands of students went to Japan and to Western countries, where they studied not only science and technology but also Western political thought. It was in this context that Yan Fu translated Thomas Huxley's *Evolution and Ethics* and brought social Darwinism to China,[8] and Liang Qichao claimed that "even if a government system deprives the people of much or all of their freedom, it is a good system so long as it is founded on a spirit of meeting the requirement of national defense."[9] During the late nineteenth and early twentieth centuries, intellectuals introduced various Western social theories to China. These theories were introduced to a single end—saving China from imperialism.

The intellectuals of the late Qing dynasty also persistently urged the state to reform. By the early twentieth century, however, mounting social and political problems made conservative reforms an increasingly irrelevant solution.[10] After the Hundred Day Reform failed, more and more intellectuals favored the idea of revolution.[11] Yet the Republican Revolution in 1911 failed to solve many of the problems inherited from the Qing monarchy. China was as weak as before. In 1919, when the news arrived in China that the Versailles Peace Treaty would transfer all Germany's Shandong rights to Japan rather than return them to China, Chinese intellectuals staged the May 4th Movement. The

---

6. For the history of intellectuals during this period, see Chang Hao (1971), Philip C. Huang (1972), Yu (1992), Schwartz (1964), Pusey (1983), and Meisner (1967).

7. Pusey (1983, 7).

8. In translating Huxley, Yan Fu virtually wrote a new book; his notes are about half of his volume's length. His major purpose to translate the book was to call for a strong state to save China from Western imperialism.

9. Cited in Nathan (1986, 62).

10. Fairbank and Reischauer (1978), Skocpol (1979), and Spence (1990).

11. Lin (1990).

May 4th generation championed the slogan "Mr. Democracy and Mr. Science" primarily because it believed that democracy and science were the bases of a strong state. Over time, especially after the Japanese invasion in the early 1930s, more and more of the younger generation of intellectuals saw communism as the avenue toward their dream of a strong state.[12] The behavior of Chinese intellectuals up until the communists took power was thus primarily shaped by the dream of having a strong state to defend China from Western and especially Japanese imperialism.

After the communists took power, the Chinese intellectuals' dream finally came true. Most of them surrendered their autonomy to the state. The consequences have by now become clear. The "strong state" for which the intellectuals wished did not succeed in its efforts at modernization, but it did quite efficiently punish intellectuals who showed even the slightest independence. The repression of intellectuals reached its peak during the Cultural Revolution. Chaotic communist rule during Mao's era pushed intellectuals, who now desired to limit the power of the state, toward a new affirmation of democracy— the hallmark of the May 4th generation. But after over thirty years under a communist government, Chinese intellectuals had acquired some new characteristics that would have a fundamental impact on their political behavior during the 1980s.

Under the Shadow of Mao

When Mao Zedong stood on Tiananmen and proclaimed before the cheering masses that "From now on the Chinese have stood up," the excitement of Chinese intellectuals was tangible. The dream of a strong state that could defend the nation from foreign aggression had finally come true. During the early 1950s, many Chinese intellectuals who had lived in the United States returned to China enthusiastically, although for some their enthusiasm meant first enduring hardships under McCarthyism.[13] Even established scholars, whose own philosophies and scholastic approaches were remote from or even opposite to Marxism, such as Jin Yuelin, Feng Youlan, and Zhu Guangqian, sincerely tried to convert themselves into Marxists.[14] For the younger generations, acceptance

12. See Cheek (1997) for how Deng Tuo turned into a communist during that period.

13. Qian Xuesen, the father of the long-range missile in China, is the best-known example. Before finally returning to China, he was held in custody by the United States government for several years.

14. Li Zehou (1989, 151).

of communist rule was unconditional. Fang Lizhi, the leading dissident of the 1980s, has recalled:

> Immediately after Liberation and in the 1950s I firmly believed in Marxism. When I entered the party in 1955, I was convinced that Marxism should show the way in every field and that the Communist Party was absolutely good.
>
> When I was expelled in 1958, during the Anti-Rightist Campaign, I made a sincere self-criticism. I was convinced that I had wronged the Party.[15]

Fang expresses the feeling of the majority of intellectuals of that generation.[16] It was not until the early 1970s, when the social crisis and political struggle within the CCP had reached a massive scale, that Chinese intellectuals gradually awakened. By that time Chinese intellectuals had acquired some new characteristics as a result of over twenty years of communist rule: they were greatly frightened by the negative impact of state power, they were indoctrinated by Marxist and by Maoist populist thinking, and, finally, having been isolated from the outside world, they had developed a great information deficiency. In what follows, I examine these characteristics and their impact on the intellectuals' political behavior.

A FRIGHTENED GROUP

In 1979, *Beijing Spring* published a futuristic story entitled "A Tragedy That Might Happen in the Year 2000." The story envisions the death of Deng Xiaoping in 1998 and a consequent power struggle within the party that ends with the hardliners winning the upper hand. As a result, Deng's followers are executed and leftist policies are reintroduced, including the old cult of Mao's personality, a wage freeze, strengthening of the police, heightened ideological vigilance, and a break in economic and cultural ties with the West.[17] In fact, this sober picture was widely shared among intellectuals of the time. For example, in *Penitence*, Ba Jin expresses not only the deepest sorrow for his own obedience to the state and his effort to convert himself into a communist, but also his worry about another Cultural Revolution. To preclude this from happening once again, he urges that a Cultural Revolution museum be established so that later generations will remember that event as a national tragedy.[18] Ba's view was widely

---

15. Fang (1990, 208–209).

16. Many autobiographies written by Chinese in English have given similar accounts (e.g., Chang Jung 1991; Liang 1984).

17. The story is cited from Nathan (1986, 87).

18. Ba (1986).

shared among intellectuals and brought heated discussion.[19] In fact, much writing from the "wounded literature fever" period and afterwards is filled with intellectuals' contrition for their past endorsement of the state.

After experiencing the tragic consequences of absolutist state power, intellectuals during the 1980s became extremely averse to, and had a deep-seated distrust of, the state. It was in this situation that intellectuals rediscovered democracy—this time as a tool to contain state power. Many characteristics of intellectuals and students during the 1980s—for example, their utilitarian and idealistic understanding of democracy and their radicalism—can be understood in light of these experiences. Popular proposals made by the intellectuals, such as prohibiting life tenure, separating the powers of party and state, and strengthening the power of the National People's Congress, all centered on this general concern. The theoretical exploration of socialist humanitarianism and socialist alienation during the early and mid-1980s also partook of this logic. Even the "culture fever" in the mid-1980s centered on the question: What cultural factors in China had facilitated Mao's tyrannical rule? When the state became a problem, democracy once again emerged as the solution.

Because of their deep-seated distrust of the state, the worry of a conservative revival was a key concern of Chinese intellectuals. Any state policy changes during the 1980s were liable to be interpreted as moves towards a conservative revival (which was true in some cases), and each such change thus generated widespread concern. Such concern, in turn, became a major constraint on state policy-making. In this sense, the current Chinese state actually has very limited autonomy. Distrust of the state also had a great impact on the rise and development of the 1989 Movement. When China's economy was in a crisis during 1988, the state implemented readjustment programs. However, many intellectuals treated these programs as a signal of conservative revival and argued that the problems of reform could only be solved by further reform.[20] A strong urge to stop a conservative revival led intellectuals to become deeply involved in a crisis discourse around 1988, which contributed to the rise of the 1989 Movement.

A GROUP INDOCTRINATED IN MARXISM

After thirty years of communist rule, the thinking and behavior of Chinese intellectuals bore the strong influence of Marxist and Maoist traditions, even though many of these intellectuals no longer believed in Marxism. Here I provide only

---

19. Gong (1986) and Ye (1988).
20. The distrust can be found in many places in Chen Yizi (1990).

a few examples. During the 1980s, Chinese intellectuals believed the Maoist notion that a society would not make great progress unless the masses were enlightened. The *River Elegy* TV series and the "world citizenship" discussion in
1988 (both of which will be discussed more fully later) were examples of this
Maoist legacy. Jin Guantao, a leading intellectual of that time, praised *River Elegy* for its great contributions in explaining difficult theoretical issues to the
masses in an understandable way. He applauded *River Elegy* not just because the
TV series adopted many of his views on China's past, but also because he believed that thought "can produce the strength and power to transform society"
only when it reaches the masses. He enthused that "Chinese people need this
type of thinking just as the parched yellow earth needs a sweet rain." [21]

In the 1980s intellectuals still had a mechanical faith in the Marxist principle
of the coordination of the superstructure and the economic base. They were
convinced that "democracy is the major premise or prerequisite for all developments—or modernization." [22] They believed that democracy, like scientific
laws, is unlimited by social or political conditions and therefore applies everywhere and can be sustained in any country,[23] and that "Without reform in
all spheres, economic reform will be difficult. Revitalization of the economy is
closely linked to political democracy." [24] Even the more moderate wing of this
group of intellectuals believed that "if there were no democracy, there would
be no socialism and four modernizations." [25] By the late 1980s, "no democracy,
no economic development" had become a popular belief among intellectuals.
They, therefore, consistently pushed for more political openings.

Finally, although these intellectuals no longer treated the Marxist social program seriously, they inherited a linear worldview and a strong desire for social
engineering on a grand scale.[26] They believed that "there are no unsolvable
problems as long as scientific attitudes and scientific methods are applied." [27]
They greatly admired Gorbachev's reform because Gorbachev tried hard to
work out a blueprint before the reform was conducted. They attributed China's

21. See Jin Guantao et al. (1992).

22. See Wei (1980, 54). Wei argues that the tragic "experiences of our great motherland over the
past thirty years have provided the best evidence [of this democracy-economic development coordination
principle]."

23. Fang (1990, 219).

24. Ibid., 151.

25. Li Honglin (1986).

26. Qian Xuesen was a prominent advocate of systems methodologies. Even Su Xiaokang, a brilliant
reportage novelist, claims that "[the rebuilding of Chinese culture] is a tremendously arduous and complicated cultural-philosophical systems-engineering project" (Su 1990, 6).

27. Yan Jiaqi (1992).

economic crisis to Deng's "cross the river by touching stones" style of economic reform.[28] The lack of a grand theoretical base and the incoherence of reform policies were among the major complaints of intellectuals.

A POPULIST GROUP

Chinese intellectuals and students also had a Rousseauian understanding of democracy. Some of them might not have known Rousseau or even have read any of the Western classics, but they definitely knew Mao's "Rebellion is right," the Cultural Revolution, and the four great freedoms. They thus acquired a Rousseauian understanding of democracy from Maoism.[29]

Mao was disdainful of procedural democracy. He called it *xiaominzhu* (the small democracy). In its place, he advocated *daminzhu* (the great democracy). At the center of his great democracy were the so-called "double hundred" policy and the four great freedoms. The double-hundred policy originated in 1956 after Mao claimed that letting "hundreds of flowers bloom" and "hundreds of schools of thought contend" would open the pathways to the development of the arts and sciences.[30] The four great freedoms are to speak out freely, air views fully, hold great debates freely, and write big-character posters freely. These were widely popularized and eventually written into China's constitution during the Cultural Revolution, but in reality people's rights to exercise these freedoms were never defined and guaranteed. With basic human rights and proper legal constraints unacknowledged, these "freedoms" were often used by people for ruthlessly and irresponsibly slandering others; at the same time, the state frequently mobilized people to use these "freedoms" for advancing ultra-leftist programs. As a result, the Dengist regime removed the four great freedoms in the 1979 Constitution.

However, most methods of nonprocedural democracy are ideal for collective actions, and the four great freedoms are no exception. Even though Maoism was no longer popular, the style of mass mobilization popularized during the Maoist era had penetrated into the habits of the Chinese. During the 1980s, the Chinese continuously used big-character posters and other Maoist mobilization methods regardless of the fact that the state had tried to abolish them.

28. See, for example, Chen Yizi (1990, 71) for the criticism.

29. See Li Shaojun (1988) for an analysis on the lineage of Chinese intellectuals' populist understanding of democracy.

30. In 1956, Mao advocated the "double hundred" policy to invite criticisms of the government from intellectuals. After many reassurances that their criticisms would not be punished, intellectuals responded. However, their criticisms and suggestions met with severe repression in 1957 in the so-called Anti-Rightist Campaign, when over 550,000 intellectuals were branded "rightists" and their careers were ruined.

In chapters 6, 8, and 9, I will show how Maoist mobilization methods exercised a great impact on the development of the 1989 Movement.

AN INFORMATION-DEFICIENT GROUP

During Mao's era, China cut off most Western contacts. It thus interrupted a process of enlightenment that had begun at the turn of the century. When the reform started in 1978, most intellectuals' knowledge of the West and of Western social and political theories was minimal and their scholastic attitude was opportunistic. In the following, I present two cases to illustrate this "brainwashing effect" of Mao's regime.

Case I: The Impact on the Social Sciences. In China, some social science academic publications during the 1930s and 1940s were of high quality, even by current standards.[31] After Marxism established its hegemony in China, however, many social science disciplines were labeled "pseudo-sciences" of the bourgeoisie and abolished. While disciplines such as economics and philosophy were spared, Marxist orthodoxy became the bible; other Western theories were taught only in distorted forms for the purpose of criticism. By 1978, when the reform began, the percentage of enrollment in social sciences had dropped from 6.3% to 0.2% in political science and law, and from 16.7% to 2.1% in finance and economics.[32] By the time that sociology was reestablished, most of the sociologists who had taught the subject thirty years earlier had passed away. Those who were still alive were between sixty and eighty years old. Most of those who taught sociology during the 1980s were thus not sociologists by training.[33] The situation was similar in related disciplines.[34]

Let me use a sociology textbook edited by a group headed by Fei Xiaotong to illustrate just how bad the situation was.[35] Fei is a respected sociologist, and some of his early publications are still masterpieces.[36] The book in question is also not at all bad in comparison with other social science textbooks published

---

31. See Zhao Zixiang (1986) and Yan Ming (1989) for more information on the development of sociology in China before 1949, on its abolition after 1952, and on its reestablishment after 1978.

32. Du (1992, 47); Kwong (1979, 74).

33. Fei el al. (1984).

34. Hayhoe (1989, 37) found that during the Cultural Revolution "Political science and law as fields of specialist study were [also] abolished with People's University and the four regional institutes closed down for the full ten-year period. Economics and finance went into an eclipse almost as serious."

35. Fei et al. (1984). I use a textbook because I believe that the quality of textbooks is a good indicator of the state of a discipline.

36. See his *Peasant Life in China* (Fei 1939) and *Earthbound China* (Fei and Chang 1945).

in China during that period. I have chosen it because it was the first sociological textbook compiled after 1978 and therefore best illustrates the Maoist legacy.
For simplicity, I use the number and type of references cited by the textbook
to indicate its quality. The citation rate of textbooks is not an absolute index
of their quality. However, if a textbook has not incorporated most of the recent developments in a discipline, it must not be of high quality.

The book cites only 129 references, of which 71 (55%) were written by
Western and Japanese authors and 58 (45%) by Chinese. However, among
the 71 references to non-Chinese authors, 32 (45%) are to Marx, Engels, Lenin,
and Stalin. Cited books and articles by other than Marxist authors were very
elementary. Most were either to a chapter of an elementary textbook or to an
entry in an encyclopedia. Not a single research paper from a Western journal
was cited. Correspondingly, among the 58 references from Chinese sources, 42
(72.4%) were either written by party leaders or scholars in government positions, or were government documents. Only a handful of the citations were
really to sociological literature, and most of those publications had appeared
before 1949. To compare, I casually picked an elementary sociological textbook
from my bookshelf and found about 790 citations to approximately 630 authors
in that book.[37]

Case II: The Impact on Intellectuals' Views of Chinese and Western Societies. During
the period of reform, Chinese intellectuals had chances to visit foreign countries for various academic activities. When they returned to China, they often
gave visitor reports on Chinese campuses to convey their image of the West,
generally depicting the West as a perfect society. They thus greatly aggravated
the grievances that the uninitiated young students had towards Chinese reality.
The following examples are taken from Fang Lizhi's speeches to university students; I have chosen Fang because he was the leading dissident during the 1980s,
who as an intellectual celebrity was able to visit some twenty nations after
reform started.[38]

In 1985, in a speech at Zhejiang University, Fang conveyed to the students
the message that China was an absolutely poor country in comparison with
Western countries:

> Per-capita GNP (in U.S. dollars) is $11,000 in Japan, $13,000 in the United
> States. . . . In Shanghai, per-capita GNP is $2,300. Thus, the average productivity

37. Rosenberg et al. (1987).
38. Along with Fang Lizhi, Wen Yuankai also delivered frequent visitors' reports during that period.

of five Shanghai citizens is equivalent to that of one American. Of course, Shanghai happens to be the most productive region in China, a real "singularity" [in physics parlance]. But what about the nine provinces where per-capita GNP is below $100? They represent nearly one-third of our thirty provinces.[39]

While it is true that China is a very poor country in comparison with Japan and the United States, by evaluating China's GNP in terms of U.S. dollars, Fang certainly exaggerated the differences.

Fang's presentation of the policy-making processes of the Western nations was incredibly naïve. In the same speech, he said that "when the American government was making policy, it requested the opinions of those academicians; the government wanted to know if they had obtained any relevant results on which to base policy." The statement speaks for itself.[40] Let me quote from one more speech by Fang:

> The youth of the West and of China are different; the West is a free society, and opportunities for young people are relatively great, and people who have tempered themselves are relatively many. Because opportunities are many and the competitive nature strong, you only have to go do something; there are none who cannot find opportunities. Therefore their students first temper their own independent, creative ability; you only need to have ability, then you can do anything.[41]

The standard image of America that Fang delivered to students was of a land of boundless opportunity. It is worthwhile to mention that Fang's impact on young students was enormous. His speeches made him a hero among students during the 1980s.[42]

AN OPPORTUNISTIC GROUP

A sudden relaxation of political control during the reform brought an influx of new information from the West. In a situation devoid of scholastic authorities, this influx facilitated the dominance of opportunism in intellectual life.[43]

39. Fang (1990, 102).

40. Kraus (1989) has an excellent analysis of Fang's presentation of the Western societies.

41. Fang (1990, 304).

42. It can be argued that Fang used oversimplified or distorted examples in his speeches in order to be effective before a largely uninitiated audience. This may be true, but if one reads carefully his major speeches and works, one may agree that his arguments cannot be reduced to political strategies but indeed constitute a way of thinking.

43. In game theory, it has been shown that opportunism will dominate in a frequently changing environment (Axelrod 1984). Also, in ecology, it is conventional wisdom that r-strategy (opportunistic)

I would like to stress that the intellectual opportunism discussed here was not just limited to a small group of intellectual elites, but extended to almost every sphere of intellectual life. Good scholastic work usually requires substantial amounts of time and energy. In a healthy scholastic environment, success is roughly positively correlated with energy expended. In this sense, opportunism contradicts the nature of scholarship. It demoralizes intellectuals and students and causes great confusion. When opportunism dominates, it induces grievances among intellectuals and students even if they themselves engage in this behavior.[44] Students and intellectuals during the 1980s had many such grievances. They accused others of achieving success by cheating, and they complained that their talents could not be properly developed in this opportunistic environment. Eventually, all grievances were directed toward the state, because it was the state that largely determined the rules of the game.[45]

The "book series fever" that spread after the mid-1980s is a good example of opportunistic behavior among intellectuals.[46] An informant (no. 1) explained to me how some of the book series were edited:

The so-called book series selects a set of related topics. The topics should be attractive and should look new: such as the arts of love, the secret of life, or how to reduce suffering. Then you find a publisher. When they agree to publish the series, you start to organize people to write it. . . . [The writing] is actually copying the content from other books. It is getting a number of books from the library and lifting the content. Some people do not even bother to hand copy. They just make xerox copies, cut them down, and connect them. It goes to the publisher after that.

A successful series can sometimes make a substantial profit. As the informant told me, if an author only buys a serial number of a book from a publisher and takes care of the rest from printing to distribution by himself, the author can earn up to over a hundred thousand Chinese yuan for a book.

---

species tend to dominate in a highly fluctuating environment and during the early period of community succession.

44. When chances of success are limited, only a few will succeed even if everyone behaves opportunistically. Furthermore, those who succeed will not feel secure in an opportunistic environment. Finally, most people who succeed by opportunistic means may not think that their success was based on opportunism. So they still decry opportunism.

45. Ge and Ren (1992) describe the major problems besetting historical research: the chasing of fads, the overindulgence in establishing new theories at the expense of doing solid research, the writing of poor-quality books, and various forms of plagiarism. This pretty much summarizes what dominated all spheres of Chinese intellectual life at that time.

46. Fang, Chen, and Yu (1988).

The state also encouraged people to bypass the entrenched channels of upward mobility. Two phrases frequently encountered in Chinese newspapers during the 1980s were *zixuechengcai* (to be a self-taught expert) and *bolexiangma.*[47] These phrases usually appeared in news stories profiling a person without a formal higher education who nevertheless invented something or developed a new theory and was therefore promoted to a high academic position, or an able official who hand-picked a talented young person for an important position. In the news, those who made such decisions were strongly praised, whereas those who opposed such practices were ridiculed. These practices might recruit a few talented individuals who had been unfortunately sifted out by the selection channels of the mainstream elite. But as a general practice propagated in the media, it greatly encouraged opportunism and demoralized students and intellectuals who were painstakingly climbing the ladder.

INTELLECTUALS AND STATE REFORM POLICIES

To improve the quality of its decision-making, after 1978 the state established several major consulting institutions, through which it tried to make decisions with advice from experts. The poor quality of scholarship and the great opportunism at work in scholarly pursuits thus came to affect the quality of state decision-making and even induced political instability. By 1988 China's economy had run into a deep crisis. At this moment, the government decided to launch a radical price reform (that is, the so-called *chuangjiageguan*).[48] However, even before the reform was implemented, the leak of the news led to panic buying and to great price hikes. In the end, the reform only compounded the uncertainties and grievances of an already highly aggrieved urban population. So far, most writings have blamed Deng Xiaoping for this *chuangjiageguan* decision.[49] Deng did strongly endorse price reform. However, the idea that "the crisis of reform can only be solved by more reform," which included *chuangjiageguan* as part of the general notion, was certainly not originated by Deng, but stemmed rather from the general mood of intellectuals. In the following, I select a few of the

47. Bole lived in China's Spring and Autumn Period (722 to 481 B.C.). During his life, he became well known for his talent in selecting the best horses from a large herd. Later on, *Bolexiangma* (Bole knows horses) became a saying in China that was used to describe those officials who could recognize talented people and appoint them to important positions.

48. The Chinese character *guan* means "pass" or "gate." Here, the price reform was referred to as a troop taking a strategic pass. *Chuangjiageguan* thus means getting the price right in one shot even with risks; it was Chinese-style shock therapy, and the metaphor frequently appeared in newspapers before 1989.

49. Chen Yizi (1990, 125).

problems present in a book entitled *Reform in China: Challenges and Choices* to address the issue.[50] This book is chosen because it was basically a set of policy recommendations presented to the state by the Chinese Economic Reform Research Institute, a major government think tank. Moreover, the ideas expressed in this book were widely shared among intellectuals during the late 1980s.

The central ideas of the book *Reform in China* are that past reform policies were a general success and that most Chinese had either benefited from reform or would support it even at the expense of their living standards (part 2). Although many problems had emerged from reform, the problems derived not from the public's limited capacity to endure reform but from the structures of the old economic system (part 3). Therefore, the only solution to current economic problems is to accelerate reform (part 4). In short, the book presents strong public support for reform and public willingness to risk inflation, job loss, and bankruptcy as consequences. In reality, mass grievances over issues of inflation and corruption became widespread by 1988. During the 1989 Movement, many workers even held Mao's posters to show their nostalgia for the "stable" life under state socialism. The public response pointed in the opposite direction from what the book predicted. Let me give an example to highlight where it went wrong.

The book predicted strong support for price reforms, among others, based on the respondents' overwhelmingly positive reaction to the question: "What do you think of the purpose of a price reform?" and to a follow-up question half a year later, when price reform had started: "Some people think the price reform will ultimately benefit the prosperity of the country. Do you think so?"[51] However, when the same respondents were asked whether prices should be controlled by the state, the market, or both, 61.8 percent of them preferred the state, while only 5.9 percent wanted the prices to be regulated by the market.[52] A half year later, when the price reform was under way, the respondents were asked the same question again; now 34.7 percent of them thought that the price

---

50. The book has been translated into English by Reynolds (1987).

51. See Yang, Yang, and Xuan (1987, 63). The first author wrote another paper two years later on the same issue (Yang Guansan 1989). The English translation of the paper appeared in *Chinese Sociology and Anthropology*. Faced with already mounting problems in society, the later surveys and assessments were more realistic. However, his overall evaluation of people's psychological capacity for further reform was very positive. According to him, despite various discontents, people's enthusiasm for reform remained high and their understanding of reform became deeper and more realistic. He concludes that "as long as people's subjective evaluation of their living standard and the situation of market supply remains high, there will be no social unrest caused by the problem of price increases" (38).

52. Reynolds (1987, 70).

should be regulated by the state. To my mind, the contradictory answers to the first and second set of questions indicate that the respondents initially had little understanding of the meaning of price reform, and that they reached a certain degree of cognitive consistency only after a considerable exposure to state propaganda on the subject.[53] However, the authors conclude that "after a short experience with the market economy, . . . many people got rid of some traditional concepts, [and] accepted the idea that prices can vary in a socialist country."[54] Based on these positive evaluations, the government decided to *chuangjiageguan.* The result was runaway inflation that brought massive grievances and provided the base for the mass support of the 1989 Movement.[55]

Intellectuals and the 1989 Movement

Memories of Mao's tyranny continued to haunt—and terrify—Chinese intellectuals. They therefore consistently pushed the state for more economic reform and for opening up the political system. But however radical they were, the majority of intellectuals during the early 1980s demonstrated a strong desire to act as a "loyal opposition," intent upon reforming rather than abolishing the system. Intentions aside, however, the activities and demands of intellectuals often fundamentally challenged the regime's legitimacy. Such challenges resulted in several major conflicts between the state and intellectuals, as indicated by the crackdown on "democracy walls" in 1979, the Anti–Spiritual Pollution Campaign in late 1983, and the Anti–Bourgeois Liberalization Campaign in early 1987.[56] Each of these campaigns created dissident heroes while demoralizing other intellectuals. Ironically, as China became more and more open, state-intellectual relations actually worsened. Therefore, when China's economic reform went into a crisis, intellectuals diagnosed the root cause of the economic crisis to be not too much reform but not enough reform, and the state adjustment policies during the crisis to be a conservative revival. Consequently, intellectuals indulged in a crisis discourse. This discourse immediately spread to the universities and contributed to the frequent student movements after 1986,

53. In that period, Chinese newspapers published many articles to emphasize the importance of price reform. Obviously, people were affected by the propaganda.

54. Reynolds (1987, 70).

55. However, the *chuangjiageguan* cannot be evaluated as a total failure, especially given the fact that the new momentum of Chinese reform after 1992 in many ways benefited from the earlier attempt. However, the toll was extremely heavy, as indicated by the degree of social turmoil around 1989.

56. See Goldman (1994) for these campaigns.

which culminated in 1989. In this section, I will provide a critical look at the major activities of Chinese intellectuals during the late 1980s and at their role in the rise of the 1989 Movement. I will limit my discussion to four related intellectual discourses and activities: the "reportage novel fever," the "*River Elegy* fever," the "world citizenship" discussion, and the "conference fever."

REPORTAGE NOVELS

The reportage novel arose out of the intellectuals' reaction to unsatisfactory realities. A strong sense of social responsibility revealed in some of the reportage novels was very touching. Many social problems explored therein were real, and the intellectuals' analyses were interesting. However, the rhetoric of reportage novels also showed the strong elitism, idealism, and opportunism of Chinese intellectuals.

What is a reportage novel? In its ideal form, it is a combination of a news report and a novel, that is, the content of a reportage novel should be real and have news value. No fabrication is allowed. A reportage novel is not just a piece of news, however. It should read like a novel and should therefore be artistic. In order to make their argument look more authoritative, the authors of reportage novels also employ bits and pieces from "philosophy, economics, ethics, law, sociology, psychology, and even environmental sciences and architecture."[57] Some of them even used survey data and statistics and carried out interviews and participant observation to buttress their arguments.[58]

Yet mainstream reportage novels of that time were never really intended to report a true story to readers in a novel form. Their topics ranged across the field of social problems, including inflation, official corruption, crime, prostitution, begging, suicide, brain drain, demography, rural-city migration, the one-child policy, private business, education, social ethics, marriage and divorce, history, ethnic conflicts, and so on.[59] The reportage novelists wrote out of their general concerns for social problems and their sense of social responsibility.

The reportage novel combined social sciences, journalism, and fiction into one form. In contrast to social science, data collection and analysis in reportage

57. This comment is by Su Xiaokang. It is quoted in He Xilai (1989). The *xueshuhua* (academism) of the reportage novel was also observed by Chinese literary critics (Xi 1988).

58. The best example was Jia Lusheng, *A Band of Wandering Beggars* (1988a). In order to write this reportage novel, Jia disguised himself as a beggar for quite a period of time.

59. As an example of the wide range of topics, see *Shenshengyousi* (Holy concerns) (Si 1988). In this two-volume collection, twenty reportage novels cover most of the topics that I have listed above.

novel writing is generally driven by the authors' preexisting views rather than by hypotheses. While journalists strive for distinctive effects, social scientists aim for representative results. Furthermore, novel writing contradicts the methodologies of both the social sciences and journalism, because even writers of realistic novels do not follow a true story faithfully. In reality, the fact gathering and presentation of most reportage novels has been heavily bent toward journalism or even novelizing. For example, in *Shensheng Yousilu* (A record of holy concerns),[60] Su and Zhang try to sound the alarm over China's primary and middle school education crisis and attribute the root of the crisis mainly to the poor economic status of teachers. To show how bad the living conditions were for schoolteachers, they portray two extreme cases:

> Two small rooms, only eighteen square meters in total, are a dwelling for six people. It is so low so that you can touch the ceiling by hand, and very damp; it receives no sunlight all day long, and therefore, the floor is wet; and so crude, the wind comes in winter, so does the rain in summer. . . .
>
> This was the living space of a special-grade teacher with forty years of teaching experience. He had lived here for thirty-three years. . . . The poor environment destroyed his health. He was tortured by pulmonary emphysema for many years and frequently coughed non-stop in classes. [The disease and the environment] tortured him more and more in his later years. He died in this dilapidated house.

The second story runs:

> In a southern big city, there was an old teacher with over thirty years of teaching experience. Eight family members had only twenty-one square meters of living space. When he stayed in the hospital for his liver cancer, he cried "house," "house," continuously in a coma. Before he died, his family members had to tell him a lie that they were allocated "a three-bedroom apartment." He was then able to close his eyes and went to heaven.

All big cities in China had serious housing problems during the 1980s, but was the average living condition of schoolteachers significantly worse than that of the rest of the population, as this reportage novel implied? The answer could be in the affirmative, but the question cannot be addressed by simply considering a few extreme cases. Extreme cases, however, were highly effective in agitating both already aggrieved intellectuals and many others. The above paragraphs

---

60. Su and Zhang (1987); reprinted in Si (1988).

really evoked a strong emotion in me while I was reading them, as did some additional commentaries in the reportage novel, such as: "Is it not said that teachers are the engineers of the soul of mankind? Why is it that their own souls do not even have a place to stay?"[61] "All are human, why can some live spaciously while others have to live in awkward, embarrassing, and painful ways?" My reaction was typical. "When his (that is, Su's) works were published, in some mountainous areas they were hand copied from one village to another and in some counties they were even duplicated by photocopying. Many people read them with tears."[62]

Most of the reportage novelists also adopted social theories to buttress their arguments. Words such as "sociologically," "psychologically," "linguistically," "philosophically," and "historically" sometimes appear all together in a single reportage novel. Such glosses made reportage novels more appealing to readers. For example, in *Di'er Qudao* (The second channel), Jia Lusheng uses the IQ concept to glorify vicious competition among private book dealers, and between the dealers and a state-owned bookstore, in a lawless market:

> The 1980s are an era of IQ competition. . . .
> Illiterates win the commercial competition even over the university graduates [i.e., a state-owned bookstore manager]. What does this say? It says that the IQ of lizards is higher than that of dinosaurs. . . . What we need is a little flexibility. That is why most members in the "ten thousand yuan family" have low educational levels. Education means little. Whether you can get rich wholly depends on your IQ.[63]

The following quotation from the same novel presents the same view through the mouth of a private book dealer:

> My success is mainly due to my high IQ. . . . The stronger the competition, the more conflicts between competition and morality. What shall we follow, morality or competition? Morality [only] helps the incompetent ones. However, the law of nature is [only] in favor of competition. . . . How is a baby born? Three hundred million sperm rush to an egg, and only one succeeds. I am sure it is the best one. This is how a baby is made.

61. The phrase "engineers of the soul of mankind" is a quotation from Stalin.
62. He Xingan (1988).
63. The following two passages are from an abbreviated version of the reportage novel published in *People's Daily*, Overseas edition (Jia 1988b).

Obviously, the author has no real knowledge of the IQ concept, or of IQ testing and its limitations.[64] His lizard versus dinosaur analogy shows that the speaker misunderstood the mechanisms of biological evolution. He also does not seem to understand that competition will not automatically give rise to a healthy market without a state that at least supplies collective goods such as law, education, and other infrastructures.

However, regardless of the naïveté of the novelists, the reportage novels were highly attractive to uninitiated students and to an aggrieved urban population. In fact, a "reportage novel fever" rose as soon as reportage novels became popular in the mid-1980s. They achieved great popularity in part because of the persistence of social problems. However, the manner in which the novelists presented social problems was also important. The novel style allows a "true story" to be modified and exaggerated into a more effective form. The journalist's attitude makes the goal that of effective presentation rather than of accurate representation. The social science approach seduces naive students into treating these authors as sophisticated thinkers.[65] Through their literary effectiveness, the politicized reportage novels effectively directed unhappy students toward certain ways of thinking.[66]

THE *RIVER ELEGY* TV SERIES

The *River Elegy* series was a combined outcome of the culture fever and reportage novel fever. It presented a critique of Chinese culture in a style that resembled that of reportage novels. The first author of the script (Su Xiaokang) was one of the most influential reportage novelists of that time. However, more than a typical reportage novel, the TV series combined modern television, arts, journalism, history, and sociology into one form.

The series essentially argues that China's inward looking, river- and land-based "yellow civilization" has led to conservatism, ignorance, and backwardness. In order to survive, China has to learn from the maritime-based "azure

64. For an excellent description of the history of the IQ test and its problems, see Stephen Jay Gould (1981).

65. As a matter of fact, Chinese intellectuals and students also treated Western pop sociologists very seriously. Kraus (1989, 300) notices that "*Future Shock* has been widely read in Chinese translation. Many intellectuals find it appealing, because it purports to demonstrate their growing importance. Many Chinese accept Toffler uncritically as a serious Western social scientist, much as they mistake Herman Wouk, Irving Stone, and Eric Segal for serious novelists."

66. In my view, reportage novels also became popular because of China's weak legal system. Otherwise, the potential of libel suits alone might have made their publication much more difficult.

civilizations" and to establish a market-based economy. To make the general argument of the TV series appear more authoritative, the authors adopted many Western theories, such as Wittfogel's irrigation-despotism thesis, Hegel's argument that land-based Chinese civilization leads to conservatism, and Toynbee's early notion that all civilizations had either been extinguished or were in the process of being extinguished except for Christian civilizations. In addition, the authors invited over ten "academically accomplished young and middle-aged [Chinese] scholars" from various disciplines to sit in a "studio" to "briefly explain or express their opinions on certain topics." [67] Finally, much historical evidence was marshaled to support these theories.

Because of its careless citations of historical evidence, uncritical adoption of some highly questionable Western theories, and poorly thought out conclusions, the TV series received criticism from scholars in both mainland China and Taiwan.[68] Some of their criticisms were well founded. Nevertheless, critics might have taken the matter too seriously, because even though the authors had intended to make the series look scholastic, it was not a truly scholarly work in terms of its nature, quality, and attitudes.

In terms of the extent to which the *River Elegy* TV series caught the attention of the general public, and especially of the students, it was extremely successful. Its immense passion, elegant prose, and sobering tone were fully extended by its temporally and spatially unbounded moving pictures, further adding to its theoretical flavor, and showcasing a way of thinking that was novel to most Chinese. The series captured the attention of millions of Chinese as soon as it was televised by the China Central Television Station (CCTV) during prime time in June 1988. A *"River Elegy* fever" developed immediately. Students in universities discussed and debated various issues raised in the series. After watching the program many people wanted to have a copy of the script, leading to the rapid sale of over five million copies of it.[69] Pushed by high demand, as well as supported by the then CCP general secretary Zhao Ziyang, the CCTV retelevised the whole program.[70] The viewing rate among intellectuals and students was incredibly high. Among fifty-eight informants to whom I posed the

67. Su (1990, 3).
68. See Fu (1992), Wang and Qiu (1992), Zhang Guozuo (1989), and Zhao Guangxian (1989). For interested English readers, Rosen and Zou (1991–92) have put together an excellent collection that includes the translated *River Elegy* script and several articles from both mainland China and Taiwan that argue for or against the series.
69. Cao Fang (1989).
70. Jin Ren (1989).

question: "Did you watch the TV series *River Elegy?*" fifty had watched the complete TV series, five had watched part of it, and only three had not watched it at all.

As expected, students' assessments of the TV series were very positive. When I asked: "What did you think about the TV series when you watched it?" among the fifty-five informants who watched the series, only six expressed negative feelings. Among the forty-nine informants who evaluated the series positively, thirty reported that the series provided them with a new angle with which to look at history and that they totally believed the arguments which it presented. Another nineteen more or less insisted that although the series was scholastically less than sound, it elicited a sense of crisis among Chinese that was positive for the development of the country. The series was also highly praised by some China specialists on the same grounds. For example, Madsen praised how "with an extraordinary sophisticated use of video images to convey a sweeping historical and philosophical argument about the state of Chinese culture, the series achieved a level of rhetorical power and conceptual complexity rarely reached by television documentaries in the West."[71] Madsen is right. A similar TV series would have never been televised by the mainstream Western media because of Western media's conformist nature.[72]

THE WORLD CITIZENSHIP DISCUSSION[73]

In 1988, when China's economic reform faced serious problems, Chinese intellectuals were actively looking for solutions. At the beginning of this unusual year, an article was published in the *World Economic Herald* of February 15, entitled "Facing the Last Year of the Dragon of the Century: The Most Urgent Problem for Chinese is still the Problem of World Citizenship."[74] The subtitle of this article is "Alarm: The Economic Gap is still Widening Between China and the Developed Countries, and even Some Developing Countries."[75] Coinciding with the economic downturn, this article sparked a huge surge of crisis

71. Madsen (1990, 256).

72. See chapter 10 for more discussion of the issue.

73. Mao once said that China as a big nation should contribute more to world civilization, otherwise China should be deprived of its world citizenship. The world citizenship idea originated from Mao's romantic metaphor.

74. The *World Economic Herald* was a liberal newspaper published in Shanghai and a major mouthpiece of Chinese economic and political reform. It was forced to close down after the June 4 military crackdown.

75. The conclusion made in the subtitle was based on the reported GNP in U.S. dollars: in reality the economic gap between China and the West was narrowing, a fact obscured by a great depreciation of the Chinese yuan in the 1980s.

discourse centered on the world citizenship discussion. In the *World Economic Herald* alone, at least fifteen articles on the topic appeared in 1988.[76] Many other Chinese newspapers were also involved, including the leading official paper, the *People's Daily*.[77] A panel discussion was held in Beijing in August to discuss the issue. The *World Economic Herald* compiled discussions from different sources into a book series.[78] Even Taiwan and Hong Kong media were eventually involved in the discussion.[79]

The crisis consciousness was widely praised. For example, China's most renowned scientist, Qian Xuesen, argued that the "world citizenship" discussion could strengthen a sense of national solidarity.[80] An article published in the *People's Daily* also states that "Crisis consciousness is an engine for a country's development."[81] The title of another article in the *World Economic Herald* of May 16, 1988 claims that "China has to have people to speak out." During the discussion, "letters rushed to the *World Economic Herald* like snow flakes."[82] The following are two examples cited from those letters: "The world has given China a yellow card. China has to have a general mobilization!" and "Stand up, those who do not want their world citizenship to be revoked!"[83] In the summer of 1988, the discussion had created another fever on a scale that matched the contemporaneous *River Elegy* fever. A pervasive sense of crisis formed, extending beyond intellectual elites to the wider sphere of intellectuals and students.

THE CONFERENCE FEVER

During the 1980s, China's university students were considered, and considered themselves, to be intellectuals. The relationship between intellectual elites and university students was very close. In Fang Lizhi's speeches and writings,[84] for example, it is easy to see that his main audiences were first students and then

76. That is: Feb. 15; Mar. 7, 29; May 15, 16, 30; June 6, 20, 27; July 4; Sept. 5, 12, 19; Oct. 24; and Dec. 19. I say "at least" because a few issues of the newspaper from 1988 were missing in the Shanghai Academy of Social Science library, where I located the paper.

77. Sept. 5, 1988.

78. See the report in the Dec. 19, 1988 *World Economic Herald*.

79. On Sept. 12, 1988, the *World Economic Herald* reported the involvement of the media in Hong Kong and Taiwan. An article by Nian (1988), which appeared in *Zhongyang Ribao* (The Central Daily, Taiwan), was also reprinted in the *World Economic Herald*.

80. *World Economic Herald*, May 30, 1988.

81. Zi Chao (1988).

82. Cao Fang (1989).

83. Ibid.

84. Fang (1990).

Westerners. Other intellectual elites were also highly popular on campuses. The following is a report on students' enthusiasm toward Liu Binyan when he made a speech at a university in Shanghai:

> Invited by the Student Union of Tongji University, Liu Binyan delivered a speech on November 6 [1986] at the Tongji auditorium. The auditorium can hold three thousand people; however, students from many other universities also wanted to attend the meeting. Finally, even the passageway of the auditorium and the area outside were jammed with students. At least over five thousand students attended the event.[85]

The same situation was repeated when Fang Lizhi spoke at the same university two weeks later.[86] In 1986, this kind of campus speech was still uncommon. By 1988, however, as China's economy declined, making speeches in universities became a major channel for intellectuals to spread their ideas. Consequently, a "conference fever" formed in China's major universities. As an informant told me (no. 68), between 1988 and early 1989 several conferences would be held each day in Beijing University. Some of his classmates spent most of their time in attending conferences rather than in classroom study.

Speeches at conferences are not the same as formal publications. Government censorship of formal publications pushed most intellectuals to hide some of their views. However, intellectuals spoke frankly in the conferences. For example, Jin Guantao once said in a conference at Beijing University that "one of the heritages of the twentieth century is the experimentation and failure of socialism."[87] He definitely would not and could not have published this kind of comment formally. One of the frequent attendees of the conferences at Beijing University told me (no. 63): "In the conferences, they all tried to challenge the government. [During that period], if one wanted to complete a speech at Beijing University, one had to attack the communists. Otherwise, the students would simply jeer the speaker off the stage."

The impact of the conferences on the rise of the 1989 Movement is obvious. Among the forty-two valid informants whom I asked about the frequency of their conference attendance, twenty-three reported low attendance and nineteen reported high attendance (table 2.1). However, among the low conference attendance group, nineteen (82.6%) had a lower or median level of participation during the movement. In contrast, among the high conference attendance

85. Li Xinhua (1988).
86. Fang (1990, 157–88).
87. Cited in Wu Ren (1990a).

TABLE 2.1   The Relationship between Conference Attendance
             and Level of Activism during the 1989 Movement

Conference Attendance	Level of Activism				
	Low	Moderate	High	Organizers	Total
Lower	8	11	4	0	23
Higher	2	1	10	6	19

Note: Among the seventy informants, forty-eight were students during the 1989 Movement. Forty-two of these students provided information on their level of movement participation and conference attendance (see appendix 1 for details). The table shows a very strong correlation between conference attendance and student activism ($gamma = 0.82$, $p < 0.001$; $gamma$ has properties similar to the regression coefficient). Conference attendance: Lower = never attended or only attended a few times; Higher = attended many times. Level of activism: Low = remained only as adherents throughout the 1989 Movement; Moderate = participated only in a few demonstrations or other events; High = participated in the hunger strike or heavily participated throughout the 1989 Movement; Organizers = student leaders in the 1989 Movement.

group, sixteen (84.2%) informants were either activists or organizers during the movement. There is a very strong correlation between students' level of conference attendance and level of movement participation during the 1989 Movement ($gamma = 0.82$, $p < 0.001$).[88]

The *River Elegy*, world citizenship discussion, and conference fevers caused major theoretical thinking and concerns to spread from small scholastic circles to a wider population. They narrowed the political orientations of students to several key issues, and fostered the establishment of politically oriented student networks. By 1989 Chinese society was ripe for a large-scale movement.

Conclusion

I argue that the patterns of intellectuals' political activities during the 1980s were shaped by state-intellectual relations during the hundred years following the emergence of modern Chinese intellectuals, and particularly by the way

88. The data should be interpreted cautiously. Other factors related to the level of student activism, which will be discussed later, are the prestige of a university (chapter 4) and the existence of social sciences in a university (chapter 3). They are confounded with the above result because many conferences were held in a few comprehensive universities or institutions specializing in the social sciences and humanities.

intellectuals were treated by the state during Mao's era. Under imperialist pressure, Chinese intellectuals during the late Qing dynasty and the Republican era persistently sought a strong state that could defend the nation, an action that finally led to the rise of communism. Yet the communist state, the strong state of which intellectuals had dreamed, became a problem because the state performed less well in economic modernization than it did in implementing political repression. The painful experiences of intellectuals during Mao's era pushed them to fight for democracy. Still, the intellectuals themselves also inherited strong Maoist legacies: the unchecked state power under Mao had frightened Chinese intellectuals and drove them to take democracy as the prerequisite of Chinese modernization; the long-standing Marxist mode of education had given them a utopian vision; Mao's mass mobilization had nourished a populist understanding of democracy; and thirty years of repression and isolation had created an educated class with a great information deficiency and with opportunistic attitudes. All these factors contributed to the dominance of idealism, opportunism, and radicalism among Chinese intellectuals, forming an ethos which in turn shaped intellectual discourses during the 1980s and facilitated the rise of the 1989 Movement.

three

ECONOMIC REFORM,
UNIVERSITY EXPANSION, AND
STUDENT DISCONTENTS

In the last chapter, I discussed how relationships between the
state and society before and during the 1980s facilitated the
formation of a group of radical intellectuals and students, and
how the activities of this group and its interactions with the state
paved the way for the rise of the 1989 Beijing Student Movement. This group, variously called the liberal intellectuals or the
intellectual elite, was a small minority among Chinese intellectuals. Nevertheless, the 1989 Movement was eventually participated in and supported by the majority of students and intellectuals. Why did this larger group support the movement? My
research indicates that this had much to do with a set of state
policy changes during the period of reform. In the late 1970s,
the state adopted a policy that strongly emphasized the role
of intellectuals in China's development, but by the early 1980s
state policy had shifted to a market-oriented developmental
strategy.[1] This policy change was accompanied by an overexpansion of university enrollment. Consequently, by the late 1980s

1. China has gone through frequent policy changes (Lin and Xie 1989; Whyte 1981).
Skinner (1985) identifies eleven major policy cycles just between 1949 and 1977.

the perceived standard of living and social status of students and intellectuals had greatly declined, and university students were experiencing more and more difficulty finding satisfactory jobs after graduation. Higher education became a poor investment. The change in state policy thus created an alienated academy ripe for activism. In this chapter I examine this whole process and its negative impact on intellectuals and students. On a theoretical level, I also suggest that an overexpansion of enrollment had a greater impact on China than on developed nations because in China the university is a radical institution.

The University Expansion

Following Mao's death in 1976, the Chinese government then headed by Hua Guofeng launched a "new leap forward," aimed at achieving "four modernizations" by the end of the century.[2] The short-term goals of the "new leap forward" were laid out in a Ten Year Plan (1976–85) that aimed to achieve "at least 85 percent mechanization of all major agricultural activities," to produce "400 billion kilograms of grain and sixty million tons of steel," and "to build or complete 120 large-scale projects, including ten iron and steel complexes, nine nonferrous metal complexes, eight coal mines, ten oil and gas fields, thirty power stations, six new trunk railways, and five key harbors."[3] This neo-Stalinist strategy of economic development required big science and high technologies. Thus the role of intellectuals was greatly emphasized, as a means to these ends.[4]

In the late 1970s and early 1980s intellectuals found themselves highly praised, in sharp contrast to their experience during the Cultural Revolution. They were no longer labeled as the "stinking ninth" (*choulaojiu*), but as brain

2. They were the modernization of industry, agriculture, the military, and science and technology. It was originally Mao Zedong's own vision back in the 1950s, and it was restated by Zhou Enlai at the Fourth National People's Congress in January 1975. Deng Xiaoping also supported the development strategy at least in its early stage of implementation.

3. Quoted from Hua Guofeng (1978) in his report to the fifth meeting of the National People's Congress.

4. Hua (1978) argued that "we must supply modern science and technology on a broad scale, make extensive use of new materials and sources of energy, and modernize our major products and the processes of production." Deng Xiaoping (1983, 86) declared more explicitly: "The key to the four modernizations is the modernization of science and technology. Without modern science and technology, it is impossible to build modern agriculture, modern industry, and modern national defense. Without the rapid development of science and technology, there can be no rapid development of the economy."

workers.[5] They were also given greater academic freedom. Mao's policy of enrolling university students from the ranks of workers, peasants, and soldiers through the recommendation of local authorities was abandoned and the entrance examination system was reinstated.[6] The seeming promise of a future as intellectuals led to such keen competition in the first several years of university admission entrance examinations that the first major social fever after Mao was the "study fever."[7] Therefore, after Mao's death and before the mid-1980s, intellectuals and students in China were cheered for their contribution to "the springtime of the sciences."[8]

The mutual reinforcement of state policy and social demands thus led to a great expansion of higher education. Between 1977 and 1985, while middle school enrollment in China was declining, both the number of universities and general university enrollment increased rapidly.[9] In 1977 China had only 404 universities. The number rose to 1,075 in 1988. The first expansion occurred in 1977 and 1978, when universities that had been shut down during the Cultural Revolution were reopened. The second surge occurred between 1982 and 1985.

5. The number nine came to be associated with intellectuals in two ways. First, Mao used the phrase "brother number nine" in the 1960s to allude to intellectuals; his inspiration was a line from the revolutionary opera *Taking Tiger Mountain by Strategy*, in which the protagonist, a People's Liberation Army soldier who joins a group of bandits to learn their ways, is called "brother number nine" to denote his junior status. Second, the term "the stinking ninth" was used to refer to intellectuals during the Cultural Revolution when their low political status found them added to an existing set of eight bad social groups (landlords, rich peasants, counter-revolutionaries, bad elements, rightists, renegades, enemy agents, and capitalist roaders). See Han and Hua (1990, 14).

6. Students enrolled during the Cultural Revolution were called "worker, peasant, and soldier students." They entered the university through the recommendation of local officials. In reality, the basis of recommendation was often a candidate's personal relationship with local leaders, and most importantly the connections of the candidate's parents with local officials.

7. For example, over 5.7 million people competed for 278,000 positions in the first nationwide university entrance examination in 1977 (Huang and Mou 1990). The acceptance ratio was 1:20.5. The competition was so keen mainly because this was the first entrance examination in more than ten years. Yet the general enthusiasm was very clear. The "study fever" turned into a "diploma fever" after 1980 and died out in the mid-1980s (Liu Xiangyang 1989).

8. "The springtime of the science is arriving" is a line from a breathtaking speech by the then president of the Academy of Science, Guo Moruo, at the Conference of Science and Technology held in March 1978. It became a catchphase in the late 1970s and early 1980s.

9. Because of a general emphasis on higher education as well as the decline of public education in rural areas after the dismantling of the commune system, middle school education experienced a huge decline in the 1980s. Henze (1992, 115) reports that the rate of transfer from elementary school to junior secondary schools was reduced from 94 percent in 1976 to 76 percent in 1980 and to 69.4 percent in 1988. The transition rate from junior to senior secondary school was 71 percent in 1977, 37 percent in 1980, and 21.2 percent in 1988. For general information on Chinese education in the 1980s and its emphasis on higher education, see Hayhoe and Bastid (1987), Hayhoe (1987, 1988, 1989, 1992), and Pepper (1984, 1990).

TABLE 3.1   Expansion of Chinese Universities during the Reform

Year	No. of Universities	Total Enrollment (1)	Economics and Finance (2)	Politics and Law (3)	Liberal Arts (4)	Arts (5)	Politics and Law as Percentage of Total	Social Sciences and Humanities as Percentage of Total	Teacher/ Student Ratio in Universities
1977	404	625,319	7,992	576	35,038	4,783	0.09	7.71	0.298
1978	598	856,322	18,190	1,229	46,153	5,662	0.14	8.32	0.241
1979	633	1,019,950	21,597	3,315	57,244	5,319	0.33	8.56	0.232
1980	675	1,143,712	37,082	6,029	58,054	6,023	0.53	9.37	0.216
1981	704	1,279,472	47,895	9,944	69,076	7,326	0.78	10.49	0.195
1982	715	1,153,956	55,980	14,635	59,663	5,540	1.27	11.77	0.249
1983	805	1,206,823	71,100	18,286	67,909	6,266	1.52	13.55	0.251
1984	902	1,395,656	97,450	25,237	89,146	7,501	1.81	15.72	0.226
1985	1,016	1,703,115	147,543	36,129	126,828	12,644	2.12	18.97	0.202
1986	1,054	1,879,994	169,384	43,178	128,091	13,175	2.30	18.82	0.198
1987	1,063	1,958,725	180,398	42,034	113,423	14,012	2.15	17.86	0.197
1988	1,975	2,065,923	206,088	43,654	111,683	16,685	2.11	18.30	0.190

Data source: China Statistical Yearbook (1990). The numbers listed from columns (1)–(5) are the total numbers of students in universities (column [1]) and in different majors, as indicated in the head of each column.

In these three years, the number of universities rose from 715 to 1,016; a new university was formed every three or four days. As a result, the total student enrollment in universities rose by 3.3 times in eleven years (table 3.1).[10]

The greatest increases in enrollment occurred in the social sciences and humanities. Such enrollment rose 7.8 times between 1977 and 1988. In disciplines categorized under politics and law, it increased 75.8 times in the same period (table 3.1).[11] If, as I have argued in the introduction, the university in underdeveloped nations is typically a radical institution, social science and humanities departments in underdeveloped nations hone the leading edge of this radicalism. This is in part because many of these disciplines teach ideas derived from Western civic culture and political thinking that are revolutionary in relation to indigenous political traditions. That is why in underdeveloped nations

10. *China Statistical Yearbook* (1990). Please note that the great increase of adult higher education is not reflected in table 3.1.

11. All the figures in this section that are not taken directly from table 3.1 are calculated based on the data in table 3.1.

TABLE 3.2   The Relationship between Students' Major and
Level of Conference Attendance during the 1989
Movement

| | Conference Attendance | |
Discipline	High	Low
Social	14	7
Nonsocial	5	16

Note: Forty-two out of a total of forty-eight student informants provided information on their level of conference attendance (see appendix 1, "A Methodological Note," for details). The result shows that students of the social sciences and the humanities attended significantly more conferences than students of other majors (χ^2 test, $p < 0.01$). Social = social sciences and humanities; Nonsocial = any disciplines other than social sciences and humanities.

students in social sciences and humanities are much more likely to be involved in activism.[12]

During the 1980s, universities with social science disciplines held more seminars and conferences to introduce Western political thinking and discuss current Chinese politics than those universities without these disciplines. We know from the previous chapter that conference attendance and student activism were highly correlated. I have also found that while most students majoring in the social sciences or the humanities reported frequent conference attendance, the reverse was true for students in other majors (table 3.2, χ^2 test, $p < 0.01$).

During the 1989 Movement, social science and humanities students were highly over-represented among movement participants. In 1988, for instance, 18.3 percent of university students in China were in the social sciences and humanities, and a similar proportion also held for the student population of Beijing. Yet of the twenty-one Beijing student leaders on the most-wanted list published by the Public Safety Ministry after the military crackdown, fourteen (66.7%) majored in those areas.[13] The University of Political Science and Law is a small university, whose enrollment in 1988 was only 3,141; but that university contributed two student leaders to the most-wanted list, and its student activism reached a level that only a few universities in Beijing could match.

12. Altbach (1968a, 58; 1989, 8); Nasatir (1967, 324–26).
13. *Guangming Daily,* June 14, 1989.

Obviously, by disproportionately recruiting students into the social sciences and humanities, the Chinese government unintentionally magnified the political impact of the enrollment expansion.

From Four Modernizations to the Preliminary Stage of Socialism[14]

The "four modernizations" development strategy soon proved to be unsustainable. Although the "new leap forward" brought high economic growth of nearly 11 percent in 1977 and of more than 12 percent in 1978, the scale of investment far exceeded the state's financial capacity. At the same time, a rapid growth in imports—85 percent in the two years of 1977 and 1978—was not matched by an increase in exports. China ran its largest trade deficit since the First Five-Year Plan.

With such economic failures came power struggles within the CCP. Hua's influence faded while Deng's power rose. In September 1980 Hua had to give up his position as premier of the State Council to Deng's supporter Zhao Ziyang. A year later Hua resigned his position as party chairman; he was replaced by another Deng supporter, Hu Yaobang, who took the title of General Secretary of the CCP. Hua's "four modernizations" program was gradually dropped; it was replaced by Deng's newly articulated economic development policy, which aimed to quadruple China's GNP by the year 2000. This was not just a change of economic goals; the overall approach to the economy was also fundamentally altered. The new policy emphasized the role of the market, the importance of agriculture, light industry, and the service sector, and private initiatives and foreign investment in economic development. If the goal of the new reform program was not initially clear even to Deng, by now everyone knew that it was a move toward a market economy in China.[15]

14. The preliminary stage of socialism, a concept available by the early 1980s and formally adopted by the Thirteenth Party Congress in 1987, holds that socialist states at their initial stage should greatly emphasize the role of the market in the economy and allow the existence of multiple forms of property ownership, ranging from private economy to state ownership.

15. Many scholars have tried to explain this transition (e.g., Harding 1987; White 1993), and their arguments all sound plausible. What I want to stress is that the impetus of reform did not come just from the state leadership. The two most important early reform measures, the household responsibility system and the private economy, were actually accepted by the state after people in some areas were already practicing them. The household responsibility system started in Anhui province in 1978. Its initial purpose was to maintain the crop yield after an extreme drought. Even though the measure spread quickly because of its effectiveness, especially in poor regions, the state did not formally accept it as a legitimate form of organization until 1981. Similarly, the private economy started in densely populated areas such as Wenzhou as early as the mid-1970s when Mao was still alive (Chen Yizi 1990, 25–35; Fei Hsiao-tung 1986; Kate Xiao

Chinese students and intellectuals were extremely ambivalent toward this policy change. Their pro-Western pretensions led them to strongly support the new policy, but they were unhappy about their economic status under it. Of the newly burgeoning sectors under the new policy, collective industries employed only petty technologies, private businesses were run by people with little or no education, and joint-venture and foreign firms brought in their own technologies. Therefore, big science and high technologies did not have immediate importance, and intellectuals and students became marginalized. Moreover, with the development of the market economy, wealth and education came into a negative relation. Most Chinese perceived that private entrepreneurs and individuals in entertainment professions had little formal education but earned many times more than university graduates.[16] Two popular sayings of the 1980s—"Those who produce missiles earn less than those who sell tea eggs" and "Those who hold scalpels earn less than those who hold eel knives"—revealed the general attitude of students and intellectuals toward private entrepreneurs.[17] Students' grievances toward the economic status of the people in the entertainment business are reflected in a comment by one of my informants:

> My feeling was that those who really became rich were either *daoye* or movie stars.[18] Honest people like my parents worked hard their whole lives . . . but did not get proper rewards. My mother, for instance, prepared and taught classes every day; the energy she spent was definitely no less than that of a pop star who sang a song on the stage. Anyhow, I felt everything was unfair if [those who were] hard working could not get good pay. (no. 30)

In the 1980s, Chinese students did not quite understand capitalism and market forces. They thought that a market economy would bring the country

---

Zhou 1996). The state initially adopted the private economy mainly in order to solve acute problems of unemployment (Rosen 1987; Shi 1992).

16. Bai (1987, 163) reports that among eleven types of jobs (or careers), "individual laborers" (see ch. 1, n. 20) were ranked the highest in economic rewards but only ninth in perceived social status. On the other hand, university and graduate students were ranked highest in their perceived social status but ninth in their possible future economic benefit. This conclusion is based on a regionally stratified random sample of 3,340 people in 29 provinces and municipalities.

17. Chinese phrases are so formed that missile (*dao-dan*) and egg (*ji-dan*) share the same pronunciation in their last character, as do scalpel (*shoushu-dao*) and knife (*dao*). This made these sayings humorous, sarcastic, and easy to remember. Other similar sayings can be found in Chai (1988) and Xiao Qinfu (1989, 240).

18. *Daoye* can be directly translated as "brokers," but during the 1980s *daoye* became a derogatory name for those involved in commercial activities.

prosperity, but they never expected that market forces would also degrade the prestige and privileges that intellectuals in traditional societies had enjoyed. This discrepancy was a major source of grievance for students and intellectuals.

Decline in the Quality of Higher Education

While total university enrollment expanded 3.3 times between 1977 and 1988, educational expenditures as a percentage of the total government budget only increased by 2.4 times, from 1.35 to 3.27 percent, between 1978 and 1987.[19] This increase was also greatly eroded by high inflation as well as by the state's declining capacity for revenue generation in the same period.[20] Thus, even though the Chinese government put great emphasis on higher education, its increases in funding lagged far behind the growth of enrollment.

The consequent decline in quality of higher education could first be observed in the drop of the teacher/student ratio from 0.298 in 1977 to 0.190 in 1988 (table 3.1).[21] Moreover, as the economic status of intellectuals declined, universities were unable to keep talented young teachers.[22] Between 1981 and 1989, Beijing University, Fudan University, Qinghua University, and two other key universities recruited a total of 6,104 young teachers; by the end of 1989, about 32 percent of them had gone abroad.[23] Because government regulations required new graduates to pay a fine if they went abroad without completing a number of years of service (two years for master's and Ph.D. degree holders, and five years for bachelor's degree holders), many young teachers were only temporarily retained.[24] Were this factor accounted for, the actual extent of the brain drain could be seen to be even higher.

Many young teachers who were unable to go abroad left the universities to work for various new companies. One informant (no. 2) recalls that among the sixteen classmates retained by his university after graduation, eight went to the United States and Canada, seven to various companies, while only one still teaches there. This was by no means an anomalous experience. A survey con-

---

19. Calculated from Min (1991, table 2). Also, see Pepper (1990, 147–52) for more discussion of the issue.

20. Min (1991).

21. On the declining quality of university education and the rise of student movements in relation to the decreasing teacher/student ratio in India, see DiBona (1968, 131–71).

22. Zhang and Deng (1989).

23. Gao Zi (1990).

24. Pepper (1990, 169–70).

ducted at a Chinese university indicated that among fifty-six newly recruited young teachers, fifty-four of them expressed a strong wish to leave.[25] The declining quality of higher education was a particularly acute problem in the social sciences and humanities, because while most of these departments had only been lately formed, after the Cultural Revolution, with poorly trained teachers,[26] they had a much greater expansion in enrollment. In any event, under such conditions even those who were still working in the universities tended not to work hard.

Increasing Economic Dependence

One result of inadequate state funding was that after the mid-1980s university students were no longer able to support themselves financially and had to depend on their parents. Before the early 1980s, university students in China were financed under a *zhuxuejin* (stipend) system. The monthly stipend ranged from zero to 27 yuan, based on the average income of their family. Most students received between 10 and 27 yuan. By the living standards of that time, a thrifty student could manage to live independently on twenty yuan a month.

Between 1985 and 1986, the state changed the stipend system to a scholarship system in most universities. Under the new system, the amount of money that a student could receive depended on his or her academic performance rather than on family income. While most students did not receive a scholarship, the best could get as much as 500 yuan a year. This new distribution system was not just intended to stimulate students' learning. Because of inflation, the amount of stipend that a student could get had become trivial in comparison with the cost of living, yet the state did not have the financial capability to adjust the stipend for inflation. Therefore, the state redistributed the money to the best students. By 1988, however, a student in Beijing needed about 100 yuan a month. This meant that even the first-class scholarship holders could no longer live independently on their award alone. University students were in their late teens and early twenties—at an age when one usually has a strong desire to free oneself from the control of one's family and be economically independent. Hence the new scholarship system created widespread grievances among students.

25. Zhang and Deng (1989).
26. See chapter 2.

The Problems of Job Placement after Graduation

Immediately after the Cultural Revolution, there was a high demand for university graduates in the big cities. Universities and research institutes in China had not recruited qualified members for over ten years. Government agencies at various levels also needed to recruit new cadres after the Cultural Revolution, when a large number of Maoist cadres had been purged and when most revolutionary veterans had already passed the age of retirement.[27] Thus between the early and mid-1980s about three and half million university students got jobs in universities, research institutions, large-scale state enterprises, or high-level government agencies, all located in a few big cities. In the meantime, a great number of adult universities were established, whose graduates also found a huge number of jobs awaiting them.[28] Therefore, in the course of only a few years, big cities and good positions became saturated.[29] Yet the state was no longer able to assign university graduates to remote areas where they were most needed, as it had done during Mao's era,[30] and the recently prospering industrial sectors, that is, the rural collective industries and private businesses, did not really need and could not attract university graduates. Nevertheless, enrollment was still expanding, while the university curricula lagged behind the needs of society.[31] After the mid-1980s, it became increasingly difficult for university graduates to get jobs that satisfied them.

27. Yang and Cui (1989, 39).

28. Between 1980 and 1986 adult education expanded sixteenfold. The expansion of adult higher education contributed to most of the increase. In 1985 there were already 1,216 adult universities, with a total enrollment of 17.25 million (Liu Xiangyang 1989, 106). In 1986, 450,000 students graduated from adult universities—a number that surpassed the number of graduates from ordinary universities (Li Wu 1988). These adult students took away good jobs from students in ordinary universities, and moreover lowered their sense of being elites.

29. Yang and Cui (1989) report that in 1981 through 1983 sixty percent of social science and humanities majors were assigned cadre jobs in high-level government agencies after graduation. In 1984 and 1985, about 30 percent still got cadre jobs, although most were in provincial- or lower-level governments. In these years, the state over-recruited a half-million cadres; it subsequently had to cut the size of the bureaucracy.

30. Many graduates simply refused assigned jobs if they were in remote areas. For example, in 1982 the state assigned 109 university graduates to Daxinganling district in Heilongjiang province, but only 42 went. In 1985, another 86 university graduates were assigned to the place, and 31 of them actually went (Yang and Cui 1989, 73).

31. Even in the late 1980s, the university curricula still bore the strong influence of the past. Of the 826 areas of specialization in the Chinese university system, about 200 focused on basic theories (Li Wu 1988). (Chinese scholars generally called mathematics, physics, chemistry, biology, astronomy, and geology the six primary theoretical disciplines.) Graduates with degrees in such disciplines were largely irrelevant to the Chinese economy, which was at a labor-intensive stage.

In 1987 over 3,000 graduates in China were rejected by the employers to which they were assigned.[32] Although this constituted only one percent of total graduates, it created a panic in universities and in society, since this had never occurred before.[33] A 1989 study indicated that 21.9 percent of university students were greatly disturbed by the news.[34] Once again, the impact was much stronger on students in the social sciences and humanities than on students in other majors. Enrollment expanded on a greater scale in the social sciences and humanities, even though their learning was particularly useless in the new market economy. The result was that students from these majors were highly overrepresented among those whom employers refused to accept. In Beijing, of the 600 university graduates refused by employers in 1987, 10.5 percent were students in political science and law, although those majors only constituted 1.9 percent of the student enrollment.[35]

To make the situation worse, the state started to reform the job assignment system at this moment. In 1988 a new job assignment policy, called the "two-way selection system," was implemented in many universities. Under the new system, both students and employers could shop around, and each could veto any proposed match by the university, but the university remained responsible for assigning jobs to students who failed to find an employer. Most students initially welcomed this policy because they were unhappy about the old job assignment system. Yet just after the new job assignment policy was implemented, 80 percent of students in a university answered "no" to the question: "Do you agree that the state should no longer take care of job allocation for university students?"[36] This was in part because in the late 1980s good jobs were few and competition was high: these were circumstances under which "two-way selection" became "backdoor selection," that is, a system in which employers only took students who had acquaintances in their unit regardless of students' academic performance. Students complained that "children were responsible for their studies, and parents were responsible for their children's jobs."[37] Many of my informants who graduated between 1988 and 1990 expressed similar feelings. They gave examples of how poor students got good jobs because of powerful parents, while good students failed. One informant

32. Liu Xiangyang (1989, 126).
33. Li Wu (1988).
34. Yang Liwei (1989).
35. *Guangming Daily* (1987).
36. Liu Xiangyang (1989, 127).
37. Wang Dianqing et al. (1990, 131).

insisted that resentment toward the new job allocation policy had been a major source of grievance among his classmates at the beginning of 1989.

Some students in social sciences and humanities had to compete for jobs as flight attendants or as waiters in big hotels.[38] An account by one of my informants sums up the impact of this "two-way selection system" on her cohort:

> We students from the Beijing University Department of Economics had great difficulty finding suitable jobs. Some of my classmates became shop assistants in department stores after graduation; some went to construction companies; some went to very small research institutions. I felt very sad because good jobs in state ministries, trading companies, and banks were only given to those who had backdoor access.[39] Thus, even if there was a good job, there would be several hundred people competing for it, and eventually only those who had the best backdoor access could get it. (no. 30)

Decline of Enthusiasm for Study

To be enrolled in a Chinese university, one has to pass highly competitive entrance examinations. This system selects a student population with high expectations and elitist pretensions.[40] It is, therefore, reasonable to expect that students would feel frustrated when they saw the value of their diplomas, the quality of university education, and above all their future economic status all in great decline. Students became less and less interested in their studies during the late 1980s.

When I asked informants to describe their typical daily activities on campus, the answer was uniform and simple for those who entered universities in the late 1970s and early 1980s. Except for sleep, they spent most of their time on their studies. However, when students of the late 1980s were interviewed, the variation became huge. While some still worked reasonably hard, others could

38. Hua and Cao (1988); Dong (1990).

39. A person who has backdoor access is one who can get a good job through personal (most probably his/her parents') connections.

40. In a study by Li Guoqing (1988), students of several Beijing universities were asked: "How many honors did you receive in school prior to university?" Eighty percent had received one or more honors; in key universities, the figure was 90 percent. In one key university, among 45 classmates, one out of every 3.7 students had received state- and provincial-level honors for excellence in their studies, each student had earned 1.5 district- and county-level honors, and almost everyone had multiple school- and class-level honors. Even those who had less than impressive entrance examination scores were actually the very top students in a county or even a district.

spend on average as little as two or three hours a day on their studies.[41] The following answer gives a picture of how these students spent their time:

> I got up at eight or nine. Usually I read something. But, if someone came and asked me to play mah-jongg, I would go. At noon when my girlfriend finished classes, . . . we went to have lunch together. If she had classes in the afternoon, I might continue to play mah-jongg. When she did not have classes, we went out together. After dinner, she usually went to the library. I then found an excuse to play mah-jongg again. (no. 48)

This informant told me that he seldom went to classes after the second year of university life, yet he claimed that most students in his class were similar to him.[42] According to another informant (no. 45), absenteeism in some of the courses that he took could run as high as 70 and 80 percent. The problem indeed became a matter of general concern during the late 1980s.[43]

In my interviews, I asked informants to recall approximately how many hours a day on average they had spent studying. The average study hours per day decreased continuously from the late 1970s to the late 1980s (figure 3.1). Between 1978 and 1979 students on average spent nine to ten hours a day on their studies. This decreased to five and half-hours a day in 1988. Four periods were obvious. The first period covers the students who entered university between 1978 and 1979.[44] Many students of this period were former Red Guards and sent-down youths.[45] They were older and felt they had lost much valuable time during the Cultural Revolution. Almost invariably, they studied very hard. This period was that of the "study fever" in Chinese society at large. Students of the second period entered the university between 1980 and 1982. Most of them entered the university directly from high school. They apparently studied a little less hard than had the Cultural Revolution cohort, but their overall enthusiasm for study was still very high. This period roughly corresponded to that of the

41. Here "studies" means any course-related activities, including class attendance and homework. The low number of hours reported here shows that these students did not attend class very often.

42. The informant reported that he spent on average four hours a day on study. The lowest reported number of average daily study hours in my interviews was two.

43. See Cao Rida (1989) and Zhu Wentao (1988).

44. The year 1978 had two university enrollments, the delayed 1977 enrollment in spring and the normal summer enrollment. The spring enrollment was usually called the 1977 cohort.

45. During the 1960s and 1970s, mainly as a measure to solve unemployment problems in urban areas, the Chinese government sent about seventeen million urban youths to the countryside in the name of receiving "re-education" from the peasants. Most of these youths returned to the cities after the Cultural Revolution. They were called "sent-down youths." See Bernstein (1977) for further details.

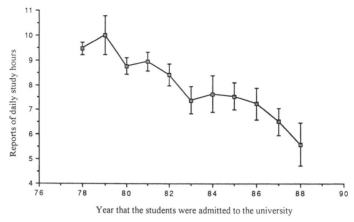

FIGURE 3.1. Relationship between reports of daily study hours (mean ± s.e.) and year that the informant was admitted to the university. The majority of my informants entered universities in the mid- to late 1980s. In order to account for this bias, a small-scale survey was implemented among those who were admitted to Chinese universities in the late 1970s and early 1980s in 1993 in Montreal, Canada. Therefore the sample size for the data in this figure is 119. (See Zhao Dingxin [1996] for the Montreal survey.)

"diploma fever." The students in the third period entered university between 1983 and 1986. They were affected by the urban economic reform that had started in 1984. As a result, their interest in study declined greatly. The fourth period is that of the students who entered the universities in 1987 and 1988. During this period, China's economic reform ran into deep crises; inflation soared, and corruption became rampant. Society as a whole, and the students in particular, were demoralized. Many students were tired of studying. The time was ripe for major social unrest.

During the late 1980s, a popular saying divided Chinese students into the "Ma," "To," "Xuan," and "Yuanyang" factions. The "Ma faction" comprised the students who indulged in playing mah-jongg, poker, or other games. The "To faction" included those students actively preparing for TOEFL and GRE examinations in order to go abroad. The "Xuan faction" was made up of those students who were party animals. Finally, to the "Yuanyang faction" belonged those students who spent most of their time with their girlfriends or boy-friends.[46] In the interviews, I asked respondents whether this described the real situation of their class or university. Among the twenty-eight students who en-

46. *Yuanyang* (mandarin ducks) is a metaphor for an affectionate couple in classical Chinese literature and folk tales.

TABLE 3.3   Relation of Students' Majors to Their Agreement with the Proposition That Chinese Students in the Late 1980s Could Be Divided into To, Ma, Xuan, and Yuanyang Factions

	Social Sciences and Humanities	Natural Sciences and Engineering
Agree	12	4
Disagree	3	9

Note: Since the grouping of students into these factions was most prevalent between 1986 and 1989, in the interview I only probed the students who entered the university between 1986 and 1988. Twenty-eight out of thirty-four qualified students were questioned. Significantly more of the students majoring in social sciences and humanities than those in natural sciences and engineering agreed that Chinese students in the late 1980s could be characterized as belonging to the To, Ma, Xuan, and Yuanyang factions (χ^2 test, $p < 0.01$).

tered the university between 1986 and 1988, sixteen answered yes, and another twelve students answered yes with various qualifications, but none replied negatively. Among the sixteen students who answered most positively, twelve had majored in the social sciences and humanities. On the other hand, among those who gave qualified answers, only three were social sciences and humanities students (table 3.3, χ^2 test, $p < 0.01$). This also confirms that students of social sciences and humanities studied less than other students.[47]

Among the so-called "four factions," playing mah-jongg and preparing for the TOEFL test dominated the narratives of my informants.[48] One informant (no. 26) recalled that students in her university indulged in mah-jongg to such an extent that they not only played it during the day but also sometimes played all night long. She told me that at 11:00 P.M., when the curfew started and dormitory lights were shut off by the university, students moved the table to the hallway and played under the corridor light. Few would have objected to the noise they made because others were either playing or watching. Mah-jongg playing often involved gambling, and sometimes gambling could lead to fighting between students. Another informant (no. 30) recalled that such conflicts

47. Students also spent a lot of time chatting in dormitories, and some students spent much time attending or organizing conferences and seminars. These activities had great significance for students' political behavior. For more discussion, see chapters 2 and 4.

48. The impact of going abroad on students' political behavior will be discussed in chapter 5.

had been a major source of tension among the male students in her class. Students engaged in other activities as well. Some worked part-time on or off campus. Others started doing business. A few political students were involved in dissident activities.

Higher Education and Student Activism

In this chapter I have shown that university enrollment expanded greatly in China during reform, and that this expansion created many problems that contributed to the widespread grievances among students before the rise of the 1989 Movement. Great expansion in university enrollments has been related to student activism in other countries as well. In Latin America, for example, in both of the revolutionary surges (between 1956 and 1960, and 1965 and 1975), those countries that showed stronger student-guerrilla linkages were also the countries in which universities experienced greater expansion in student enrollments.[49] We also know that enrollment overexpansion in West European and North American universities after World War II caused a "credential crisis" that contributed to the widespread student activism in the 1960s.[50] However, regardless of how "radical" the 1960s students were in the eyes of contemporary observers, very few student movements in the West reached even a fraction of the scale of the 1989 Movement.[51] Why?

In this section I will give a comparative answer to the question.[52] My central idea, as stated in the first chapter, is that before World War II and the

---

49. Wickham-Crowley (1992, chs. 3, 9).

50. See Collins (1979), Lipset (1972), and Scott and El-assal (1969). Also Hall (1985b) argues that in the 1960s Britain had weaker student activism than did other developed nations because Britain had more conservative enrollment policies and because the British education system provided more opportunities to junior academics.

51. In terms of scale, for example, during the 1989 Movement the participation rate for events such as the April 27 demonstration (chapters 6 and 8) had reached about 90 percent in several major Beijing universities. No student movement in Western countries ever reached this level of participation.

52. Lipset (1967) and Altbach (1981, 1989) argue that university students in underdeveloped countries are politically more powerful because they are disproportionately from higher socio-economic groups than their compeers in industrialized nations, that they make up a disproportionately large section of public opinion because of their close affinity with actual elites, and that they are special because only a small fraction of the total population has the privilege of receiving a university education. In making these claims, Lipset and Altbach obviously compare contemporary students in underdeveloped countries with those in developed countries. What they neglect is that traditional Western aristocratic students had shared almost all these characteristics, yet had been politically passive, and that Western students had become widely politicized precisely when higher education lost its aristocratic character.

rise of mass university education, the university in the world of Western Christendom was by and large a conformist institution. On the other hand, the university in underdeveloped countries initially emerged as, and tends to remain, a radical institution.[53] This has been a major factor behind the different political orientations of the students in the West and in most underdeveloped nations.

The earlier universities in Europe, such as those of Paris, Bologna, and Oxford, evolved out of the cathedral schools that appeared during the twelfth century.[54] After the fourteenth century most medieval universities were brought under the firm control of the church and the state.[55] Before the nineteenth century the major function of the university was to produce clerics and state bureaucrats.[56] Its curricula—mainly canon law, civil law, medicine, and theology—were indigenous to Latin Christendom. Its students were almost exclusively from upper-class families.[57] In short, the medieval university was essentially an indigenous product of Western Europe.[58] Since it was founded, it had always been "a means of embodying the existing authority, whether ecclesiastical or secular, in knowledge." [59]

In Europe, it was the mutual efforts of the state and the middle class that finally compelled church power to retreat in the university.[60] Thereafter, the medieval university was gradually converted into a modern institution. This transformation occurred rather smoothly over a long historical period. The enrollment of middle-class children in the university, the decline of church

53. A qualification must be made. When I say that the university in the historical West was a conformist institution, I do not mean that aristocratic students were not involved in any kinds of collective action. For example, fighting between town and gown for rents or other issues was common in early European universities (Haskins 1971; Rait 1971). Also, conflict between students and faculty had been a characteristic of American universities (Horowitz 1987). Yet, except for 1848 Germany, students in the West were never involved in national politics before the 1960s.

54. For the origin of Western Universities, see Haskins (1957) and Rashdall (1936).

55. Baldwin and Goldthwaite (1972), Lytle (1974), and Riddle (1993).

56. Lawson and Silver (1973), Lytle (1984), and Ringer (1979).

57. Variations existed across Europe and over time. For example, in the history of early Oxford, plebeian students actually surpassed students of noble and clerical origins in number. Yet by the time of the Industrial Revolution, plebeian students had all but disappeared (Stone 1974). As Vaughan and Archer (1971, 213) argue, it was not that middle-class families were unable to pay the educational cost but rather that middle-class children frequently found themselves barred on either social or religious grounds.

58. Cobban (1975).

59. Riddle (1993, 48).

60. As Max Weber has rightly commented: "Behind all the present discussion of the foundations of the educational system, the struggle of the 'specialist type of man' against the older type of 'cultivated man' is hidden at some decisive point" (Vaughan and Archer 1971, epigraph).

domination, and the introduction of modern curricula all occurred gradually.[61] By the time that the admission of middle-class children into the university had become more commonplace, the middle class had already become one of the dominant classes. Its members tended to admire aristocratic culture and were not interested in radical changes. The modern curricula themselves were more-over also a natural development of Latin Christendom's culture and thus had less revolutionary impact at home than they did on university students of un-derdeveloped nations. The Western university continued to be a conformist institution until after World War II, when university education was further plebeianized by market forces, much as other luxurious commodities were.[62] Even now, after the New Left movement of the 1960s, Western universities still bear many of the characteristics of a conformist institution.

To most underdeveloped countries, however, the university was a foreign in-stitution with few or no indigenous cultural roots. Universities were founded as part of the package of forced development. Most universities were founded by colonial powers, with the aim of either spreading Western religions or train-ing lower-level bureaucrats to help manage the colony. If a university was in-digenously founded, its aim was to learn from the West and to transform the nation. The content taught in the university was therefore foreign and even revolutionary to any non-Western high culture. In most underdeveloped coun-tries university students have been predominantly recruited from upper-class families.[63] Yet unlike their counterparts in historical Western universities, where young idealists have been able to mature and to integrate into the establish-ment, students in underdeveloped countries have tended to perceive their own culture as dying. Under forced social change, they were economically unable to maintain their old aristocratic way of life even if they so wished. Western aris-tocratic students never had a sense of crisis commensurable with that experi-enced by their counterparts in underdeveloped countries.

Universities in underdeveloped nations play a double role: they transmit Western culture to help spur economic development, and they encourage stu-dents to identify with domestic culture to help maintain political stability and

61. Although education reform in France was more radical, the church domination of the university remained strong many years after the French Revolution (Vaughan and Archer 1971). It was not until be-tween the First and Second World Wars that middle-class children in France started to enter the univer-sity on a great scale (Worms 1971).

62. As Halsey notes, "the history of European and American universities in the age of coal and steam industrialism is one of successful resistance, by ideological and other elements in the 'superstructure,' to the pressures set up by economic change" (quoted in Ringer 1979, 7).

63. For the case in China, see Israel (1966, 5) and Yeh (1990).

a sense of nationalism.[64] These two tasks are essentially contradictory. Once students have acquired the "magic" of Western civilization and face a society in which most of the population still lives in a traditional manner, they tend to become radicalized in their thinking. Under a colonial presence and weak domestic government, students tend to turn to nationalistic, communist, and even fascist movements. After independence, they tend to attribute poor economic conditions and the low standard of living in their country to the backwardness of their culture, to the corruption of the leadership, and to the inefficiency of institutional arrangements. This makes students in underdeveloped nations especially susceptible to political preoccupations.[65]

Beyond culture, the nature of the university is also, and perhaps more importantly, shaped by the nature of the state. In comparison with those under authoritarian regimes, universities under democratic regimes tend to be conservative for two political reasons. First, as is argued in the introduction, most democratic states do not have to legitimize themselves through a mega-scale transformative social project, as some authoritarian states do. Therefore, they are less likely to generate state-centered grievances. Second, democratic states do not place strong sanctions upon freedom of thought and association, which are vital to intellectual life. However, in the long run such freedom brings multiple issues, perspectives, and political forces into the political arena. Because of this, under democratic regimes conflicts tend to rise and be solved locally, people are likely to be both horizontally and vertically divided, and multiple political discourses and forces nurture a sense of reality or even lead to apathy. Thus, the university in an authoritarian regime like China is not simply born as a radical institution; it is maintained as radical by certain state-society relations. The argument becomes clearer if we compare Chinese universities with those in India, the next largest underdeveloped nation. Although student militancy has been a tradition in both India and China, Indian students after independence were less and less able to organize into a unified movement aimed at national issues, whereas Chinese student movements have always kept a state-centered nature.[66]

---

64. Lipset (1967).

65. In India, for example, students were a major force in the independence movement (Altbach 1968b; Shils 1968). In South Korea and Thailand, student movements have repeatedly resulted in the downfall of regimes (Douglas 1971; Kim 1989; Samudavanija 1989). In Iran, students and secular intellectuals were a major force during the early phase of the Islamic Revolution (Bashiriyeh 1984; Malani 1994). In China student movements recurred in response to Japanese aggression before the communists took power.

66. See Altbach (1974) and Shils (1968) for further discussion of the Indian case.

Conclusion

This chapter has examined the mood of rank-and-file intellectuals and students who were normally not very interested in politics. I argue that state policy changes during the 1980s created massive grievances among students and intellectuals, the most relevant of which was the shift of reform strategies from "the four modernizations" to the "preliminary stage of socialism." This new policy immediately lowered the economic benefits of being an intellectual or a student. The impact of this policy shift was magnified by other state policies—one of which had been the great expansion of university enrollment since 1978. The expansion not only further devalued intellectuals but also provided human resources for student movements.

The enrollment expansion also created other problems. Since it was accompanied by inadequate state funding, the quality of education and student life greatly declined. It also led to a relative surplus of university graduates, making students unable to find satisfactory jobs after graduation. As a result Chinese students after the mid-1980s became less and less interested in studying. As a sign of massive discontent, more and more students spent time playing mahjongg and poker, preparing for the TOEFL test, holding parties, or simply spending time with their boy/girl friends.

I also argue that in comparison with the university in the West, the university in an underdeveloped nation like China was radical for cultural as well as political reasons. First, the university in an underdeveloped nation tends to be a foreign institution with few indigenous roots. It teaches a foreign culture and is an engine for forced modernization and against tradition. It is born as a radical institution. Moreover, such a university will be particularly radical when it is situated in a transformative authoritarian regime, because this kind of regime is more likely to generate state-centered grievances.

While the 1989 Movement was popularly considered as a "pro-democracy movement," some scholars, based on the traditional language that the students used during the movement, have questioned the movement's democratic nature.[67] In my study I found that movement participants could be placed into two categories. While a few radical activists did take democracy as a primary goal (chapter 2), most students participated in the movement in reaction to

---

67. For example, for Pye (1990), the students during the 1989 Movement were just using democracy as a lofty claim to fight for self-interested grievances, which if openly addressed would be labeled as "selfish" and censured in Chinese culture.

China's rising market economy. The latter population constituted the majority of students and intellectuals. I found that students by and large loved the political freedom that the reform had brought to them. Many of them also considered themselves supporters of the market-oriented reform. However, they did not trust the state and did not understand the market economy. They believed that the reform would bring intellectuals more benefits, and when it turned out that the opposite was true, they were very angry. Therefore, when a few political students started the movement, the rest of the students were sympathetic and soon joined in it. To this population, however, democracy remained more a "borrowed language" than a clearly understood political program—one very similar to Marxism for the early working-class movement in the West.[68]

68. See Calhoun (1983).

four

THE DECLINE OF THE SYSTEM
FOR CONTROLLING STUDENTS IN
UNIVERSITIES

In chapters 2 and 3, I discussed the role that intellectual elites played in the rise of the 1989 Beijing Student Movement and the sources of grievances particular to the student population. However, history has repeatedly demonstrated that a regime can still avoid large-scale social movements or revolutions as long as the regime can effectively control the aggrieved population. Indeed, since de Tocqueville, many scholars have noted that revolutions do not occur when a state is truly repressive but instead break out when the state has to relax or change its control methods in response to international competition or domestic pressure.[1] In this chapter I look into the student control system in Chinese universities during the 1980s, showing that because of changes in social structure brought about by the reform, the student control system in universities was greatly weakened. This weakening facilitated the spread of nonconformist ideas from intellectual elites to the aggrieved students, thus contributing to the actual rise of the movement.

1. See Collins (1981b), Huntington (1968), and Skocpol (1979).

This chapter starts with a general overview of the structure of the student control system and of the basic routines of student control personnel in Chinese universities. It is followed by a section on the foundations and problems of the political control system in China. I then examine how a campus environment which had once facilitated control over students became conducive to student mobilization, and how political control institutions in Beijing universities were captured for mobilizational purposes after the decline of political control. Finally, I substantiate the major arguments made in this chapter with some quantitative evidence that directly links the effectiveness of political control to the level of student activism and that shows which facets of weakening control coincided with the spatial patterning of student activism.

The Structure and Routines of Student Control Systems

Since the mid-1950s, state control in China has been largely exercised by rank-and-file activists under the supervision of local communist party branches.[2] This approach, also known as internal control, is congenial to Chinese culture.[3] It also reflected Mao's distaste for institutional politics and the way that the Communists came to power. In comparison with most Eastern European communist countries, state control in China depended much less on a secret police force before 1989.[4]

In a Chinese university, the Committee of Student Affairs is the highest-level organization responsible for student management. The Committee is responsible for establishing control strategies and for assessing the mood of students and the quality of control measures. It had usually been headed by a vice-secretary of the university's Communist Party Committee; then, during the 1980s, some universities adopted the principal responsibility system, under which a vice-president, sometimes not even a party member, took charge of the office. Two organizations under the leadership of the Committee of Student Affairs undertake the daily supervision of students: The Department of Youth (or the Department of Student Affairs) takes charge of political affairs, while the Student Bureau takes responsibility for matters such as enrollment, job as-

---

2. See Schurmann (1968) for the state control system during Mao's era.

3. Parish and Whyte (1978), Whyte and Parish (1984), and Troyer (1989).

4. In contrast to their Eastern European counterparts, the gradual military victory over the nationalist government won the Chinese communists a solid grassroots base and definite legitimation. A strong secret police force was not really necessary for the safety of the newly founded communist state.

signment, registration, awards, and punishment. In some universities these two offices have been merged since the mid-1980s.

The next administrative level is that of the Committee of Student Affairs in each department. These committees usually consist of three departmental-level cadres: the departmental vice-secretary of the Communist Party, the vice-chairman of the department, and the departmental secretary of the Communist Youth League. They lead class directors (*banzhuren*) and political instructors (*fudaoyuan*). Each class director or political instructor takes charge of one entering class. Operating at the grassroots, they form the cells of the student control system in a university. Before 1978 many political instructors held their jobs professionally. During reform, the size of this professional body shrank greatly, and in some universities the professional political instructor position was formally abolished, and the jobs were taken over by young teachers or even senior students. In some other universities, the political instructor position was omitted, and the job left to class directors. The class director position was most often taken by young teachers. Normally, its role is to help students with their studies and with their daily problems, but in reality, class directors, like "mothers" of the class, may take charge of everything from psychological counseling on the traumas of a broken love affair to tasks which political instructors normally do. Thus, in the following discussion I sometimes refer to both class directors and political instructors as political workers.[5]

Political control in Chinese universities takes place either through political education or through direct control carried out by student control personnel. Political education has two components: First, students take several compulsory courses, designed to introduce Marxism and to encourage them to accept Communist Party domination as well as the basic value system of Chinese society. A typical curriculum includes the History of the Chinese Communist Party, Political Economy, Marxist Philosophy, and Politics and Current Affairs. Since 1987, in an effort to strengthen political control by new methods of inculcation, many universities have added some of the following courses: Law, Thought Cultivation (*Sixiang Xiuyang*), Ethics of Work, and Philosophy of Life. Second, students are required to spend one afternoon a week studying relevant government documents and newspaper articles. The study session is organized by a class monitor, but a class director or political instructor is required to take part in the meetings whenever possible.

---

5. The Communist Youth League is also a channel for political control over students. The Party Committee entrusts the Department of Youth to direct the work of the Youth League, whereas the Youth League supervises the official Student Union and various student organizations. See Francis (1991) for more descriptions of official student associations in Beijing University.

Political instructors and class directors take charge of daily student management. Since the 1980s, class directors have become more and more important, especially in universities where the political instructor system was abolished. Their tasks range from supervising weekly regular political meetings to disseminating and explaining new policies of the university or the state, reading and holding discussions on important newspaper articles, selecting honor students, and even criticizing and deciding the level of punishment for "backward" students who break university regulations. Political instructors also go to student dormitory rooms and talk to students. Before the early 1980s, a political instructor usually had several student activists around him or her. It was mainly through those activists that political instructors learned about students, including about their private lives. The activists were in turn rewarded with access to limited resources such as party membership, good job assignments, or even leadership positions.[6] When the political climate went bad, as during the heyday of the Anti-Rightist Campaign in 1957, even non-activists started to inform on each other.[7]

The Problems of the Political Control System

The internal political control system was highly effective during Mao's era.[8] However, it quickly declined during the process of reform in the 1980s.[9] Both its high effectiveness and its rapid decay stemmed from several distinctive characteristics of the internal control system itself. In this section, I outline the foundations and the key problems of this system.

6. For more discussion on similar topics, see Shirk (1982) and Unger (1982). Unger's subjects were secondary school students. However, some of his findings also apply to university students.

7. One informant (no. 15) reported how her father had become a rightist during the Anti-Rightist Campaign: "My father talked in his dormitory about some local famines [that he knew] in the 1950s. At the time, it seemed no one cared about what he had said. But when the [Anti-Rightist] Campaign was started, other students reported this to the authority. Because they still needed people to fill the quota, my father became a student rightist. Because of this, he was sent to the Dongbei region after graduation."

8. Rosen (1985, 1990) and Shirk (1982) have made a similar observation.

9. Political control is only one dimension of the student control system. Therefore my analysis does not suggest that the whole student control system had collapsed. During the late 1980s, student control cadres were still doing their jobs in monitoring students' moral conduct, academic performance, and other nonpolitical activities. Moreover, the government also made several attempts to strengthen the student control system, with limited success. However, in terms of political control, these efforts became rather insignificant in comparison with the general social trend during the late 1980s.

FOUNDATIONS AND CHARACTERISTICS
OF THE INTERNAL POLITICAL CONTROL SYSTEM

Four factors formed the basis of effective internal political control during Mao's era. First, and maybe most importantly, before the 1980s the communist government enjoyed a high level of ideological legitimation. Therefore, both political workers and a large number of students actively participated in mutual supervision activities, and they tended to consider their behavior as moral even if such behavior might be detrimental to other people's careers or even lives. A substantial number more or less wanted to believe that what they did was good for the country. Their interests and political beliefs converged. This was revealed in my informal interview with Ding Zilin, who became an active dissident after her son's death on the night of June 3, 1989, during the military repression. She told me: "In 1957, those rightist students were actually all good students with ideas. However, we, a bunch of naive students, criticized them heavily. Now, I feel very guilty whenever I recall the experience."

Second, to start a career as a political worker was among the best avenues of status attainment for university students. During Mao's era, student control personnel were usually free from political persecution except in the heyday of the Cultural Revolution. Higher official positions in universities were open mainly to young political workers who performed their tasks well. A young political worker who aspired to be an academician was more likely in later years to be given good courses to teach or to be appointed as a leader in a research team.

Third, as a result of communist rule, by 1989 Beijing had 67 institutions of higher learning, with over 162,576 students.[10] Most of these universities are located in the Haidian District and surrounding areas. With six to eight undergraduate students living in a dormitory room, and with up to a thousand students in any single dormitory building, the social environment greatly facilitates mutual supervision among students when most students think that such behavior is moral and profitable.[11]

Fourth, during Mao's era, student control personnel had several effective means to reward conformist students and punish "political deviants." For

10. The data are from *Educational Statistics Yearbook of China* (1989) and *Zhongguo Gaodeng Jiaoyu Daquan* (1989). The data excluded 90,927 undergraduate students enrolled as non-boarding, night school, and correspondence students in these universities.

11. The narrative by one of my informants (no.15), as cited in note 7, is a very good example of the mutual supervision function of dormitory rooms.

example, they could reward "good students" with party membership and punish "deviants" by assigning them poor jobs.[12] Once a student was considered to have made a serious political mistake, political control personnel had the power to decide the level of punishment and to record this in the individual's dossier. This dossier would follow that student to the workplace, seriously affecting his/her future life chances.

Economic reform, however, brought about swift changes in state-society relations. Among those changes, the most significant were the decline of the ideological legitimation of the state and the rise of new avenues of status attainment beyond the state. The change in state-society relations along these two dimensions made active participation in mutual supervision politically immoral and economically senseless, and therefore undermined the foundations of the internal political control system.

During the 1980s, for instance, many punishments lost their effectiveness. In 1978 the Chinese government had put the economy on the top of the agenda. Since economic development needs the cooperation of intellectuals, the political climate had to be loosened: hence political control personnel were not always encouraged to use harsh measures to punish students. Moreover, as the ideological legitimation of the state declined, a bad political record in one's dossier was no longer a nightmare, because political offenders were often respected by local people. Finally, as more and more university students found jobs in privately owned, joint-venture, or foreign companies, the job assignment system meant less and less, especially to active students. For instance, all the six movement leaders that I interviewed in 1993 had either been jailed or been dismissed by their universities after the military crackdown, but none of them reported great difficulties in finding jobs. In fact, I experienced difficulties in locating student leaders in Beijing because by early 1993 many of them had already gone to the prosperous southern provinces to look for better opportunities.

Most students did not need severe sanctions to keep them away from nonconformist political activities, however. Although the political control system was still quite effective during the early 1980s, it greatly weakened in only a few years. The decline was so quick because such internal political control has two properties that made it extremely sensitive to changing state-society relations. First, the effectiveness of internal control is highly sensitive to the ideological legitimation of the state. While the efficiency of a professional control system

---

12. Until the late 1980s, the state took responsibility for assigning every university student a job upon graduation. Under this system, students with poor marks, a bad political profile, or uneasy relations with school authorities often got poor jobs.

depends heavily on infrastructural technologies, an internal control system depends primarily on people's cooperation. Internal student control measures are effective only when most students and grassroots political control personnel cooperatively participate in mutual supervision and consider their activities as moral behavior. Secondly, the effectiveness of internal student control is also very sensitive to the economic and political reward patterns in the larger society. The state can reward professional secret police only as long as it has the financial resources to do so. This is impossible for nonprofessionals. A separate payroll for political workers and student activists is not only too expensive because of the size of this population, but it would also turn political workers and student activists into the "police" and thus alienate them from the rest of students. Internal control is effective only when it is implemented by individuals with whom the controlled population identifies. In the following, I elaborate the problems associated with the political control system in Chinese universities, along with the more general issues of how low ideological legitimation and declining economic benefits affect political control.

LACK OF MORALE AMONG STUDENT CONTROL PERSONNEL

As mentioned before, internal control was highly effective during Mao's era because a substantial number of political workers and students who had actively participated in mutual supervision more or less wanted to believe that what they were doing was beneficial to the country. This became impossible after the economic reform. A market-oriented reform requires open doors. Since the reform, more overseas Chinese and Westerners had visited China, and more Chinese had gone abroad.[13] Domestic travel also became much more frequent. The Voice of America (VOA) and British Broadcasting Corporation (BBC) were no longer treated as enemy broadcasts; instead, many university students listened to them routinely, largely as a means to learn English.[14] An affluent West, and more importantly, the economic miracles in Taiwan and South Korea, were contrasted with China's past economic performance. The communist state had delivered far less to China than what had been promised. Coupled with the bitter memories of the Cultural Revolution and with the new international wave of democracy, people's faith in state socialism and the government declined greatly, especially among students and intellectuals.[15]

13. See chapter 5 or Zhao Dingxin (1996) for more details.

14. Quan (1990); He and Zhu (1994).

15. See Hayhoe (1989) and Ho and Huenemann (1984) for other descriptions on the "open door" policy.

The state's decreasing ideological legitimation among students and intellectuals was confirmed by my interviews. Of the sixty informants asked the question "What was your view of the Four Cardinal Principles before the 1989 Student Movement?" twenty-one (35%) claimed to have been strictly against them, whereas only nine (15%) claimed that they had accepted them. The remaining 50 percent accepted them with various reservations. Moreover, most people who conditionally accepted the Four Cardinal Principles did so not because they agreed with them but for pragmatic reasons. Only a handful of students and young teachers still accepted the ideological legitimation of the state. The following are two rather typical answers from those who conditionally accepted the Four Cardinal Principles:

> My basic view on this point was that our country should be as stable as possible. Stability does help economic development. The most important thing was that the country must be developed. This principle or that principle was only a matter of the second degree. (no. 45)

> I did not agree with the Four Cardinal Principles. But I thought that this was only a form. The content of the Four Cardinal Principles, as many people had noticed, could be developed and modified. . . . I felt OK as long as the reform is advanced substantially. (no. 68)

In both cases, the informants more or less accepted the Four Cardinal Principles not because they still had faith in the ideology itself but because they felt that these principles did not bother them as long as the state was still effective or was developing in the right direction. Such respondents would stand against the government if it went into a commonly perceived wrong direction; indeed, most informants of this type actively participated in the 1989 Movement.

As a result of this decline of ideological legitimation, young teachers were no longer willing to be political workers. When they were required to do the job, they generally no longer took it seriously, and even if some of them did treat their work seriously, not many students would cooperate with them. The nature of the job often made people associate political workers with the ultra-left past. They were not respected, and their efforts were often mocked.[16]

During the 1980s the higher-level student control agencies in China conducted many surveys to monitor the effectiveness of political control and the mood of students. As 1989 approached, these surveys often demonstrated an increasing decline of political control. For example, in 1986 Liu Qinglong

16. Quan (1990); Wu Dayuan (1993).

TABLE 4.1 Students' Responses to the Statements (1) "China Would Develop More Quickly If It Were under Capitalism," and (2) "I Have Lost Hope over the Current Reform"

Answer	1986 (%)	1987 (%)	1988 (%)
Agree with (1)	16.8	28.7	34.3
Agree with (2)	23.2	51.7	58.9

Data source: Wang Dianqing et al. (1990).

conducted a survey among 344 randomly selected students in a university in Beijing.[17] The result showed that 57.8 percent of students were dissatisfied with their political courses, whereas only 14.3 percent were satisfied and the rest were somewhere in the middle. In 1987, Liu asked the same questions in the same university, this time of 993 students. The percentage of dissatisfied students increased to 63.6 percent, whereas the size of the satisfied group dropped to 6.7 percent. Obviously, students had become increasingly dissatisfied with old-style political education. Another survey conducted in Beijing yielded a comparable result.[18] Students were asked if they agreed with two statements: (1) "China would develop more quickly if China were under capitalism," and (2) "I have lost hope over the current reform." Their responses are summarized in table 4.1. As is shown in the table, the percentage of affirmative answers to both questions increased greatly after 1986; in other words, more and more students considered capitalism to be the solution for China, and fewer had any hope for China's reform. Here the students' mood coincided with the increasing activism in Chinese universities.

Therefore, when Beijing students were asked to rank the importance of eleven potential influences on their ideological formation, they ranked their class directors and political instructors in ninth and tenth place, ahead of only the leaders of their departments and universities.[19] At the top ranked the prevailing ideological current, newspapers and magazines, parents, literature, and peers. Although comparable data on political workers' influence during Mao's era are not available, it is reasonable to assume that their influence then was

17. Liu Qinglong (1990).

18. Wang Dianqing et al. (1990). The survey was conducted in sixteen Beijing universities. The sample size for the 1989 survey was 1,104 students.

19. Liu Qinglong (1990).

much stronger, considering the power that political workers had over students before the economic reform.

The channels of status attainment in the university were also drastically altered in the wake of the 1978 economic reform. Before 1978, to be close to the Communist Party was about the best avenue for achieving higher socioeconomic status. The reform changed the avenues of status attainment, however, making political conformity to the government unessential.

Except in the early period of the Cultural Revolution, the politically conformist students of Mao's era were less likely than other students to be subject to political persecution, and they had greater chances of acquiring party membership, a golden ticket to status attainment. The politically conformist students also had higher potential for getting good jobs after graduation or after they retired from their political careers. Moreover, high official positions in universities also went mainly to young political workers who were outstanding in their job performance.

But reform changed the channels of status attainment in a way that made being politically active an increasingly unwise choice. Since the early 1980s, job assignments have been based more and more on grades rather than on political performance. By the end of the 1980s, as economic reform deepened, many universities even experimented with abandoning the job assignment system and with letting students look for jobs by themselves. The reform also opened many channels that were outside state control. Among these alternative channels, working in non-state sectors and studying abroad were the most important.

Working in a university after graduation had once been among the best jobs that a student could get. By the late 1980s, however, it was no longer true because the economic status of intellectuals had greatly declined (chapter 3). For a young teacher remaining in a university, to be a political worker was a considerably poorer choice than to be a teacher. Political workers had less chance of being sent abroad than did young teachers doing research. After the late 1980s, researchers could pay themselves and their associates through grants, while political workers had fewer alternative sources of income.

To be a political worker in the universities was also no longer a route to political advancement. Early in the 1980s, in order to recruit younger and reform-minded bureaucrats, Deng Xiaoping forced millions of cadres to retire, filling the vacancies mainly with new graduates.[20] Many higher-level officials at the time, including the general secretary, Hu Yaobang, had a Youth League background, and thus pursuing a political career by starting as a student activist and the head of a departmental-level Youth League appealed to many students. However, such hopes diminished as vacancies were gradually filled, Hu Yaobang resigned, and reform deepened. As one departmental political cadre, a party vice-secretary of a department, pointed out:

> Now it seems quite difficult to have a successful political career [through this route]. Nowadays in the university, only two routes are feasible to reach higher political posts. The first is to be academically famous, including a degree from a Western university, and then shift to the official channel. The second is to run a university enterprise successfully.[21] Once you run it well, your ability is recognized. (no. 44)

This does not mean that universities were unable to recruit a sufficient number of political workers; they filled the posts with newly graduated students. During the 1980s, rural students still considered the position to be a good one. It was otherwise difficult for these students to get jobs in cities like Beijing because of the family registration (*hukou*) system. To some students, a political job at the university was attractive because it provided more foreign contacts and also because it gave them more discretionary time to prepare for TOEFL and GRE tests. Yet while universities were able to recruit political workers, they were unable to keep them. One informant (no. 2) reported that none of his eleven classmates who were once class directors or political instructors was still working in the university. Six of them went to companies and five to the United States and Canada. This was not just true for grassroots political workers. The same departmental party vice-secretary told me:

> [After graduation in 1986, I was assigned to a job at the Youth League of the University]. Seven to eight students like me got positions of a similar rank. So far, except for me, none of them still does political work. At least, no one still works as a pure political cadre like me. Among them, one is in business, two went to companies,

---

20. Yang and Cui (1989).

21. In China, a university also runs factories and companies. Much of the profit is used to pay the bonuses of faculty members. In some universities, bonuses can outweigh wages.

and two went abroad. Another one or two have changed jobs even though they are still working in the university.[22]

After the 1989 Movement, many papers published in Chinese youth journals also noted the seriousness of the problem. With between 65 and 70 percent of young teachers spending the majority of their time studying English and preparing to go abroad,[23] and over 75 percent of political workers expressing the wish to leave their jobs,[24] it was not surprising to find it argued that the instability of the political worker personnel had become the most serious problem of university political education.[25]

Decline of Political Control and Student Mobilization

In the last section I briefly mentioned how the student living environment and campus layout facilitated student control during Mao's era. Now I will show that, after the decline of the student control systems in universities, the campus environment, which had once facilitated political control over students, instead became conducive to the growth of social movements, and that the student control institution itself in fact acquired mobilization functions.

THE CAMPUS ENVIRONMENT AND THE SPREAD OF DISSIDENT IDEAS

In this section, I show how the dormitory environment facilitated the spread of dissident ideas at the universities. (In chapter 8 of this book, I will analyze in greater detail how the campus environment assisted student mobilization and shaped the development of the 1989 Movement.) Most undergraduate students in China live in dormitories. The dense living environment greatly facilitated the spread of dissident ideas when the state was no longer able to regulate student life inside the dormitory.

22. After 1989, to stop the decay of the political control system, the Chinese government has tried to raise the status of student control personnel in universities. For example, by the time I began my interviews in Beijing in early 1993, such personnel had been awarded equivalent academic ranks and their wage levels had been increased. The problem is that most Chinese people, including the political control personnel themselves, do not usually take their academic titles seriously; and the wage increase was too little in comparison with the wage-hikes in other professions.

23. See He Sha (1992). The result is derived from a survey conducted in a polytechnic university in Beijing.

24. Quan (1990).

25. Wu Dayuan (1993).

In my study, most informants reported that they usually chatted in the dormitory room for from one to several hours each day. Although politics and political grievances were not always the topics of their conversations, they did constitute a major theme, especially when the socioeconomic situation worsened. During the late 1980s dormitory rooms were the primary location where nonconformist ideologies spread and achieved dominance. When I asked my informants: "Were you afraid that other students might report the contents to the authorities when you discussed sensitive political matters in your dormitory room?" fifty-two out of fifty-four informants responded with an unqualified no. Only two answered yes, to some extent. The following comment reflects this lack of concern:

> I was not afraid. Nowadays I do not think anybody will inform on me. Even if somebody does it, I do not think any students will be afraid of that. In my last university year, that was in 1991, one of my classmates even openly demanded to withdraw from the Communist Youth League. . . . Even though he did so, his life, including his job after graduation, was not affected. (no. 33)[26]

During the 1980s, enthusiasm for newly introduced Western philosophies and political theories occurred repetitively on Chinese campuses,[27] creating social fevers such as "Freud fever," "Nietzsche fever," "Sartre fever," "culture fever," and "political reform fever" (see chapter 1). By the time a fever passed, not too many students had actually read the original works.[28] In fact, most students got to know an interesting novel or a book when some other students reading the book in the same or a nearby room discussed their reading in a dormitory conversation. Students might also get ideas from various conferences held on campus. During the conference fever in 1988 and 1989, students in the same or nearby dormitory rooms also frequently informed each other about conferences and invited each other to go to them.

If intellectual elites spread their ideas by publishing student-oriented books and holding conferences in universities, the students who were then thus sensi-

---

26. During Mao's era, only those who had made serious political mistakes or committed crimes were asked to withdraw from the Youth League. Demanding to withdraw one's membership voluntarily would have been unthinkable, and in itself it would have been a crime.

27. Some were not actually new to China, but only to the young students.

28. Li Jinmin (1988) reports that even after the "Nietzsche fever," about two-thirds of the students had still never read any of Nietzsche's books. The survey was conducted in eight universities, with a sample size of 2,005 students and an 85.5 percent return rate.

tized to their ideas spread them further through the dormitories. As soon as one student in a dormitory room became interested in politically related matters, his reading would probably become a recurring topic of discussion there:

> The major topic in our dormitory room was reform, . . . mainly the market economy and privatization. One student in our dormitory room strongly supported the market economy. He read the *World Economic Herald* a lot. He also read many books by Fang Lizhi and Li Yining. When he read those books, he passed these messages to us [in the dormitory room]. We then debated. (no. 54)

Here, dormitory rooms have a convergence function. This, however, does not mean that students would necessarily come to agree with each other. The same informant explained: "During the debate, another student and I were strongly against his ideas, while one student supported him. The rest were in the middle." However, frequent discussions of hard-to-solve social problems made students more sensitive to a few issues, and gradually, as social problems prolonged or worsened, they came to some consensus on a few basic viewpoints. In this manner, during the late 1980s more and more students came to believe that democracy and capitalism were solutions to China's problems.[29]

MOBILIZATIONAL FUNCTIONS OF POLITICAL CONTROL INSTITUTIONS

After the ideological legitimation of the regime weakened, some student control personnel and students in universities not only resisted cooperation with the state but also captured student control institutions to spread nonconformist ideologies. Their efforts were often very effective because they held strategic positions of communication in the universities.

29. Many studies conducted in China report the existence of "core members" in student dormitory rooms (Li Guanghua 1992; Ren Jiayu 1991; Sun Xijun 1985). Students' mutual influence was stronger in those dormitory rooms with one or more core members. Xu and Liu (1985) take three typical dormitory rooms to illustrate such influence. They found that in dormitory room A, where the core member was interested in martial arts, the whole room stayed up late to learn martial arts and the core member and his/her roommates became the organizers or active members of the martial arts association in the university. Another student in the dormitory room was very interested in problems associated with China's reform, and often initiated discussion on this topic. When the students reached their third year, and as the reform wave swept the city, this student rose to become a core member. From then on, reform became a major topic and the room collectively subscribed to the *World Economic Herald*. In dormitory room B, where the core member was an academically diligent and politically conformist student, most students in that dormitory followed suit. In dormitory C, the core member was interested in playing Chinese chess and poker. Over time, the other students also became addicted to these games.

In the past, courses in politics had been a major weapon of political social-ization. When students no longer believed that Marxist dogmas were valid, ab-senteeism from such courses became extremely high. In a few cases, however, such courses actually gained in popularity; most probably, these were courses which the teacher taught in a critical way. The impact of such classes on stu-dents was revealed in this dramatic account:

> In the second semester of the first year, we had a course called the History of the Chinese Revolution. This is usually a political education course for the CCP. How-ever, the teacher taught us a true history of the CCP. Why did the CCP take power? He did not tell us the dogmas. From his own analysis, he let us know that there were qualitative differences in the history of the CCP before and after the armed rebel-lion. He solved many puzzles in my mind. . . . Usually for a political course such as this, 50 percent attendance would be considered good. But when this teacher taught, even the corridor of the classroom was filled. It was really a spectacular sight! Un-til now many of my classmates still thought that it was he who enlightened us. Af-ter that semester, everything seemed changed to me. I felt like a new man. It was re-ally a process of soul reconstruction. Yet, this was a natural process. . . . We were extremely grateful to the teacher. Once he had to move and he did not let us know. Nevertheless, more than thirty students appeared at his apartment to offer help on that day. (no. 67)[30]

Between 1988 and early 1989, intellectual elites were spreading dissident ideas in universities by holding conferences. I have found a strong correlation between students' conference attendance and their level of participation in the 1989 Movement (chapter 2). Ironically, most of these conferences were sponsored by student control agencies such as the Youth League and the Department of Youth. Before 1989, the Department of Youth in major Beijing universities seldom turned down any proposed conference organized by students or intel-lectual elites. On the contrary, in many universities the Youth League and the Department of Youth assigned a special person to organize this type of confer-ence. Most higher-level student control agencies did not intend to spread non-conformist ideas; rather, they intended to use the conferences as a method for political control. During the late 1980s, many higher-level student control cad-res held the notion that only a free political environment on campus could pre-vent students from going off-campus.[31] As a result, some liberal intellectuals,

---

30. This informant later became a hunger striker, fasting at Tiananmen Square for a week during the 1989 Movement.

31. Rosen (1991a, 439).

some students, and even some lower-level political work cadres came to spread dissident thinking.

Quantitative Evidence

I have argued that the decline of the political control system had a great impact on the rise of the 1989 Movement. I have also argued that the weakening of political control was mainly a result of the declining ideological legitimation of the state and of changing channels of status attainment. In this section, I try to test the two arguments with the available data.[32]

Table 4.2 shows the percentage of political work cadres who intended to continue their careers, the student enrollment, and the scale of student activism in eight Beijing universities. Low percentages here are taken as indicating a strong decomposition of the political control system, while high percentages imply the opposite. Among the eight universities listed in table 4.2 Beijing University, Beijing Normal University, and Qinghua University are coded as high student activism universities. These three universities had "big-character posters" on the day of Hu Yaobang's death, and students in them staged demonstrations and organized autonomous student unions much earlier than did students at other universities on the list. Between early and mid-May, when all other universities started to resume classes, Beijing University and Beijing Normal were the only two universities whose students maintained the class boycott. On the other hand, Qinghua University and Beijing University were the only two universities that established student-run broadcasting stations at Tiananmen Square during the hunger strike.[33] While Beijing University and Beijing Normal University played leading roles in initiating the hunger strike during mid-May, Qinghua University was the leading force in organizing the picket systems and

32. The effort made here is only a rudimentary step toward a quantitative analysis of the issue. First, the conclusion here only confirms a positive relation between the decline of student political control and the level of student activism, and indicates some factors that led to such a decline. It does not exclude other factors. For example, some universities, such as Beijing University, have a long tradition of student activism (Chow 1967; Israel 1966). The campus subculture in universities with an activist tradition may also have contributed to the differentiated level of student activism on Beijing campuses. Moreover, the survey data used in the analysis may not be of high quality. Some of the questions are unclear, and the people who conducted the survey may not have had formal training in questionnaire research. However, regardless of possible weaknesses, the strong and consistent results in the following analysis, together with the qualitative evidence presented in previous sections, give us confidence in the conclusion.

33. *Huigu yu Fansi* (1993, 187–93). In the universities, students ran the equivalent of campus broadcast stations. The stations relied upon extensive public address systems, in which a central station was connected by wire to speakers around campus. Students from the two universities set up similar, and competing, public address systems in the Square.

TABLE 4.2.   The Desire of Political Work Cadres to Continue Their Work in a
University and the Level of Student Participation in That University
during the 1989 Movement

University (College)	Want to Continue This Work over a Long Period of Time (X) (%)	Enrollment (Y)	Level of Student Participation[a]
1. Qinghua University	0	14,270	XX
2. Beijing University	12.5	12,682	XX
3. Beijing Normal	7.7	7,035	XX
4. Beijing Teacher	37.5	4,761	X
5. Beijing Steel	12.8	5,879	X
6. Capital Medical	50.0	2,115	X
7. Beijing Forestry	27.8	1,893	X
8. Northern Communication	37.5	4,318	X
Weighted mean (WM)[b]	14.9		
WM for rows 1–3	6.3		
WM for rows 4–8	30.3		

Data sources: The student enrollment data are from Zhongguo Gaodeng Xuexiao Daquan (1989). The interview
data are from Rosen (1991a). Here, political work cadres include political instructors and higher-level
political control cadres. Interviews were done at nine universities. Because the enrollment at an engineering
college cannot be determined, only eight universities are included. The omission does not lead to problems
because all three engineering colleges in Beijing are small colleges with lower movement participation.
[a]Here, XX = high student participation and X = low participation.
[b]In this table and in table 4.3, the weighted mean was calculated as mean = $\Sigma X_i Y_i / \Sigma Y_i$.

maintaining order at Tiananmen Square during the hunger strike. All in all,
each of these three universities contributed, on the basis of its enrollment, a
higher proportion of student leaders than did almost all of the other universities. Of the twenty-one student leaders on the most wanted list published by
the Chinese government after the military crackdown,[34] Beijing University accounted for seven, Qinghua University and Beijing Normal University each accounted for three, and the rest of the universities listed in table 4.2 had none.

In China during the 1980s, political work cadres were normally assigned to
each entering class. Variations on class size in China were small. Therefore,
we can assume that the number of political work cadres in a university was
proportional to the size of that university. Thus, although we do not know the

34. See the June 14, 1989 issue of Guangming Daily for the list.

exact number of political work cadres in a particular university, we can estimate its proportions by the proportion of share of student enrollment in that university. We can estimate the average percentage of the political work cadres who still wanted "to continue this work over a long period of time" in some universities by a weighted mean (that is, we can weigh the percentages in the second column of table 4.2 by the proportion of student enrollment in that university). The formula to calculate the mean is given at the end of table 4.2.

After the calculation, I found that, on average, only 14.9 percent of political work cadres answered "yes" to the question "Do you want to continue this work over a long period of time?" This result is itself startling. When I divided the eight universities into two groups in terms of their level of movement participation and estimated the weighted mean by the same method, the affirmative answer in the higher participation group dropped to 6.3 percent, whereas in the lower participation group it increased to 30.3 percent. In other words, activism was much more prevalent on campuses where the political control specialists were demoralized. This supports the first argument that lack of morale, and an implied unwillingness to intervene in students' dissident activities and counter the rising tide of mobilization, in part explains differential rates of activism on various campuses in Beijing.

Table 4.2 appears to show a strong correlation between the size of student enrollment and the level of student activism. This, however, is a pseudo-correlation. For example, the University of Political Science and Law, a university not on the list, is a small university; yet it had two student leaders on the most wanted list, and its student activism reached a level that only a few universities in Beijing could match. A plausible explanation is that universities with higher prestige (those universities usually having a larger enrollment) or larger faculty in social sciences and humanities often had more Western-trained professors, provided more contact with Western universities and foundations, gave exposure to more novel ideas, and therefore experienced a greater decline of political control. The University of Political Science and Law had an extremely high level of activism because it is a university which specializes in the social sciences.

Table 4.3 lists political work cadres' responses to factors that might have been attributed to their unwillingness to continue their jobs and to the level of activism in each university. All the data are from the same sources as in table 4.2. Among the four items (X_1 to X_4), X_1 ([The work] does not receive a correct evaluation from society) measures political cadres' understanding of other people's perception of the legitimacy of political work. Since a major task of political work cadres is political education or ideological indoctrination, its

TABLE 4.3   Reasons Why Political Work Cadres Do Not Want to Work as Political Work-
                   ers for Long, and the Level of Student Participation in the 1989 Movement

University (College)	Does Not Receive Correct Evaluation from Society (X_1) (%)	Fear of Future Policy Change (X_2) (%)	Cannot Develop One's Future (X_3) (%)	Low Material Benefits (X_4) (%)	Level of Student Participation
1. Qinghua University	100.0	53.3	6.7	6.7	XX
2. Beijing University	43.3	37.5	31.3	25.0	XX
3. Beijing Normal	60.0	56.4	28.2	10.3	XX
4. Beijing Teacher	55.0	35.0	30.0	15.0	X
5. Beijing Steel	15.4	46.2	7.7	15.4	X
6. Capital Medical	25.0	62.0	25.0	12.5	X
7. Beijing Forestry	22.2	50.0	11.1	11.1	X
8. Northern Communication	87.5	75.0	25.0	12.5	X
Weighted mean (WM):	61.0	49.5	20.3	14.1	
WM for rows 1–3	70.7	48.0	20.3	14.3	
WM for rows 4–8	43.5	52.1	20.0	13.9	

Data sources: Data are from the same sources as table 4.2. Enrollment data (Y) are omitted here. Explanations that appeared in the footnotes to table 4.2 also apply in this table. Since some respondents opted for two categories, the totals may exceed 100 percent in some cases.

value, and political work cadres' own perception of its value, is an index of the level of ideological legitimation of the state. X_2 measures political work cadres' concern about future policy changes (whether they worried about their future political and economic status). It is a mixed index. X_3 measures the cadres' perception of whether their own work contributed to their life chances. X_4 measures the respondents' perception of their current level of income in society. Therefore, X_2, X_3 and X_4 measure political work cadres' own evaluation of their work in terms of political as well as economic status.[35]

When I estimated the weighted mean percentages for each question by the same method used in table 4.2, I obtained results that show that on average 61 percent of political work cadres did not think that their job was appreciated by others. This is the highest percentage among the four items. If we separate

35. The original data consisted of eight statements. Items five to eight, which measured other factors that led to political work cadres' unwillingness to take on their jobs, were excluded. Statement five (that is, "not suited to this work") is excluded because while this could be one's real feeling, it could also just be an alibi apt to many interpretations. Very few respondents chose items six to eight. This in itself also confirms that political and economic factors were most crucial to the demoralization of political work cadres.

the eight universities into the high and low student participation groups again, the number of those who thought their work was not well appreciated by others dropped to 43.5 percent in the low participation group, but increased to 70.7 percent in the high group. Negative feelings were much stronger among political work cadres in high participation universities.

The next three items (X_2 to X_4) combined reach 83.9 percent, which indicates that the loss of confidence in the future of their work, politically and economically, was also a very important reason why leading political work cadres refused to take their work as a career. Respondents in the low and high movement participation universities, however, did not show much difference in their response to the statements from X_2 to X_4. This means that while political dissatisfaction was much stronger among respondents in higher movement participation universities than among those in lower ones, economic disappointment was quite uniform across all universities. This is hardly surprising. While the reform affected the economic situation of political work cadres in all universities, Western influences acted more strongly on high movement participation universities. In any event, it was precisely for moral as well as for economic reasons that the cadres were no longer willing to cooperate with the government. The second argument is, therefore, confirmed.

How did this decline of political control affect the behavior of a political worker in an actual process of student mobilization? A clue might be found in a class director's (no. 19) comparison of his own behavior in a student movement in 1986 with his activities in the 1989 Movement. In both cases he was asked by higher-level authorities to persuade students not to demonstrate on the street. He cooperated in 1986. He successfully prevented students in his class from going to the street by gathering students together before a scheduled demonstration and teaching them how to play bridge. Yet he did nothing to stop the students in 1989. He explained his inaction: "Teachers and students were both living in the same society. We had only graduated a few years earlier. . . . We shared similar feelings. We also discussed problems that the students often mentioned. We, in fact, supported the students' action."

Conclusion

Political control in Chinese universities has primarily been based on the cooperation of political workers and student activists with student control agencies at higher levels. In comparison with a secret police system, this system is more sensitive to the level of ideological legitimation of the state, as well as to the synchronization of cooperative activities with the channels of status attainment existing in the larger society. It had therefore been very effective during Mao's era, when the state enjoyed high ideological legitimation and when political workers and conformist students were well positioned for status attainment. But the system quickly weakened after 1978, when the ideological legitimation of the state greatly declined and other channels of upward mobility opened up.

This chapter shows that after the decline of the student control system in Chinese universities, a campus environment that had formerly extended state control now facilitated the communication of grievances and dissident ideologies among students. During the late 1980s, even the student control system itself was captured by intellectual elites to spread dissident ideas. The analysis here indicates that universities that experienced greater weakening in student control systems were also those that had higher levels of student activism during the 1989 Movement. In other words, the decline of the student control system in universities did make a significant contribution to the rise and development of the 1989 Movement.

five

ON THE EVE OF THE 1989 MOVEMENT

By the late 1980s, China's economic reform had gone into a deep crisis. Inflation and corruption hounded Chinese society. People's confidence in the reform was at its lowest point, and grievances mounted. The emerging economic crisis not only further radicalized the liberal intellectual elites but also alienated the rest of the students and urban residents. To help one better understand the mass support for the 1989 Beijing Student Movement, I start this chapter with a discussion of the socioeconomic environment immediately before the movement's outbreak. Joining a social movement in an authoritarian regime like China is a high-risk activity. Most students chose to "exit" before voicing their grievances politically.[1] In this chapter I also argue that, among other activities, going abroad had been a major route for Chinese students to escape from the unhappy domestic reality, and hence that the diminishing possibilities for going abroad at the end of the 1980s drew students to domestic politics. As 1989 approached, the last section shows, some intellectual elites persistently pushed for desired social changes—actions that constituted the final episode before the rise of the 1989 Movement.

1. Hirschman (1970).

Emerging Social Crises

During the late 1980s, socioeconomic problems that had emerged during reform developed to a scale that affected almost every sector of the urban population. For example, the rural reform had greatly increased agricultural produc-
tivity and had freed underemployed laborers formerly tied to the land. Even
with a great expansion of rural industry, the surplus of laborers in rural areas
was still estimated at about 200 million. Many rural laborers swarmed into big
cities looking for jobs. By October 1988 the population of migrant laborers in
Beijing had reached one million and was growing continuously.[2] In Guangzhou,
capital of Guangdong province, more than 2.5 million rural laborers flooded the
city over a short period between February and March 1989.[3] Such massive migration made the already overpopulated cities appear even more crowded, and
brought a huge increase in crime rates.[4] In some provinces organized crime
reached such an extent that passengers on crowded public buses or even on
trains were collectively robbed by armed thugs. Many Chinese, used to a very
low crime rate, now no longer dared go outside after dark.

The social problems that had the greatest impact on the Chinese and were
most directly related to the rise of the 1989 Movement were rampant corruption, high inflation, and increasing income disparities.[5] In chapter 3, I touched
on the impact that perceived income disparities had on intellectuals and students. Most Chinese also considered the increasing income gap as mainly a
result of corruption and inflation,[6] and thus these two topics deserve separate
attention.

2. Wu Ren (1990a).

3. Kristof (1990b, 35).

4. The general crime rate was reported to have increased by 26.4 percent from 1987 to 1988, with serious crime increasing by 65.7 percent (Wu Ren 1990a).

5. Almost every sector of urban population shared grievances over these problems. For example, a question was asked in a survey carried out within *Jiusanxueshe* (one of the nine satellite parties in China with
membership based exclusively on senior intellectuals) Beijing branch ($n = 280$, return rate $= 67.5$ percent):
"What are the problems of current society that concern you the most?" Respondents were instructed to
choose three out of seven items. The result is that 81.2 percent chose "corruption within the Communist
Party," 72 percent chose "the wages of intellectuals are too low," and 55.6 percent chose "high inflation"
(*Beijing Jiusanluntan* 1989). Similar studies carried out in other sectors of the urban population yielded com-
parable results (Wu Ren 1990a).

6. In a survey conducted in Shanghai in 1988, people were asked to judge the following statement:
"Most people become rich by corrupt or criminal means." Fifty-three point eight percent of the people
agreed with the statement, only 27.3 percent did not agree, and the rest gave no comment. Conclusions were

RAMPANT OFFICIAL CORRUPTION

Poor information and commodity flows in an immature market tend to produce monopoly profits. In China during the 1980s those who had power could have free access to such information and commodities, and hence to such profits. This structuration was perhaps the ultimate source of the large-scale corruption that broke out in China after the mid-1980s. For example, under the newly introduced dual-track price system for raw materials, state enterprises still received their yearly quota at the lower subsidized prices, but enterprises of other sectors had to buy raw materials at the market price. Thus, those who had access to raw materials at lower prices could make a fortune by selling lower-priced raw materials at higher open market prices. As a result, many government agencies that had the power to allocate raw materials or to issue licenses opened companies. Individuals who had good connections with people in those companies also started companies. Like the food chain in an ecosystem, such a network of corruption can extend over several links.[7] The number of registered companies increased from 170,000 in 1986 to 400,000 by mid-1988. Even the State Council, the highest administrative body in China, established more than 700 companies over a similarly short period of time.[8] Many new companies had neither capital investment nor an office. The only business in which they were involved was that of exchanging their power for money, or, in economic terminology, "collecting rents."

During the reform, managers of state enterprises and local government leaders acquired more decision-making power. These managers and local government officials did not however have long-term incentives to use this power for the collective good of the state and its enterprises. Local government therefore spent a lot of money on (often wasteful) construction projects, while enterprise managers spent much money for nonproductive purposes. For instance, enterprise managers tended to increase workers' bonuses at rates far exceeding profit increases. They also used public money for private purposes, such as buying foreign luxury cars, traveling domestically and internationally, and holding

---

based on 642 valid cases out of 670 questionnaires; among these respondents, 266 were workers, 165 were state cadres, 128 were intellectuals, and 14 were private businessmen (*Xuanchuan Tongxun* 1988).

7. For example, Wu and Zhang (1988) report that a bill of sale for fifty tons of steel traveled from one person to another five times without going outside a hotel, while the price per ton of steel went from 700 yuan to 1,500 yuan, with each middleman getting a profit of between 5,000 and 10,000 yuan on each transaction.

8. Wu and Zhang (1988).

frequent banquets where they would maintain and further their own connections. Group consumption in China grew rapidly.[9] Consequently, the state had
to print more money; this, in turn, became a source of high inflation.

The psychological impact of corruption was enormous. A survey indicated
that over 83 percent of urban Chinese believed that most cadres were corrupt,
and over 63 percent of cadres surveyed admitted that they had been involved
in some forms of corruption.[10] Between March and May of 1989, the journal
Banyuetan (Semimonthly) conducted a survey in twenty-eight provinces, asking
respondents to rank eight social problems. The result was that 78.15 percent
chose official corruption as the issue that concerned them the most, a much
higher percentage than the next social problem of common concern—the
high inflation.[11] This was understandable. High inflation gave people a great
sense of insecurity, but rampant official corruption added a sense of injustice
to their feelings. By the late 1980s, most Chinese saw state legitimation as de-
riving largely from economic and moral performance (see chapters 1 and 4).
They were thus extremely sensitive to the issue of official corruption. More
serious still was the fact that most urban Chinese believed that corruption
was something that the state could not really control. Up to the end of 1989,
after the 1989 Movement and after the government had taken strong measures against corruption, only 20.7 percent of students believed that corruption
could be effectively controlled.[12]

HIGH INFLATION

Next only to rampant corruption in the concerns of most Chinese was the
problem of high inflation. This inflation was a combined result of the financial
deficit, the overheated economy, rampant corruption, price reforms, and the
decreasing confidence of the general public in the state. The mutual reinforcement of the last two factors was especially crucial in pushing inflation up to a
rate unacceptable to most Chinese.

In 1987, facing an overheated economy, some of the more cautious members
of the government suggested economic adjustments. The suggestions were rejected by both Zhao Ziyang and Deng Xiaoping. Zhao Ziyang insisted:

9. Group consumption is the purchase of goods by state enterprises and government agencies.
10. Cherrington (1991, 122).
11. Wu Ren (1990a, 8).
12. Cang (1990, 225).

Although there was some inflation in 1987, if we look at the industrial and agricultural growth rates, at investment in capital construction, at foreign trade, or at the rate of increase of the standard of living, the economy is still in good shape. We should not see only trees and not the forest, and let people's complaints about inflation undermine our determination to reform. We must carry the reform even deeper.[13]

Zhao was primarily echoing the views of his brain trust. During the late 1980s, most of his counselors tended to overestimate people's capacity to endure the negative impact of economic reform, insisting that problems of reform could only be solved by further reform. Zhao's brain trust was also aware of the experience of Eastern European countries, where in the 1970s adjustment measures to deal with economic crises actually ended the economic reform. These counselors had a deep-seated distrust of the state due to their past experiences as intellectuals, even though they were now incorporated into the state elites. They therefore also believed that any setback to reform measures would constitute a conservative revival, signaling the failure of reform.[14]

Subsequently, calls for *chuangjiageguan* (to get the price right at one shot) grew widespread; apparently even Deng Xiaoping supported the idea.[15] Eventually, a decision to establish a market-regulated price system in China within five years was made at the Beidaihe meeting in mid-1988. Yet before the plan was released, leaked news of it brought waves of panic cash withdrawals and panic buying all over China.[16] Many urban residents bought whatever goods were available in stores. Some even bought rooms full of matches or toilet paper—enough for several generations. In some cities even big department stores were emptied. The price reform decision had to be reversed in less than two weeks—even before it was formally released—but its social impact continued to reverberate for a long time.

As a consequence, inflation soared. As officially reported, the inflation rate on retail prices was 7.3 percent in 1987, increased to 18.5 percent in 1988, and came to 28 percent in the first quarter of 1989.[17] Most Chinese believed that the real figure was much higher. Their perceptions were well founded, because inflation rates on food were disproportionately higher than on some other

13. Chen Yizi (1990, 127).
14. See chapter 2 for more discussion of the issue.
15. For Deng's support of the price reform, see Chen Yizi (1990, 125–29) and Nathan (1990, ch. 6).
16. In the first half of 1988, total private bank savings decreased by 3.6 billion yuan (Wu Ren 1990a, 5), even though total savings had been increasing at a two-digit level since 1978.
17. *China Statistical Yearbook* (1990, 226) and Selden (1993, 120).

products, yet most urban families spent at least half of their income on food.[18] As a result of the inflation, the early fruits of reform gradually withered. Prior to 1978 workers spent about 60 percent of their income on food consumption. This percentage had dropped to 42 percent by 1985. However, it rose to 55 percent in 1987, and bounced back to 60 percent in 1988.[19] Inflation thus became one of the hottest topics during 1988 and 1989. That was why, during the 1989 Movement, many workers and urban residents held Mao Zedong and Zhou Enlai's posters in their demonstrations (chapter 6). Most of them did not actually want to return to Mao's era, but they could not stand the current scale of social change and the accompanying uncertainties.

Diminishing Social Buffers

The great expansion of university enrollment lowered students' sense of elitism, while the economic crisis narrowed students' career opportunities. By the late 1980s, students were less and less interested in classroom study, indulging more and more in activities that ranged from preparing for the TOEFL test so as to go abroad, to playing mah-jongg, to simply killing time (see chapter 3). Going abroad had become one of the most important alternatives for aggrieved students and thus acted as a "safety valve" for the political stability of the regime.[20] However, by the late 1980s, while more and more Chinese students had applied to foreign universities, domestic regulations and international capacities had increasingly limited their chances of success in application. This contributed to the grievances of students before the rise of the 1989 Movement.

18. The inflation for non-staples such as pork, eggs, vegetables, and sugar was 30 to 60 percent in state-run stores and even higher in the free market where state price regulations were poorly implemented.

19. Cheng Chu-yuan (1990, 3).

20. Since World War II, more and more students from underdeveloped nations have pursued higher education in developed countries (Agarwal and Winkler 1985). The impact of this internationalization of higher education on the socioeconomic development of the underdeveloped nations has received great attention (Altbach 1991; Altbach and Wang 1989; Hayhoe 1990). Most research has focused on some unintended consequences of foreign study on underdeveloped nations, such as the effects of brain drain (Adams 1968; Das 1972; Howland 1967; Rao 1979), the problem of reintegration into native societies after studying abroad (Goodwin and Nacht 1986), and the political impact of foreign study on student-sending nations (Hayhoe 1988; Zhao and Xie 1992), although in other areas, Gabaccia (1988) argues that the massive migration of Italians to the New World functioned as an important safety valve for Italian domestic politics.

GOING ABROAD AS A "SAFETY VALVE"

To understand the importance of going abroad to the life of students, we need to know how many students had gone abroad by 1989.[21] According to China's official statistics, over 90,000 students and intellectuals had studied abroad by 1989, including over 20,000 who were privately sponsored.[22] Yet these statistics may greatly underestimate the size of this population. The government obtained statistics from Chinese embassy-sponsored student associations in foreign countries or from various universities in China. But many privately funded students did not join such associations and applied for their overseas studies not from universities but from their work-units. Finally, a large number of non-state-sponsored students for various reasons went abroad not as students but as visitors.

To have a better estimate of the scale of the phenomenon in question, I asked informants to report, to the best of their knowledge, the number of their classmates who had gone abroad.[23] Data obtained in Montreal were divided into four groups under two dichotomous categories (key versus non-key, and coastal area versus interior, universities). The result is that 35.9 percent of students ($s.e.$ = 4.1, n = 48) in the key national universities went abroad, a much higher proportion than the 11.4 percent ($s.e.$ = 1.3, n = 24) of students of non-key universities who did so (table 5.1). On the other hand, 34.9 percent of students from coastal area universities went abroad, which is also a higher number than the 17.8 percent rate for students in interior universities. The highest percentage of students going abroad came from coastal area key national universities. In this category, the reported percentage of classmates who went abroad reached 40.3 percent ($s.e.$ = 5.0, n = 35). There are six cases where the reported percentages were over 70 percent. This indicates the importance of foreign study to the regime's stability, since most major student protests were initiated by students of coastal area key national universities.[24] Between 1979 and 1989,

21. Since a majority of students went abroad either by applying for North American universities or for visitor's visas to join their spouses who were studying in North America, my analysis will mainly focus on this population.

22. Li Tieying (1990).

23. Due to their close-knit campus life (chapters 4, 8), Chinese students develop close relationships which last many years after university. Therefore, most students were able to answer the question.

24. The reported rate of going abroad was 7.4 percent for coastal region non-key universities and 13.1 percent for students of interior non-key universities. Since most respondents from interior non-key universities were government sponsored, the result may reflect the Chinese government's efforts to allocate scholarships to students and young teachers in small interior universities to enhance their academic level.

TABLE 5.1   Reports of Percentage of Classmates Going Abroad by Students in Different
               Types of Universities

	Coastal Area Universities	Interior Universities	Coastal Area and Interior Universities Combined
Key universities:			
Mean	40.3	24.1	35.9
s.e.	5.0	5.3	4.1
n	35	13	48
Non-key universities:			
Mean	7.4	13.1	11.4
s.e.	1.6	1.6	1.3
n	7	17	24
Key and non-key universities combined:			
Mean	34.9	17.8	
s.e.	4.5	2.6	
n	42	30	

Note: The table includes data from my Montreal interviews and from a small-scale survey. The survey was implemented to obtain information on students who entered Chinese universities in the late 1970s and early 1980s (see fig. 3.1). The Beijing interview data were not used here because the Beijing interviews were conducted mainly among students who were in undergraduate programs during 1989. When I conducted the interviews in 1993, this group of students were either still bound by the five-year working prerequisites (see the text for explanation), or had just started to enter the foreign study application process. The proportion of reported classmates gone abroad for the Beijing group was 9.4 percent, s.e. $= 2.5$, $n = 29$.

3.82 million students graduated from universities.[25] These figures give us a better indication of the number of students who went abroad in the 1980s.

Going abroad helps to channel grievances of university graduates in several important ways. First and foremost, it provides hope and a way of escape. In a study of the "going abroad fever" in China, it was found that most Chinese applied for foreign study because of their economic or political dissatisfactions with domestic reality.[26] This finding is congruent with a survey conducted in Beijing in 1990. Responding to the question "What is your view on the current going abroad fever?" 56.5 percent of the respondents chose the item "Since there is no future in China, it is the only alternative." On the other hand, only 18.7 percent chose "After finishing my studies, I will return and render service

25. *Educational Statistics Yearbook of China* (1989, 14).
26. See Xiao (1989).

to the country."[27] A recollection by one of my informants (no. 10) shows how students tried to escape from China immediately after the 1989 Movement:

[TOEFL centers in Beijing] started to accept the January 1990 applications for the TOEFL test in October 1989. There was a rumor that this would be the last test held in China. The other testing centers were already full. Qinghua center was the only one that had not started taking applications. The scene was unforgettable. Many people waited in line overnight simply to be registered. Yet the situation had become so chaotic by the morning that the registration had to be canceled. Then they decided to hold the registration at the university education bureau. . . . At least three to four thousand people showed up. Many people came not for themselves but for their classmates or friends to make sure that if the applicant had failed to register, they could register for him/her. . . . Terrified by the situation, the TOEFL center decided to let everybody register and created a new testing site at the centennial hall of Jingxi Hotel. I took my test there.

Students' levels of eagerness to go abroad were closely related to their domestic opportunities. Between the late 1980s and early 1990s, TOEFL and GRE applicants in Beijing generally scored much higher than applicants in southern cities like Shanghai and Guangzhou.[28] The photos in figure 5.1 show two rather representative advertisement boards in 1993: the top one at People's University in Beijing, and the bottom one at Fudan University in Shanghai. While boards at People's University were filled with advertisements from TOEFL and GRE preparation schools, boards in Fudan were dominated by posters for dance parties, concerts, and movie schedules. This was not a coincidence, since—as I was told by two administrators of the TOEFL testing center in Jiaotong University in Shanghai—1993 was also the first year that the number of TOEFL applicants dropped drastically in that city. Obviously, by 1993 Shanghai's booming economy was providing students with great opportunities, whereas Beijing could not provide enough opportunities for its students.

Most students had to spend a great amount of study time to get competitive marks on TOEFL and/or GRE tests, which meant that they had much less energy to involve themselves in other activities. Moreover, if a person feels that he/she will leave very soon, that person will probably view his/her stay in China as temporary and therefore become less concerned with domestic politics.

27. Rosen (1991b, 178).
28. Two informants (nos. 10 and 18) voluntarily provided this piece of information.

FIGURE 5.1. A comparison of the campus advertisement boards at People's University, Beijing (*top*), and Fudan University, Shanghai (*bottom*), in spring 1993. The two pictures were taken at about a two-week interval in the spring of 1993. They show that while the campus advertisement board in Beijing was still filled with ads for various TOEFL and GRE training schools, in Shanghai the campus advertisement board was covered by announcements of dance parties, American movies, and so on. (Photographs by the author.)

Indeed, during the 1989 Movement the only two groups in People's University that did not take part in the class boycott during late April were foreign students and students in various TOEFL preparation courses.[29]

In China, before being allowed to go abroad, one has to be examined by a CCP local to determine one's political profile. Since the early 1980s such political examination has gradually become a formality, but its persistence means that the authorities still have the power to withhold permission if a person is considered a political deviant. For this reason, most TOEFL students in the 1980s tended to avoid "political troubles." As a rather extreme example, even student leader Shen Tong had, for a period of time before 1989, tried to stay out of political trouble in order to get to America.[30]

DECREASING CHANCE OF GOING ABROAD AND THE RISE OF GRIEVANCES

Going abroad became increasingly difficult after the mid-1980s. Over 95 percent of students sponsored by the government did not show any sign of returning. As a result, the state gradually stopped sponsoring graduate students and set more and more rules to restrict the wave of studying abroad.[31] Although in the end none of these state policies were rigorously enforced, they led students to suspect that the state was going to change the foreign study policy. Rumors resulting from these suspicions had a great psychological impact on students.

More important than new domestic restrictions was the increasing difficulty that Chinese students had in being accepted by North American universities. Before the early 1980s, very few Chinese students knew the procedures for applying for admission and financial assistance at North American universities. Yet, as those who had gone abroad earlier became familiar with the admissions systems, they started to help their friends or relatives in China. More and more students became familiar with application procedures for foreign universities and for financial assistance. Table 5.2 lists the percentages of different cohorts of students who learned about foreign study application procedures in a given period of student life. In each column, the largest number is

---

29. Feigon (1990, 146–47) was told by a student: "I'm not going to abandon an opportunity of going to the United States just for a chance to save China."

30. Shen Tong (1990, 145).

31. The rule that bothered students the most concerned the work prerequisites, according to which a bachelor's degree holder had to work in China for at least five years, and a master's or doctoral degree holder for at least two years, before going abroad. See Pepper (1990, 169–70) and Zhao Dingxin (1996) for discussion of other regulations.

TABLE 5.2   Percentages of Different Cohorts of Students Who Learned How to Apply for Foreign Universities in a Given Period of Student Life

Time Students Learned to Apply[a]	Year Students Were Admitted to Universities									
	1978	1979	1980	1981	1982	1984	1985	1986	1987	1988
In high school	0	7	0	25	18	10	30	*50*	25	*60*
In junior university	23	15	27	12	18	*50*	30	37	*60*	20
In senior university	23	7	*36*	25	*36*	0	38	0	5	0
After graduation	*46*	*69*	*36*	*37*	27	40	0	12	10	20
Abroad	7	0	0	0	0	0	0	0	0	0
Sample size	13	13	11	8	11	10	13	8	20	5

Note: Part of the data in this table was from a small-scale survey conducted in Montreal in 1993 (see table 5.1). Among the students who reported this piece of information, three were admitted into a university in 1983 and two in 1989. Since the sample sizes for these two years are too small to detect any trend, these students were treated as part of the 1984 and 1988 cohorts, respectively. Italic numbers indicate the highest percentage at a given stage of student life.

[a] This column indicates the time in which the informants learned how to apply for foreign study. For example, "in senior university" means that the students learned the procedure of application for foreign universities in their third or fourth year of university life. "After graduation" means that students acquired the knowledge after they graduated from the university. "Abroad" means that students did not know how to apply for foreign study on their own until they had gone abroad.

italicized to show when most students became knowledgeable about the application procedures. For example, it shows that while 46 percent of students who entered university in 1978 learned the ropes of application procedures only after their graduation from the university, 60 percent of those who entered the university in 1988 had become familiar with the routine in their high school years.[32]

The trend was reflected in the number of students who took the TOEFL test. In Beijing, 285 students took the test in 1981, 2,500 in 1983, and 5,000 in 1985; the number then rocketed to 18,000 in 1986, and to around 35,000 in 1988.[33] Beijing had the first TOEFL testing center in 1981. By 1989, Beijing had seventeen testing centers.[34] Even this scale of development could not

32. After the late 1980s even the coastal area elite middle school students started to apply for fellowships for undergraduate studies in North American universities. As Jin (1993) reports, among 99 graduates from a key middle school in Shanghai, 27 students refused to take domestic entrance examinations because they had already taken TOEFL and GRE and were preparing to go abroad.

33. Xiao (1989, 141).

34. *China International Examinations Coordination Bureau* (1990).

satisfy growing demands. In the late 1980s, TOEFL test applicants in Beijing had to line up in front of a testing center overnight just to get an application form.

Chinese students became by far the fastest growing community in North American universities. In the United States alone, their numbers increased from 2,770 in 1980 to 33,390 in 1989, multiplying by over twelve times. In comparison, the total number of foreign students in the United States increased only 24 percent in the same period.[35] The scale of increase in the number of Chinese students was very impressive in itself, but it was dwarfed each year by the exponential increase in the absolute number of Chinese applicants. Almost all of the non-state-sponsored Chinese applicants required full financial assistance. After 1986 the Chinese government started to grant only one-year scholarships to government-sponsored students studying in North American universities (which means that they also needed financial assistance a year after). North American graduate schools faced increasing difficulty in accepting more Chinese students, even though many of them had impressive academic records. In any event, by the end of the 1980s, more and more students had experienced and been frustrated by repeated rejections by foreign universities or in the visa offices of destination countries.[36]

In 1988, when the Japanese government restricted the entry of Chinese students to Japan's language schools, riots and demonstrations immediately took place at the Japanese Consulate in Shanghai.[37] Similarly, in 1989, when the Australian government limited entry for language school applicants, sit-ins and demonstrations went on for weeks in front of the Australian Consulate in Shanghai.[38] Although some language school applicants were not university graduates, the intense desire to go abroad and the feelings of frustration could easily be observed. During the 1980s, rumors about students protesting in front of foreign embassies and about conflicts between students and visa officers could be frequently heard; the above examples are cases that I saw reported in an internally circulated official publication.

However, the students' main discontent was not with foreign embassies. Although experts consider China's foreign study policies to be "fairly liberal,"[39] most Chinese students did not perceive them that way. In Beijing University, when students were asked "What is your view regarding the current policy of

35. *National Center for Education Statistics, Digest of Education Statistics* (1989, 1993).
36. Xiao (1989).
37. *Xuanchuan Tongxun* (1988).
38. Ibid.
39. Altbach (1991, 313).

sending students abroad?" 80.2 percent thought that it was unreasonable or extremely unreasonable, whereas only 5.4 percent considered it reasonable.[40] It is noteworthy that this survey was conducted in 1990, when most students in the university were still experiencing the trauma of the military crackdown. However, students already had a critical attitude towards the government's regulation of foreign studies before 1989. One of my informants (no. 22) claimed that a major reason Li Peng was so unpopular among students was that many restrictions on foreign studies were set when Li was in charge of the Higher Education Commission. Facing repeated rejections, students shifted their attentions back to the unhappy Chinese reality.

The Turbulent Wind before a Mountain Storm[41]

Before the 1989 Movement, intellectual elites had two diagnoses of China's socioeconomic crisis. A few of them located the root of the problem in the weakness of the government and advocated a "new authoritarianism." The majority of intellectual elites and radical students saw the origin of the crisis in a lack of political reform and advocated democratization.[42] Both groups, however, viewed the state's economic adjustment policy as a sign of the revival of the conservative faction within the government, and both believed that problems of reform could only be solved by further reform. The year 1989 also coincided with the anniversaries of three historical events that had had a great impact on modern China. It had been two hundred years since the French Revolution, seventy years since the May 4th Movement, and forty years since the founding of the People's Republic. Intellectual elites and students wanted to mark this symbolic moment.[43] Without much coordination, dissident activities, including conferences and salons, big-character posters, and small-scale demonstrations and petitions, mushroomed from 1988 into 1989. These activities eventually led to the 1989 Movement. Let us now examine how intellectual elites and radical students orchestrated the prelude to the largest student movement in history.

40. Rosen (1991b, 179).

41. Beside my own interviews, the major data sources for this section are from Leng and Miao (1989), Oksenberg, Sullivan, and Lambert (1990), Wu Ren (1990a), and *Wushitian de Huigu yu Fansi* (1989).

42. For the new authoritarian versus liberalism debate in English sources, see Zhao Dingxin (1994) and Rosen and Zou (1990–91).

43. Most petitions by members of intellectual elites at the time emphasized these historical events.

STUDENT ORGANIZATIONS AND STUDY GROUPS

We already know, from chapter 2, that political conferences were frequently held on Beijing campuses before the rise of the 1989 Movement. Besides the conferences, small-scale study groups among students also formed on major campuses.[44] The most famous of these was Wang Dan's Democracy Salon and its precursor the *Caodi* Salon (the Salon on the Lawn) organized by Liu Gang. Many members of the intellectual elites, including Fang Lizhi, Li Shuxian, Xu Liangying, and Wu Zuguang, held talks in the salon. Even the American ambassador and his wife participated in one of their gatherings. Salons and study groups trained many student activists and were the major organizational base for the coming student movement. Many of the student leaders at Beijing University, such as Wang Dan, Liu Gang, Feng Congde, Yang Tao, Xiong Yan, and Guo Haifeng, were either active participants or organizers at the *Caodi* Salon and the Democracy Salon. Several of my informants, all active participants of the 1989 Movement, were frequent patrons of these two salons.

THE PETITION MOVEMENT

In 1989 the intellectual elites assumed a more active role in laying the groundwork for the coming movement. One of their actions was to petition Deng Xiaoping and other state leaders to urge amnesty for all political prisoners. The petition movement was initiated on January 6, 1989, when Fang Lizhi wrote an open letter to Deng Xiaoping suggesting the release of all political prisoners, including Wei Jingsheng, to mark the fortieth anniversary of the founding of the People's Republic, the seventieth anniversary of the May 4th Movement, and the two-hundredth anniversary of the French Revolution. More and more intellectual elites joined in this petition movement.[45] The following lists a few major petitions, later actions often being in support of the earlier ones:[46]

February 13: Bei Dao and thirty-two other people write a letter to the National People's Congress and the CCP to recommend amnesty, especially for Wei Jingsheng and other political prisoners, on the fortieth anniversary of the founding of the People's Republic and the seventieth anniversary of the May 4th Movement.

44. These study groups thus functioned as what McCarthy and Zald (1973) call "transitory teams" in the movement's initial mobilization, even though they failed to take control of the movement.

45. The petition movement also involved people from Taiwan, Hong Kong, the United States, and some other nations.

46. Wu Ren (1990a); Leng and Miao (1989, 1–15).

February 16: Chen Jun holds a press conference in Beijing with foreign journalists. He releases the letter by Fang Lizhi and the letter by Bei Dao and the thirty-two other intellectuals.

February 19: Chen Jun, in the presence of foreign journalists, announces the establishment of the petition liaison center for the release of Wei Jingsheng.

February 26: Zhang Xianyang, Li Honglin, and forty-one others write a letter to the CCP Central Committee to ask for the release of all political prisoners.

March 8: Beijing University and some other universities post a letter by Xu Liangying and forty-one other intellectuals to urge the state to avoid further political tragedies in China and to release all political prisoners.

March 24: Beijing University and some other universities post a letter by Dai Qing and forty-two other intellectuals to the National People's Congress to ask for amnesty to prisoners, especially Wei Jingsheng, on the fortieth anniversary of the founding of the People's Republic.

These letters repeatedly mention the fortieth anniversary of the People's Republic, the seventieth anniversary of the May 4th Movement, and the two-hundredth anniversary of the French Revolution. They strongly suggested to students and to the general public that 1989 was an unusual year that one should not let pass by quietly.

PROTEST ACTIVITIES PRIOR TO THE 1989 MOVEMENT

Because of the worsening economic situation of intellectuals and students, and of the country as a whole, student protests repeatedly broke out in universities after 1986. Table 5.3 lists some major protest activities prior to 1989, selected on the basis of the scale of the activities as well as of their impact on later student movements.[47] The protests can be grouped into two blocks, separated by the Anti-Bourgeois Liberalization Campaign of 1987. The first wave of student protests started in September 1985. It was triggered by the Japanese government's intention to commemorate the "Mukden Incident" of 1931, which marked the beginning of its annexation of China's Dongbei region. In the demonstrations students called for a boycott of Japanese goods, accusing the government of "selling its soul" with its open-door policy and of doing business

---

47. All the student protests are also described by Cherrington (1991, chs. 4 and 6). In addition, Schell (1988) discusses the major student demonstrations before 1987. Wu Ren (1990a) depicts the shining shoes protest and the Chai Qingfeng incident.

TABLE 5.3 Major Student Movements, 1985 through 1988, and Their Targets

Place	Time Started	Major Targets
Beijing	Sept. 18, 1985	Anti-Japanese; critical to various reform policies.
Hefei	Dec. 4, 1986	Poor food quality in university; against the manipulation of election in the local People's Congress; more democracy.
Shanghai	Late Nov. 1986	Initiated as a protest against the arrest and beating of students after many students danced on the stage with the American surf-rock band Jan and Dean in the city's 18,000-seat Stadium. Gradually shifted to democracy and other issues when the news of the Hefei demonstration arrived at Shanghai in December.
Beijing	Dec. 23, 1986	Democracy was the main issue.
Student movements were interrupted by the Anti–Bourgeois Liberalization Campaign and the resignation of Hu Yaobang.		
Beijing	April–June 1988	Shoe shining protest and Chai Qingfeng incident; elitist sentiment.
Beijing	April–June 1988	Against rampant corruption and high inflation; demand for democracy.

with anyone.[48] A few months later, however, the center of activism shifted to Hefei and Shanghai and the main issue of the movement shifted to democracy.

The second wave started in April through June 1988.[49] During the first meeting of the Seventh National People's Congress, students at Beijing University posted a big-character poster that read "Academics are useless, and shining shoes can also serve the people." Afterwards, a few Beijing University students repeatedly went to Tiananmen Square and declared that they wanted to "shine shoes" for deputies of the congress in order to make a living. Meanwhile more big-character posters appeared at Beijing University. Many of them called on students to make a living by manual labor (*shengchan zijiu*). Less than two months after these activities were stopped by the police and university authorities, Chai Qingfeng, a Beijing University graduate student, was killed during a row at a snack bar near the campus by some "unemployed youths." That "unemployed youths" dared to brawl with and kill a graduate student was treated by students as an indication of their declining status in society. Demonstrations broke out immediately. The government responded swiftly. To satisfy the students, the university set up a memorial hall and held a highly elaborate ceremony for the

48. See Cherrington (1991, 78–79) for more details of this movement.

49. It is reported that 210 student protests and over 1,100 wall posters appeared on Beijing campuses in 1988 (Ren Yanshen 1990, 127).

victim. Within forty hours of the incident, six suspects were arrested. Their arrest was broadcast on TV and the suspects were pronounced guilty even before a trial. Very quickly, one of the six was executed and the others were given long sentences. At the same time, the state put policemen on maximum alert on all the main roads leading to Tiananmen Square and repeatedly warned students to restrain themselves. It was only by these measures that the students' agitation subsided.

The general sentiment expressed in these protest activities was elitist rather than democratic. During the Chai Qingfeng incident, for example, no students questioned the legal procedure involved in sentencing the six suspects, who supposedly had rights equal to those of the students. Yet both waves of protests ended with demands for democracy. This had a lot to do with the existence of intellectual elites and radical students. During the quiet times they organized various study groups, salons, and conferences to spread nonconformist ideas. At moments of social activism, they wrote big-character posters to link various "social ills" with the lack of democracy. This active core also provided the organizational base and leadership for the student movement.[50] Many protest activities failed to concentrate on political issues only because they failed to direct the mood of students to their ends. As a leader of the 1989 Movement recalled (no. 69): "The Chai Qingfeng incident was an aborted student movement. . . . We were very excited when it started, but things did not turn our way. We were very sad and depressed."[51]

By early 1989, small-scale campus protests became even more frequent. For example, on March 1, a big-character poster entitled "Down with Deng—A Memorandum to the Whole Nation" appeared at Beijing University as well as other universities. It argued that "communist politics equals empty talk, the power of the mighty, authoritarianism, arbitrariness, and power greater than the law. Therefore, party domination and the Four Cardinal Principles must be abolished." On April 13, Wang Dan and some other students in Beijing University spread some leaflets which stated that China was once again at a crossroads, that it could either go back to the dark and ignorant old authoritarian

50. For example, one of my informants (no. 60) reported that he and a few of his friends ran a political salon and organized demonstrations prior to 1989. During the 1989 Movement he tried to make the movement confrontational from the very beginning. He also had very close relations with young intellectual elites in Beijing. Once, when he felt that the targets of the movement as indicated by the slogans and the big-character posters were too diffuse, he went to a young intellectual for suggestions. The young intellectual told him to try to narrow their claims to ten Chinese characters, those for: democracy, freedom, science, rule of law, and human rights.

51. According to the informants, Liu Gang—an organizer of the *Caodi* Salon—had been a major agitator during the Chai Qingfeng incident.

system or march toward a free, democratic, egalitarian, and fraternal new world. But the power to make a choice did not belong to the government or its leaders, it only belonged to the people. On the same day, another letter from the "Student Union of Guangxi University," entitled "Calling upon the Attention of Students of all the Universities," appeared in Beijing as well as on university campuses in many other cities. It claimed that China had entered a most critical and dangerous period and called on students "to learn from their fellow students seventy years ago and to march in the street and to Tiananmen Square" on May 4.

At this moment, that is, on April 15, Hu Yaobang, the former general secretary of the CCP, died of a heart attack. Hu's sudden death was significant to students and intellectuals in several ways. First, he was considered by most intellectuals and students as the most outspoken and reform-minded leader within the highest echelons of the CCP. Secondly, Hu had lost power in 1987 in part because of his soft attitude toward the 1986 Student Movement. Many students still felt sorry that their early movement activities had actually brought down a reform-minded leader. Third, Hu was widely respected for his austere lifestyle and as a disciplined father whose children had never been involved in corrupt commercial activities. Fourth, there was also a widespread rumor that Hu suffered his heart attack during a Politburo meeting in a dispute with Li Peng in which he urged an increase in state education expenditures. Li Peng was viewed as a conservative figure in the foreign and Hong Kong media and in Chinese rumor circles. This also added a sense of martyrdom to Hu's sudden death. Finally, by the time of Hu's death, he was still one of the seventeen members of the CCP Politburo and thus a top state leader. Since to mourn a top state leader is a legitimate action, to start a social movement at Hu's death greatly lowered the possibility of immediate repression.

Antithetical couplets and big-character posters appeared in major universities on the day of Hu's death. The contents of the big-character posters were initially centered on memorials for Hu but soon extended to other issues. Only two days later, on April 17, the first wreath from the University of Political Science and Law arrived at Tiananmen Square. On the same evening, students at Beijing University marched off the campus. The 1989 Movement had begun.

PART TWO

THE DEVELOPMENT
OF THE 1989 BEIJING
STUDENT MOVEMENT

six

A BRIEF HISTORY OF THE 1989 MOVEMENT

Before analyzing how state-society relations contributed to the development of the 1989 Beijing Student Movement, we need to know more precisely how the movement unfolded. To this end, this chapter offers a narrative of the movement, chronologically arranged into four major sections which correspond to the movement's major periods. This narrative does more, however, than just give a general description of the movement. It highlights a few major events and issues that were important to the development of the movement but that nevertheless have not received enough attention in previous writing. Also, since the next four chapters focus on the events in their structural aspect, this chapter pays particular attention to the contingencies that also shaped the 1989 Movement. Most of the contingent factors and activities discussed here—Hu's sudden death, the three students kneeling in Tiananmen Square, the conflict and lack of communication among student activists before the hunger strike, the hunger strike, and the arrival of large numbers of students from other cities in Beijing—were significant only in the context of a particular state-society relationship. Yet their contingent occurrences did have a significant impact on the trajectory of the movement.

To avoid repetitiveness, I do not give lengthy accounts here of events covered in the analytical chapters. For example, I do not go into government and media responses to the movement because I deal with them in chapters 7 and 10, respectively, and I do not elaborate on the April 27 demonstration since I discuss it in chapter 8. Also, I do not pretend to present a complete historical account; I center the narrative on a few activities that became important to the later development of the movement, while omitting many other competing movement activities. I hope this choice will not give the impression that the dynamics of the movement were shaped by the activities of a few well-organized elite students. In fact, as can be seen in this and the following chapters, even the activities of radical student activists were often spontaneously initiated.

A word is in order about "spontaneity," a term that will frequently appear in my description of the 1989 Movement. I do not use this word because my informants used it to characterize their experience through a sort of moralizing "historical memory."[1] In fact, they seldom used it. In the interviews, I asked the informants to focus on their personal experiences and activities during the movement. Most informants followed this instruction, and when they gave general comments that extended beyond personal experiences and activities, I did not give those comments much credence. Rather, I use the word "spontaneity" analytically, to capture the individual or small-group-based nature of their activities in relation to the movement as a whole. My choice is based on the following observations (or carries the following connected meanings). First, the movement was initiated by many individuals and small groups through independent actions and mutual influences without a general coordination. Second, during the movement many independent or semi-independent activities competed for significance. These movement activities were thus situated in a highly competitive environment, where the domination of certain activities in the movement was determined more by a particular activity's power to move unorganized audiences than by the motivation of actors. Third, the movement saw the emergence of many organizations and leaders. None of its organizations had a prehistory, however, and none of its leaders were elected by a reasonable number of movement participants via a recognized procedure. Therefore, the leaders of the organizations did not really respect each other, or even the organizations they supposedly led; the movement participants did not respect the organizations and the leaders; and organization leadership changed

1. See Polletta (1998) and Tilly (1994).

very frequently during the course of the movement.[2] Fourth, when I read the personal accounts which the student leaders gave in my interviews and in published memoirs,[3] I found many of them were in the form "I walked down the road and saw X (or, I woke up in the morning and thought of Y), and then I decided to do Z." In other words, many of their activities represented spontaneous and individualistic responses to events rather than conscious decisions arrived at collectively by their organizations. Finally, through the narrative and analysis in this and the following chapters, I want to show that because of the students' massive grievances and the social ecology of the campus and Tiananmen Square, while the leaders and organizations that emerged during the movement could usually effectively stage radical movement activities, such leaders and organizations were absolutely unable to exercise effective control over the movement. Whenever movement leaders or organizations wanted to make strategic moves rather than take more radical actions, they were immediately marginalized. In other words, the leaders and organizations that emerged during the movement had only a *unidirectional effectiveness* vis-à-vis the movement. Although I cannot present all the evidence that I have collected in this regard, much of the material in this chapter certainly illustrates this unidirectional effectiveness. In fact, the second part of this book is in great measure intended to reveal and analyze the origin and impact of the movement's unidirectional nature.

The Rise of the Movement

On April 15, 1989, Hu Yaobang died of heart attack. Hu had been pushed to resign from the CCP general secretary position in 1987, in part because of his lenient attitude toward a smaller scale student movement in 1986. After his resignation Hu became a widely respected figure among students and intellectuals. Although a few students and intellectuals had been preparing the movement long before Hu's sudden death, that event certainly provided an ideal occasion on which to start a movement (chapter 5).

At Beijing University, about eighty posters appeared on the evening of Hu's death.[4] Most of these mourned his passing, but a few also attacked the

2. For example, as a student leader told me (no. 69), the Beijing Students' Autonomous Union changed its leadership at least seven times in only the first few weeks of its existence.

3. For a memoir in English, see Shen Tong (1990).

4. Wu Ren (1990b).

government.[5] The content of the posters changed quickly over the following days. By April 19, most of the 570 posters that had appeared on the 31 university campuses in Beijing had themes centered on free press, free association, political democracy, and official corruption.[6]

The first demonstration started at noon on April 17, when about 600 young teachers and students from the University of Political Science and Law went to Tiananmen Square to lay a wreath for Hu. Knowing that these other students had already demonstrated in the streets, students in Beijing University marched to the Square that same evening, arriving early the next morning. However, most students had no idea of the specific purpose of this demonstration. For example, before they arrived Zhang Boli asked Wang Dan about the purpose of this demonstration (both later became major leaders of the movement), and Wang Dan replied: "I do not know either. It is you guys who initiated this."[7] Zhang said: "Then we should set several demands." Zhang suggested three: reevaluation of Hu Yaobang, press freedom, and an increase in educational expenditures. After they stopped at the Monument to the People's Heroes, a student named Guo Haifeng stood up and asked for more suggestions, and eventually seven demands emerged:

(1) reevaluate Hu Yaobang, especially in relation to his prodemocratic views;

(2) renounce the [1987] Anti–Bourgeois Liberalization Campaign and the [1983] Anti–Spiritual Pollution Campaign, and rehabilitate all the people prosecuted in these campaigns;

(3) reveal the salaries and other wealth of government leaders and their families;

(4) allow the publication of nonofficial newspapers and stop press censorship;

(5) raise the wages of intellectuals and increase government educational expenditures;

(6) turn down the "Ten Provisional Articles Regulating Public Marches and Demonstrations" promulgated by the Beijing municipal government; and

5. The following are two examples of posters that appeared at Beijing University on the day of Hu's death: "Incompetent government, corrupted society, dictatorship, and depreciation of intellectuals: this is our society, the reality, and our tragedy!" "Our demand: dismiss the incompetent government, overthrow autocrats, establish a democratic state, and found our society on education."

6. Wu Ren (1990b, 35).

7. Zhang Boli (*Huigu yu Fansi* 1993, 50–51).

(7)   provide objective news coverage of the student demonstration in offi-
       cial newspapers.

At this stage, however, only a few students actively participated in the movement. Many joined demonstrations to get away from classroom studies that
bored them and to enjoy the carnival-like spirit. A student from People's University (no. 14) described his first experience of a demonstration:

> I remember it was April 19. . . . I saw many students marching. . . . I asked a female
> student what they were doing. She told me that they were demonstrating. At this
> point, I knew that the student movement had started. I followed them by bicycle.
> Many people were *qihong* on the way.[8] [For example], when students chanted "down
> with official corruption," a few people on the street shouted back "we support
> you!" Then we laughed together. The whole situation made me very excited.[9]

A few days later, however, the festival spirit gave way to a militant mood.
Here rumors played a crucial role. In the early period of the movement, students were effectively mobilized by rumors centered on Li Peng's failed promise to meet students after Hu's state funeral and on police brutality around the
Xinhua Gate.

THE XINHUA GATE INCIDENT

After April 17, many protest activities were centered on the Xinhua Gate, inside which the CCP Central Committee and State Council are located. Outside, students shouted slogans attacking government leaders and demanded
dialogue with them. Some of them threw bottles and shoes at the policemen
who guarded the gate. The police tried to restore order in front of the gate
several times.[10] Finally, in the early morning on April 20, after several hours of
efforts at evacuation, only about 200 students remained; these refused to go.

---

8. A literal translation of *qihong* is "gathering together to create a disturbance."

9. In fact, a carnival-like spirit was common in other student movements in China during the 1980s. Li
Xinhua (1988, 15) observed a student demonstration in Shanghai in 1986: "On December 19, three thousand
students from Jiaotong University marched to the People's Square. I followed them. They walked with
a cheerful mood, just like in a spring outing. They chatted with each other on the way on topics totally
irrelevant to their demonstration and cheered when some of their actions received attention from
bystanders."

10. The police's strategy was to first surround a group of people and then discharge them by opening
an outside circle. Those who were left out of the circle gradually went home. The whole process went on
peacefully.

Policemen dragged the students into a big bus and sent them back to Beijing University. There were skirmishes during the process. However, back at the university some of students held up bloodstained clothes and angrily shouted slogans. The whole event was labeled by students as the Xinhua Gate Bloody Incident (*Xinhuamen Canan*). Rumors about police brutality and arrests spread immediately.

The government denied the accusations. Through the media, it claimed that the blood was from some students who cut themselves accidentally when they smashed the windows of the moving bus. Although the evidence that I have collected shows that the government's account could be true,[11] most students believed that the police did in fact brutally beat their fellows and that the government was lying about the incident. This is how a student from Beijing University recalled her personal feeling after the news of police brutality (no. 30):

> I was never interested in politics. . . . When Hu Yaobang died, a lot of antithetical couplets and posters appeared at the Triangle. I read them with great pleasure because I was unhappy about the general situation at the time, but I still went to class and did not join any movement activities. . . . In the early morning of April 20, I saw several students with blood on their faces and big-character posters in their hands rushing to the Triangle. Students had been beaten by policemen! This made us very angry. Demonstration is a constitutional right. The students just wanted to raise some objections to the government. Yet, they beat us when we went to demonstrate. We were greatly annoyed. I went to demonstrate on that same day and joined the class boycott.

After the Xinhua Gate Incident, a few universities started a class boycott, more demonstrations took place, and students became highly mobilized.[12]

HU YAOBANG'S STATE FUNERAL

The government planned a state funeral for Hu Yaobang for April 22, at the Great Hall of the People, west of Tiananmen Square. However, to block the students from entering the Square, the Beijing municipal government announced on April 21 that the Square would be sealed off to minimize traffic during the funeral. On the same day, an announcement by "The Provisional Action Committee of Beijing Universities" appeared on many campuses. It

---

11. For details, see the last section of the introduction.

12. In chapter 10, I will explain why people wanted to believe in unfounded rumors even though the government's versions of events were sometimes more accurate.

asked students to meet at Beijing Normal University and march to the Square to participate in Hu's funeral.

Students from over twenty universities gathered at Beijing Normal. They left for Tiananmen Square at around 10:00 P.M. and picked up students from some other universities along the way. One of my informants estimated that around 50,000 students joined the march, not including students and Beijing residents who were already in the Square. After they arrived, a young teacher from the University of Political Science and Law went to various universities and asked them to send someone to have a coordination meeting. Between twenty and thirty representatives gathered in a corner of the Monument to the People's Heroes and discussed what demands they should make of the government. My informant (no. 60) suggested three. The government should (1) guarantee the safety of students in the Square, (2) allow students to send their delegates to attend Hu Yaobang's funeral, and (3) promise never to *qiuhou suanzhang* with students.[13] The rest of the students agreed.

At about 4:00 A.M. on April 22, policemen arrived at the Square and lined up between the students and the Great Hall of the People. A government officer went to the students and asked them to move back to the Monument to the People's Heroes to yield some space for the buses and cars of those who were invited to the state funeral. My informant (no. 60) rejected the demand. He told the officer: "They come for the funeral. We are staying here for the same purpose. We all want to pay our last respects to Yaobang, but we, over a hundred thousand students, have been sitting on the ground overnight. We are no less sincere than those who come here by car. I am unable to persuade students to leave just for them to park their cars here." The informant then raised the three demands. The officer replied, after a while, "Your safety is guaranteed. As long as there are no major accidents on the students' side, the government will not interfere. As to sending student delegates to attend the funeral, we can't decide. That the government will not *qiuhou suanzhang* with the students, I can guarantee now. Of course, my guarantee may not be useful, but I will forward the message for you."

The negotiation went on for quite a while. At about 6:00 A.M. the officer suggested that students send a delegation to talk inside the Great Hall of the People. Five students went in; at this point the third demand was changed to "The government should make an unbiased report on the Xinhua Gate

---

13. *Qiuhou suanzhang* literally means "to square accounts after the autumn harvest." It is used here to refer to the government's possible revenge taking after the movement's end.

Incident." Some student activists and young teachers, wanting to make a gesture of good faith, led students back to the Monument to the People's Heroes as the officer required.

At 7:15 A.M. the five representatives received a five-part formal reply from the Office of the Hu Yaobang Funeral Service saying that: (1) Hu Yaobang's funeral ceremony will be broadcast live to students; (2) the buses for those who attend Hu's funeral will not block the view of students; (3) students' safety is guaranteed as long as students do not become highly disordered; (4) the Office has no authority to decide whether to allow students to send their own delegates to the funeral but will raise the issue with higher-level authorities; (5) the "Xinhua Gate Incident" is beyond the jurisdiction of the Office, but the students' demands in that regard will also be reported to the higher-level authorities. The student representatives were satisfied with the reply.

Before the five representatives had received this formal reply, however, my informant (no. 60) became impatient. He shouted that "the three demands are non-negotiable. If they are not met, I am going to bring students university by university to the original place every ten minutes starting from seven o'clock." When the time came, the informant led students from the University of Political Science and Law in a rush toward the police lines. As soon as they moved forward, the police retreated. Seeing that nothing happened, my informant and a few students brought all the students to their original position, disregarding the other activists' attempts to prevent them.

After a while, a long corridor about five to seven meters in width was formed between the students and police. The corridor became a giant stage for any students who wanted to express themselves. There were always some students shouting slogans, raising demands, and giving speeches in the corridor.

The funeral started at 10:00 A.M. and proceeded for an hour. Many students did not treat the ritual seriously. My informant (no. 60) noted that quite a few students were enjoying popsicles when the dirge was sounded. Students did not go away after the funeral. Many competing activities went on simultaneously. In one corner of the Square, for example, one could see some students paint a fishnet on a giant cloth and then rip apart the cloth with scissors and their bare hands, crying emotionally all the while.[14] At the same time, synchronized voices from a distance gradually became dominant. One could hear waves of voices from different directions shouting chants, such as "Make a decision Beijing University! Make a decision Beijing University!" "Sit down students in the

14. The fishnet symbolizes the heavy control of the Chinese state, from which the people (the fish) are desperately trying to free themselves.

front! Sit down students in the front!" "Dialogue! Dialogue!" "Come out Li Peng! Come out Li Peng!" and "Send our wreaths inside! Send our wreaths inside!" Observing more carefully, one could also see many individual actions. For example, at one point, my informant (no. 60) became so angry that he even hit himself in the face, bloodying his visage. The students became increasingly emotional as the event moved on in this manner.

Among numerous competing activities, two not only attracted most students' attention but also shaped the further development of the movement. One was the kneeling of three students in front of the Great Hall of the People, and the other was a speech made by Wuer Kaixi, a student from Beijing Normal University.

At about 11:40 A.M., the students asserted that while they had now dropped all the original demands, they still wanted to have a dialogue with Premier Li Peng. After about twenty minutes, there was no sign that Li Peng was going to come out. At this point, several student representatives were allowed to pass the police line to hand in a petition. However, when they arrived at the stairs of the Great Hall of the People, three of them—Zhou Yongjun, Guo Haifeng, and Zhang Zhiyong—knelt down, with Wuer Kaixi standing alongside. Holding the petition over their heads, the three students were crying and begging to see Li Peng. Several government officials tried to receive the petition, but the three students refused. They insisted that Li Peng must come out to get the petition himself.

After a while, Wuer Kaixi stood up with a big electronic amplifier in hand and said "I am Wuer Kaixi. I am Wuer Kaixi," repeating the same sentence until students gradually calmed down. Then he continued: "Today, our students have stayed in the Square for over ten hours without taking food. What do we want? We have thought of many things, but now we have only one thought and demand: that is, to beg o-u-r Premier to come out and talk with us even if it is for only one sentence."

Wuer then said, as if begging: "Our premier, why do you still not come out?" The students' emotions were boiling. The whole Square echoed with: "Come out Li Peng! Come out Li Peng!" "Dialogue! Dialogue!" Students rushed toward the police. The police and students were pushing each other back and forth. The whole situation became almost uncontrollable. Then Wuer Kaixi stood out again. He asked students to calm down and announced that Li Peng would see them in fifteen minutes. The three representatives still knelt there and students were waiting, but Li did not come out as Wuer had said he would. Now every student felt greatly insulted. Students shouted: "Come back representatives! Come back representatives!" Some students even shouted "Down with Li Peng!" Many cried like babies. The students left greatly disappointed, many vowing a class boycott as they returned to their universities.

THE EMERGENCE OF STUDENT MOVEMENT ORGANIZATIONS

Movement organizations now began to emerge. To be sure, these were very weak organizations, with no grassroots membership. The first was formed at Beijing University on the evening of April 19, when Wang Dan and a few others held a "democracy salon" at the Triangle. Around 1,000 students were in the area. At the meeting they discussed the failures of past student movements. Attributing these failures to the lack of organizations to lead the movement, they decided to establish a Beijing University Autonomous Student Union Preparatory Committee. On that day, as Shen Tong has recalled, "anyone who had the courage to get up, give his name, his major, and what class he was in" automatically became a leader of the organization.[15]

Several major universities followed step in the next few days. Yet in most cases the autonomous student unions formed without even an open meeting. In Beijing Normal University, for instance, such a union was created through Wuer Kaixi's almost single-handed efforts. During the movement, the only attempt to elect leaders through a popular vote was made at Beijing University. On April 24, around ten thousand students gathered at the university's May 4th Stadium to elect the standing members of the Autonomous Student Union Preparatory Committee. Unfortunately, during the meeting "the milling crowds could not hear or would not listen to the speakers; various self-appointed student leaders vied for control of the bullhorns."[16] The activists fought each other so viciously that Xiong Yan even accused Zhang Zhiyong of being a spy for the school authorities. Most students left greatly disappointed. No general election was ever attempted.

On April 21, an announcement by "The Provisional Action Committee of Beijing Universities" asked students to take part in Hu Yaobang's state funeral. There was no other information about this "organization." In fact, the first Beijing-wide organization, The Beijing Students' Autonomous Union Preparatory Committee, was established on the evening of April 23. Over forty students from 21 universities participated in the meeting. They elected Wang Dan, Wuer Kaixi, Ma Shaofang, Zhang Kai, and Zhou Yongjun as standing members of the organization. Zhou Yongjun, from the University of Political

15. Shen Tong (1990, 172).
16. Wagner (1990, 52).

Science and Law, received the most votes and thus became chairman.[17] A major decision made at the meeting was to start a citywide class boycott. Within eight days of Hu's death, Beijing students thus achieved a great mobilization and established several formal—albeit self-appointed—social movement organizations. The movement had entered the next stage.

Student Protests and the Government's Concessions

THE APRIL 26 PEOPLE'S DAILY EDITORIAL
AND THE APRIL 27 DEMONSTRATION

After Hu's state funeral, the government turned its attention to the movement. On the evening of April 25, the China Central Television Station (CCTV) and the Central Broadcast Station broadcast an April 26 *People's Daily* editorial entitled "It is Necessary to Take a Clear-Cut Stand against Turmoil." The editorial labeled the movement as a planned conspiracy to create antigovernment turmoil staged by an extremely small number of agitators. It called on the people to stand up and oppose the movement and predicted that the whole country would have no peace if the movement lasted.[18] The editorial sent Beijing students a clear message that any further activism would no longer be tolerated by the government.

Historically, a government reaction of this kind had been enough to deter further student activism. But this time, partly because the government reaction had been delayed by Hu's death, the editorial failed to achieve its purpose. Instead, most students felt insulted. An informant (no. 68) explained: "The April 26 editorial made every student at Beijing University very angry. Until then, we really did not want to overthrow the communist government. We felt that such a task was impossible. Many of us felt that our great patriotism was insulted."

In many universities, students gathered together angrily and discussed what to do. The newly formed Beijing Students' Autonomous Union Preparatory Committee decided to stage a large-scale demonstration on April 27 to defy the editorial. To get more support, they also reframed their strategies. Many radical demands appearing in early slogans and petitions were avoided during their mobilization and the demonstrations. Meanwhile, the students added such slogans as "Support communist government!" and "Support socialism!"

---

17. According to my informant (no. 60), Zhou received the highest vote because that small university had six students in the meeting.

18. For an English version of the editorial, see Oksenberg, Sullivan, and Lambert (1990, 206–208).

The government also staged countermobilizations to try to stop the demonstrations. Yet the government countermobilization efforts could not penetrate very deep. For even traditionally loyalist elements of the university, such as the party members and grassroots-level student control personnel, shared grievances with students (chapter 4). An informant (no. 63) remembered:

> On the afternoon of April 25, student cadres, party members, and teachers attended a meeting. In the meeting, the department party secretary informed us of the major contents of the editorial to be aired in the evening. They asked us to persuade students not to support the movement. After listening to this, a young teacher who was a party member jumped up and said: "We are unable to persuade students. Nowadays, television has been highly developed. It is simple. You just need a state leader to talk on the TV. Why do you ask us to do the job?"

Putting pressure on a few student leaders was another tactic that the government used to stop the demonstration. Through various channels, the authorities tried to persuade student leaders to call off the demonstration. Under enormous pressure, many well-known activists, including Zhou Yongjun, Wuer Kaixi, and Shen Tong, hesitated and wanted to make some compromises. However, these student leaders could not really control the movement. While they intended to make some compromises, most other activists still wanted to see the demonstration happen. In the end, tens of thousands of students marched on the street on April 27 (chapter 8).

THE GOVERNMENT'S CONCESSIONS

Due to the determination of the students, the restraint of the government, and a favorable campus physical environment, the demonstration achieved a stunning success. Since hardliner rhetoric had proved useless, and because the government at this stage wanted to end the movement peacefully, concession became its only alternative. On the noon of April 27, when the students were still marching toward Tiananmen Square, State Council spokesman Yuan Mu expressed the government's intention to have a dialogue with students. The next day, the *People's Daily* and some other major official newspapers reported the demonstration on the front page and with a slightly positive tone. Starting on April 29, the government held several dialogues with students, the most well known of which occurred on that day.

On April 28, the government asked the Association of All China Students, a government-sponsored student organization, to organize the dialogue. The

Association invited forty-five students from sixteen universities. Four leaders of the newly established independent student unions, including Zhou Yongjun, Guo Haifeng, and Wuer Kaixi, and many other movement activists were invited to the dialogue, but they were not allowed to represent or speak for the newly founded independent student unions.

It should be noted that although the participants were invited by an official student union, the dialogue was not as phony as many have subsequently described it to have been. In fact, compared with the numerous later dialogues, this was the one where students and government officials had the most substantive discussion. In the dialogue, students raised issues concerning official corruption and its causes, biased news reports, the putative police brutality on April 20, Li Peng's refusal to meet the students after Hu's funeral, the April 26 *People's Daily* editorial, and the reevaluation of Hu Yaobang. They thus covered most of the seven demands raised earlier. Moreover, Xiang Xiaoji, a student from the University of Political Science and Law, challenged the validity of the dialogue itself. His major point was that those who participated in the dialogue could not represent students because they were not elected, and that the meeting was thus just a preliminary contact between students and the government. He made three suggestions for achieving a more substantial dialogue: (1) a student dialogue delegation should be formed, with two elected representatives from each university; (2) before the dialogue, there should be some preparatory dialogues to discuss the time, location, number of people, topic, and form of the formal dialogue; and (3) the students would end the class boycott when the substantial dialogue began. Xiang later emerged as the head of the Dialogue Delegation.

However, the dialogue did not satisfy many students, especially student activists. Wuer Kaixi refused to attend. Some participants protested the form of the dialogue and left the room in the middle of the proceedings. After the dialogue, Zhou Yongjun and Xiang Xiaoji asserted that their participation and speeches represented only themselves. Many student activists thought that the dialogue was a plot aimed at dividing the students. That evening, many big-character posters in major universities attacked the government, the dialogue, and the students who had participated in the dialogue.

Nevertheless, the atmosphere of confrontation eased as the government continued to make concessions. The government's willingness to make concessions reached its peak on May 4, when Zhao Ziyang met the delegates of the Asian Development Bank Conference.[19] In the meeting, Zhao said that since

19. Zhao Ziyang (1990a).

the basic slogans used in student demonstrations were "Support the Communist Party!" "Support Socialism!" "Uphold the Reforms!" "Push Forward
Democracy!" and "Oppose Corruption!" the majority of students were "by
no means opposed to our basic system." Meanwhile, Zhao Ziyang asked Hu
Qili and Rui Xingwen, the two top state leaders in charge of China's official
media, to open up the media. He told them that there was "no big risk in opening up a bit by reporting the demonstrations and increasing the openness of
news."[20] The government almost completely reversed the evaluation of the
movement made in the April 26 *People's Daily* editorial. The student movement
thus achieved a major success.

THE DIALOGUE DELEGATION

Beijing students were in a victorious mood. Most student leaders were also
happy to offer some compromises to the government. On April 30, the Beijing
Students' Autonomous Union held a meeting, at which, since it was unlikely
that the government would hold a dialogue directly with them, they approved
Wang Chaohua and Feng Congde's motion to organize an independent dialogue delegation.[21]

The Dialogue Delegation held its first meeting on May 3. In the meeting
Xiang Xiaoji suggested three dialogue agendas: (1) on the nature of the current student movement; (2) on strategies for future economic and political
reform; and (3) on how people's constitutional rights could be truly realized
in China. Xiang's suggestions impressed the other delegates. He was elected in
a voice vote as the chairman of the delegation, and Shen Tong became Xiang's
associate.

Following Xiang's suggestion, the delegates were divided into three groups,
each preparing one topic. In the following days, the Dialogue Delegation held
numerous meetings. As more and more universities added their representatives,
its size grew to about seventy students.[22] The delegates contacted the government several times in order to set up a dialogue, while the government, through
various channels, also expressed a willingness to talk.[23] Around May 10, the

---

20. Faison (1990, 156).

21. Shen Tong (1990, 215) and Feng Congde (*Huigu yu Fansi* 1993, 68).

22. Supposedly, the delegates from each university were to be elected, and in a few universities students
treated this quite seriously. But at most universities, including Beijing University, the representatives were
decided upon by a very small circle. In fact, quite a few students in the Dialogue Delegation meetings were
neither elected nor invited. They went to the meetings on their own.

23. See Shen Tong (1990, 229–31) for how the government contacted the Dialogue Delegation through
university authorities.

government even went into technical details, asking the delegation to restrict its formal dialogue members to twenty. On the evening of May 12, Xiang Xiaoji told my informant (no. 59, a member of the Dialogue Delegation) that the first dialogue with the government had been scheduled for May 15. Yet the next day, the hunger strike started. To understand why a hunger strike was initiated when the students and the government were approaching each other, we have to examine in greater detail the movement during early May.

THE DECLINE OF THE MOVEMENT

After the April 27 demonstration, the government started to hold dialogues with students, Zhao Ziyang reevaluated the movement, and the official media reported positively on movement activities. The government's concessions satisfied the majority of students. During the May 4 demonstration, Zhou Yongjun, on behalf of the Beijing Students' Autonomous Union, formally announced that the class boycott would end that day. After May 4 all of the universities except for Beijing University and Beijing Normal University resumed classes. Although most students in Beijing University had voted for continuing the class boycott after May 5, more and more students actually went to class. In fact, by May 9 and 10, radical students in the university had to picket in front of classrooms to stop others from attending classes.[24] Even those who were not attending class were no longer so concerned about the movement. Many students, movement activists among them, traveled or visited home. Those who stayed on campus began to enjoy themselves by playing poker and mah-jongg. The Triangle at Beijing University, which had been full of people since the start of the movement, was no longer congested. Student leaders had to continuously make speeches at the Triangle to keep up students' interest in the movement.[25] In fact, much of the momentum of the movement in Beijing during this period was sustained by the protest activities of Chinese journalists (chapter 10).

Meanwhile, the leadership of the movement was becoming increasingly problematic. Partly because all the student organizations had been established in a hurry, the problems of the student movement organizations went beyond disagreement over movement strategies. Many student leaders did not seem to respect the organizations they founded. They announced personal decisions in the name of organizations and disregarded organizational decisions with

24. Wang Chaohua (1992a, 77).
25. Wu Ren (1990b, 57–58) and Shen Tong (1990, 226).

which they personally disagreed.[26] In the following, I summarize crucial divisions among student activists during early May and explain how these divisions contributed to the rise of the hunger strike.

Student activists in this period can be categorized into three groups. The first was the Dialogue Delegation group. These students were eager for the coming dialogue with the government. The leaders of the delegation had also openly or privately contacted the government and were almost certain that the dialogue would take place. They therefore had the most moderate position.

The second group was the Beijing Students' Autonomous Union, which included student activists such as Wang Chaohua, Zhou Yongjun, and Wang Zhixin. These students regularly attended the meetings of the Autonomous Union. Some leaders of the Autonomous Union and the Dialogue Delegation attended each other's meetings, and thus most students in the former group knew the Dialogue Delegation and some of its activities. The students in the two groups had certain conflicts, however. While students in the Dialogue Delegation thought that the movement had reached a stage where demonstrations and class boycotts would be replaced by dialogues, in which they would play a major role, the students in the Autonomous Union group thought that it was their fight that had created opportunities for the Dialogue Delegation.[27] Therefore, the leaders of the delegation saw their contacts with the government as a special privilege and kept them secret. Meanwhile, the leaders of the Autonomous Union, not wanting the delegation to be the mouthpiece of the students generally, had independently come up with many petitions and demands different from those put through by the Dialogue Delegation. Naturally, the government was confused as to whom it should deal with, while the students in general came to believe that the government was not interested in talking with students at all.[28]

Nevertheless, the union group was more or less aware of the interactions between the Dialogue Delegation and the government. It believed that its focus

26. A well-known example at this stage was Zhou Yongjun's personal decision to call off the April 27 demonstration under the name of the Beijing Student's Autonomous Union Preparatory Committee, of which he was the chairperson.

27. See Wang Chaohua (1992b) for more discussion of relationships among student leaders of the two groups.

28. For example, Zheng Xuguang, a leader of the Beijing Students' Autonomous Union, attended a Dialogue Delegation meeting on May 11. In the meeting, he said: "This is the first time that I have attended a Dialogue Delegation meeting. I now feel that a dialogue between students and the government is highly possible. However, the Autonomous Union and students knew nothing about it. They feel that the possibility of having a dialogue has not increased since May 4, and have thus decided to go on a hunger strike. You should let the students know about the dialogue as soon as possible" (*China News Digest* 1994, 16).

should be on consolidating campus democracy, a major achievement of the movement.[29] Thus it can be seen that the general orientation of the leaders in the Beijing Students' Autonomous Union group was also not radical.

The third group, the charismatic group, consisted of a few radicals, among whom were such legendary student leaders as Wang Dan and Wuer Kaixi. While most of this group's members at one time or another held standing member positions in the Beijing Students' Autonomous Union, they tended to do things in their own ways. Most of them did not regularly attend the Autonomous Union's meetings, and they were therefore even less informed about the negotiations between the Dialogue Delegation and the government than the Autonomous Union leaders. An extreme example is that of student leader Wang Dan; he told me in an interview that he did not even know of the existence of the Dialogue Delegation until the hunger strike began. To this group, the government's concessive strategies were simply tricks.[30] Trapped between what they perceived to be an uncompromising regime and a student body with a decreasing enthusiasm for activism, a few activists in this group decided to stage a hunger strike.

THE HUNGER STRIKE MOBILIZATION [31]

Hunger strikes had been considered and indeed used many times leading up to and during the movement. Before the movement began, some agitators from outside Beijing had planned a hunger strike for April 5.[32] On April 18, two

29. For example, the moderate approach was reflected in the Beijing Students' Autonomous Union's May 6 announcement: "Democratization is a gradual process. The Beijing Students' Autonomous Union will no longer use demonstrations as a major means to advance democracy in China. In the following days, our first step is to organize conferences and seminars and to invite renowned scholars such as Yan Jiaqi and Yu Guangyuan to present talks. . . . The second step is to run newspapers and magazines. . . . [About the dialogue between student and the government], we are flexible. The dialogue can be achieved through a third party, that is, through the newly formed Dialogue Delegation" (Wu et al. 1989, 153). According to Wang Chaohua (*Huigu yu Fansi* 1993, 94), on May 11 the Autonomous Union decided that "Considering the recent [positive] responses of the government to the Dialogue Delegation, the Beijing Students' Autonomous Union should oppose any large-scale activities while promoting small- to moderate-scale actions," and that no demonstrations should be held during Gorbachev's visit to Beijing (Wu et al. 1989, 180).

30. The mood of radical students in this period was reflected in a big-character poster posted on May 7: "The tiger-headed, snake-tailed democratic student movement has been gradually calmed down with no fruitful results. . . . People have great hope in us. We have been highly praised and supported, but what can we offer in return? . . . Our faces were slapped (e.g., conspiracy, turmoil). We were then rewarded by sweet dates (e.g., the youth are patriotic). So, we forget the pain and start to enjoy the dates" (*Bajiu Zhongguo Minyun Ziliaoce* 1991, 153):

31. The origin of the hunger strike will also be discussed in chapter 7.

32. Shen Tong (*Huigu yu Fansi* 1993, 14).

students from Beijing University staged a hunger strike in front of the Xinhua Gate.[33] In Beijing Normal University, Liang Er remembered that in early May an activist even argued: "We absolutely must start a hunger strike. It will be ideal if the hunger strike leads to bloodshed."[34] Chai Ling, a major hunger strike leader, also recalled:

> We had the idea of the hunger strike at the beginning of the movement. One day when I was talking with Zhang Boli, he said: "Do you know that the hunger strike has been and is a very effective weapon [of protest]? . . . If we are really hungry, we can go to the dormitory or the washroom to eat something in secret. You are the treasure of the country. When the university authorities see that you are on a hunger strike, they will hold you like babies."[35]

However, although there were discussions about it, the hunger strike did not become a reality until May 11. On that evening, Wang Dan, Wuer Kaixi, and four other students dined in a small restaurant, where they discussed the movement. They all agreed that the movement was in crisis but that the government did not have any sincere desire for a genuine dialogue and was playing for time.[36] In light of the situation, Wuer Kaixi proposed a hunger strike. They decided to start the hunger strike on May 13 in Tiananmen Square. The date was chosen for two reasons: first, they had no time to waste, since students were rapidly losing interest in the movement, and second, they predicted that to make Gorbachev's state visit successful, the government would have to make major concessions once students occupied Tiananmen Square.[37]

The hunger strike mobilization started after the students went back to

---

33. Bai Meng (*Huigu yu Fansi* 1993, 57).

34. According to Liang Er (*Huigu yu Fansi* 1993, 126–28), Wuer Kaixi started to talk about a hunger strike in a speech on May 8. Wuer's major concern was also that the movement needed a push. Wuer only made up his mind, however, after a meeting with Tian Jiyun, a deputy prime minister, and Zhao Ziyang's secretary on May 10. While Tian was talking with Wuer, he from time to time turned around to whisper with Zhao's secretary. Wuer took this as a sign that the government might be able to make a major concession if students applied more pressure. Thus, he decided on the hunger strike.

35. Chai Ling (*Huigu yu Fansi* 1993, 89).

36. Chai Ling justified the hunger strike with a similar reason: "[After Zhou Yongjun announced the end of the class boycott on May 4], the student movement lost momentum; more and more students were returning to classes. Arguments over whether we should return to class or continue the class boycott consumed a lot of the student movement's time and resources, and the situation was getting more and more difficult. We felt then that we had to undertake a hunger strike" (Han and Hua 1990, 197).

37. Wang Dan told Chai Ling after the meeting that: "[We will start the hunger strike] two days before Gorbachev's state visit to give the government enough time to respond." See Chai Ling (*Huigu yu Fansi* 1993, 89).

school. It was not an easy process. Even at Beijing University, the most radical of the universities, after a whole day of effort only about forty students volunteered to be hunger strikers. It was not until Chai Ling made her emotional speech at the Triangle on the night of May 12 that the number of students signed up for the hunger strike rose to about three hundred (Chai's speech will be discussed in chapter 9).[38]

The Beijing Students' Autonomous Union tried to stop the hunger strike. For example, Wang Chaohua, on behalf of the union, tried to persuade Chai Ling to call off the hunger strike. Chai replied: "The hunger strike was spontaneously initiated by students. No one has the right to stop it!"[39] When Wang accused hunger strike leaders of abusing the name of the Beijing Students' Autonomous Union to mobilize students, Zheng Xuguang jumped up with the rejoinder "Do you still believe that the autonomous union has authority over students?"[40] To some extent, Zheng was right. Since the rise of the hunger strike, movement organizations had less and less capacity to control the movement. In the end, the Beijing Students' Autonomous Union failed to stop the hunger strike.

The Hunger Strike Period

When the hunger strikers had just arrived at Tiananmen Square on the afternoon of May 13, they numbered only a little over three hundred. Including supporters, no more than 3,000 students stayed over the first night in Tiananmen Square. Most students and Beijing residents did not yet support or even seem to care about the hunger strike. Moreover, since the hunger strike had been organized in a hurry, with most of the participants not thinking that it would last very long, the students in the Square had come with no extra clothes and with nothing to sleep on. On the night of May 13 the temperature dropped to five degrees Celsius. Therefore, all my hunger strike informants described the first night of the hunger strike as an extremely cold, hungry, and lonely one. However, within two days the fasting population grew to over 3,000, drew millions of sympathizers, and induced a leadership crisis within the government that led to Zhao Ziyang's step-down and to martial law. The hunger strike turned out

38. Eventually about two hundred students from Beijing University participated in the hunger strike on its first day.

39. See Wang Chaohua (1993, 25).

40. Wang Chaohua (*Huigu yu Fansi* 1993, 95).

to be a great success of movement mobilization—but it also set the stage for the movement's bloody ending.

DIALOGUE AND INTELLECTUAL MEDIATION

May 13 and 14 were crucial days for the eventual outcome of the movement. The hunger strike was still at an initial stage, and the government desperately wanted it to end before Gorbachev's state visit. Besides, the intellectual elites and moderate student leaders also wanted the hunger strike to end quickly so that they could have time to consolidate what they had gained over the previous few days. As a result, many contacts were made among students, intellectual elites, and the government.[41] However, despite the good faith of some movement organizers, intellectuals, and top government leaders, they all failed to end the hunger strike. In its wake, the situation in Tiananmen Square became much less controllable, and most top state leaders grew uninterested in compromising. The following focuses on these two most dramatic days.

The government reacted immediately to the news of the hunger strike. On the morning of May 13, Yan Mingfu, the head of the CCP Central Committee's United Front Work Department, met with several intellectuals and asked them to gather the student leaders and some intellectuals influential among students (as mediators) for an emergency meeting in the afternoon. Eventually, such student leaders as Wuer Kaixi, Wang Chaohua, Xiang Xiaoji, Shen Tong, Wang Dan, Chai Ling, Feng Congde, and Zhou Yongjun went to the meeting, along with a few intellectuals including Liu Xiaobo, Chen Ziming, and Wang Juntao.[42]

Yan Mingfu spoke first. He told the participants that the purposes of this meeting were, first, to get the opinions of students and intellectuals and pass them in the quickest way to the Central Committee, and second, to persuade students to withdraw from the Square before Gorbachev's arrival. Then, starting with Wuer Kaixi and Wang Dan, students and intellectuals in turn aired their views on the movement and the hunger strike. In sum, they stressed that their actions were lawful, peaceful, and patriotic. While most of them welcomed the recent changes in the government's attitude toward the move-

---

41. Up to this point, for fear that their involvement would invite head-on government repression, most of the intellectual elites who had been highly active before the rise of the movement were actually trying to distance themselves from the students.

42. See Liu Xiaobo (1992, 99), Wang Chaohua (1993, 26), and Shen Tong (1990, 239–40) for details of this meeting.

ment, they accused the government of lacking sincerity. They wanted the government to openly change the verdict of the April 26 *People's Daily* editorial. They also demanded immediate talks between the Dialogue Delegation and the government. A few also demanded that the government recognize the Beijing Students' Autonomous Union and punish the policemen who beat the students during the Xinhua Gate Incident. Yan Mingfu responded to the students as follows:

> I will report what you have said to the Central Committee as soon as the meeting is over. The student movement is a patriotic movement. It was brought about by many cultural, social, and educational problems in our country. Some of the problems have been extremely serious. The Central Committee has felt a great sense of urgency in dealing with these problems. . . . After the April 27 demonstration, the Central Committee seriously considered students' demands. All the problems can be solved by seeking common ground while respecting our differences. Dialogue is a major component of democracy. It is acceptable to both students and the government. It was probably the lack of transparency that led to students' suspicion of the government's sincerity about having a genuine dialogue. . . . [Therefore] the government should take responsibility for it and make self-criticism. China is currently in a transition from a closed society to a modern society. Different social groups cannot get the same benefits in this process. The whole society is full of contradictions and conflicts. To solve these problems, we need constructive efforts from different social groups. The April 27 and May 4 demonstrations by students were very successful, and the hunger strike is also not an unlawful action. What the Central Committee is concerned about is that the hunger strike will be in conflict with Gorbachev's coming visit. The Central Committee, therefore, hopes that our fellow students will put the interest of our nation in the first place. . . . I hope that the students could restrain their behavior by a sense of historical duty. I know that you will do it because history has dictated that you are a generation that still concerns itself with our country and our people, not a generation that leads a life of pleasure.[43]

Yan Mingfu's frankness won over the majority of the student leaders. By the end of the meeting, both Wuer Kaixi and Wang Dan had guaranteed that the students would withdraw from Tiananmen Square before May 15. Yet if Yan had won over most, he had not persuaded all. Shortly after the meeting started, two hunger strike activists, Chai Ling and her husband Feng Congde, told the students beside them that they had something to do in the Square and left quietly.

43. Yan Mingfu's speech is cited from Liu Xiaobo (1992).

On the early morning of May 14, Yan Mingfu met again with the student leaders Wang Chaohua, Wang Dan, and Wuer Kaixi.[44] Yan told them that the government had agreed to hold a dialogue with the Dialogue Delegation. The government representatives included Li Tieying, Yan Mingfu, Luo Gan, and ten deputy ministers of the State Council. Wang Dan and Wuer Kaixi said that the ranks of the government representatives were not high enough. Yan replied: "Li Tieying is a deputy prime minister and a member of the Politburo, I am the secretary of the Central Secretariat of the CCP. Do you really think that our ranks are not high enough?" The three student leaders had nothing more to say, so they started to discuss technical details of the dialogue. Eventually, they broached the idea of broadcasting the dialogue live on CCTV. Yan Mingfu said this was impossible because the United Front Work Department had no such equipment and the equipment of the CCTV station was being used to prepare Gorbachev's state visit.[45] The three student leaders countered that they might not be able to persuade the hunger strikers if the dialogues were not broadcast live. After some discussion, Yan agreed that "the meeting could be video-typed by CCTV staff . . . and completely broadcast in the evening. Meanwhile, students can also record the meeting themselves and broadcast it in Tiananmen Square."

The three student leaders accepted the arrangement, but they also hemmed and hawed in front of Yan Mingfu. Yan apparently understood their hesitation. He continued: "The Central Committee had decided not to hold the welcome ceremony for Gorbachev's state visit at Tiananmen Square regardless of whether the students withdraw from the Square or not. Now, the decision is completely up to the students. Even if you decide to leave, are you certain that you can bring the students out?" According to Wang Chaohua, they immediately sensed the danger if they could not bring students out, and started to discuss how to bring the students out in front of Yan. At one point, Wang Chaohua criticized the hunger strike, orchestrated by Wang Dan and Wuer Kaixi, as an irresponsible action, and asked Wang Dan whether he could really persuade Chai Ling and other radical students to leave. After some thought, Wang Dan replied that they would leave if some renowned intellectuals would go there to persuade them. Then, Wang Chaohua said that she knew of a meeting of some such intellectuals in the afternoon, where they might be asked to help. Wang Chaohua volunteered for the job herself.

44. The following description of the meeting is based mainly on Wang Chaohua (1993, 28).

45. In Shen Tong's (1990, 245) autobiography, he says that the meeting could not be broadcast live because it was in conflict with a soccer game. I am inclined towards Wang Chaohua's version of the story since Wang got the information directly from Yan Mingfu, while Shen Tong heard it from someone else.

The meeting that Wang Chaohua mentioned had been organized by Dai Qing, a controversial journalist at *Guangming Daily*. It had been arranged the previous day, May 12, when Dai Qing attended a dialogue between Hu Qili and several communication theorists and senior journalists.[46] Dai Qing told Hu Qili that having been interviewed many times by foreign journalists regarding the movement had led her to wonder, "Why can't the *Guangming Daily* publish our views directly?" Hu Qili agreed. Dai Qing then said: "Our newspapers often invite scholars to participate in panel discussions and to publish their views in a summary. Could we do the same this time?" Hu Qili replied: "You can decide the form yourself."

With a positive answer, Dai Qing started to prepare the meeting. She eventually invited ten people, including Yan Jiaqi, Su Xiaokang, Bao Zunxin, Liu Zaifu, and Li Zehou. Before the meeting started, Wang Chaohua went in, and after a while Wen Yuankai also joined in, together with several private entrepreneurs. The meeting started at about 2:00 P.M. At the same time, Tiananmen Square was already packed with some 300,000 people, as more and more students joined the hunger strike.[47] With the arrival of Wang Chaohua, the meeting shifted focus. Wang Chaohua cried, begging them to use their influence to persuade the hunger strikers to leave the Square. Many intellectuals sobbed with Wang; they agreed to take on the task. Before they went to Tiananmen Square, Su Xiaokang wrote an "urgent appeal" to be read in the Square on behalf of these intellectuals.

At around 4:45 P.M., while the twelve intellectuals were still in the meeting, the dialogue between the government and students started. The conference room, set up as suggested by Xiang Xiaoji,[48] had a long table in the middle. Thirteen government officials sat on one side of the table and the same number of speakers from the Dialogue Delegation sat on the other side. Behind the speakers sat the other members of the Dialogue Delegation and observers from the hunger strike group. On both sides there were journalists from China's major news agencies and newspapers.

However, although some government officials and student leaders had been working very hard to make the dialogue possible, the dialogue was from the very beginning a chaotic one. First, the members of Dialogue Delegation were eager to attend the meeting whether or not they had been selected as speakers.[49]

46. The description of the meeting is mainly based on Dai (1993).

47. Li Lu (1990, 136).

48. Xiang (1995).

49. The following narratives concerning the dialogue are mainly based on reports by three informants (no. 57, 58, 59). As members of the Dialogue Delegation, they all attended the meeting.

No one wanted to miss this historic moment. As a result, over forty students from the Dialogue Delegation participated in the meeting, although the plan had been for only twenty to attend. Second, the hunger strikers did not trust the Dialogue Delegates and therefore sent observers to sit behind the speakers. Shortly after the dialogue started, Wuer Kaixi asked Cheng Zhen, a hunger striker from Beijing Normal University, to read a letter entitled "A Letter to Mama." While she was reading, most of the people in the room, including journalists and government officials, burst into tears. Students in the room became very emotional thereafter.[50] Third, although the students had been demanding dialogue for over ten days, they were not really prepared for it. Most of the student representatives in the meeting were unknown to each other a few days previously. There was little consensus or coordination among them. Once in the limelight of what they had perceived to be a historic moment, many of them could not even behave normally. Their speakers often made excessively long speeches with contents only remotely related to the dialogue agenda. Those who were not selected as speakers either jumped in to talk or passed endless notes prompting speakers to raise issues which they saw as more important. Sometimes, students even fought to grab microphones.

Finally, before the dialogue started, the student broadcasting station at Tiananmen Square had announced: "Please go to the United Front Work Department to support the dialogue students. Some people there wanted to sell our fellow students out."[51] Hence hunger strikers and supporters were continuously arriving at the United Front Work Department. From time to time these students demanded that Xiang Xiaoji or even Shen Tong go out of the conference room to make various requests or add more demands. They also jammed the door of the United Front Work Department and blocked the crew of the CCTV when they tried to send the videocassette to the station for broadcast. Yet after the students found out that the dialogue was not being broadcast on TV, they repeatedly shouted outside the United Front Work Department to demand an immediate termination of the dialogue.[52] Eventually, at

50. One informant (no. 59) told me that this action had been decided upon beforehand. Initially, they asked my informant to read it. She was requested to read with emotion and tears. Eventually, in order to better touch the hearts of the listeners, they decided to let a female hunger striker read the letter.

51. Chai Ling (*Huigu yu Fansi* 1993, 107).

52. Most students treated the failed CCTV broadcast of the dialogue as a government conspiracy. Shen Tong (1990, 247–48) wrote that the dialogue was not broadcast because someone more powerful than Yan Mingfu stopped the process. My understanding is that during that period government control over the media almost collapsed and that more inflammatory reports appeared everywhere in the major official media (chapter 10). I therefore accept Xiang Xiaoji's version of the story (Xiang 1995, 72).

7:15 P.M., a group of students headed by Wang Chaohua rushed into the meeting room to demand that either the meeting be immediately broadcast live or that it be stopped.[53] Students in the room immediately stood up and accused the failed broadcast of being the result of a government conspiracy. At this moment, Chai Ling turned on a cassette player to play the "Hunger Strike Declaration." The dialogue ended in chaos.

While the dialogue was still in process, the twelve scholars headed to the State Council's Bureau of Complaints, where they arranged to meet with some hunger strike organizers in order to persuade them to bring the students out of Tiananmen Square.[54] To Dai Qing's surprise, the hunger strikers expressed their total agreement with the view of these "teachers" and invited them to talk directly with the rest of the students.

The twelve intellectuals were also warmly welcomed when they entered the Square. After they arrived at the broadcasting center, one of them read the "Urgent Appeal."[55] The appeal greatly praised the students and the movement. It demanded that the government recognize the movement as a patriotic democracy movement and the Beijing Students' Autonomous Union as a legal organization. Meanwhile, it also suggested that the students withdraw from the Square to let the Sino-Soviet summit proceed smoothly.[56] While the appeal was well received, the students did not withdraw. In fact, a few radical students even thought that the real intention of the scholars was to help the government. Li Lu recalled his feelings after having listened to the "Urgent Appeal":

> It sounded good. They were voicing our main demands. But when we calmed down and thought, we realized that they were actually acting on behalf of the government. Chinese intellectuals are always apprehensive and timid. These [intellectuals], though they openly said they supported the students, actually spoke for the government. The intellectuals might be able to persuade students to leave the Square

53. According to Wang Chaohua (*Huigu yu Fansi* 1993, 102–103), she went in because she saw many students jammed in front of the United Front Work Department shouting: "Stop the dialogue! Start the live broadcast immediately!" She agreed to deliver their message. She was escorted into the conference room by two students because the students did not trust her either. Therefore, she had to act radically after she went in.

54. Unless otherwise specified, the following account of the activities of the twelve scholars at Tiananmen Square is based on Dai (1993), Su Wei (1992), and Shu (1990).

55. There were two versions of the story. Su (1992) remembered that it was Wen Yuankai who read the appeal, while Dai (1993) claimed that she had read it. Both of them were among the twelve scholars. I have to rely on Dai Qing's account because one is less likely to mistake someone else's speech as one's own.

56. The appeal was broadcast on CCTV News and published on the front page of *Guangming Daily* the next day. The English version of the text appears in Han and Hua (1990, 207–208).

but they didn't have the power to guarantee that the government would not mete out punishment later.[57]

While the scholars were trying to persuade the students to withdraw, Chai Ling passed a note to Feng Congde which said: "Please read the hunger strike declaration three times in the broadcasting station." As Feng read the declaration, the emotions of the students in the Square came to a boil. The situation soon spiraled out of control. The twelve scholars had to flee from the Square amid a hostile crowd. As they left, the students hurled insults at them: "Get the hell out of Tiananmen Square! We do not need the Savior!" "This is our business! Nobody can represent us!" "We are risking our lives to let you harvest the fruits? Only in your dreams!"[58]

Thus, the students still occupied Tiananmen Square when Gorbachev arrived in Beijing on May 15.[59] This was the first state visit between the former Soviet Union and China in thirty years. It marked the ending of hostile relations between two countries that shared a common border of over 4,000 kilometers. Therefore, the visit had been for a long time portrayed in the Chinese media as a major diplomatic breakthrough. Yet, the welcome ceremony was rearranged to take place at Beijing Airport, and the first meeting between China's president Yang Shangkun and Gorbachev in the Great Hall of the People was delayed for two hours. Moreover, the government had to cancel a few other activities because of the Tiananmen Square occupation.[60] To Deng Xiaoping and many other top state leaders, the students' action was a great insult and an indication that a moderate approach was not going to work. At this point the so-called conservative/reformer struggle within the party intensified greatly (chapter 7).

MASS SUPPORT DURING THE HUNGER STRIKE

It was against this background that the hunger strike entered its third day— May 15. On that day, the Hunger Strike Headquarters (hereafter the Headquarters) was founded. Chai Ling became the general commander. Feng Congde,

57. Li Lu (1990, 138).

58. Liu Xiaobo (1992, 122). The line about the savior echoes "L'Internationale." A literal translation of the Chinese words to that line reads: "There has never been a savior, / Nor should we rely on gods and emperors."

59. In fact, another dialogue was held between government officials and student leaders on the morning of May 15. Yet, many important hunger strike organizers did not even participate in this dialogue.

60. See Brook (1992, 38) and Schell (1994, 85).

Li Lu, and Zhang Boli became vice commanders.[61] Most Beijing students were not in favor of a hunger strike at first. Yet as the hunger strike continued, students and Beijing residents became more and more concerned about the health conditions of the students and antagonized by what they perceived to be the lack of response on the part of the government. An informant (no. 3) who had acted as a guard for the hunger strikers since May 15 remembered:

> I was very much against the idea of a hunger strike. . . . Before the hunger strike, we had resumed class. It seemed that everything was going to be over soon. . . . However, as soon as the hunger strike started, the government's reaction really disappointed us. On the first day of the hunger strike, we were very surprised that the government did not try to remove the strikers. However, after the second and third days, we became more and more sympathetic to them. The key was sympathy. Many of my friends told me that they came to Tiananmen Square because they were moved.

Therefore, Beijing students returned to the political concerns they had been preoccupied with earlier. By May 16 the number of hunger strikers had increased to 3,100. Each university started to set up camps in the Square to support the hunger strikers. Finally, many students also volunteered to do different services in the Square, including guarding the hunger strikers and serving as picketers to keep the life-lines unblocked by the waves of visitors and supporters.

After May 15, the sirens of ambulances could be heard day and night in Tiananmen Square and along the roads to the hospitals. Inspired by the extremely positive coverage that China's official media was giving to the movement in those days (detailed in chapter 10), Beijing residents of all occupations—including such traditionally loyal elements of the government as lower- and middle-rank government bureaucrats, police, and PLA officers—demonstrated to urge the government to negotiate with the students and solve the crisis. On both May 17 and 18 the size of demonstrations reached well above a million people.

This mass support has generally been treated as a sign of the rise of civil society or of working-class consciousness in China. What I want to emphasize is

---

61. According to Li Lu (*Huigu yu Fansi* 1993, 136), this was how the Headquarters was formed: "Because it was urgent, we had no time to hold a meeting to discuss how to establish such an organization. I set a condition that those who were willing to stand out and to dedicate their lives to the hunger strike and the democratic movement should be the leaders. . . . At that moment, there were a dozen or so students around. Later, they all became key members of the Headquarters' Secretary Department. Then, Chai Ling made a speech and the Hunger Strike Headquarters was formally established."

that most people who participated in this part of the movement did so primarily out of sympathy with the frail hunger strikers. Moreover, most demonstrations in this period were organized semi-officially. The following narratives from two of my informants provide examples:

> [During the hunger strike] many people at our institute had demonstrated at the Square; most of these were young persons. Before the demonstration, some people in the Communist Youth League announced the date of the demonstration on the broadcasting station owned by our institute. The demonstration was organized by the Communist Youth League of the institute. . . . The CCP general secretary in the institute did not order us to participate, but he by no means had tried to stop us. . . . Instead, the general secretary assigned several buses to take us to the Square (no. 5)

> In the parade of Beijing Automobiles, I saw my schoolmate. I asked him how he came to be there. He told me that the director of his unit had told them: "You can join the march if you want. I will provide you with drink if you go." He then came. (no. 11)

Eleven of my informants described their experiences during these demonstrations. Strikingly, they all give similar accounts. During the hunger strike period, demonstrations were usually organized by the cadres of such organizations as the Communist Youth League or the official worker union of a given work-unit; they were generally tacitly approved of by the leaders of the work-units.[62] The authorities in the work-units also allowed demonstrators to use such work-unit resources as money, the flag of the unit, materials to make banners, communications equipment, and buses or trucks. Most demonstrators also got paid while marching in Tiananmen Square.[63]

In these days supporting hunger strikers became a moral imperative, putting enormous pressure on the people in those work-units that had not yet marched on the street. By May 18 the Office of News and Publication, a very conservative institute, had still not demonstrated. Many of its staff members were very unhappy. As one person said publicly at the institute: "Even the State Council and the handicapped people have demonstrated in Tiananmen Square. In Bei-

---

62. In some cases, leaders in work-units even personally led demonstrations. For example, the manager of the Beijing Cookware Plant personally led his entire workforce out to march in the Square (Walder 1991a, 485). The vice chancellor of Nankai University also personally led doctors and teachers from Tianjin to demonstrate in the Square under the banner "sympathy delegation" (*Shengyuantuan*) (informant no. 27).

63. In 1997, I went to Beijing again and interviewed nine workers from different factories who had participated in demonstrations during the hunger strike. They all provided very similar accounts of how they had joined the demonstrations, which I have summarized above.

jing only two institutions have not yet marched on the street: one is the CCP Politburo and the other is our institute." These and similar comments made the leaders of the unit extremely uncomfortable. Eventually, they allowed the people in their unit to demonstrate during work time and provided them with resources, including transportation.[64]

WORKERS' PARTICIPATION DURING THE MOVEMENT

The phenomenon of mass participation has made scholars strongly emphasize the importance of independent union activities during the movement.[65] My study, however, shows that independent union activities played a minimal role. Since the Beijing Workers' Autonomous Union (*gongzilian*) was known as the most important independent work union established during the movement, the following narrative mainly focuses on that organization.[66]

The Beijing Workers' Autonomous Union was formally established on May 18.[67] It reflected the fact that some student leaders had started to mobilize workers during the hunger strike period. Li Jinjin, a graduate student from Beijing University, played a crucial role in the formation of the organization. Alongside Li were student activists, including Zhou Yongjun and Xiong Yan, who were also deeply involved in organizing and who also held important positions in the Workers' Union. Li Jinjin acted in the union as a legal consultant, and Zhou Yongjun as the Minister of Organization.[68] In fact, most of the

64. This piece of information was provided by informant no. 5, who was herself a journalist in that unit.

65. See Calhoun (1994, 94–97), Perry (1992), Walder (1991a, 1991b), Walder and Gong (1993), and Wang Shaoguang (1990b). For example, Walder (1991a, 467) evaluates worker participation during the movement in one of his articles thus: "In May of 1989 urban workers burst suddenly onto the Chinese political scene. They marched by the tens of thousands in huge Beijing street demonstrations, in delegations from hundreds of workplaces—acts repeated on a smaller scale in cities throughout the country. While organized strikes were rare, small groups of dissident workers formed dozens of independent unions and other political groups from Sichuan to Shanghai, and from Inner Mongolia to Guangdong. The most visible, the Beijing Workers' Autonomous Union, set up in mid-April, had an organized presence on Tiananmen Square beginning in the week of the student hunger strike, claimed thousands of members, published dozens of handbills and political manifestos, and played an important role in organizing demonstrations after the declaration of martial law. The workers' unprecedented political response helped transform a vibrant student movement into the most severe popular challenge to Communist Party rule since 1949."

66. In the early period of the movement, Tiananmen Square became a place for public speeches. Many Beijing residents, including workers, went to the Square in the evening. Some Beijing residents even made occasional speeches along with the students or vowed to establish some new organizations. Their activities had no impact in the Square, however.

67. See Walder and Gong (1993, 7).

68. Many other students were involved in the Beijing Workers' Autonomous Union. For example, a movement activist from Qinghua University in a subsequently published diary wrote that the Beijing

documents of the Beijing Workers' Autonomous Union were prepared by Li and other students.[69] Since the Beijing Workers' Autonomous Union's rhetoric was thus to a great degree crafted by the students, it is misleading to argue, on the basis of the Worker Union's published documents, for the workers' significance during the movement.[70]

Furthermore, most of the resources used to run the Beijing Workers' Autonomous Union were obtained from or through students. Zhou Yongjun recalled how he helped establish a broadcasting station for the Beijing Workers' Autonomous Union: "The Stone Company helped me; they gave me 10,000 yuan. Adding to it some 'run-for-life' money that a Hong Kong journalist had given me, I bought a generator. I then installed a broadcasting station on a bus and gave it to the Beijing Workers' Autonomous Union. . . . Because of its broadcasting station, the Workers' Autonomous Union achieved a prominent position among other organizations."[71] Li Lu remembered: "Whether it be the Workers' Picket Corps, the Beijing Citizen Picket Corps, or the Beijing City People Dare-to-Die Corps, students helped organize these groups and provided them with money. In particular, we assisted the Beijing Workers' Autonomous Union in its preparation and formation. Even their broadcasting equipment and announcer were from the Headquarters. At that time, we worked together every day. Their headquarters was very close to ours. We had very close contacts."[72]

A student leader whom I have interviewed gave a similar account of how another non-student movement organization was established:

> The Beijing Citizens' Autonomous Alliance was organized by Wan Xinjin, a young teacher in our university. He said that we needed to have such an organization and I agreed with him. After trying for a while he eventually established the organization and made himself the general commander. Between ten and twenty workers followed him. Financing the alliance depended entirely on me. They were unable to raise money because they were not good at making effective fundraising speeches (no. 60).

Workers' Autonomous Union held a press conference at the Square on June 1 in which, of the three people in charge, one was from People's University and another from Beijing Agricultural University—only Han Dongfang was a worker (*China News Digest* 1994, 2.).

69. See Black and Munro (1993, 222) for how Li Jinjin helped the Beijing Workers' Autonomous Union to prepare various documents.

70. For example, Walder and Gong (1993) have cited the Workers' Union's published documents to argue for its importance.

71. Zhou Yongjun (1993, 58).

72. Li Lu (*Huigu yu Fansi* 1993, 371).

When the Beijing Workers' Autonomous Union formally announced its establishment, its declaration was read by Li Jinjin.[73] Li also asked Zhang Boli for help. Zhang let them use the broadcasting equipment belonging to the Headquarters, sent picketers to maintain order for them, and even provided food for the workers who attended the ceremony.[74] Even the banner with the giant characters "The Beijing Workers' Autonomous Union" on it was prepared by Zhang Lun, another student leader.[75]

On May 29, three members of the Beijing Workers' Autonomous Union were arrested. On May 30 the Beijing Workers' Autonomous Union confronted Beijing security forces, demanding their immediate release. This action caught the attention of the Western media and has been used to argue for the importance and strength of the Beijing Workers' Autonomous Union during the movement.[76] Yet the action was actually initiated by students and involved heavy student participation. When students at Tiananmen Square were informed about the arrests, they went to factories to mobilize workers to rescue the three workers. However, their attempts were unsuccessful.[77] Therefore, on the morning of May 30 Li Jinjin and Han Dongfang led some people to the Beijing Public Security Bureau to demand an immediate release of the three workers. Among their large number of followers, only around twenty were workers.[78] Meanwhile, students also went to Tiananmen Square to gather more supporters.[79] My informant (no. 60) recalled:

[Some students] came and told me that the Beijing Public Security Bureau had arrested several workers and asked us to go there and demand an immediate release. At the moment, there were only nine students in our tent. I led them to the Public Security Bureau. On the way, we made a lot of fuss to attract people. When we arrived, several thousand people had followed us. I made a speech and demanded that they release the workers. Some people from the Bureau came out to take photographs. They asked us to send in representatives. However, I did not know when, who, and how many people were kidnapped. I also had no idea about the overall plan of this action. Thus I refused to go in. I said that I wanted to go in, but I dared not. . . . [Instead] I asked them to send people out. I said that I could guarantee their

73. Xiong Yan (1992) recalled that it was he who read the declaration.

74. Zhang Boli (1994a).

75. Zhang Lun (*Huigu yu Fansi* 1993, 297–98).

76. Walder and Gong (1993, 13–14).

77. Yan and Li (1989, 132).

78. Black and Monro (1993, 229).

79. Zhang Boli (1994a) recalled that Wang Chaohua also brought many students there. Their arrival raised the number of protestors at the Beijing Public Security Bureau to several thousand.

safety. This went on for over two hours. Meanwhile, I asked some people to look for Zhou Yongjun to ask who had been kidnapped and how. . . . After some time, I saw a large crowd of people coming from the east. I saw flags of at least twenty universities. In the front was Xiong Yan. When they arrived Xiong announced "I am Xiong Yan. I am the general commander of tonight's action. We have the following demands . . . " Once Xiong declared himself the general commander, I left the scene.[80]

In sum, if we examine the role of the Beijing Workers' Autonomous Union through such criteria as leadership, sources of material resources, and major activities and participants, it becomes obvious that the union was basically only an appendage of the student movement.

THE FINANCIAL RESOURCES OF THE TIANANMEN SQUARE OCCUPATION

At Tiananmen Square, over three thousand hunger strikers needed shelter, drink, medicine, and medical support; the encamped students and the students on picket lines also needed food; students from other provinces were arriving in Beijing on an ever larger scale; student leaders needed communications equipment and printing materials. Where did the money come from for all this? An answer to this question will help us to understand the nature of the movement and of the state-society relationship behind the movement.

It is not easy to estimate how much was needed to run Tiananmen Square each day. Liang Er, the head of the Financial Department of the Beijing Students' Autonomous Union, recalled that they spent a maximum of 200,000 yuan a day in cash on their logistics.[81] Considering that the Headquarters had its own financial system, that each university had independent financial sources, and that many donations were in kind, the occupation might easily have consumed several million yuan a day at its peak.

During the hunger strike the major financial resources were donations from individual Chinese as well as aid from government and public institutions. The following report from *Guangming Daily* gives us a clue to how people in Beijing financially supported the Tiananmen Square occupation:

80. The validity of this narrative can be cross-verified by Xiong Yan's brief mention of the event (Xiong 1992): "On May 30, after the Beijing Public Security Bureau arrested three workers, I mobilized students and organized a sit-in in front of the Bureau." Because Xiong Yan claimed his leadership publicly, the event was even recorded in a government document (Leng and Miao 1989, 187).

81. Liang Er (*Huigu yu Fansi* 1993, 244).

At the headquarters of the Beijing Students' Autonomous Union, located at the south-east corner of the Monument to the People's Heroes, a massive number of people were pushing their way through in order to contribute money or food to students. They included workers, peasants, teachers, government cadres, and private businessmen. A cadre from the Ministry of Culture donated three hundred and sixty yuan; a vice division commander in the PLA donated a thousand; Lei Jieqiong, the chair of China's Progressive Democracy Party, donated a thousand. . . . Workers from Beijing General Textile Company collectively donated ten thousand. . . .

Meanwhile the All-China Federation of Trade Unions and All-China Social Welfare Lottery Fundraising Committee had each donated 100,000 yuan, and the All-China Hardware and Mineral Products Import-export Corporation had donated 50,000 yuan.

Our journalists also saw fast food and bread sent by restaurants and private businessmen; timbers from a timber factory, bundles of plastic films from the Institute of Planning and Designing under the Ministry of Light Industry, and even a whole truckload of mattresses from somewhere.[82]

Perhaps surprisingly, a huge amount of resources actually came from the state or from public institutions. The following description by Nan Lin may give us a picture of this:

With the tacit approval of the government and the command of the city government, the Red Cross, city hospitals and clinics, and ambulance services coordinated the transport of the fainting strikers to hospitals and clinics, then returning them to the Square. On May 17, eighty Red Cross members, sixteen ambulances, and two buses were permanently stationed at Tiananmen to provide health and emergency services not only to the strikers but also the encamped students. On May 18, the sixth day into the hunger strike, more than 3,500 trips had been provided by the ambulance services. Because of impending weather (rain was expected), the city government, on the recommendation of the city Red Cross, dispatched seventy buses to Tiananmen to provide shelter for the strikers.[83]

Another instance of government support occurred on May 17, when the Beijing Police answered an emergency call from students of Qinghua University and sent several thousand police to help student picketers keep the order along the life-lines.[84] Similarly, although Li Lu has written that he stole many bottles of

---

82. Wu et al. (1989, 296).

83. See Lin (1992, 85–86). According to Zhang Boli, there were eighty buses (Zhang Boli 1994b, 76). On the same day, students also received over 10,000 raincoats and much other rain gear (Wu et al. 1989, 264).

84. Wu et al. (1989, 268–69).

normal saline from a hospital to feed fellow hunger strikers,[85] in fact, most of the bottles of normal saline were provided by the government. By May 16 the Beijing Emergency Treatment Center alone had already sent 5,000 bottles of normal saline to the Square.[86]

Major universities in Beijing also made great efforts to help the students. Liu Xiaobo has recalled:

> I asked the general secretary of the CCP and the head of the General Affairs Department in Beijing Normal University to send quilts, winter jackets, umbrellas, raincoats, boots, and other necessities to Tiananmen Square as soon as possible. General Secretary Fang Fukang quickly came with a few other people. They pitched tents for us. They also brought much rain gear and things to keep the students warm during the cold night.[87]

The same university authorities, in response to the call of student activist Liang Er, let students use the cars and buses that belonged to the university for free. The university also supplied a huge amount of food for students who had traveled to Beijing from other provinces.[88]

The abundance of monetary and material resources could also be seen from the tremendous waste in the Square. All the informants who mention the issue tell similar stories. However, none of the accounts is as striking as Liu Xiaobo's:

> [In Tiananmen Square] almost all the drinks were thrown away before they were emptied. Countless bottles of normal saline were thrown away while almost full. Half or a whole boxes of fast food, half or whole loaves of bread, and other foodstuff were spread everywhere. The cigarettes that students smoked became more and more expensive, as did the liquor they drank. . . . There was no way to probe into corruption and squandering due to the lack of financial control. The amount of garbage itself testified to the wasteful habits. Different movement organizations and various hunger strike groups constantly fought, sometimes physically, to get more materials. Every group was desperately trying to get more. They would rather store things up now and throw them away later than share with others. . . . I saw with my own eyes a female student who one time opened thirteen bottles of normal saline and threw them away one by one after only a few sips.[89]

85. Li Lu (1990, 136).

86. Wu et al. (1989, 216). Li Ximing (Wu et al. 1989, 332), a top government official, has also described how the government provided material resources for hunger strikers.

87. Liu Xiaobo (1992, 129).

88. Liang Er (*Huigu yu Fansi* 1993, 181).

89. Liu Xiaobo (1992, 142).

Obviously, extensive monetary and material support from ordinary Chinese, the government, and public institutions sustained the Tiananmen Square occupation. The government made great efforts to help because they did not want to see students die or an epidemic break out in a congested and extremely unsanitary Tiananmen Square. Yet public institutions had provided more than what the government intended.

MOVEMENT ORGANIZATIONS AND LEADERSHIP

During the hunger strike conflicts between student leaders in the Headquarters and other movement activists were intense. For instance, on May 14 Feng Congde and several other students from Beijing University established a broadcasting station in the Square, which became the mouthpiece of the Headquarters.[90] However, on the next day, students from Qinghua University constructed a more powerful broadcasting station known as the Voice of the Student Movement.[91] Student leaders of the Autonomous Union group had more control over this station. Conflicts between these two groups never stopped. "The two stations turned on and started to broadcast at the same time. They both made announcements and gave orders. Their broadcasts interfered with each other."[92] Major leaders from these two centers, Feng Congde and Zhou Fengsuo, twice even fought physically.

After the hunger strike started, the Dialogue Delegation gradually lost its influence, and the Beijing Students' Autonomous Union's influence over the movement declined. The hunger strike leaders achieved domination over the movement. However, the hunger strike leaders were also divided. There were two types of hunger strike leaders. The first type, including Wuer Kaixi and to a less extent Wang Dan, had taken the hunger strike as a political action. To them, an event such as Gorbachev's visit was a good occasion to boost the movement and to push the government toward more concessions. To other leaders, however, the hunger strike was just a means of expression and a chance to sacrifice for a better China. They did not care much about Gorbachev's state

90. Feng Congde (*Huigu yu Fansi* 1993, 151) has described how this broadcasting center was established. Li Lu (*Huigu yu Fansi* 1993, 138) claims: "Our Headquarters was maintained mainly because of Feng Congde's broadcasting center. Without the broadcasting center, the Headquarters would have existed only in name."

91. One of the student initiators of the broadcasting station has given a detailed account on its formation and activities (*China News Digest* 1994).

92. Zheng (1993, 95).

visit and the accompanying arrival of a large number of foreign journalists,[93] and they decided to continue the hunger strike until the government completely accepted their demands. The nature of the hunger strike (by which I mean the amount of personal sacrifice involved) determined that those students who joined the hunger strike tended to belong to the latter group. This was reflected by the initial hunger strike mobilization at Beijing University, which contributed the majority of the hardcore hunger strikers. As will be discussed in chapter 9, the mobilization at Beijing University was not very successful until Chai Ling recast the purpose of the strike from "for democracy" to "to see the true face of the government and test the consciousness of the Chinese."

Therefore, though student leaders such as Wuer Kaixi and Wang Dan played a crucial role in initiating the hunger strike, they were, from the outset, unable to control it. In fact, because of their relative flexibility in negotiating and in dealing with government officials, their credentials among hunger strikers quickly declined. After the hunger strike began, the Square was controlled by idealists such as Chai Ling, Feng Congde, Zhang Boli, and Li Lu. "Dedication," "Reform needs sacrifice," "China needs a second Tan Sitong,"[94] "We face death, fight for life": such slogans dominated the discourse of the hunger strike students. Some hunger strikers even refused to drink water and planned to burn themselves alive. As a result, such important events of this period as Gorbachev's state visit and the concomitant arrival of a large number of foreign journalists failed to make a fundamental impact on the course of the movement. This was because the students who dominated the Tiananmen Square occupation in this period never treated those events in the first place as political opportunities.

Even student leaders in the Headquarters were not the most radical ones. Although they were extremely idealistic, their leadership position caused them to have more concerns than the rest of the hunger strikers. Therefore, they sometimes also thought of ending the hunger strike to avoid possible unintended consequences. However, the Headquarters leaders could not really control fellow fasting students. Zheng Yi, who was in the Headquarters from May 16, observed:

93. This was indicated by the behavior of student leaders. For example, while Wuer Kaixi and Wang Dan attended dozens of press conferences and interviews with foreign journalists, student leaders such as Li Lu, Feng Congde, and Chai Ling participated in very few of them.

94. Tan Sitong was a key figure in the Hundred Day Reform (1898) during the late Qing dynasty. When the reform failed and all key figures were ordered to be arrested, Tan had a chance to go into hiding, but he refused to do so. He said that he wanted to dedicate his life to awakening more people. Tan became a legendary figure after being killed.

Although the leaders at the Headquarters had endless meetings, the real decision-making power was not in the hands of these earthshaking young leaders. . . . Whenever the hunger strikers were asked about the idea of ending the fasting, the answer was a flat no. One night, that the hunger strike should end became the dominant opinion among the leaders. However, this was impossible to implement. Hunger strikers suspected that students in the Headquarters were going to sell out the fruit they had struggled to obtain. The government's negligence had pushed hunger strikers to make up their minds to fight till death. . . . Many students even claimed that if the Headquarters decided to end the hunger strike, they would immediately kill themselves. The mood to fight with their lives was spreading and intensifying every hour. A common identity nurtured by the already 100-hour long hunger strike also unified the 3,000 hunger strikers. As long as one student refused to eat, the rest would follow.[95]

However, though student leaders had lost effective control over the direction of the movement, Tiananmen Square became more hierarchical and orderly as the movement went on. Many student leaders were now followed by several bodyguards to protect them. Picket lines were formed so that ambulances could enter and leave the Square quickly.[96] Along with the picket lines was an elaborate security system. People were no longer able to move freely inside the Square without valid passes, which could be updated many times in a day. Even leaders and activists of the movement had difficulties moving around.[97]

END OF THE HUNGER STRIKE

After the negotiation with students failed, the conflicts among top government leaders intensified. Between May 15 and 17, the CCP Central Committee held a series of meetings. In these meetings, most leaders except for Zhao Ziyang wanted to end the movement by martial law (chapter 7). After May 17 the

95. Zheng (1993, 70).

96. Li Lu (*Huigu yu Fansi* 1993, 139) has claimed that the picket lines were mainly his effort, while Calhoun (1994, 73) has reported that they were largely the work of Zhang Lun. During that period, almost every university had its own pickets, while some pickets had independent origins. Although the pickets of different universities were coordinated, they might not necessarily be led by a single person or organization. As informant 3, a student who acted as a picketer, told me: "I did not know who was taking charge of the pickets, but we all knew what to do. There were some people who came over and asked us to do this or that, but it was not always the same people. Sometimes I also thought of something and went to tell other people what to do. The key was that if you had ideas, you shared them with others."

97. Liu Xiaobo (1992, 131–32) has described how this elaborate security system worked; student leader Liang Er (*Huigu Yu Fansi* 1993, 241) has recalled his difficulty in passing through some security lines.

government again approached students. However, unlike the earlier attempts, these later contacts were aimed not so much at reaching an agreement with the students but at placating the public.[98] For example, at the meeting between Li Peng and hunger strike organizers on May 18, while the students still demanded a dialogue and a positive evaluation of the movement as preconditions for ending the hunger strike, Li Peng was only interested in issues of how to end the hunger strike and send hunger strikers to the hospital.[99]

By May 19 most student leaders knew that the government was going to declare martial law. Therefore, many student leaders and activists wished to end the hunger strike so as not to give the government any excuse for employing martial law. On the late afternoon of May 19, two intellectuals went to the Square and found Zhang Boli.[100] They brought Zhang to the Workers' Cultural Palace, where some fifty intellectuals were waiting. They told Zhang that martial law was going to start at 12:00 A.M. that night. They suggested that the hunger strike be ended immediately so that the government would have no excuse to resort to martial law. Zhang Boli agreed to persuade the other student leaders at the Headquarters. Meanwhile he asked the intellectuals to prepare for them a declaration marking the end of the hunger strike.

When Zhang Boli went back, he discussed thus with Li Lu and Chai Ling. Both of them agreed with him. At 7:00 P.M., they held a meeting to vote for the issue. About two hundred students came to the meeting, some of them handpicked by Zhang Boli to come and support him. The meeting was held inside a big bus. Zhao Boli particularly ordered those who guarded the bus not to let Wuer Kaixi in. He was concerned that if Wuer did not agree with him, his charisma could reverse the opinion. Zhang Boli spoke first. He emphasized that many people were going to die if the hunger strike did not stop. He did not convey his exact intentions because he believed that the threat of martial law was still a secret.[101] Others wanted to speak after Zhang. However, Zhang only

98. Zhao Ziyang's visit to hunger strike students on the morning of May 19 is not counted because it was obviously for a different purpose (see chapter 7).

99. Detailed reports on the meeting appeared in many sources. For English versions, see Oksenberg, Sullivan, and Lambert (1990, 269–82) or Han and Hua (1990, 242–46).

100. The following story is based mainly on Zhang Boli's account (*Huigu yu Fansi* 1993, 195; Zhang 1994c, 46–47). I also incorporated the accounts of Li Lu, Chai Ling, Feng Congde, and Liu Yan in *Huigu yu Fansi* (1993, 164–70, 199–201, 204, and 201–203).

101. Around the time of the meeting, the Headquarters broadcasting center had already broadcast news reports that announced: "At 12:45 tonight the government will send troops to Tiananmen Square" (*Bajiu Zhongguo Minyun Ziliaoce* 1991, 185). Therefore, most students would have known the news of impending martial law.

called on students whom he had already lined up before the meeting. Then when Zhang asked students to vote on the proposal, the majority of participants voted in favor of ending the hunger strike.[102]

Student leaders then organized a meeting to announce the decision to the rest of the hunger strikers. Chai Ling presided over the meeting. As soon as she announced the decision, many students stood up and accused the leaders of selling out the fasting students. Feng Congde, Chai Ling's husband, also came forward, arguing that this decision was invalid and that another vote should take place. The student leaders then fought bitterly. Li Lu and Wang Wen even fought physically. Eventually, Feng resigned his position in the Headquarters and went out to hold another vote on the same issue. He got the opposite result: "I held another vote after I left. . . . Over eighty universities sent representatives. At least eighty percent of those students said that between eighty to a hundred percent of their students did not want to end the hunger strike."[103]

It would be senseless to try and judge which vote was more valid. Most hunger strike students still fasted after the announcement. Nevertheless, Zhang Boli immediately informed Beijing journalists that the students had ended the hunger strike. Half an hour later, at about 9:30 P.M., the CCTV stopped normal programming to broadcast the news. Student leaders thought that this was a great victory because it illegitimatized the use of martial law.

Then, at 10:00 P.M., the official loudspeakers at Tiananmen Square turned on to broadcast live a special meeting of top state leaders, Beijing municipal leaders, and army cadres. In the meeting, Li Peng vowed that the government would "take firm and decisive measures to end the turmoil to safeguard the CCP's leadership and the socialist system." Yang Shangkun stated that: "To maintain social order in the capital and restore the normal routine, we have no alternative but to call some troops to Beijing."[104] That same night troops started to approach Beijing from the suburbs. Early the next morning, martial law was

---

102. The same evening another group of student leaders, including Wuer Kaixi, Liu Yan, Wang Dan, Ma Shaofang, Cheng Zhen, Liang Er, Shen Tong, Xiang Xiaoji, and many others, also had a meeting that decided to end the hunger strike. Liu Yan recalled that she and Wuer went to see Yan Mingfu in the afternoon (*Huigu yu Fansi* 1993, 201–202). Yan Mingfu told them that martial law would be declared that night. Wuer asked Liu Yan to go to the Square to find all the student leaders that she could and ask them to come to the United Front Work Department to have a meeting. In that meeting, Yan told all students the news of martial law and asked them to end the hunger strike. Eventually, they all started to eat. When these students went back to Tiananmen Square, the meeting held by Zhang Boli was about to end. These two groups both appeared at the meeting that announced the end of the hunger strike. For other descriptions of the meeting at the United Front Work Department, see Shen Tong (1990, 287–88).

103. Feng Congde (*Huigu yu Fansi* 1993, 204).

104. For English versions of both speeches, see Han and Hua (1990, 255–58).

formally declared. Some students fasted until May 20, but attention had turned to the coming troops.

From Martial Law to Military Repression

POPULAR RESISTANCE

While the government's special meeting was still in process, martial law troops moved on Beijing from all directions. By May 20 about seven or eight divisions of ten to fifteen thousand troops each had attempted to enter the city by railway, subway, and, mostly, by highway.[105] Most Beijing residents were outraged by the news of martial law and the army advancement. They massed to block the troops and protect the students. On the major roads, people used every available material, such as sewer tubes, concrete posts, bicycle-lane dividers, garbage bins, steel bars, and buses, to build barricades.[106] Such popular resistance usually started with a few students or residents who were walking on the road and spotted army movement. They either directly went to block the troops or went to inform residents nearby. People then arrived by the hundreds, thousands, and then tens of thousands, eventually outnumbering the soldiers.

At this stage most of the soldiers were unarmed. They simply stayed where they were after being stopped. When the people stopped the army, they went over or even climbed up into the military trucks to inform soldiers about the "truth" of the movement and to ask them to leave. The soldiers appeared bewildered by the popular reaction. Facing harangues or even ridicule, they generally kept silent. When they were asked why they had come to Beijing, their answers ranged from "to join a military exercise" to "to guard Tiananmen Square" to even "to make a movie." Many of them told the people that they had not read anything for a week and knew very little about what had happened in Beijing after the start of the hunger strike.[107]

In most cases, the soldiers were nicely treated. Because of the barricades, the logistics of the army broke down. Local residents and students made efforts to

---

105. See Brook (1992, ch. 3) on the troop movements during this period.

106. Since most of the armies entered by highway, I focus on what happened on the highways.

107. Most published sources have taken these answers literally. In fact, it was likely that some soldiers just played innocent to avoid conflict. For example, a low-ranking officer from Dongbei Military Region wrote that they had watched the movement on a video before going to Beijing (Gao Zirong 1989, 8). During martial law, many soldiers also waved the V-sign or shouted pro-movement slogans to make their infiltration easier or to lessen the conflict (Chen Guishui 1989, 13).

send food and drink to soldiers. Moreover, in places close to the university district where students dominated the resistance, students even held parties to entertain them.[108] However, soldiers were also humiliated by some young Beijing residents. "All the soldiers are bastards!" "Go home, your mothers are dying!" "Your sisters are being raped by turns, hurry home!" Many soldiers were bruised by this sort of verbal abuse,[109] and tension and resentment started to build up among them.

Occasional violence also erupted at this stage. The most serious incident happened in the Fengtai area, where at noon on May 20 a few hundred policemen turned their clubs on a crowd. Forty-five people were hurt in the conflict, among whom three were seriously wounded.[110] In the same region, on the evening of May 22, soldiers from the 113th Division of the 38th Army were starting to withdraw, as had been agreed upon by troop and student negotiators, when a few people in the crowd shouted: "Beat them, beat these soldiers to death!" "Do not let them enter the city!" Bricks were cast at the soldiers. Early the next morning similar conflicts occurred, again in the same region. According to government sources, a total of 116 soldiers were wounded in these conflicts, and 29 were seriously injured.[111] The soldiers did not fight back, but they were very angry as a result.[112] After two days of stalemate, the government had to order the troops to withdraw on the morning of May 22. The popular resistance went on successfully.

The amazing fact is that this successful resistance was conducted with little coordination. To be sure, there were some efforts to coordinate the resistance. For example, on the night of May 19, several members of the Dialogue Delegation formed a Bureau of Coordination of Beijing Universities. The bureau owned a military map, donated by an army officer, and two hotlines. As an informant (no. 59) recalled, they received phone calls every three minutes reporting army movements. They then called each university asking them to send students to particular locations. On May 20, Wang Chaohua also sent small contingents to several places where a large number of soldiers were stopped. The Beijing Students' Autonomous Union later even produced a map of Beijing showing troop positions and major barricades, and the union assigned each

108. Informant no. 63 joined a party of this kind near the Summer Palace.

109. See Yang Qingfu (1989) for a description of how soldiers were humiliated or even beaten by local youths during this period.

110. Wu Ren (1990b, 69).

111. Ibid., 75.

112. Ren Bin (1989).

university an area to take charge of.[113] Finally, members of the Flying Tigers—
a motorbike team loosely formed by some private businessmen—were also
highly conspicuous because of the awful noise their bikes made while traveling
through the city. On the way they often passed news of troop movements as
well as rumors.

However, these coordination efforts were largely ad hoc, and the role they
played in the popular resistance was minimal. The following narratives show
how Beijing residents were typically mobilized into a popular resistance:

> I was at home that evening. At midnight, I was awakened by extremely loud noises.
> Outside somebody shouted that the troops were coming and asked neighbors to
> block the military carriers. A lot of people went out. . . . Someone also shouted
> "Please bring wet towels to protect yourselves from tear gas." People then went
> back to fetch towels. When we went out to the street, we saw some concrete sewer
> pipes laid along the roadside. We immediately pushed them to the middle. That
> night, a huge number of people went out. All my family went out as well. Many stu-
> dents were at the Square, some of them the children of this neighborhood. Even if
> their own children were not at the Square, people still went out because we all felt
> that the students would be beaten if the soldiers entered the Square (no. 8).

Along with the Beijing residents, students and teachers also spontaneously initiated various actions. A young teacher (no. 36) told me how a group of them
had been involved in the action:

> On May 19 we knew that the army would come that night. Many young teachers
> came to my dormitory. We discussed what we should do when the troops came.
> Eventually we decided to persuade the soldiers to withdraw. We decided to write a
> statement, print it on handbills, and record it on a cassette. When we met the troops
> we could give them the handbills and turn on our cassette players. . . .
>
> In the night, we headed toward Liuliqiao. . . . When we arrived at Liuliqiao, we
> found that the troops had arrived and that some people were already there trying
> to stop the troops. We went over and turned on our cassette players. Somehow, we
> were separated and I was now alone. Then I met two students from our university.
> We three became a new team. The two students told me that there were more
> troops in Babaoshan, so we went there.

---

113. Wang Chaohua (*Huigu Yu Fansi* 1993, 212).

Nine of my informants talked about their personal experiences on the night of May 19, but none of them indicated that they were mobilized by, or coordinated through, any organizations.

OUTSIDE STUDENTS AND MOVEMENT DYNAMICS

After the hunger strike began, students from all over the country began arriving in Beijing in large numbers. Between May 16 and 26, around 172,000 outside students arrived at Beijing by train, while only 86,000 left.[114] Considering that outside students also went to Beijing by bus, air, bicycle, or even on foot, the numbers should be even larger. Therefore, after May 20, when more and more Beijing students felt tired and left, the Square gradually became dominated by outside students.

Most outside students got free rides to Beijing by persuading or even forcing the officials at a station to let them on a train. If this did not work, some would even lie down on the tracks to stop the train. As an informant (no. 27) recalled, the Tianjin railway station even added several special lines on May 17 so that anyone could ride for free to Beijing. Over 10,000 Tianjin students went to Beijing that day.

A large number of outside students stayed in the Square while in Beijing. However, an even larger number of outside students spent their nights in university dormitories with new acquaintances or old high school classmates. Most of my student informants remembered that there were some outside students living in their own or nearby dormitories. One informant (no. 33) told me that by late May half of the students staying in the dormitories of his university were outside students. Another informant (no. 68) told me that he himself had arranged accommodations for more than a hundred outside students.

The arrival of a large number of outside students made voluntary withdrawal from Tiananmen Square very difficult. For the most part, outside students came to Beijing for one of two reasons: they were local activists who wished to support the movement in Beijing, or they simply wanted to take a free trip to the capital. Either way, they were reluctant to return home after only a couple

---

114. See Wu et al. (1989, 474). The government may well overestimate the outside students' return rate. During late May, every outside student could get a free return ticket from the Beijing railway station just by showing his/her university ID. This could be what the government statistics were based on. However, many Beijing students whose home town was not Beijing took advantage of this policy, borrowing a university ID from an outside student from their home town to get a free ticket to visit home. One of my informants (no. 10) told me that he got a free ticket back to Guangzhou this way.

of days. Thus those who still remained in the Square were either energetic new-comers or committed radicals.

STUDENT LEADERSHIP DURING THE EARLY PERIOD OF MARTIAL LAW

After martial law was declared, Tiananmen Square was no longer the center of attention, and the hunger strike became meaningless. By noon on May 20, even the most stubborn hunger strikers had started to eat, and most of them had also returned to school. The hunger strike leaders were still lingering at the Square, but they did nothing to organize students or Beijing residents to block the troops.[115] Overwhelmed by the number of troops, the hunger strike leaders were in a gray mood. On May 21 rumors led them to believe that the troops would fight their way to the Square that night. Therefore, all the major leaders except for Li Lu, including Chai Ling, Feng Congde, and Zhang Boli, went into hiding.

The night of May 21 was nerve-wracking for the students remaining in the Square.[116] However, the troops, instead of arriving, started to withdraw on May 22. The event immediately changed the students' mood as well as their es-timate of the future of the movement. Zhang Boli described the change:

> On May 20 a very important person told me that a massacre would start that night. . . . He persuaded us to leave the Square immediately to avoid bloodshed. . . . He told me that the army had produced 10,000 Beijing road maps. From the num-ber, I estimated around 10,000 squads or platoons of troops were coming! We were all terrified. However, we did not ask students or local residents to block the troops. . . . On the second day, we all received some emergency money and ran away. I went to hide at Xu Gang's home. . . . To my surprise, the troops did not come and everything was as usual. When some people called and informed me about this, I said that it was really good news. If they did not repress us this time, everything would be fine. We then discussed what we should do immediately. Finally, we all arrived at the same conclusion. If the troops dared not to use force this time, it would be more difficult for them to repress us by force later on. Guided by this be-lief, we went back to the Square.[117]

Not just the student leaders but also most students and Beijing residents became optimistic; that the army would not shoot civilians became a common belief.

115. Zhang Boli (*Huigu yu Fansi* 1993, 207).
116. See Wu et al. (1989, 364) for the mood of the students in the Square that night.
117. Zhang Boli (*Huigu yu Fansi* 1993, 207–208).

However, on the late afternoon of May 22, when the hunger strike leaders went back to the Square, they found that it no longer belonged to them. In the days after the Headquarters had stopped functioning the influence of the Beijing Students' Autonomous Union had increased, and many new organizations had sprung up. Most seriously, while the hunger strike leaders were in hiding, Wang Chaohua went around tent by tent to persuade students to leave. When students in each tent agreed, she then asked a representative to sign a paper. By the time that the hunger strike leaders went back to the Square, students from over two hundred universities had consented to leave.[118] To reduce the influence of the Beijing Students' Autonomous Union in the Square thus became the most urgent issue for the hunger strike leaders.

Since Wang Chaohua now had a sheet that contained signatures from representatives of over two hundred universities, the first thing that the hunger strike leaders did was to obtain the sheet. Zhang Boli tricked Wang into letting him see the sheet and then refused to return it.[119] Meanwhile, the hunger strike group organized a meeting on the night of May 22. They managed to get "representatives" from eighty-nine universities.[120] During the meeting, they bashed the Beijing Students' Autonomous Union and other student organizations. Chai Ling declared:

> Since its founding, your Beijing Students' Autonomous Union has never done a single good thing. In particular, you occupy the leadership position without showing leadership quality. You were against the hunger strike from the very beginning. However, after the hunger strike started in spite of your objections, you moved your headquarters to the Square and expressed your support. I have absolutely no understanding of what you have done.[121]

Zhang Boli added:

> We are under martial law. The CCP Central Committee has established Martial Law Headquarters to command several hundred thousand soldiers to go against us. Yet, the situation in the Square is very disappointing. There are over ten student organizations in the Square, all claiming the highest command and all being irresponsible. The Beijing Students' Autonomous Union has only one leader, Wang

118. Ibid., 208.
119. Ibid.
120. The number was from Li Lu (1990, 175). Please note that during the movement, student leaders frequently manipulated meetings by various means. Therefore, the result could swing considerably depending on who had organized a meeting.
121. Chai Ling (*Huigu yu Fansi* 1993, 224).

Chaohua, in the Square; leaders of the Federation of Students from Outside Beijing are indulging in power struggles. They changed their general commander four times in a day and even wanted to take over the broadcasting center. If this goes on, even if the martial law troops do not attack us, we will defeat ourselves. . . . Therefore, I propose to establish a provisional headquarters to lead the Square for forty-eight hours. Meanwhile, the Beijing Students' Autonomous Union will pull back to Beijing University to rectify itself. After forty-eight hours, the provisional headquarters will end its mission and hand power back to the Beijing Students' Autonomous Union.[122]

According to Zhang,[123] most students in the meeting raised their hands to show support. Zhang then continued:

The leaders of the Hunger Strike Headquarters have already established their prestige, and are trusted by students. Therefore, leaders of the Headquarters should hold major positions in the Provisional Headquarters. The members of the standing committee include Chai Ling, Wang Dan, Wang Chaohua, Li Lu, Feng Congde, Guo Haifeng, and me. The Provisional Headquarters still has one commander, Chai Ling; three vice commanders, Zhang Boli, Li Lu, and Feng Congde; one secretary general, Guo Haifeng.[124]

The participants applauded to show their approval. Wang Chaohua was very upset after the meeting, accusing the hunger strike leaders of staging a coup. Zhang Boli replied: "The motion was passed. It is useless for you to try to get more support. This is democracy." [125] The hunger strike students reclaimed the Square.

THE JOINT FEDERATION

After the imposition of martial law, leading intellectuals further increased their presence in the movement. On the night of May 22 a meeting was held at the Square to discuss the possibility of establishing an organization that would combine all of the political forces that had emerged in the movement. Wang Juntao, Chen Ziming, Bao Zunxin, Yan Jiaqi, Liu Xiaobo, Wang Dan, Liang Er, and Zhang Lun were among the participants. Also in the meeting were some

---

122. Zhang Boli (1994d, 57).

123. Ibid.

124. Wang Chaohua was included in the leadership because the hunger strike leaders wanted her cooperation. See Zhang Boli (*Huigu yu Fansi* 1993, 209).

125. Ibid.

leaders of the newly established non-student organizations and a few individuals from Hong Kong.[126] Since the meeting was inconclusive, another meeting was called for the next day at an office in the Institute of Marxism-Leninism-Mao Zedong Thought. Hunger strike leader Chai Ling also attended the meeting. The participants there decided to establish an organization to coordinate and lead the movement. They named it the Joint Federation of All Circles in the Capital (hereafter the Joint Federation) to indicate its broad base, although in fact the organization was dominated by intellectuals and students.

The Joint Federation raised high expectations at the time of its establishment. Yet because the radical students did not trust the intellectuals and the intellectuals differed among themselves, the organization failed to control the movement.[127] A student leader (no. 69) remembered:

> In those days, I spent almost every day in the meetings of the Joint Federation. Each meeting lasted half a day or even a whole day. We discussed the current situation and exchanged information. Although many suggestions were made, the students at the Square never adopted them. So the meetings eventually turned out to consist of a group of people sitting in a big room making empty talk.

The intellectuals nevertheless did help the hunger strike leaders to establish their nominal authority inside the Square. After the withdrawal of the martial law troops, the intellectuals were for a short period no less optimistic than the students. They believed that the movement was "The Final Showdown between Darkness and Brightness."[128] They also believed that "As long as the flag of Tiananmen Square does not fall, a chain reaction will soon start all over the country."[129] They therefore supported the Tiananmen Square occupation and decided to establish a "Defending Tiananmen Square General Headquarters" (hereafter the General Headquarters) to manage the Square. They appointed Chai Ling as its general commander, Zhang Boli, Feng Congde, and Li Lu as its vice-commanders, and Guo Haifeng as its secretary general. The next day, May 24, the General Headquarters held an oath-taking rally at the Square. Wang Dan and Chai Ling presided over the meeting. In that meeting, Wang Dan announced the formation of the General Headquarters

126. See Black and Munro (1993, 206) and Zhang and Lao (*Huigu yu Fansi* 1993, 232).

127. See Li Lu (1990, 176–77) for hunger strike leaders' attitudes toward the intellectuals and the Joint Federation during this period.

128. This is the title of a statement prepared for the first Joint Federation meeting. It was drafted by Gan Yang.

129. Zheng (1993, 96).

and the appointment of the Joint Federation. The leaders of the Provisional Headquarters established the day before by the hunger strikers monopolized its leadership positions.[130]

According to the earlier agreement, the hunger strikers were to return the leadership of Tiananmen Square back over to the Beijing Students' Autonomous Union after forty-eight hours. This appointment therefore helped the hunger strike leaders defeat the leaders of the Beijing Students' Autonomous Union and achieve domination in the Square. Li Lu described Chai Ling as being thrilled when she came back from the meeting of the Joint Federation: "On May 23 Chai Ling came to me full of excitement. She told me that we no longer needed to worry about the forty-eight hour deadline . . . [because] we had now been appointed by an even larger organization called the Joint Federation of All Circles in the Capital."[131] Zhang Boli also used the appointment to fool Wang Chaohua. On the evening of May 24, with a rectified leadership and a new plan of the movement, Wang Chaohua went to Zhang Boli to demand that leadership in the Square be returned to the Autonomous Union. Zhang recalled:

> When Chaohua came to me, I avoided confronting her. I told her: "Go and discuss the issue with the Joint Federation." Chaohua said: "You have gone back on your words. We have rectified ourselves. We now have a nine-student leadership." . . . I replied: "First, you and I did have an agreement to return power to you after forty-eight hours. However, Chai Ling is the general commander and I am not. So, I can only make suggestions not decisions. Secondly, the Joint Federation is headed by Wang Dan. Wang Dan is currently our most renowned and powerful man. He now leads an organization that includes both intellectuals and students. I think their decisions carry greater authority. Moreover, I heard that the Joint Federation could make suggestions to as well as command the General Headquarters. I think that they have the mandate to lead us. . . . We do want to return the power back to you. It was the Joint Federation that started another organization."[132]

Thus, by supporting the student leaders of the hunger strike group, the intellectuals helped the continuation of the Tiananmen Square occupation. Afterwards, although the General Headquarters fell far short in commanding the Square, it did become its single most important symbol.

130. On one occasion Li Lu denied that the leaders of the General Headquarters were appointed by the Joint Federation (*Huigu yu Fansi* 1993, 238), while he elsewhere acknowledged the appointment (ibid., 219–20). Here, I adopt Lao Mu (ibid., 272–74) and Zhang Boli's (1994a, 59) version of the story. This is not just because of Li's inconsistency. Lao Mu attended the meeting, and Zhang Boli had the appointment sheet after the meeting, whereas Li Lu did not attend the meeting.

131. Li Lu (*Huigu yu Fansi* 1993, 219–20).

132. Zhang Boli (*Huigu yu Fansi* 1993, 210–11).

TO WITHDRAW OR NOT TO WITHDRAW

By late May it had become more and more clear that the Tiananmen Square occupation had created many problems and that if continued would lead to a
head-on confrontation between the people and the government. At this stage,
most intellectuals and Beijing students believed that the students should leave
the Square.[133] However, neither the Joint Federation nor the Beijing Students'
Autonomous Union could control the students there. The fate of the movement was now in the hands of those who refused to leave.

On May 27 the Joint Federation held a meeting. Whereas in previous Joint
Federation meetings the participants virtually could not agree on anything, this
time all of them, including Chai Ling and Feng Congde, voted that the students should leave the Square.[134] They decided to hold a large-scale demonstration to celebrate their victory and then withdraw from the Square on May 30.
It seemed that the deadlock between students and the government could be
loosened. Many were greatly relieved. However, Chai Ling and Feng Congde
changed their minds. In the press conference that evening, Chai Ling claimed
that the meeting had been a plot and that they had voted for the motion only
because of pressure from the rest of the people in the meeting. She also announced that her General Headquarters had decided to withdraw from the
Joint Federation. People were disappointed. Three Hong Kong journalists expressed their distress in a report: "Although the proposal [to withdraw from
the Square] was passed by a majority vote, it has no force. What surprises us is
that the suggestions of various movement organizations, including the decision
of the highest-level organization—the Joint Federation—must have the final
approval of the Defending Tiananmen Square General Headquarters. The majority must follow a minority, which is absurd." [135]

How could this happen? In general, Chai Ling was infamous for changing
her mind, first saying one thing in a meeting and then saying something else
in front of the public.[136] This time, however, it seemed that Li Lu had influenced Chai Ling. According to Li Lu himself, when Chai informed him about
the decision, he argued that the Joint Federation was only an organization
for coordination, and that the General Headquarters was obliged only to the
"Tiananmen Square Parliament" (the term will be explained later). In his view
the Joint Federation's decision was in fact undemocratic because two days ear-

---

133. For the changing mood of Beijing residents, also see Wu et al. (1989, 533–34).
134. For other details about the meeting, see Liu Xiaobo (1992, 179–81).
135. Zhao, Ge, and Si (1990, 135).
136. Both Wang Chaohua (1993, 31) and another student leader (no. 69) report having this impression.

lier the Tiananmen Square Parliament had voted for continued occupation.[137] Yet according to Chai Ling, Li Lu persuaded her by warning her that the government had been colluding with the Joint Federation people, trying every possible means to trick the students out of the Square.[138]

Li Lu's objection, of course, was just an excuse. Only four days earlier, when Chai Ling had excitedly told Li Lu that they were no longer obliged to return power to the Beijing Autonomous Union because the Joint Federation had appointed them as leaders of the General Headquarters, Li did not seem worried that the appointment was against democratic procedure or a government plot. Nevertheless, Li Lu's personal role in the fate of the movement should not be overstated. Even if Li had not raised his objections and Chai Ling had not changed her mind, the chances of leading students out of the Square were slim. To understand why, one must examine the micro-level decision-making in the Square. I will focus on the so-called "Meetings of the Tiananmen Square Parliament" that Li Lu played off against the Joint Federation.

Under martial law, numerous organizations held frequent meetings in the Square. Li Lu referred to the meetings called by the General Headquarters as "Meetings of the Tiananmen Square Parliament," [139] a phraseology that had given many scholars writing about the movement the false impression that some such stable institution existed inside the Square, its relation to the General Headquarters being similar to the relationship between the congress and the executive branch in a democratic nation. This is misleading, not least because few of the meeting participants were elected, but moreover because of the high fluidity of the participants in the General Headquarters' public meetings.

During late May around four hundred universities had camps in the Square (excluding the camps established by students from special technical schools). Yet at each of these meetings only some universities had their students present, and the universities that had students in the meeting changed every time.[140] More broadly, during the martial law period, especially given the arrival of huge numbers of students from outside Beijing, Tiananmen Square had a very high rate of turnover. A student who attended one day's meeting might the next day leave Tiananmen Square for good. The representatives from each university were also constantly changing. The constant change of meeting participants meant

---

137. Li's argument is summarized from his own narratives in Li Lu (1990, 179–180) and *Huigu yu Fansi* (1993, 238–40).

138. Chai Ling (*Huigu yu Fansi* 1993, 227).

139. Please note that no student leaders other than Li Lu used this term to describe those meetings.

140. For example, according to Li Lu himself, the May 22 meeting involved students from only 89 universities, but the May 24 meeting had over 400 representatives from 300 universities (Li Lu 1990, 175, 177).

that soon most of those who thought that the students should leave the Square had actually already left, while those who stayed at the Square and attended the so-called "Meetings of the Tiananmen Square Parliament" were more likely to be hardcore radicals and energetic newcomers from outside Beijing. Therefore, any effort at moderation became very difficult. Li Lu recalled that the debate over whether or not to end the Tiananmen Square occupation was the primary topic of every "Tiananmen Square Parliament Meeting," consuming most of their time. Yet the overwhelming majority of participants, most of whom were outside students, continually refused to leave.[141] Therefore, Li Lu and Chai Ling's rejection of the Joint Federation's decision might actually have been the only choice they had. Otherwise, the decision would not have been carried out in any case, and they themselves could have been ousted from the leadership. Wuer Kaixi made this point clearly when he was interviewed by Li Peier, a Hong Kong journalist, on June 2:

> We have thought about leaving the Square many times, but each time we changed our mind. For example, on May 27 we wanted to announce that we would leave the Square on May 30, but our decision was repudiated. Here, the most important reason was that students, especially the outside students, were not willing to leave. Anyone in charge had to support the Tiananmen Square occupation. Were you to ask students to leave, they would certainly try to get rid of you.[142]

In fact, Wuer Kaixi had been expelled from the leadership because he asked students to leave the Square on the early morning of May 22. Wang Chaohua was also squeezed out of the Square because she had persistently tried to bring the students out. On June 1, Lian Shengde, the head of the Federation of Students from Outside Beijing, also urged the students to leave the Square and was therefore dismissed from the leadership as well. To play the radical was the only way to keep one's influence.

HONG KONG MONEY

After martial law was declared, most state-owned factories and public institutions in China stopped their financial endorsement of the students. During the course of the movement, more and more student organizations and even individual students had engaged in fundraising activities.[143] Since none of the

---

141. Li Lu (*Huigu yu Fansi* 1993, 303).

142. Li Peier (1989, 211).

143. For example, one informant (no. 18) described to me how several of his schoolmates went out to raise money and used it to buy imported cigarettes for themselves.

student organizations had a good accounting system, scandals about student embezzlement and corruption were widespread.[144] By late May Beijing residents became reluctant to contribute money. During late May, individuals who brought donations in person from other cities or even from other countries were arriving at Beijing every day. Nevertheless, facing a chaotic student leadership and a widespread concern with student corruption, many people had to hold such money before finding a trustworthy person to whom to deliver it. Eventually, most of this money did not reach students in the Square.

Due to the intensive international media coverage after Gorbachev's state visit, overseas Chinese had been increasingly involved in the movement. They held demonstrations as well as fundraising activities. However, most of their money did not reach students in the Square either. This was, among other reasons, because a large amount of money from such sources was sent to China as checks or money orders made out to "the Students' Autonomous Union," "Hunger Strike Headquarters," "Tiananmen Square Headquarters," or even just "Tiananmen Square"; such donations, even if delivered, could hardly be redeemed.[145]

Because of the amount of money involved and its numerous sources, quite a bit of money still reached the students. The main problem was that most overseas Chinese did not know of the newly established General Headquarters. Therefore, when people did deliver money to students, they most likely gave it to the student leaders of the Beijing Students' Autonomous Union and the autonomous unions of the major universities. Because of the intense conflicts among movement activists, the General Headquarters had great difficulty getting money from them.[146]

By the end of May, there were still between 10,000 and 20,000 people staying overnight at the Square, while the daytime population usually multiplied. Feng Congde, who was in charge of the General Headquarters' finances during

144. For student leaders' own accounts of the chaotic financial system and possible corruption among student leaders, see *Huigu yu Fansi* (1993, 241–62).

145. Many donations were also sent to the students through China's Red Cross, the CCTV, or even through renowned intellectuals such as Yan Jiaqi and Liu Xiaobo. To my knowledge, only a small amount of them eventually went to students.

146. For example, on May 27, while the General Headquarters had only 5,000 yuan left, the Beijing Students' Autonomous Union and the Beijing University Students' Autonomous Union still had a considerable amount of money. In the Joint Federation meeting that day, Feng Congde pledged that the Beijing Students' Autonomous Union would transfer 100,000 yuan to the General Headquarters. Liang Er agreed to do so in the meeting but never delivered the money. Eventually Feng Congde had to borrow 30,000 yuan from the Beijing University Students' Autonomous Union to tackle the financial crisis. For more details, see *Huigu yu Fansi* (1993, 241–62).

late May, remembered that while after May 24 he still needed around 40,000 yuan a day just to buy food, his daily income from donations was only between 20,000 and 30,000 yuan.[147] By May 27 the General Headquarters had only 5,000 yuan left; meanwhile, it already owed much larger amounts to various stores.[148] It seemed that students might have to leave the Square just because of financial problems. At this point the infusion of Hong Kong money became critical.

People in Hong Kong had supported the movement enthusiastically ever since it started. The Hong Kong University Student Association sent a delegation to Beijing as observers as early as April 20.[149] Hong Kong residents held many fundraising activities. The largest one was on May 27, when over three hundred Hong Kong singers, actors, and actresses performed at a stadium for twelve hours to raise money. About thirteen million Hong Kong yuan was collected just at this single event.

What was crucial about the Hong Kong money in comparison with that from other sources was not its quantity, however, but its quality. During the hunger strike, some Hong Kong students stayed at the Square with Beijing students, and Hong Kong professors and students also attended various meetings of the Joint Federation and the General Headquarters. They therefore had a deep knowledge of what was going on in Beijing and where the money should go and be used.

The leaders of the General Headquarters first solicited Hong Kong money in a Joint Federation meeting on May 23. In the meeting, Chai Ling asked Qiu Yanliang, a professor in Hong Kong, to help her improve students' living conditions at the Square. Only two days later, the first stock of modern tents and sleeping bags from Hong Kong arrived in Beijing. By May 30, hundreds of tents were set up on the Square and more were still coming. A movement activist who left the Square on May 24 due to the deteriorating sanitary conditions described his impression in a diary when he returned to the Square on June 3:

> I saw that the environment in the Square has been drastically improved; it is much cleaner now. I also saw that many tents . . . have been set up to the north of the Monument to the People's Heroes. Each of these tents is about a man's height and ten meters in length, with a mountain-shaped roof. On two sides, two triangle windows are wide open. This kind of tent has an excellent ventilation for helping students to endure Beijing's hot summer. The tents are arranged row after row into a square array. Anyone could comfortably live in one for ten days or half a month.

147. Ibid., 256, 262.
148. Wu et al. (1989, 466–67).
149. Li Lu (*Huigu yu Fansi* 1993, 323).

No wonder that the government is so desperate. I admire those who reorganized a chaotic Tiananmen Square into such great order![150]

Not just the tents but all the other major events happening in this period, such as the creation of the Statue of the Goddess of Democracy, the establishment of the Democracy University, and even the four intellectuals' hunger strike, were more or less made possible by the monetary contributions from Hong Kong.[151]

Hong Kong students also established a Hong Kong Material Supply Center at the Square to provide food, blankets, sleeping bags, walkie-talkies, and other essentials. The importance of financial and material support from Hong Kong to the continuation of the Tiananmen Square occupation can be seen from the response to a small interview conducted by Hong Kong students themselves. When thirty students were asked "Will you still stay at the Square without the supplies from the Hong Kong Material Center?" seven said "no," four replied "it depends," one refused to answer, and the rest said "yes." Even taken at the face value, it shows that eleven or 36.7 percent of the students could have left the Square if deprived of supplies provided by the center.[152] However, the thought of having no food to eat or place to sleep is totally different from actually living in that condition. The question, when asked by rich Hong Kong students, could also have been taken as an insult by the proud local students. Some respondents might have been motivated to downplay the importance of the financial and material support from Hong Kong. Indeed, we know that many Beijing students left the Square in this period primarily because of the deteriorating conditions.[153] If there had been no Hong Kong money, the Tiananmen Square occupation could have ended in a financial crisis.

FINAL EPISODES

After May 22, although radical students still occupied Tiananmen Square, more and more Beijing students went back to school or home. At the occupa-

---

150. *China News Digest* (1994, no. 39 [4], 6).

151. Hong Kong students gave 8,000 yuan to build the Statue of the Goddess of Democracy. The Democracy University also received much help from Hong Kong students, starting from its very first day of preparation.

152. Li Lu (*Huigu yu Fansi* 1993, 325).

153. After ten days of occupation, Tiananmen Square had become an unlivable place. The terrible smell, a mixture of ammonia, night soil, rotten food, and body odor, was still vivid in the minds of those of my informants who were forced to leave the Square by the bad smells in late May.

tion's peak over a thousand students from the University of Political Science and Law usually stayed at the Square over night. By late May, the number had dropped to about ten (no. 60). Even from Beijing University there were only a few dozen students still staying overnight at the Square by the end of May (no. 68). The overall number of students who stayed at the Square overnight dropped from between 100,000 and 200,000 during mid-May to around 10,000 by the end of May,[154] and over 90 percent of the students continuing at the Square were from outside Beijing.[155] This, however, does not mean that Beijing students and residents no longer cared about the movement. As is suggested by the popular slogan "If Li Peng does not step down, we will visit the Square every day," a huge number of people in Beijing still visited the Square daily, swelling the daytime population.

While the government was preparing for a military operation, radical students were preparing to hold Tiananmen Square as long as possible. In this period, several episodes drew people's attention and helped extend the Tiananmen Square occupation. On May 27, students of the Central Academy of Fine Arts were asked to make a sculpture modeled after the Statue of Liberty. The students had originally planned to withdraw from the Square on May 30, and the sculpture was at first intended to be used in a final march to celebrate victory. Once the students refused to leave, it too stayed to become another rallying point for the movement. On May 30, tens of thousands of people went to the Square to see the sculpture. Tiananmen Square was once again congested.

In the final days, two other events also attracted public attention. The first was a four-man hunger strike organized by Liu Xiaobo and the second the establishment of the Democracy University in the Square. On May 29, Liu Xiaobo invited Zhou Duo and Hou Dejian to stage a seventy-two-hour hunger strike. In the process, Liu's friend Gao Xin also joined. The original purpose of this hunger strike was complicated.[156] Essentially, it reflected the intellectuals' ambivalence toward the movement. They supported the movement but were greatly worried about its direction of development. Through the hunger strike, Liu intended to win the hearts of students and gain control over the movement. The hunger strike was started at the Monument to the People's Heroes on the afternoon of June 2. Hundreds of thousands of people went to the scene. Many went to see Hou Dejian, a famous singer and composer best known for his song "Descendants of the Dragon." The hunger strike was terminated by the

154. Wu et al. (1989, 416, 465).
155. Ibid., 535.
156. See Liu Xiaobo (1992, 189–200) for his own account of the purpose of the hunger strike, and Han and Hua (1990, 349–54) for an English translation of the "Hunger Strike Declaration."

military crackdown. Although they failed to achieve their original goal, their heroism did win the respect of students, making it possible, as we shall see later, for them to take on the role of mediators between the martial law troops and the students, thus helping to bring students out of the Square peacefully.

The last event that showed the students' determination in continuing the Tiananmen Square occupation was the establishment of the Democracy University. Although during the movement Zhang Boli and most other student leaders were often condemned for being "power maniacs," "undemocratic," and "corrupt," these same student leaders were also very upset at other leaders and activists for the same reasons.[157] Therefore, Zhang Boli decided to establish a Democracy University in the Square to deepen people's understanding of democracy. Zhang was supported in this by Zheng Yi and other leaders in the General Headquarters. Later on some students from Hong Kong also provided him with support and money.

The university was originally scheduled to open on May 28. However, its opening was delayed until June 3. Zhang Boli named himself the president of the university and Yan Jiaqi as honorary president. Again, a large crowd was attracted. To maintain order, the organizers had to use a rope to divide the "students" of the university from the crowd. According to Zhang, around 10,000 people were inside the rope during the opening ceremony. The ceremony ended at 0:50 A.M. on the early morning of June 4. By that time, the martial law troops had already arrived at the Square.

THE MILITARY CRACKDOWN[158]

While students were still lingering at the Square, the second military operation started (chapter 7). In the beginning, soldiers infiltrated into the city disguised as civilians. As early as May 26, one regiment of the army had entered Beijing this way.[159] By early June, troops were infiltrating Beijing on an ever-larger scale,

    157. Zhang Boli (1994e).

    158. Many of the references in this section are to contributions to a two-volume work entitled *Jieyan Yiri* (Under martial law). The contributions are personal experience narratives written by over two hundred soldiers who participated in the military crackdown. The government's intention in publishing this book was, of course, to legitimize the crackdown. However, since the government had assured the soldiers that they had done the right thing, the soldiers tended to be frank in describing their conflicts with civilians. The book's impact in China was not entirely what the government had expected, and the government put a stop to the book's distribution shortly after it came out. I have compared the soldiers' accounts with others from unofficial sources, and I have found that the descriptions are strikingly similar, despite their different viewpoints. Since the book brings together accounts from soldiers who were in different military units, it is one of the richest sources of information on the military repression.

    159. Li Shaojun (1989), the commander of the regiment, has given a detailed description of the operation.

and local residents and students became alert to the military moves. As a result, more and more plainclothes soldiers were stopped along the road by residents and students. Skirmishes were frequent.

The turning point came on the evening of June 2, when people on the western side of Beijing, especially those in between the Muxidi and Liubukou intersections, became very emotional. Possibly this was because three civilians had been killed by a speeding military jeep at Muxidi. According to the government, while the jeep belonged to the Beijing police, it had been borrowed by CCTV for civilian use for the last ten months. Therefore, this was just a traffic accident. However, people tended to believe that the three people were killed by martial law troops on purpose. From then on, local youths, especially those who lived in the Muxidi vicinity, not only verbally insulted the soldiers but also started to beat them up. A Qinghua student (no. 38) described what she saw:

> On the evening of June 2, the government broadcast was criticizing the Statue of the Goddess of Democracy. We were curious and went to see it. . . . When we were close to Tiananmen Square, we saw some military trucks being stopped. Many workers were trying to break tires and smash the trucks. They also cast bricks at soldiers and pulled them out to beat them. It was around midnight at the Xidan intersection. At that time, the soldiers did not fight back. . . . I felt that this was not right, so I asked a male classmate to stop them. However, several people came over and asked who he was. They suspected him of being a secret policeman. To avoid further conflicts, I had to rush forward and tell them that we were students. Then they let us go. My classmate still wanted to argue with them. I saw the situation was quite tense, so I pulled him away.[160]

Many soldiers have told of how they were beaten up by local residents between the nights of June 2 and June 3.[161] Yet, because most people, including journalists, were against martial law, civilian brutalities, and especially those that happened before the military repression, have generally been ignored.

On June 3 the army infiltration was on a greater scale and some units were advancing in uniform. Soldiers and plainclothes soldiers could be seen almost everywhere. They were asked to take up certain positions but often did not

160. This student's action was not unique. During this whole period, countless numbers of students, most of them movement activists, tried to stop civilian brutalities. Many of them saved the lives of soldiers in peril. For example, Zhou Yongjun (1993, 59) gave an account of how he saved the life of an officer who turned out to be a regiment-level commander. Because of the testimony of that officer, the prosecution of him after the military crackdown was eventually dropped. For soldiers' accounts of how students saved them, see Ren Bin (1989, 36), Ni (1989, 65), and Dan (1989, 120–46).

161. See Huan Xiaoping (1989), Kong (1989), Ni (1989), and Wang Hongwei (1989).

know how to reach their destinations. Many of them behaved erratically on the street and were easy to identify. In some places the confused soldiers were caught, rounded up, and taken to certain locations where they were encircled and lectured at, spat upon, and kicked by local residents. From time to time, people from the outside threw in one more soldier and shouted: "Here, we caught another one!"[162]

Residents and students also started to find weapons. Rumors said that the troops were deliberately sending weapons to the street to let civilians seize them, in order to create excuses for a repression.[163] From what I have reconstructed, the martial law troops did send many weapons into Beijing in civilian vehicles. However, they did so mainly because their soldiers had infiltrated Beijing in plainclothes and unarmed. Therefore, they had to ship the weapons separately. After June 2, residents and students were on the alert for suspicious civilian vehicles. As a result, they caught several such vehicles with military equipment. For instance, on the morning of June 3 students and Beijing residents stopped three tourist buses carrying military equipment at the Liubukou intersection.[164] In a rage, some people in the crowd took out guns, machine guns, grenades, bullets, helmets, and gas masks, and displayed them on the street to show that the government was going to use live ammunition against the people. The Martial Law Headquarters had to send about five hundred riot policemen and soldiers to recover the weapons. Conflict immediately broke out. In the process, the riot police used clubs and tear gas, and many people were wounded.[165] In the afternoon, soldiers and riot police attacked civilians in other places for similar reasons. Both sides became increasingly hostile.

The final assault started on the evening of June 3. Around 9:00 P.M., soldiers advanced on Tiananmen Square from all directions. They were ordered "to clear all the obstacles by force and reach the destination on time."[166] With regard to the use of live ammunition, the record is complicated. General Zhang Kun, a vice political commissioner of a group army entering Beijing from the south, stated that his army had received a clear order not to use live ammunition. Because of communication problems, the army never received any further

162. For soldiers' accounts, see Zhao Lumin (1989) and Yan Dongyin (1989).

163. Li Lu still insisted on the theory several years later (*Huigu yu Fansi* 1993, 306).

164. Both pro- and antigovernment sources reported the incident. See He Zhizhou (1989) and Li Shengtang (1989).

165. Simmie and Nixon (1989, 173) also give an eyewitness account of the incident.

166. The order is translated from the account of General Wang Fuyi (1989, 84), the political commissioner of the 38th Army.

orders and therefore never distributed bullets to soldiers.[167] Yet, according to Zhao Xiaoqiang, a special commissioner sent by the Martial Law Headquarters to a group army also from the south, the headquarters gave him a personal order that soldiers could shoot into the air to disperse the crowd when it was absolutely necessary. Thus when the army was not able to move and its communication with the Martial Law Headquarters was interrupted, Zhao called a special meeting to convey this order.[168] These two accounts show that while the military order itself might not mention anything about the use of live ammunition, the Martial Law Headquarters had determined to take over the Square by any means necessary, live ammunition included.

It seemed that there was no consensus among different armies on how the live ammunition should be controlled. In some army units bullets were controlled at the regiment level, while in others it was at company level. In some regiments or companies, the commander let only one person carry bullets, while the rest had only unloaded rifles. In other units, the commander distributed bullets to several trusted officers. There was also evidence that a few army units distributed bullets to many, if not all, officers before or during the repression.[169]

Although the troops advanced in all directions, most deaths that night occurred in the west between the Muxidi and Liubukou intersections. Among the ninety-two recorded deaths in Ding Zilin's painstakingly constructed "June 4

167. See Zhang Kun (1989, 294). General Zhang was beaten almost to death by local residents because he did not allow his bodyguards to fight back.

168. See Zhao Xiaoqiang (1989, 208).

169. The above variations were constructed from soldiers' accounts, in particular Li Huxiang (1989, 136), Liu Xinli (1989, 224), Peng (1989, 216), Zhang Xibo (1989, 169), Zhao Xiaoqiang (1989, 208), and Zhu Shuangxi (1989, 209). Their narratives are generally consistent with the observations of my informants. One of my informants (no. 70), who had stayed on the west side of Beijing on the night of June 3, told me that he saw a battalion of soldiers holding an intersection. They stood back-to-back three in a group and were very nervous. When my informant approached them, they immediately raised their rifles and ordered him to stop. My informant then held up his university ID and said: "I am a teacher at People's University. I have come to look for my students!" When he got closer, however, he started to accuse them of killing. The commander of the battalion got very upset. He rushed to my informant and yelled at him: "Who killed people? We do not even have bullets!" Meanwhile, the commander grabbed the rifles from the nearby soldiers and disassembled them one by one, showing that they were unloaded. That same night, the same informant also followed local residents chasing a military truck. People were stoning the soldiers and trying to get closer to the truck. The soldiers on the truck shot at the ground to create distance between the truck and the chasing crowd. From time to time, however, there were people wounded by the rebounding bullets. Both sides were unspeakably emotional. Once a soldier threw his helmet and rifle on the ground and cried: "I am not going to do this any more!" and jumped off the truck. As soon as he reached the ground, however, people ran over and beat him to death. My informant tried to stop the tragedy, but was only pushed aside.

Death List,"[170] fifty (54.3%) of them occurred along Changan Avenue and its extension, Fuxing Road. At Muxidi intersection, the death toll listed by Ding reached sixteen, or 17.4 percent. Assuming that Ding's list includes between 20 and 25 percent of the total actual deaths,[171] we can estimate that between sixty-four and eighty people died at the Muxidi intersection alone and between two hundred and two hundred fifty people died in the west side of Beijing during the night of June 3 and early June 4.

It is not completely clear why most of the deaths occurred on the western side of the city. For some reasons, popular resistance in the west had always been more violent than in other places. I mentioned earlier how during the first military assault, between May 19 and 22, the only place where significant violence occurred was in the Fengtai area in the west of Beijing, and how on the evening of June 2 three civilians were killed by a military jeep in an accident on the west side. The scale of popular resistance on the western side of Beijing could also be seen in the casualties of the 38th Army. On the night of June 3 and early June 4, the 38th Army had six deaths, one hundred and fifty-nine critical injuries, over eleven hundred other injuries, and about three thousand beaten up. It also lost forty-seven armed vehicles and sixty-five trucks, most of them burned by street fighters.[172] The civilian resistance was so strong that the 38th Army spent over an hour just taking over the Muxidi intersection.

It is not clear whether the 38th Army had received special orders. There was evidence that the 38th Army distributed bullets to the lower-ranking officers and even to rank-and-file soldiers much earlier than did most other armies. This certainly could induce a high death toll. The high death rate may also be attributable to the fact that the soldiers of the 113th Division of the 38th Army, now in the vanguard, had been attacked by civilians as early as May 22 and therefore might have borne more resentment. The high death toll could also be attributed to the fact that some soldiers went out of control when caught between a military order and a vicious civilian attack. Indeed, both sides were extremely emotional. One informant (no. 43) told me with an unforgettable expression: "I had only read in novels that soldiers' eyes will turn bloodshot in a

---

170. See Ding Zilin (1994). Ding lists ninety-six deaths. However, one of them died in Sichuan and another three deaths occurred many months later for reasons not directly related to the military repression itself. Therefore, they are excluded here.

171. On June 6, the Chinese government acknowledged a little over 300 deaths during the repression, including both civilians and soldiers (Yuan 1989). On the other hand, Brook (1992, 161) counts at least 478 deaths by June 4. These were roughly taken as low and high estimates of the number of deaths, although the actual number of deaths could be even higher.

172. *Sanshi Bajun Junshi* (1994, ch. 7).

fierce fight, but that night I saw that the eyes of many soldiers and local residents had turned blood-red!" The fact that a few soldiers might have been out of control could also be seen from how civilians were shot during the repression. Of the ninety-two victims listed by Ding, twenty-two (24%) of them were injured while in unquestionably passive positions. Some people were shot while just taking pictures (i.e., nos. 2, 5, and 27) or hiding behind something (i.e., nos. 1, 11, 15, and 75).[173]

The troops from the west arrived at Tiananmen Square at about 1:30 A.M. on June 4. Other troops also gradually arrived. As soon as they had arrived, the soldiers immediately blocked the major roads to the Square to prevent people from coming in. Meanwhile, the government-controlled loudspeakers in the Square repeatedly announced an "Emergency Announcement." It claimed that troops had to be called in to suppress an antirevolutionary rebellion in Beijing, and that local civilians should immediately leave the Square and stay at home. Otherwise their personal safety would not be guaranteed. More and more people left the Square. At the end, about 4,000 people still clustered around the Monument to the People's Heroes. By 2:00 A.M. the troops had completely encircled the Square. Both outside and inside of the circle, people sang "L'Internationale" repeatedly. Students inside the circle also repeatedly swore to stand or fall in Tiananmen Square.

At this moment, the four intellectuals who were still fasting at the Square played an important role.[174] To avoid violence, they went from place to place to ask students and local residents to get rid of the rifles and other weapons that they had collected in order to defend the Square.[175] Meanwhile, Hou Dejian and Zhou Duo went to negotiate with the troop commanders to ask them to open a path along which students could leave the Square. At about 3:30 A.M., Hou Dejian and Zhou Duo met with Ji Xinguo, a regiment-level political commissioner.[176] They said that they would persuade students to leave the

173. See Ding Zilin (1994). Ding's list contains only between 20 and 25 percent of the total of deaths. However, of the thirty-six Beijing students who died during the crackdown, thirty-two were included in the list, and of the eighty-three victims with known identities on the list, sixty (72.3%) were students, intellectuals, or cadres. We know that the intellectuals and students were much less involved in the physical confrontation with soldiers than were local residents. Therefore, the estimate could inflate the percentage of passive deaths during the repression.

174. See Gao Xin (1990), Hou (1989), and Liu Xiaobo (1992).

175. Many other students were also trying to persuade people to lay down their weapons. See Li Lu (1990, 197) and *China News Digest* (1994, 4:13) for other accounts.

176. The negotiation was documented by both Hou Dejian (1989) and Ji Xinguo (1989). Except in tone, their accounts were strikingly consistent.

Square and asked the army to create a path. Ji Xinguo reported Hou's request
to the Martial Law Headquarters. The headquarters immediately agreed and
informed Hou Dejian that south was the direction.[177] When Hou and Zhou
went back, the Martial Law Headquarters repeatedly announced: "Students, we
appreciate that you will leave the Square voluntarily. Students, please leave in
the southeastern direction."

The action of the four intellectuals also met with resistance. "Shame on
you!" "Get out of here!" and other insults frequently rang in their ears as they
were persuading students to leave.[178] At one point, as Liu Xiaobo recalled, a
worker even tried to hit him with an iron bar while accusing him of being a traitor.[179] Yet as more and more soldiers arrived, leaving became the only option.
Therefore, the intellectuals' persuasion was also effective to a certain degree.[180]

The soldiers began to get restless. At about 4:15 A.M. Hou Dejian went back
to Ji Xinguo to request a little more time. Ji guaranteed that they could still
have a peaceful retreat but told Hou that there was not much time left, and he
suggested that Hou leave alone if he was unable to persuade the students to ac-
company him. When Hou went back, the remaining students finally decided to
take a voice vote on the issue. Feng Congde asked the students for a voice vote
for or against the withdrawal. According to several of my informants, they
could not really tell the difference,[181] but Feng announced that the voice vote
for the withdrawal was louder.[182] Therefore, the students started to leave, dragging along with them those who refused to go.

At 4:35 A.M., only several minutes after the students started to retreat, all the
lights at the Square were turned on. The army started its final operation. Soldiers marched forward to squeeze students to the south. Meanwhile, a squad
charged up to the Monument to the People's Heroes and shot down the loudspeakers belonging to the students.

At this point, the students astonishingly still maintained a good order. They
marched about five to ten people in a row, under the banners of their own universities. They also arranged for local residents and females to stay in the

177. This was obviously the safest path. A few students who left the Square in the western direction
were immediately caught up in still ongoing fighting between local residents and soldiers. The most tragic
event occurred in the Liubukou area, when a speeding tank crashed into a crowd; several students who had
just left the Square were killed or wounded as a result. See Ding Zilin (1994) for more details of this event.

178. Li Lu (1990, 199).

179. Liu Xiaobo (1992, 228).

180. Ibid., 230–31.

181. Hong Kong student Lin Yaoqiang remembered that the voice vote for staying was louder (Fang
1989).

182. See Feng Congde (*Huigu yu Fansi* 1993, 318) for his justification of the decision.

middle, for better protection. They cried along the way and sang "L'Internationale." After reaching the Qianmen area, the students dispersed in several directions. Yet, at the very rear there were still about a hundred or so people who
refused to go further. Gao Xin, one of the four hunger strikers, happened to be
there.[183] According to Gao, when they arrived at Qianmen, they met thousands
of local residents and students and stopped. Together, they shouted slogans
against the soldiers. However, when they shouted "Fascists! Fascists!" the soldiers rushed forward and started to shoot. They all ran to hide. Soldiers actually shot at the sky, but one student was still wounded, according to one of my
informants. It was 6:00 A.M. on the morning of June 4. Gao Xin saw the soldiers wave their guns, toss their helmets, jump high, and shout with excitement.
After seven most dramatic weeks the movement was repressed.

183. Gao Xin (1990).

TOP, A demonstration in front of the Xinhua Gate, the south entrance to the government compound. The event led to the "Xinhua Gate Incident" on the early morning of April 20. See the introduction and chapter 6. BOTTOM, The April 27 demonstration. The student protesters held hands to keep the order of the march. See chapters 6, 8, and 9. (Photographs from Huang Tian, ed., *Zhonghua Minzhu Xuelu* [Hong Kong: Limin Chubanshe, 1989]. Reproduced with permission.)

TOP, The characters on the back of the hunger striker read: "Fasting to the death is only a small deed." The statement is a slightly modified version of half of a traditional Chinese couplet that was an exhortation to Chinese widows to remain faithful to their dead husbands. The other half of the couplet goes: "Keeping one's chastity is the most important matter." See chapter 9. (Photograph © Sing Tao Limited. From Beijingxueyun Editorial Committee, eds., *Beijingxueyun —Lishi de Jianzheng*, 1989. Reproduced with permission.) BOTTOM, Often led by cadres of work-units, workers received paid leave and used state-owned resources such as the trucks in the picture to demonstrate in support of the hunger strikers, a phenomenon that I characterize as "semi-official mobilization." See chapter 6. (Photograph from Huang Tian, ed., *Zhonghua Minzhu Xuelu* [Hong Kong: Limin Chubanshe, 1989]. Reproduced with permission.)

The two photographs contrast the physical environment in Tiananmen Square before (TOP) and after (BOTTOM) the arrival of "Hong Kong money." See chapter 6. (Photographs from Huang Tian, ed., *Zhonghua Minzhu Xuelu* [Hong Kong: Limin Chubanshe, 1989]. Reproduced with permission.)

While public resistance to martial law troops was peaceful on and around May 20 (TOP), it became highly emotional when the soldiers tried to enter the city the second time in early June (BOTTOM). See chapter 6. (Top photograph © Sing Tao Limited. From Beijingxueyun Editorial Committee, eds., *Beijingxueyun—Lishi de Jianzheng*, 1989. Reproduced with permission. Bottom photograph from Huang Tian, ed., *Zhonghua Minzhu Xuelu* [Hong Kong: Limin Chubanshe, 1989]. Reproduced with permission.)

seven

STATE LEGITIMACY, STATE BEHAVIORS, AND MOVEMENT DEVELOPMENT

During the 1989 Beijing Student Movement, the Chinese government went back and forth several times between policies of concession and repression, neither of which was successful. Eventually, the government suppressed the movement with military force, and the movement ended tragically. Both the frequent changes in state policy and the eventual repression have been commonly explained as the outcome of power struggles between reform and conservative factions within the government. In this chapter, I argue that the key factor underlying these policy changes and the consequent development of the movement was the ineffectiveness of previous state control measures, an ineffectiveness which in turn had resulted from the presence of conflicting views of state legitimacy in the minds of top state elites, the movement activists, and the rest of Beijing's population.[1]

This chapter is organized into three sections. First, I provide

---

1. There are many accounts of intraparty struggles, published in Hong Kong-based newspapers and magazines, that were supposedly leaked by high-level leaders or their associates. There is no doubt that some of these news items were true. However, I decided not to rely on this source of information in the analysis because of the existence of a substantial quantity of unreliable news in these publications.

a critical review of theories of factionalism in Chinese politics, which are the most popular explanations of Chinese politics in general and of the 1989 Movement in particular. Then, I present a model that reveals the Chinese state's fundamental social control problems by bringing into focus the nature of the regime and its sources of legitimation. Finally, I provide an empirical account—with some interpretation—of the state's behavior during the 1989 Movement.

Elite Factionism and Dynamics of the 1989 Movement

Currently, most writings on Chinese politics emphasize its factional nature.[2] This is particularly true of the analyses of the state's behavior during the 1989 Movement.[3] Although such analyses vary in their details, they generally argue that the shifts in state policy during the movement were the consequence of struggles between reform and conservative factions within the government.[4] Most models of factionalism are not based on theories of the state. Such arguments imply, however, that the state is not composed of a unitary elite with cohesive interests but rather of different elites fighting for power and policy significance. Logically, factionalism is indeed the only possible outcome when political conflicts are organized around clientelist ties rather than through formal organizations.[5] Yet when such models are used to explain the behavior of the Chinese state during the 1989 Movement, they encounter some problems.

First, such models of elite factionalism simplify the interpersonal networks within the CCP. Because open factions are illegal in the CCP, a strong, stable faction is very difficult to establish. The "factions" within the CCP are embedded in networks formed through such sources of affiliation as regional ties, nepotism, friendships, ideological similarities, and common past work experiences. Moreover, ideological factions may not correspond to the lines of division within such networks, and thus divisions based primarily on ideology have only occasionally become dominant in the CCP's history.[6] Second, while the

2. Baum (1993), Dittmer (1990a, 1990b), MacFarquhar (1974, 1983, 1993), and Teiwes (1990).

3. Chen Yizi (1990), Cheng Chu-yuan (1990), Dittmer (1990a, 1990b), Kristof (1990a), and Nathan (1990).

4. For example, Cheng Chu-yuan (1990, 38) argues: "The demonstration in Tiananmen Square can be interpreted as a reflection of the mounting popular discontent of the people. But the decision to crack down on the protesters can be understood only as having occurred within the framework of an intraparty power struggle."

5. Nathan (1990).

6. As Ding Xueliang (1994, 40) has illustrated, Wang Zhen and Deng Liqun were commonly thought to belong to the hard core of conservatives. However, they had close relations with, and were trusted by, Deng Xiaoping.

theory carries some validity for analyzing Chinese politics during Mao's era, when the state could make policy choices relatively free from societal demands and then impose its policies in ways that generated a deep impact on society, it is weak when it comes to explaining the development of the 1989 Movement.[7] After the reform started, state-society relations in China entered a process of continuous metamorphosis (chapter 2). By the late 1980s, China had developed into a performance-based authoritarian regime. At this stage, most of the urban population no longer believed in communist ideology, so the state had to rely increasingly on economic and moral performance to survive. Under this regime, although there were no institutional checks and balances as in a democracy, extra-institutional pressures from Chinese society narrowed the regime's policy choices. Factionalist theories overestimate the autonomous power that the Chinese state had during the late 1980s. They assume that the Chinese state could still shift its policies at will, which was not true.

The factionalistic explanation of the rise and development of the 1989 Movement can be summarized as follows: The rise of a conservative faction hampered economic as well as political reform in China, which gave rise to the movement. During the movement, government policies toward the movement shifted back and forth between concession and repression as a result of factional struggle. Eventually, hardliners gained the upper hand in the power struggle, which brought military repression. The military repression marked the consolidation of the conservative faction and the failure of reform.

This explanation has at least two empirical difficulties. First, the model cannot explain the timing of some important events. For example, it is believed that Zhao Ziyang was a leader of the reformist camp and that the repressive April 26 *People's Daily* editorial was made possible because Zhao Ziyang had left for North Korea.[8] However, the state shifted back to a concessive strategy on April 27, immediately after a successful student demonstration that defied the April 26 *People's Daily* editorial. By April 29, the government had held the first dialogue with students. Zhao visited North Korea between April 23 and April 30; thus, if he was not responsible for the April 26 editorial, he should also not be given credit for the state's concessions that occurred before he went back to China. Second, what happened after 1989 was not what the model predicted. There was no extensive purge of the so-called reformers in the CCP. Most importantly, the economic reform in China actually renewed itself, gathering a new momentum after 1992.

7. In fact, as Teiwes and Sun (1999) convincingly argue, Chinese politics even during Mao's era should not be treated simply as the result of factional struggles between Mao and his opponents.

8. See Chen Yizi (1990) and Chen Xiaoya (1996, 206–207).

The weaknesses of the model become clearer if we pose a hypothetical question: would the state have acted differently if factionalism were not the driving force of the state policy change? The answer is probably no. During the 1989 Movement, the state dealt with the movement in the following ways. First, it tolerated the movement. When tolerance did not work and the movement escalated, the government verbally threatened the students with a *People's Daily* editorial. However, when the editorial did not work, the government adopted limited concessions in order to contain the movement. Unfortunately, limited concessions could not co-opt the students; therefore the state implemented martial law and deployed a huge number of troops to Beijing. Martial law and soldiers were initially aimed primarily at intimidating the students and Beijing residents. It was only when a show of force was unable to end the Tiananmen Square occupation that the government ordered the repression.

The above discussion shows that the state tried every control measure in its repertoire, to no avail. In the end, the state leaders were left with only two choices, either to repress the students or to face the prospect of eventually stepping down, as the communist leaders in Eastern European countries had done. However, since most top leaders in China during the late 1980s had joined the revolution long before the communists took power, it was almost impossible for them, "reformers" and "hardliners" alike, to give up the power for which millions of their revolutionary comrades had died. Thus, military repression became their only choice. I would like to make it very clear that this chapter does not argue that there was no power struggle among the top state leaders or that the power struggle had no impact on the development of the 1989 Movement. What this chapter argues is that in this particular case models based on factionalism have less explanatory power than does the state-society relations model. This analysis also does not justify the killing—an action in itself unjustifiable. But it does show that by overemphasizing the role of factionalism in state policy formation during the 1989 Movement, the factional model underestimates the fundamental problems that an authoritarian state like China confronts in times of crisis.

Legitimacy and State Control

In the introduction I have defined legal-electoral, ideological, and performance legitimacy as the three basic sources of state legitimation. However, in a given country at any particular time people can have widely different views of the basis of state legitimation, depending on their positions in society and their personal experiences. Therefore, to apply this theory to the 1989 Movement we need to further specify the sense and levels of state legitimacy as perceived by the state elites and relevant Beijing populations. We also need to understand how the legitimation structure reduced the effectiveness of state control during the 1989 Movement. My discussion focuses on four important groups: top state elites, intellectual elites and radical students, university students, and Beijing residents. This grouping does not imply the existence of cohesive players or actors during the movement. Rather, it is based on the conviction that the majority of individuals in each group had a perspective on state power that was quite distinct from those of individuals of other groups, and that this perspective could to some extent shape their behavior.

TOP STATE ELITES

This group included most Politburo members, especially the standing members of the CCP Politburo. It also included a few veterans who had joined the revolution before the Long March and who were actively involved in major policy-making processes during the movement and who had a significant say in them. The CCP Politburo had seventeen members in 1989.[9] It consisted of both CCP veterans and younger leaders who had joined the party as late as the 1950s. Most individuals in the group had started their revolutionary careers in the 1930s or 1940s (table 7.1). They were considered the second or third generation of the CCP leadership. All the veterans joined the communist movement in the 1920s. By the late 1980s, only a few of them were still politically active. Among them, the most powerful ones are listed in table 7.1. Except for Deng Xiaoping and Yang Shangkun, in 1989 none of them held formal positions within the CCP, nor did they take charge of the daily routine of the government. However, because of their legendary revolutionary experiences and due to the fact that most current leaders in the government and the army had been their subordinates and had been promoted through the ranks by them, they still enjoyed a great deal of influence—even veto power over state policies. The first eight individuals on the list are known to have played a crucial role in the final crackdown on the 1989 Movement. They were sometimes called the eight octogenarians.[10]

Most writings on the 1989 Movement have emphasized the factional nature of this group. What has been neglected is the fact that the majority of the

9. Some of them were not in the core decision-making group in dealing with the movement. However, since I explore the political nature of the leadership as a whole, a slight change of the list should not affect my analysis and conclusions.

10. Cheng Chu-yuan (1990, 209–21).

TABLE 7.1   Time When the Politburo Members and Some of the Most Powerful Veterans
Joined the Communist Revolution

Politburo Members[a]	Year Joined the Revolution[b]	Veterans	Year Joined the Revolution[b]
Yang Shangkun	1926	Yang Shangkun	1926
Qin Jiwei	1929	Deng Xiaoping	1922
Hu Yaobang	1930	Peng Zhen	1923
Zhao Ziyang	1932	Deng Yingchao	1924
Yao Yilin	1935	Chen Yun	1925
Wan Li	1936	Bo Yibo	1925
Song Ping	1937	Li Xiannian	1927
Wu Xueqian	1938	Wang Zhen	1927
Qiao Shi	1940	Nie Rongzhen	1922
Li Peng	1941	Lu Dingyi	1925
Tian Jiyun	1945	Song Renqiong	1926
Jiang Zemin	1946	Liu Lantao	1926
Hu Qili	1948	Xi Zhongxun	1926
Li Ximing	1948	Xu Xiangqian	1927
Yang Rudai	1952		
Li Tieying	1955		
Li Ruihuan	1959		

[a] These were the seventeen Politburo members immediately before the rise of the 1989 Movement.
[b] The year when the individual joined either the Communist Party, the Communist Youth League, or the army led by the communists.

group had one thing in common—they were absolutely loyal to the CCP and believed in the current political system. Among the thirty top elites listed in table 7.1, only three had joined the CCP in the 1950s, and only four in the 1940s. The rest started their revolutionary careers in the 1920s or 1930s, long before the communists took power. They had fought hundreds of battles and seen many of their friends and associates die for the cause. Their life-long dedication to a common cause had certainly shaped their views and strengthened their loyalty to the CCP.

Besides their unique life experiences and identities, we also have some other evidence to support this argument. During the movement, many senior leaders, especially the octogenarians, repeatedly expressed their high loyalty to the CCP. For example, in a meeting with the CCP Central Advisory Commission Standing Committee, Chen Yun declared: "Everyone knows that the Chinese revolution went through decades of hard struggle and saw the sacrifice of more than twenty million people, and only then was the People's Republic of China founded. The victory did not come easily." [11] Their loyalty to the CCP can also be seen by considering the behavior of Xu Jiatun as a deviant case. Xu joined the CCP in 1938. Between 1983 and 1989 he was the chief-of-staff of the Xinhua News Agency's Hong Kong Branch. During this period, his understanding of capitalism and the West underwent a fundamental change. Xu fled from China to the United States in the 1990s for fear that he might be punished because he had expressed sympathy with the student movement while in Hong Kong. However, even after three years in the United States, he still professed his loyalty to the CCP and expressed his grievances only in regard to a few top state leaders that he did not like personally. [12] Obviously, most of the top state leaders listed in table 7.1 had a longer career and more central positions in the CCP than Xu. They also did not have Xu's experiences in Hong Kong and the U.S. to divide their loyalty and identity. It is unlikely that the majority of this group during the late 1980s would lose their faith in a regime for which they had fought so hard.

Individuals in this group knew that China's economic performance was poor when compared, for example, with that of Taiwan or South Korea. They were also aware of the widespread corruption and high inflation in China before the rise of the 1989 Movement. However, they tended to attribute China's poor performance to inexperience and to Mao's personal mistakes, [13] believing that the current economic crisis was a short-term setback. Their overall evaluation of the state's performance was still positive. Also, although the top state elites were not popularly elected, they insisted on the right to command their whole society by legal and constitutional means because they were committed to an ideology—an insistence which was consistent with the general tendency for ideology to be a higher-order legitimation than legal-electoral legitimation. My estimate of this group's perspective on its ideological and legal mandates as well on the state's performance is listed in the first row of table 7.2. [14]

11. Chen Yun (1990).

12. Xu Jiatun (1993).

13. Deng Xiaoping (1983, 291–301).

14. The top military elite is another group that played an important role in the final military repression. Most top military commanders during the late 1980s also had joined the CCP in the 1920s, 1930s, and 1940s. Their military careers led them to establish strong loyalties to the CCP. For example, Qin Jiwei, who joined the Red Army in 1929, was Minister of Defense in 1989. He had fought hundreds of battles and seen the deaths of thousands of his associates. Qin was also under the long-time leadership of Deng Xiaoping and Xu Xiangqian. Both were veteran elites by 1989. Therefore, in this chapter, this group is treated the same as top state elites in its loyalty to the CCP. See Qin (1996) for his military career.

TABLE 7.2   State Legitimacy as Perceived by Different Sections of the Beijing Population
                during the Late 1980s

	Ideological Legitimacy	Performance Legitimacy (Economic)	Legal-Electoral Legitimacy
Top state elites	+	+/−	0
Intellectual elites and radical students	−	−	−
Students	−	−/+	−
Beijing residents	0	−/+	0

Note: Here, +, +/−, −/+ and −, respectively, represent positive, somewhat positive, somewhat negative, and negative perceptions of state legitimacy, and 0 is entered when the dimension of state legitimacy was not very important to that population.

INTELLECTUAL ELITES AND RADICAL STUDENTS

This group included both major dissidents and liberal intellectuals. A few individuals from this group, such as Fang Lizhi, Liu Binyan, Wang Ruowang, Yan Jiaqi, Chen Ziming, and Wang Dan are well known in the West, thanks to the writings of China specialists. I discussed some of the major characteristics of these people in chapter 2. I will summarize a few relevant arguments here. This group was composed of politically ambitious intellectuals who had been interested in politics even during Mao's era. Most of them also had once been true believers in communism and Mao. Due to the disastrous outcome of the Cultural Revolution and their unpleasant personal experiences at that time, by the end of the 1970s many of this group's members had some skepticism about Marxism and China's political system. The size of this group increased to include some young students, and its ideas crystallized over time. By the late 1980s, its members generally believed that all the tragedies of Mao's era resulted from the lack of human rights, of an independent legal system, and above all of democratic politics. They also believed that China was still one of the poorest countries in the world after forty years of communist rule, and that China's backwardness was a result of its rigid planned economy and the political system. Finally, they insisted that China's economic reform had experienced a deep-seated crisis whose source was the slow pace of political reform.

Therefore, most individuals from the group did not really consider the regime to be ideologically or legally-electorally legitimate.[15] They also had a very

15. Burns (1989, 497) has an excellent account of the Beijing intellectuals' skepticism regarding the Four Cardinal Principles during the late 1980s.

negative opinion of the regime's economic performance during the 1980s (table 7.2). Within the group, the differences were mainly over their views on how to bring about changes in the current regime.[16] The core of this group's radical wing was small, probably no more than a few hundred in Beijing. However, since most of them were professors, writers, journalists, and students in major universities, they were able to communicate their ideas extensively and effectively. Their influence on the rest of the intellectuals and students was enormous. By the late 1980s, as China's economic crisis deepened, their ideas turned into a dominant intellectual discourse. The 1989 Movement was initiated by a few radical intellectuals and students who had actively engaged in this discourse.

UNIVERSITY STUDENTS

While radicals initiated the movement, it was the rank-and-file students who sustained it. This is also a group that I have interviewed extensively. As I have described in chapter 4, during the 1980s most students did not see the state as ideologically legitimate, even though they believed that the state was effectively leading economic development. Moreover, in chapters 3 and 5 I have argued that high inflation, rampant official corruption, and the declining status of intellectuals during the late 1980s had greatly eroded the students' confidence in the regime's performance. As 1989 approached, more and more students became critical of the regime.[17] My evaluation of this population's sense of the state's legitimation along the ideological, legal-electoral, and performance dimensions is represented in table 7.2.

BEIJING RESIDENTS

This group consisted of workers, rank-and-file government employees, private businessmen, primary and middle school teachers, shop assistants, the unemployed, and so forth. The 1989 Movement was initiated as a student movement. However, during and after the hunger strike, more and more Beijing residents

16. Their debate was centered on the liberal versus "new authoritarian" strategies of modernization. While liberals insisted on "no democracy, no economic development," advocates of new authoritarianism emphasized the necessity of authoritarian tutelage at the lower level of economic development before democratization. However, as China's economic crisis deepened, the ideas of liberal intellectuals became popular. For a detailed discussion of the debate, see Zhao Dingxin (1994).

17. For example, to the question: "China would develop more quickly if it is under capitalism," the "yes" answer increased yearly from 16.8 percent in 1986, to 28.7 percent in 1987, and to 34.3 percent in 1989. See table 4.1.

joined the movement. They played a crucial role in stopping the martial law troops in late May. Many of them fought street battles as the troops advanced to Tiananmen Square on June 3 and 4. Their participation had a great impact on the development of the movement especially during the martial law period.

It has been demonstrated that an individual's capacity to understand and articulate an ideology is strongly correlated with his/her level of education.[18] Therefore, it is argued that the question of legitimacy is essentially an intellectual question.[19] However, a lower capacity for articulation does not mean that an individual has no feelings about and never passes judgment on the state. This population certainly had some feelings about the changes in the market prices of everyday consumer products. During the late 1980s, when China's economic crisis deepened and inflation soared, this immediately became a major grievance of all the urban populations. As with the students, the general population's perception of the state's economic performance during the late 1980s leaned toward the negative (table 7.2).

More importantly, in its long history China had developed a stable moral dimension of state legitimation centered on the Confucian political theory of "governing by goodness" or "the mandate of heaven."[20] According to this theory, rulers had to fulfil certain moral, ritual, and material obligations to show their responsibility for and love of their subjects; in exchange the subjects offered conformity and loyalty.[21] After the ideological legitimation of the state declined, moral and ritual performance reemerged as popular criteria for the people to judge their government. Therefore in the 1980s, many novels became best sellers in China not because of their quality but because they dealt with morally upright officials (*qingguan*).[22] Similarly, popular sayings such as "If an official is not able to stand up for his people, he should go home to sell sweet potatoes" (*Dangguan buwei minzuozhu, buru huijia maihongshu*) became the currency of the time.[23]

18. Converse (1964).

19. Mann (1975).

20. See chapter 1. Also see Creel (1953) and Yang Chung-fang (1991).

21. For an excellent account of how an emperor in Ming China was trained through intensive ritual activities, see Ray Huang (1981).

22. The most famous of this type of novel is perhaps *Xinxing* (A new star), written by Ke Yunlu. This story is about how a young head of a county acts as a traditional upright official for the benefit of local people. When the novel was turned into a television miniseries, each Saturday evening when the miniseries was broadcast the major streets in Shanghai were emptied of people. Except for *River Elegy*, no television program produced in China during the 1980s created a reaction among viewers to match the response given to this drama (Lull 1991, ch. 6).

23. This sentence is from *Qipin zhimaguan* (A seventh-rank official), a play about an upright official in traditional China who risked his career to serve his subjects. The play became very popular as soon as

DISCREPANCIES IN THE PERCEPTION OF STATE LEGITIMATION

Based on the above discussion, table 7.2 summarises the level and type of state legitimacy as perceived by different urban populations during the late 1980s. The scales in the table, that is, positive ($+$), somewhat positive ($+/-$), somewhat negative ($-/+$), negative ($-$), and not relevant (o), are intended to catch qualitative distinctions in the perception of state power on the part of the different urban populations that I have analyzed above. Unfortunately, the moral aspect of performance legitimacy is not included in table 7.2. People's perception of the state's moral performance during a movement mainly depends on how the state treats the social movement. The interactive nature of the moral aspect of state legitimacy makes it difficult for it to be included in a table, even though, as I am going to show, it was extremely important to the dynamics of the 1989 Movement.

Table 7.2 vividly shows a huge discrepancy among the four groups' understandings of the ideological and legal aspects of state legitimation. While the state elites asserted strong ideological and legal claims to power, intellectual elites and radical students, and to a lesser extent the Beijing residents, did not see things that way. This discrepancy had two consequences. The first results from the fact that, ruthless killing aside, most state control measures require some understanding and some degree of cooperation from the target population. The discrepancy among the Chinese population groups' understandings of state legitimation suggests that the people did not trust the government, and were hence less likely to cooperate with the state if a control measure carried ideological or legal claims. Thus, the Chinese government had a very limited repertoire of effective control measures to use when dealing with a social movement. Second, given their strong commitment to an ideological and to a legal aspect of state legitimacy, the top state elites were not going to hand over their power, as the state elites in Eastern European countries had done.[24] Thus, if protestors confronted the state head-on, they were going to face repression.

Most importantly, once the government came to be judged mainly by its performance, the economic aspect of this performance could not be its sole dimension. As I explained earlier, moral and ritual performance had also been important grounds on which the Chinese had historically judged their government. During the late 1980s the top state elites and the people differed greatly

---

it came out, and the quoted sentence became a catchphrase in the mouths of urban Chinese during the mid-1980s.

24. Chirot (1991, 3–32).

in their perception of this dimension of state legitimacy. While top state elites often too easily dismissed moral challenges from society, Beijing residents and students took the moral and ritual performance of the state seriously. This does not mean that top state elites sought to impose an image of an immoral government; rather, their loyalty to the CCP made communist ideology a morality more important than traditional moral and ritual observance. The consequence was chaotic: the government's ideological and legal claims only irritated the people, because they did not view them as legitimate, while on the other hand when the people strongly demanded moral responses from the government they did not receive them, because the state elites' moral base lay primarily in the ideology to which they were committed. Therefore, the conflict between the state and society deepened as the movement proceeded.

State-Society Relations, State Behavior, and Movement Dynamics

I have discussed how the top state elites and the other Beijing populations viewed state legitimacy. I have also touched, very generally, on the logic of why this cognitive structure affected the mutual understanding between, and the behavior of, state and society. Now I will present a case study to illustrate how the state's behavior and the dynamics of the movement were shaped by this cognitive structure. While my focus is on the state's behavior, the activities of other populations will also be briefly mentioned when they become helpful to understanding the whole process.

THE STATE'S HESITATION AND THE MOVEMENT'S DEVELOPMENT

The movement started immediately after Hu Yaobang's sudden death. Before Hu's state funeral on April 22, the state acted very cautiously. However, this restraint was probably not a result of struggles among top state elites, as many have tended to believe.[25] At this stage none of the top state elites seemed to have a clear picture of the movement, and it was not suppressed for several

25. After Zhao Ziyang stepped down, even China's official documents accused Zhao Ziyang of delaying the government's efforts in dealing with the movement. But in communist China those in power always exaggerate their struggles with the ousted leaders. For example, during the Lushan Meeting Peng Dehuai expressed his personal views to Mao, and a few other state elites who were not at all related to Peng happened to express similar views. Later, however, they were together all labeled as an antirevolutionary faction. For the government accusation of Zhao, see Chen Xitong (1989). For the Lushan Meeting, see Li Rui (1994).

reasons. First, before his death Hu was still a CCP Politburo member. Since mourning a top leader was a legitimate action that the state would itself carry out even without a grassroots initiative, it was very difficult to repress a movement disguised by mourning activities. Second, there were widespread rumors about Hu's death. It was said that Hu died of a heart attack while Li Peng confronted him in a Politburo meeting. Others even believed that Deng Xiaoping's bodyguard shot Hu. The government was concerned and wanted these rumors put to rest. Finally, the movement started when China was experiencing high inflation and widespread official corruption. While mourning Hu, many individuals also expressed concerns over these problems. The government certainly did not want to further antagonize such a public.

The Beijing Municipal Party held an emergency meeting on the day that Hu died. In the meeting the municipal leaders demanded that school authorities actively lead students' mourning activities, adroitly guide students' activities according to the circumstances, and be alert to the small number of people who intended to use the occasion for political agitation. They also asked school authorities to inform students of the "truth" about Hu's sudden death and to set up memorial halls in many key universities to accommodate the needs of various mourning activities.

Although the government tolerated the protest activities and praised Hu Yaobang in the media, it was unable to directly admit that Hu's 1987 dismissal was a mistake. Doing so would mean also acknowledging the legitimacy of the 1986 Student Movement, its prodemocratic political claims, and the seven demands made by the students in the current movement (chapter 6). These demands for democracy were indeed challenges to the regime's ideological legitimation. Their acceptance would have marked the beginning of the regime's final collapse. Naturally, the top state elites would not concede. By April 23 the students had staged many demonstrations, initiated a citywide class boycott, and established several university- and city-level movement organizations. In the end, the government's limited concession only encouraged mobilization.

THE APRIL 26 *PEOPLE'S DAILY* EDITORIAL

The government was first able to respond seriously to the student movement on April 24, two days after Hu Yaobang's state funeral. At 4:00 P.M. the Standing Committee of the Beijing Municipal Party held a meeting to discuss the situation. The Beijing government concluded that the movement was aimed at overthrowing the CCP leadership. They made four suggestions to the

CCP Central Committee: (1) that the Central Committee express its views on the current situation to the public, taking a clear-cut stand; (2) that all the newspapers and propaganda workers follow the orders of the Central Committee; (3) that the Central Committee authorize the Municipal Party Committee to deal with the student turmoil; and (4) that the Central Committee and the State Council take firm measures to calm the student turmoil as soon as possible.

Four hours later, Li Peng presided over an emergency session of the Standing Committee of the Politburo.[26] President Yang Shangkun was also invited to the meeting. Based on the conclusions and suggestions of the Beijing Municipal Party as well as on their own observations, the Central Committee determined the student movement to be an "organized, planned, and premeditated antiparty and antisocialist action." They therefore decided to: (1) establish a Student Turmoil Management Committee headed by Qiao Shi and Hu Qili; (2) authorize Hu Qili to write an antimovement editorial to be published in the *People's Daily* on April 26; (3) inform all the provinces that this editorial represented the view of the Central Committee; (4) authorize Yan Mingfu, the minister of the United Front Work Department, to inform all the democratic parties of the current situation regarding student turmoil and the decisions of the Central Committee; and (5) mobilize Beijing's citizens to fight with the tumultuous elements and safeguard the capital.

Early next morning Li Peng and Yang Shangkun went to Deng Xiaoping's residence to report the Politburo's decision. Deng not only agreed with the decision but also made a long and harsh comment on the nature of the movement. Many of Deng's comments were later incorporated in the April 26 *People's Daily* editorial.

To date there have been two main interpretations of the process. One was that the Beijing government fed the Politburo distorted information, which led to its harsh decision. Another was that there was a conservative backlash while Zhao Ziyang was away.[27] However, these interpretations cannot explain the following facts. In the first place, although the Beijing government's briefing of the Politburo was indeed full of hardline rhetoric,[28] it was not the only source of the information on which the CCP Central Committee would make a decision. Since the movement's start, Qiao Shi and Hu Qili (both regarded as reformers) had been the two standing Politburo members on the front line in

---

26. Li took charge of the meeting because Zhao Ziyang was away for a state visit to North Korea.
27. Chen Xiaoya (1996, 204–206).
28. The briefing is summarized in *Zhonggong Beijing Shiwei Bangongting* (1989, 41–42).

dealing with the movement. They had other sources of information. For example, they met with some school authorities before they heard the report of the Beijing government.[29] Second, the interpretations also cannot explain why the same government (still without Zhao Ziyang's presence) resorted to concessive strategies again after the April 27 demonstration successfully defied the *People's Daily* editorial.

Chen Xitong, the mayor of Beijing, has claimed that the individuals who attended these meetings all believed that they "[had] been confronted with a planned and organized antiparty, antisocialist political struggle."[30] This may be overstated. However, it does indicate that top state elites were not that divided during this period. They were more or less in favor of a hardline strategy, mainly because earlier concessive measures had failed to contain the movement. The problem stemmed from the huge gaps between how the top state elites and how the people perceived state legitimacy. What students demanded was not what the government could or would give.

The state elites suspected the existence of a small but well-organized force behind the students. The suspicion was possibly derived from the fact that the CCP itself had started with well-organized underground activities. It was also possible that the state elites simply lacked the proper information to understand what was going on inside the movement. In my study I found that the government lacked information for proper decision-making.[31] With no adequate information and with a rigid mindset, many movement activities could only be understood as organized conspiracies.

In a way, the government was not so wrong to spin conspiracy theories since rumor mongering was so widespread at the time. Guo Xiangdong, a student at Beijing Normal University, was hit by a bus and died, but rumor said that a police car hit her; Li Peng never agreed to meet students after Hu Yaobang's funeral, but rumor said that he had agreed but then did not come out; the government believed that policemen were actually quite restrained during the Xinhua Gate evacuation, but rumor insisted on the existence of a "Xinhua Gate Bloody Incident." Such widespread rumors must have had some impact on the top state elites, as they had had on students. Yet, by labeling the movement as

29. Ibid., 37.

30. Chen Xitong (1989, 967).

31. For example, when the hunger strike started, the government did not even know who its organizers were. Hurriedly, the government officials had to hold a dialogue with student leaders that the intellectuals had found for them (chapter 6). In the end, many of these student leaders were not involved in the hunger strike (chapter 6).

antirevolutionary turmoil, the top state elites made two mistakes. First, they lost sight of the fact that most rumors were not invented by organized forces but were instead created spontaneously by more or less anonymous individuals. Second, they underestimated the strong sympathy that the radical students enjoyed among the rest of the students and Beijing residents as a result of the growing social problems.

Once the state no longer enjoyed a high level of ideological legitimation among most urban populations, basing justifications of actions on ideology led only to antagonism. The April 26 *People's Daily* was extremely unpopular as soon as it hit Beijing on the evening of April 25. Since students and Beijing residents had little trust in the state, they believed that the rumors were true and that the government had overreacted. The April 26 editorial only reminded them of totally outmoded Cultural Revolution rhetoric. While the government's counter-mobilization of April 25 and 26 proved ineffective, a massive April 27 student demonstration went off successfully.

THE GOVERNMENT'S CONCESSIONS

To try to stop the students participating in the April 27 demonstration from entering Tiananmen Square, the state deployed all mobilizable Beijing police forces, including students from the police academy. They also called in 5,100 soldiers from the 38th Army to act as a reserve for the police force and to guard Tiananmen Square.[32] However, as more and more information reached the top decision-makers, it became clear to them that a large-scale demonstration was inevitable. At this point, they faced a dilemma. They could order repression; but with the potential size of the demonstration, Beijing police might not be able to stop the demonstration without using excessive violence. To avoid the extremely negative social consequences of violent repression, the top state elites ordered the police to block the demonstrators without violence. However, given the size of the student population and the spatial layout of the campus, this task was simply impossible (chapter 8).

Some scholars have credited the government's restraint to the lobbying efforts of some "reformers," especially Yan Mingfu.[33] Yan and some other top state elites did possibly lobby for a peaceful handling of the April 27 demonstration, but such lobbying should not be seen as the most important reason for the government's initial restraint. My interpretation is instead that the govern-

---

32. *Sanshi Bajun Junshi* (1994, ch. 7).
33. Kristof (1990a, 174); Alan Liu (1990, 513).

ment was still deeply concerned about the negative consequences of repression and did not see repression as the only way for the regime to survive. Could Yan Mingfu still have successfully lobbied for a peaceful resolution during late May? Certainly not. On April 25, Deng Xiaoping told Li Peng and Yang Shangkun that "we must do our best to avoid bloodshed, but we must foresee that it might be impossible to completely avoid it."[34] Deng's speech should be understood literally—the government would try to avoid bloody repression, but if made to choose between repression and a possible loss of power, they would choose the former without hesitation.

After the April 27 demonstration, whatever had been said in the April 26 editorial became hollow rhetoric. Short of repression, the only solution was concession. Therefore, on April 27, the State Council spokesman Yuan Mu expressed the government's intention to hold a dialogue with students. The next day, the *People's Daily* and other major official newspapers reported the April 27 demonstration on the front page with a slightly positive tone. On April 29 and April 30, government officials started to hold dialogues with students. By the time Zhao Ziyang returned from North Korea, a policy of concession was well under way. Again, if Zhao Ziyang was not responsible for the hardline April 26 *People Daily* editorial, he should also receive no credit for the state's policy of concession before he returned.

However, Zhao Ziyang did carry the policy further after his return. When Zhao was in North Korea, the Politburo sent the minutes of the April 24 meeting and Deng Xiaoping's April 25 speech to Zhao. Zhao responded that "I completely agree with the decision made by comrade Deng Xiaoping in dealing with the current turmoil."[35] When Zhao came back on April 30, he further expressed his support of the *People's Daily* editorial in a meeting with the standing members of the Politburo.[36] But meanwhile, as Zhao met with his aides to review what had happened while he was away,[37] his views began to change.

In the following days, Zhao made two public speeches. The first was on the evening of May 3, in a meeting to commemorate the seventieth anniversary of the May 4th Movement,[38] and the second was on May 4, in a meeting with the

34. Oksenberg, Sullivan, and Lambert (1990, 204).

35. Zhao Ziyang (1994).

36. Chen Xitong (1989, 969).

37. For example, Xu Jiatun was one of the people Zhao met after coming back from North Korea. For details on Zhao's meeting with Xu, see Xu Jiatun (1993, 370).

38. Zhao Ziyang (1990b). This speech was circulated among Politburo members for suggestions. According to Zhao Ziyang, two members of the Politburo suggested adding the phrase "against bourgeois liberalization" to the speech. Zhao did not follow the suggestion. He justified his position in a later report to

delegates of the twenty-second Asian Development Bank Conference.[39] The second speech (which was written by Zhao's secretary Bao Tong) made a big splash. In that speech, Zhao argued that the majority of the students were "by no means opposed to our basic system" because their basic slogans were "Support the Communist Party!" "Support Socialism!" "Uphold the Reforms!" "Push Forward Democracy!" and "Oppose Corruption!" Zhao asserted that some people were using the students to create turmoil, but he added that "this is only a tiny minority even though we must always be on guard against them, and I believe that the majority of students understand the point as well." Zhao predicted: "At this point, some students in Beijing and a few other cities are still demonstrating, but I firmly believe that the situation will gradually quiet down. China will not have large-scale turmoil." In the same speech, Zhao also appealed to the students for "calm, reason, restraint, order, and solutions to the problems based on democracy and law." Although his speech also used the word "turmoil" and stressed the importance of political stability, its basic tone was totally different from that of the April 26 *People's Daily* editorial.

CONFLICTS BETWEEN THE CENTRAL AND BEIJING
GOVERNMENTS AND THE RISE OF THE HUNGER STRIKE

Scholars tend to treat Zhao's May 4 speech as a sign of open conflict among top state elites. After the military crackdown Li Peng and Chen Xitong also criticized Zhao's speech for having encouraged the student movement, and they emphasized their own struggles with Zhao.[40] There was no doubt that different opinions and conflicts existed among the top state elites. However, this should not lead us to deny the fact that Zhao's May 4 speech was at the time well received among the top state elites, including those commonly identified as hardliners. For example, Yang Shangkun, who was to play an important role during the military repression, praised Zhao's speech highly in front

---

the CCP Central Committee: "I thought that the whole manuscript had already made an elaborate argument for the Four Cardinal Principles, and the concept 'against bourgeois liberalization' was meant to support the Four Cardinal Principles. They are virtually the same. Moreover, technically, the speech was a positive appraisal of the May 4th Movement. Thus, the phrase would have been quite out of context anywhere in the text" (Zhao Ziyang 1994). In my reading of it, the speech, written by Hu Sheng, the president of the Chinese Academy of Social Sciences and the number-one authority on China's modern history, is indeed an orthodox document.

39. Zhao Ziyang (1990a).
40. Chen Xitong (1989).

of Xu Jiatun.[41] According to Zhao Ziyang, even Li Peng was positive about the speech:

> After the speech was published, it was widely praised for a period of time.... Comrade Li Peng also told me that it was a very good speech and that in his meeting with the Asian Bank delegates he would make a speech concurrent with mine. He did make a speech with a mild tone. At that time I did not feel that we were in a great conflict.[42]

In fact, Li did as he told Zhao he would. The next day, when he met with the Asian Development Bank delegates, he made the following comment:

> [Our] government has adopted certain correct, proper, and calm measures in dealing with the movement, which has prevented its further development. This is a result of mutual efforts of the government and students including both of those who did and those who did not participate in the demonstrations.[43]

What I want to stress is that despite their differences, the top state elites still had a certain consensus at this stage. None of them wanted to see a military repression happen; yet the success of the April 27 demonstration had made verbal intimidation useless. Other than verbal intimidation or military repression, the only choice was concession, albeit at different possible levels. At this stage none of the top state elites were very clear about the consequences of a partial concession. Therefore most of them, including Deng Xiaoping, wanted at least to put up with Zhao Ziyang if his move could bring an end to the movement. Given Deng's power, if he had been totally against Zhao's move, it is highly unlikely that Zhao would have been able to maintain a soft attitude until the hunger strikers drove the movement to a point of no return.[44]

However, Zhao Ziyang's May 4 speech did draw criticism from the Beijing municipal government as well as from school authorities who were in the front lines of the efforts to quiet down the movement. Chen Xitong summarized their reactions to Zhao's speech thus:

41. Xu Jiatun (1993, 373).

42. Zhao Ziyang (1994, 10).

43. Li Peng (1989).

44. As revealed in Zhao's letter (Zhao Ziyang 1994), Deng still supported Zhao when Zhao and Yang Shangkun reported to Deng on May 13. According to Dittmer (1989, 7), Zhao went to see Deng in May, when Deng reportedly told him that "the most important thing you should do is to stabilize the situation.... If the situation is under control, you can implement your plans if they prove feasible, disregarding whatever I have said."

> Zhao Ziyang's speech resulted in ideological confusion among leading officials at various levels, party and youth league members, and the backbone of the masses, particularly those working in universities and colleges. They were at a loss in their work as many voiced their objections. Some people asked, "There are two voices in the central leadership. Which is right and which is wrong? Which are we supposed to follow?" Some queried, "We are required to be at one with the central leadership, but with which one?" Others complained, "Zhao Ziyang plays the good guy at the top while we play the bad guys at the grassroots." Cadres in universities and colleges and backbone students generally felt "betrayed" and had heavy hearts. Some of them even shed sad tears.[45]

When I first read the above description I doubted its truth. To my surprise, however, during my interviews I found that the feeling described in Chen's speech was indeed quite common. Those who had the feeling experienced it not because they were hardliners but because they felt that Zhao's speech literally "sold them out."[46] For example, a student control cadre (no. 44) of a university told me of how he had invited liberal and radical intellectuals to various salons and conferences that he had organized in the university before the 1989 Movement. This narrative naturally led me to identify him as a younger generation reform-minded cadre. However, when we talked about Zhao's speech, he reacted in a way that I did not expect:

> Zhao's speech has always been a great puzzle to me. Although the students during the April 27 demonstration raised slogans that were supportive of the government, what they did was clearly in contempt of the government. They had stabbed the government, but Zhao said that they supported the government. Many of us cannot understand. . . . To those of us who had been trying really hard to calm the students down, Zhao's speech was a turning point. After that we really did not know what to do. How could we talk with students? If we supported Zhao's speech, all we have done before became pointless. On the other hand, we could not say that we did not agree with Zhao, since he was the general secretary of the party.

Zhao's speech stirred up a great deal of contention among those who were taking charge of the attempts to exercise day-to-day control over the students. In my interviews, I found that many of these people had quite liberal personal views and were sympathetic to the movement. However, their institutional positions made them directly responsible for dealing with the students and the

---

45. Chen Xitong (1989, 970).
46. Ibid.

movement, and the change of government attitude embarrassed them and greatly eroded their authority. Thus, within a few days any top-level state officials were "attacked" when they met the university-level student control cadres. That is why when Zhao Ziyang met with school authorities, he was accused of having sold them out. The same informant that I have just mentioned told me what he did when he met with He Dongchang, Minister of Education:

> When He Dongchang came and met with us, I told him that we were puzzled by Zhao's speech. . . . I also asked him whether the Beijing Provisional Articles Regulating Public Marches and Demonstrations were still in effect. When he said yes, I mocked him that this was only in name. In reality, when the students demonstrated you could do nothing. I also asked him what we should do. He could only address my questions in an abstract way. He told us that Zhao Ziyang also agreed with the April 26 *People's Daily* editorial, and that we should use a Marxist point of view to understand the problem, should trust the masses, and should learn to use legal means in dealing with conflicts.[47]

However, as I have argued, while at this stage some top state elites had reservations about Zhao's speech, they still would have followed Zhao if his strategies had worked. The above differences of opinion—which have been cited as evidence of intense factionalism among the top elites both by scholars and in the Chinese government documents aimed at attacking Zhao—were not yet very critical. They were probably more the unhappy reactions of Beijing and university authorities than the challenges of hardliners to Zhao Ziyang. Yet the top state elites did clearly differ over how much they were willing to compromise. While Zhao might go as far as to openly change the verdict of the April 26 *People's Daily* editorial, the majority of state leaders definitely were not willing to go that far.[48] The nature of the consensus made Zhao's action look like a gamble. Were the student movement to quiet down, Zhao would have proved the effectiveness of his strategy. Otherwise, he would be cornered. Unfortunately, Zhao lost badly, because of the hunger strike.

There are two opposing views regarding the hunger strike's origins. The government later asserted that Zhao's May 4 speech encouraged radical students

47. On May 6 Li Peng met with school authorities from eight universities and told them that Zhao's May 4 speech was only his personal opinion. This response is generally cited as evidence of an intense power struggle among top state elites (Chen Xiaoya 1996). However, there is a possibility that Li made this comment under pressure from the school authorities.

48. For example, on May 4, when Zhao Ziyang (1994, 11) tentatively discussed with Li Peng the idea of changing the verdict of the April 26 *People's Daily* editorial, Li rejected the idea.

and brought about the hunger strike.[49] On the other hand, some activists countered that the government had provoked it. They claimed that government leaders, including Zhao, intended only to buy time to let the movement die out before taking revenge on students.[50] In reality, neither was the case. Zhao's May 4 speech certainly did not escalate the movement in itself. Nor did most Beijing students consider the government to be provoking them.

In fact, most Beijing students took Zhao's speech as a significant gesture and were satisfied. The view that the government concession was a conspiracy was actually created by a few radical students and teachers in order to prolong the movement, and it was shared only among a small number of people.[51] After May 4, all the universities in Beijing gradually resumed classes, with the exceptions of Beijing University and Beijing Normal University. For those students who continued to boycott classes, the time off provided an opportunity for travel or for other leisure activities. The movement was no longer their major concern. In order to renew students' interest in the movement, a few radical students started a hunger strike (chapter 6). In short, the government's concessive measures, including Zhao's speech, were highly successful, and the hunger strike was a reaction to that success.

For a government concession to push a few movement activists to act more radically is nothing new—this is in fact routine. In the United States during the 1960s, for example, after the state had made limited adjustments to its policies on civil rights, the Vietnam War, and student campus life, the majority of the American people turned away from the New Left Movement. This drove a few radicals (e.g., the Weathermen) to adopt more and more extreme strategies which broached the use of violence. But in the United States, when these few students went radical, the whole society further turned away from them, the media reported negatively on the movement, and the government's legal actions went against them: all of which contributed to the further decline of the movement.[52] In China, however, what was at first a highly unpopular hunger strike soon drew the support of almost all the urban population. Why?

Again, the key lies in how students and Beijing residents perceived the legitimacy of the state. The hunger strikers set two demands as conditions for end-

49. Chen Xitong (1989).

50. Several radical students and intellectuals whom I have interviewed expressed this view.

51. For example, one teacher went to Chai Ling and told her: "I am a party member. I have received many letters from friends outside Beijing. We are all worried that you will be confused by Zhao Ziyang's talk. The government just wants to calm you down and then to catch you in one net" (*Huigu yu Fansi* 1993, 90).

52. Braungart and Braungart (1992); Gitlin (1980, 1987).

ing the hunger strike: "First, we demand that the government promptly carry out a substantive and concrete dialogue with the Beijing Student Dialogue Delegation with sincerity and on an equal basis. Second, we demand that the government set straight the reputation of this student movement, give it a fair evaluation, and affirm that it is a patriotic student movement for democracy."[53] The first demand was not a big problem for the government. Even before the hunger strike was announced, the Dialogue Delegation and the government had had many contacts. The problem was the second demand. On the surface, it seems that Zhao Ziyang's May 4 speech almost did what the students demanded. Yet radical students also wanted the government to formally denounce the April 26 *People's Daily* editorial, which the government would not do. Most top state elites knew that although most students had joined the movement out of grievances relating to various social problems, the central themes of the movement were prodemocracy and anti-establishment. Therefore, to formally acknowledge the movement would immediately give a legal status to what might be called a "disloyal opposition." When the force of a "disloyal opposition" operates on an aggrieved population, the outcome is a domino effect in which the government makes one concession after another until it totally collapses, as happened in Soviet bloc Eastern European countries. Since most top state elites were still strongly committed to the ideological legitimacy of the regime, there was no way that they would accept the second demand and risk setting such a process in motion.[54]

However, a hunger strike is not like other forms of demonstration, such as a class boycott. A state can tolerate a class boycott without accepting the boycotters' demands. But hunger strikers will die if their conditions are not met. As mentioned before, most students and Beijing residents during the late 1980s cared about the regime's moral and economic performance, not about its ideological commitment. Moreover, their hearts were naturally inclined towards the students due to their shared grievances over recent economic crises. Thus the students and Beijing residents cared much less about what demands the hunger strikers made or what the consequence of the action might be than about how the state treated them. It was now the lives of the hunger strikers that were at stake. The state had to take care of them, for if the hunger strikers' health conditions deteriorated, the people would get very angry. Therefore the hunger

---

53. For one version of translation of these two demands, see Han and Hua (1990, 202).

54. A reader of this chapter questioned why the Chinese state survived after it rehabilitated the "April 5th" Movement in 1976. My answer is that the "April 5th" Movement was mainly aimed against the Maoists and not against the communist regime as such. Therefore, it was still a "loyal opposition" and could be easily rehabilitated without fundamentally undermining the regime.

strike also posed a moral challenge to the state. Indeed, since the only way that the state could end the hunger strike was to concede to students' demands that it found unacceptable, the hunger strike cornered the regime. The hunger strike was a highly effective action because it challenged the regime ideologically as well as morally, and thus fundamentally. However, the hunger strike also turned the movement into a moral crusade and a zero-sum game. From then on, a head-on collision was almost inevitable.

INTENSIFICATION OF THE POWER STRUGGLE AMONG TOP STATE ELITES

Before May 15, government officials tried to negotiate with students, even directly appealing to the students in Tiananmen Square to end the hunger strike for the sake of the Sino-Soviet summit. The hunger strikers refused to leave. On May 15, Gorbachev arrived in Beijing. Many activities planned for this historic visit had to be rescheduled or even canceled because of the occupation of Tiananmen Square. The disruption of Gorbachev's state visit made Zhao Ziyang's strategy increasingly unpopular among top state leaders. Moreover, since the students would not go away without the acceptance of their demands, the top state elites had to make a clear-cut decision immediately. Thus, the leadership conflict intensified.

On the night of May 16, the standing members of the Politburo held an emergency meeting.[55] In that meeting, Zhao Ziyang argued for further concessions, including a direct change of the verdict of the April 26 *People's Daily* editorial. On the other hand, Li Peng and Yao Yilin insisted that further concessions would only lead to more demands and eventual chaos.[56] The meeting lasted

55. Old veterans, mainly Deng Xiaoping, Yang Shangkun, Li Xiannian, Chen Yun, Peng Zhen, and Wang Zhen, had urged the Central Committee to hold this meeting. As is indicated in Yang Shangkun's speech to an emergency meeting of the Military Commission of the Central Committee held on May 24, they all believed that any further concessions would inevitably lead to a total collapse of the regime (Yang Shangkun 1990). Their view had a strong influence on the meetings of standing members of Politburo in the following days.

56. This is reflected in Yao Yilin's June 13 speech in a meeting with the ministry-level cadres of the CCP and the State Council (Yao 1989, 17): "When you study [Deng Xiaoping's speech], you may raise questions such as, what if we took a step back—admitted that the student movement was a patriotic democratic movement, and legalized their organizations. I think many comrades here have this question in mind. In fact, we have pondered this question many times. If we took a step back, then an opposition party would appear in China. . . . If we made such a concession, our country would go along the same path as Poland. What happened in Poland and Hungary was a combined result of pushes and concessions. Whether our party, our country, would change its color depended on this crucial and decisive step. . . . Therefore, we had repeatedly and carefully thought it over. This was the concession we could not make—absolutely not." During Yao's speech, Li Peng also added a comment: "If we legalized the Students' Autonomous

until early the next morning, with no decision. The only conclusion reached was a written speech, read by Zhao Ziyang on the May 17 morning news. The speech positively evaluated the students' demands and patriotic enthusiasm. It appealed to students to stop the hunger strike for the sake of their own health and to withdraw from Tiananmen Square. It also promised that the government would not subsequently punish movement leaders and that the government would still hold dialogues with students after their withdrawal. However, the students in the Square did not even take particular notice of the speech.

Since the first meeting was inconclusive and Zhao's speech was ineffective, another meeting was scheduled at Deng Xiaoping's home for late at night on May 17. Yang Shangkun and Li Xiannian attended the meeting as well. Deng Xiaoping started with a very brief remark: "The situation can no longer go on like this.[57] What should we do? Do we still have some leeway, and how many concessions do we still need to make?" After Deng's remark, Yang Shangkun added: "This is the last dam of a reservoir. The government would collapse if we make further concessions."[58] When Zhao Ziyang started to talk, he still advocated a further concession. Then, Yao Yilin took out a previously prepared note and started a long speech against Zhao. In turn, Zhao fought back with his own reasoning. The meeting again lasted for several hours. Eventually those present had to take a vote to decide whether or not to employ martial law to end the Tiananmen Square occupation. In the meeting, Zhao Ziyang and Hu Qili were against the idea while Li Peng, Yao Yilin, and Qiao Shi supported it.[59] Therefore, the motion to employ martial law was approved.

A comment must be added that martial law might still have been employed even if the standing members of the Politburo did not endorse it. After the hunger strike began, almost all of the veterans that I list in table 7.1 rushed back to Beijing. These retired and semiretired veterans were all strongly against further concessions. With their power and influence in the CCP, they would have

---

Union as students insisted, what about the workers? Do we legalize a solidarity workers' union upon the workers' insistence?"

57. Here, "the situation" may refer both to the situation in Tiananmen Square and the situation of a divided opinion among the standing members of the Politburo.

58. Wu et al. (1989, 390).

59. There are three versions of the story of the vote. Chen Yizi said that Qiao Shi and Hu Qili abstained. Gao Xin concluded, after some interviews, that no people in the meeting had abstained from voting. Finally, according to Yang Shangkun, only Zhao voted for a further concession in that meeting. Yang's account is supposedly the most authentic one because he was in the meeting. However, Yang did not make clear whether the rest had all voted in favor of martial law, or some had abstained from voting. I have adopted Gao Xin's version. See Chen Yizi (1990, 161), Gao Xin (1995), and Yang Shangkun (1990).

been able to mobilize the troops even without the approval of standing members of the Politburo. Yet a formal approval certainly gained a great deal of legitimacy for the action among the rank-and-file CCP members.

In these days, there were also signs that Zhao Ziyang might no longer intend to cooperate with his colleagues. For example, on May 16, in a televised meeting, he told Gorbachev that Deng Xiaoping still had the final say on the most important matters in the country. At this point, most students and Beijing residents were very angry about the government's reaction to the hunger strike. Thus, Zhao' speech invited many attacks on Deng Xiaoping from demonstrators in the following days. On the morning of May 19, Zhao insisted on visiting the hunger strikers at Tiananmen Square and trying to persuade them to stop the hunger strike. Zhao disappeared from the scene after his May 19 appearance.

What can we conclude from all this? First, the struggle among the top state elites did intensify in the period. However, the conflicts were less between two factions than almost exclusively between Zhao Ziyang and the rest of the top elites. Therefore, Zhao was easily defeated. Secondly, the struggle was not so much between conservatives and reformers than between different estimates of the cost of a further concession. While Zhao still believed that by a further concession the movement could be contained as a "loyal opposition,"[60] the rest of the top state elites, including many of his early supporters such as Yang Shangkun and Qiao Shi, thought that the regime would collapse with one more concession.[61] Finally, the state's shifting back to hardliner strategies (even if achieved through a power struggle) reflected more the nature of the state and of state-society relations in China than the factionalist nature of the government. Differently put, the state turned to a hardline approach because it lacked a mechanism to institutionalize elements of a loyal opposition while marginalizing the radicals.

60. A loyal opposition has been considered a key to the stability of democracy. The essence of the idea is that the stability of any political system lies in the fact that rival political forces accept the same fundamental value system, competing only within the normative bounds of politics. The concept is an extension of the British idea of "Her Majesty's opposition." See, for example, Linz and Stepan (1978, ch. 2).

61. In a meeting on May 22, Qiao Shi said that for "over a month, the movement has been continuously escalating. In the process, we have been restrained and tolerant. We have accepted all that the student leaders have demanded, so long as the concessions did not forfeit our basic principles. . . . In short, step by step they have had many opportunities to extricate themselves from the situation. I have for a long time believed that we can no longer concede any further. The only problem is to find a proper way to end the situation. If one more concession can solve the problem, we have made the concession already. There is indeed no way out of this situation" (Wu et al. 1989, 392–93).

MARTIAL LAW AND MILITARY CRACKDOWN

During the night of May 19, martial law troops moved toward Beijing from all directions. However, the students and Beijing residents successfully stopped them. After several days of stalemate, the troops had to retreat to the Beijing suburbs.

Since the troops were unable to enter Beijing peacefully, the only solution available, short of accepting the students' demands, was to order the troops to advance at any cost. The order did not come early only because things were not quite ready. First, in the early stages of martial law, although most senior military commanders generally supported the decision, the majority of lower-level commanders and soldiers were definitely not ready to fight their way into Tiananmen Square. The government had to further unify them. Second, the top state elites also needed to gain the support and understanding of other state officials for a policy of military repression. After May 22, the government held a series of meetings to unify various elites. The meetings had different stresses for different audiences. For example, on May 24, when Yang Shangkun met with senior military leaders, he capitalized on the radical slogans used in the movement and on the fact that martial law had been decided upon by Deng Xiaoping, backed by a group of Long March veterans.[62] When Chen Yun met with veterans in the Central Advisory Commission, he emphasized the hardship and sacrifice that they had endured before they took power, warning that if students succeeded, "not only is there the danger of losing the achievements of ten years of reform but there is also the danger of losing all the fruits of revolution, which were won with blood."[63] When Peng Zhen met with noncommunist government elites, he stressed that students had good and constructive motives but had adopted the wrong methods to address social problems, that the government also had the same concerns, and that the students were being used by a very small number of people with ulterior motives.[64] With powerful figures speaking in concert, more and more lower-level leaders openly expressed their support of martial law in the newspapers.

However, the top state elites were still concerned about the cost of military repression. They still frequently contacted student leaders through official and semi-official channels to persuade (or even threaten) them to withdraw from the Square voluntarily. Let me list some accounts by student leaders as examples.

62. Yang Shangkun (1990).
63. Chen Yun (1990).
64. Wu et al. (1989, 455–56).

Deng Pufang, the son of Deng Xiaoping, sent his associates to Beijing University. They told student leader Chang Jing that if the students withdrew voluntarily from the Square and no longer insisted on going against martial law and on changing the verdict of the April 26 *People's Daily* editorial, Deng Pufang could persuade Deng Xiaoping to resign after everything was over.[65] Also, according to student leader Li Lu, on May 26 a representative of Li Peng and the whole Politburo went to Tiananmen Square to persuade the students to leave.[66] He told the students that martial law was not aimed at them, that the soldiers were not going to harm them, and that the government would not punish students after the movement ended. If the students were stubborn and did not leave the Square, however, they would have to be removed and bloodshed might not be avoidable.[67] These efforts showed that even after it imposed martial law, the government still tried to avoid a bloody confrontation. This was not because of the particular influence of reformers but rather because everyone in the government knew the potential cost of military repression.

As the students did not leave the Square, the Martial Law Headquarters ordered the second advance. Again, the army met with strong resistance from Beijing residents. The whole process was complicated and disturbingly violent. However, with a resolute order from the central government, the troops, who were now better prepared, fought their way to Tiananmen Square. The movement ended tragically.

Why did the students and Beijing residents ignore the harsh warnings from the government and risk their lives in order to resist the martial law troops?[68] Many factors came into play. For example, during the movement the state had used hardliner strategies several times. Each time, however, they had backed off when movement participants stood their ground. Since the government had already played the "chicken" several times in a "chicken-hero game," the people expected the government to play the chicken again. Therefore, in my interviews several informants told me that even after some people in the crowd were shot, the people beside them, including themselves, still believed that they were actually hit by rubber bullets; for a while, they showed no fear. But, the key here

65. *Huigu yu Fansi* (1993, 265, 292).

66. Li Lu (1990, 179).

67. According to Zhang Boli (1994e), the last contact between students and the government was made on the afternoon of May 30 at Beijing Hotel. Li Lu and Zhang Boli went to the meeting. No agreement was reached. Eventually, the government representatives warned that students must return to the university as soon as possible because the army was going to clear the Square very soon.

68. Before the repression, the government continuously broadcast warnings that urged Beijing residents to stay at home for their own safety.

was perhaps not the existence of a so-called "information gap" between the two actors, as has been argued.[69] First, the Beijing students and residents did not together constitute a cohesive actor. By the end of May they were more like a huge, unorganized crowd. More importantly, the government did not really intend to hide the military repression as private information. In fact, the government tried in many public and private occasions to warn the people that they had run out of patience and that a repression was imminent. Yet the students and residents simply did not respond to the message. Now, again, let me explain this in terms of the model of state-society relations centered on sources of state legitimacy.

As stated before, when Zhao Ziyang's concessive strategies failed to work, the government had to go back to a hardline approach. However, this time it could not just use ideological means, because the April 26 *People's Daily* editorial had proved not only useless but also provocative to the students. Between ideological attacks and military repression, the only measure that the government could rely on was to institute a sanction against the movement by legal means. This was martial law. The problem was that, in the past, top state elites in China treated laws not as part of the social contract to which they were also subject but as a tool that could be used to advance ideological programs or possibly even for personal purposes. Therefore, legal practices and interpretation of laws changed frequently with the ideological currents, and the authority of laws diminished when the ideological legitimation of the state declined. Understandably, given this legal tradition martial law was neither able to convince students and Beijing residents nor to convey a clear message to which the opposition forces could make a rational and calculated response. In the end, martial law was as counterproductive as the April 26 *People's Daily* editorial.

By now, all the control measures that the government had tried had failed. The only measure left was brutal military repression. There was hardly anyone among the top state elites, regardless of whether they be so-called reformers or conservatives, who wanted to see it happen. Yet, ironically, this appeared to be the only effective method that the regime could use to stop the wave of large-scale mobilizations, the core of which was anti-establishment. It was effective because by the end of the 1980s most of the top state elites, including most senior commanders of the army, were still committed to a revolution which they had fought for decades and in the meantime were still able to keep the soldiers under their firm control.

69. Deng Fang (1997).

Conclusion

The government initially tolerated the 1989 Movement, while trying to confine it to mourning activities for Hu Yaobang. After Hu Yaobang's state funeral, the government's policy shifted to a more hardline approach, as was indicated by the April 26 *People's Daily* editorial that labeled the movement antirevolutionary turmoil. When students successfully organized the April 27 demonstration that defied the editorial, the government came back with a soft strategy and tried to contain the movement through a policy of limited concessions. On May 19, however, after a week of the hunger strike, the government declared martial law and brought a mass of troops to Beijing, first trying to scare the protestors away. When this did not work, military repression followed.

These policy changes and the consequent development of the movement have hitherto been explained as outcomes of factional struggles between reformers and conservatives within the highest echelon of the Chinese government. In this chapter, I offer an alternative interpretation of the same process. I argue that while the existence of power struggles among top state elites is a truism, the key factor underlying these state policy changes was the ineffectiveness of various state control measures, an ineffectiveness that resulted from the conflicting views of state legitimacy held by the top state elites, the movement activists, and the rest of the Beijing population. The logic of my argument is that each state control measure needs a legitimacy base in order to be effective. During the 1980s, while the majority of top state elites still believed in the ideological legitimacy of the regime, most students and Beijing residents evaluated the state mainly for its economic and moral performance. In the course of the movement, the students challenged the government ideologically and morally, and the larger society sympathized with the challenges. On the other hand, the government either relied on ideological or legal dimensions of state authority to deal with the movement, which only antagonized Beijing students and residents, or made limited concessions, which could not satisfy the radicals. In the end, the only viable alternative appeared to be military repression, on which the government could still rely because most top state elites, a group that included military leaders, had joined the CCP long before the communists came to power and still perceived state power as ideologically legitimate.

eight

ECOLOGY-BASED MOBILIZATION
AND MOVEMENT DYNAMICS

Having examined how the state's behavior and people's perceptions of it shaped the development of the 1989 Beijing Student Movement, we now turn our attention more fully to the movement participants. A central question in social movement research has been that of the mechanisms of participant mobilization. Since the 1970s, social movement scholars have put great emphasis on the role of formal organizations and movement networks in movement mobilization.[1] Currently, the idea that organizations and pre-existing networks are the basis of movement mobilization has become conventional wisdom. Therefore, when I started my research I designed questions to probe in that direction. As expected, I found many signs of organization- and network-based communication and mobilization. Yet many of these instances could not be understood without taking campus ecology into account; moreover, the ecology of university campuses in Beijing facilitated student mobilization beyond its encouragement of movement organizations and student networks. Let me provide an initial example.

---

1. For recent reviews of literature, see Roger V. Gould (1991, 1993), McAdam and Paulsen (1993), and Zhao Dingxin (1998).

Almost all campuses in Beijing are separated from the outside world by brick walls with only a few entrances, which are guarded by the university's own security forces. During the 1989 Movement, no policemen or soldiers ever went inside a campus to repress students. After talking to students, I found that the existence of campus walls was important for the development of the movement. Because of the walls, roads on campus were not part of the public road system, and thus the police could not get inside without clear consent from school authorities. Here, even school authorities that were unsympathetic to the movement might not be interested in calling in the police to handle students. For if they did so, they would alienate the students and would have more troubles in dealing with students after the police left. Therefore, the simple existence of walls created a low-risk environment and facilitated student mobilization.[2]

This type of finding pushed me to look more seriously at the role of campus ecology in student mobilization. I found that campus ecology affected student mobilization during the movement in the following ways: (1) It facilitated the spread of dissident ideas in the period before the movement and the transmission of news about particular events during the movement. (2) It nurtured many dormitory-based student networks. These networks were the basis of mutual influence and even coercion among students and therefore sustained a high rate of student participation. (3) It shaped students' spatial activities on the campus, creating a few places that most students had to pass or stay in daily. These places became centers of student mobilization. (4) The concentration of many universities in one district encouraged mutual imitation and inter-university competition for activism among students from different universities. (5) The ecology also facilitated the formation of many ecology-dependent strategies of collective action. Those actions patterned the dynamics of the movement.[3] The above findings and their theoretical implications will be the focus of this chapter.

Before moving on, let me note that it was not just student mobilization during the movement that was heavily based on ecological factors. Resident mobilization during the martial law period was primarily centered in the neighborhoods, and the movement was able to sustain itself after martial law largely because of the ecology of Tiananmen Square (chapter 6). However, this chapter deals strictly with student mobilization (especially during the early stage of the movement). This is, in part, because since the early mobilization faced

---

2. See McAdam (1986) for a distinction between low-risk and high-risk activism.

3. Ecology-dependent strategies are a relatively stable set of mobilization strategies in that their effectiveness and their likelihood of being adopted by movement activists rest largely on particular ecological conditions.

strong efforts at repression and involved more uncertainties, campus ecology was crucial to sustaining it. After the students had successfully challenged the regime, the perceived risk of joining a movement greatly declined. In fact, the risk diminished to the point when after mid-May going to Tiananmen Square became a common pastime and a fun activity.

State-Society Relations and Mobilization Structures

The question immediately arises of why the 1989 Movement had a mobilization structure that was distinctively different from that of most social movements occurring under democratic settings in the West. My main argument is that the mobilization structure of social movements is first shaped by state-society relations. In addition, the structure of movement mobilization is also related to the type of social movement. The mobilization of a student movement, for example, tends to depend on the conditions of the students' unique living and studying environment. Let me briefly discuss three ideal types of mobilization structures in reference to state-society relations and the types of social movements.

Some social movements mobilize primarily through formal organizations. This happens, for example, in mainstream contemporary Western society, where associational life is highly developed and politically sensitive individuals are situated under what some scholars call "multi-organizational fields."[4] Since many such organizations are not territory-based and have infrastructures with which to reach their members that are more effective than interpersonal networks, ecological conditions are less likely to be a major factor in their movement mobilization. Many social movements in the contemporary West, especially some of the new social movements, have a mobilization process approximate to this type.

Most mobilization processes, however, involve a mixture of formal organizations, interpersonal networks centered on people's immediate living and working environments, and direct ecological exposure. Thus ecology plays various roles in different mobilization processes. Due to university students' unique living and studying conditions, the impact of campus ecology on movement mobilization has drawn a certain amount of attention. For instance, many observers of student movements in the 1960s have noticed the facilitating effect of

---

4. See Curtis and Zurcher (1973), Fernandez and McAdam (1989), McAdam and Paulsen (1993), and Rosenthal et al. (1985) for the concept.

the American campus on students' participation in them.[5] Max Heirich, in particular, has convincingly described how a series of changes in campus layout at Berkeley during the 1950s made Berkeley students more available for political recruitment during the 1960s.[6] The fact that campus ecology is conducive to student movements has also been noticed by scholars who have studied such movements in other nations. Kassow, for example, has written that the dining halls built by Nicholas II to provide students in Moscow with cheap meals turned out to be meeting places where students could trade news, make new contacts, and hold assemblies,[7] and both Chow and Wasserstrom have observed that the congested living conditions on Chinese campuses facilitated student activism in early modern China.[8]

In addition to student movements, many other cases also point to the importance of ecology for movement mobilization. For example, in nineteenth-century Western Europe, when a nascent civil society coexisted with traditional communities, most social movements, such as Chartism in England and the Paris Commune, were staged by formal organizations. However, these formal organizations also relied heavily on the physical environment of the local community to extend their mobilizational potential.[9] In the contemporary West, some collective actions, such as community movements or the urban riots in America, also involved a process of mobilization that was dependent on ecology.[10] As Feagin and Hahn and Fogelson mention, the sudden and massive riots in some American cities were made possible in part because of the densely populated black ghettos and because of the fact that the residents of those ghettos tended to spend a great deal of their leisure time out on the street.[11]

Finally, some social movements tend to have mobilization structures that are mainly based on ecology. This typically occurs in places where intermediate associations are underdeveloped and associations beyond state control are illegal. In such cases, ecology and ecology-based networks and communications become

5. Berk (1974), Heirich (1971), and Lofland (1970).

6. Heirich (1971, 59–65).

7. Kassow (1989).

8. Chow (1967) and Wasserstrom (1991).

9. See Roger V. Gould (1995) and Mann (1993, ch. 15). Tilly (1976), Bezucha (1974), and Aminzade (1993) have also discussed the characteristics of traditional communities and their importance to movement mobilization in Western Europe. In particular, Tilly and Schweitzer (1982) have an excellent analysis of how the redistribution of economic activities, administrative activities, and residents in London in the years between 1758 and 1834 affected the spatial routine of the people and consequently the geographic locations of collective contentions.

10. For the community movement examples, see Delgado (1986) and Perry, Gillespie, and Parker (1976).

11. Feagin and Hahn (1973); Fogelson (1971).

the only means on which a movement mobilization can count. Many social movements occurring in strong authoritarian regimes have a mobilization process close to this extreme because those states repress voluntary associations.

In the past, scholars have generally thought that communist regimes were highly stable because their repression was assisted by modern infrastructural and military technologies. This "totalitarian myth" disintegrated after revolutions swept across Eastern Europe in the late 1980s. Thereafter, the question "How can autocratic regimes that appear to have such awesome power over their citizens collapse so quickly?" became a puzzle.[12] Thus far, most scholars have tried to address this question by emphasizing the role of "civil society" during Eastern Europe's Revolutions.[13] Yet judging by the nature of the former Eastern European regimes, it is conceivable that even in Hungary, Czechoslovakia, and Poland, where civil society was more developed, initial movement mobilization might have depended more on ecology and ecology-dependent strategies than on formal organizations or political networks. For example, I see similarities between mobilization structures in the 1989 Movement in Beijing and the strikes in Gdansk and Gdynia in 1970. According to Roman Laba, the strikes in Gdansk and Gdynia were initiated by a few activists who moved from one workplace to another, chanting to attract followers.[14] They also pushed a sound car to different shipyards to draw more people. The existing organizations at the time, such as the Workers' Defense Committee or the church, had nothing to do with the strike at this stage. The importance of shipyard ecology is clearly revealed by Laba's book even though it does not focus on the issue of movement mobilization.

An authoritarian regime may crush intermediate associations, but it cannot destroy ecology-centered human interactions. In fact, as it is revealed in this chapter, the process of centralization under an authoritarian regime often strengthens ecology-based human interactions. The huge capacity of ecology-centered mobilization at the time of political crisis explains, in part, why the seemingly mighty communist regime is actually fragile.

Universities in Beijing

Before presenting a case study of how campus ecology in Beijing facilitated student mobilization, we need some knowledge of the physical layout of Beijing

---

12. The question is posed by Olson (1990, 16).
13. See, for example, Di Palma (1991), Ost (1990), Poznanski (1992), and Tismaneanu (1990).
14. See Laba (1991, ch. 2).

campuses as well as of typical student life on campus. I start with the university district in Beijing.

THE HAIDIAN UNIVERSITY DISTRICT

In Beijing, most universities are located in and around the Haidian District. This immense university compound was the legacy of the planned economy in the 1950s. Aimed at "learning from the Soviet Union" and at establishing an educational system suitable for the massive reconstruction of the country, the giant university district acquired its current shape in two separate phases during the 1950s. The first step was to restructure the existing universities and to establish People's University. The two best and largest universities in the capital—that is, Beijing University and Qinghua University—acquired their current structure and location at this time. The second effort was to build a large number of Soviet-style polytechnic institutions in the same area.[15] A major event was the construction of *bada xueyuan* (the eight big institutions of higher learning), when eight polytechnic institutions were simultaneously built along a single road. By 1956, when the second project was completed, Beijing already had thirty-one universities with an enrollment of 76,700, compared to thirteen universities and a total enrollment of 17,442 in 1949.[16] The university district continued to expand: by 1989 Beijing had sixty-seven institutions of higher learning, with 162,576 boarding students at the undergraduate and graduate levels.[17]

CAMPUSES IN BEIJING

University campuses in China are structurally similar to each other. Since Beijing University is the center of student activism in Beijing as well as in China as a whole, this section uses Beijing University to illustrate the typical campus in Beijing.

As shown on the map of Beijing University (figure 8.1), most universities in China are separated from the outside by a brick wall. Each university has its own restaurants, student dining halls, cinema, hospital, post office, barbershops, grocery stores, sports facilities, recreational areas, and other such facilities. They are so self-contained that diligent students can live on campus for a whole semester without ever going outside.

15. Du (1992).
16. Zhang Jian and Zhou Yuliang (1989).
17. *Educational Statistics Yearbook of China* (1989); *Zhongguo Gaodeng Jiaoyu Daquan* (1989).

FIGURE 8.1. A map of Beijing University, showing the ecological concentration of students on campus.

FIGURE 8.2. The master's student dormitories at Beijing University. (Photograph by the author.)

Most university students in China board and live in campus dormitories. Classmates are usually assigned to several connected rooms in a dormitory. At Beijing University, the student dormitories occupy forty-nine buildings. They are located at the lower right side of the map. Buildings numbered 28 to 43 are for undergraduate students. With six to eight students living in each dormitory room, these dormitories held a total of 9,271 students in 1988. Buildings numbered 45 through 48 are for master's students, whereas doctoral students live in dormitories 25 and 26. With four master's students or two doctoral students living in each dormitory room, 2,893 students lived in these six buildings in 1988. Finally, buildings numbered 16 through 24 are dormitories for young unmarried teachers. The remaining dormitories housed foreign and special students in short-term training programs. Figure 8.2 is the exterior of the master's student dormitories in Beijing University.

STUDENT LIFE ON CAMPUS

According to my informants, in the late 1980s many students in Beijing University (and other universities as well) did not devote much time to studying. Many students, especially males, got up only a few minutes before their first class began and went to class without breakfast. Class absence was especially

FIGURE 8.3. An undergraduate student dormitory room at People's University. (Photograph by the author.)

high for students majoring in the social sciences and humanities or in those courses designed for political education (chapter 3). The first classes at Beijing University started at eight, but some students got up as late as ten, missing three or four classes in the morning. These students might stay in the dormitory until lunch, at about twelve. A nap was common after lunch. Diligent students got up at two, but others might get up at three or even four. Dinner started at five. Activities after dinner varied. Some went to the library or to conferences. Others went to dances, to movies, or out with their boyfriends or girlfriends. Still others remained in the dormitory rooms chatting or playing poker or mahjongg. Most students returned to the dormitories around ten. Curfew was at eleven. Chatting after curfew was a common pastime; students called this *wotanhui*, which means meeting while lying in bed. Such *wotanhui* could go on as late as 2:00 A.M.

Some students described the dormitory, classroom, and dining hall as the "iron triangle" of their lives. According to a study of student dormorites, the time that students spent in their dormitory rooms during a day was more than the time they spent on all other activities combined.[18] Figure 8.3 shows the inside of a typical undergraduate student dormitory room in People's University.

18. Xu and Liu (1985).

Campus Ecology and Patterns of Mobilization

In the interviews, I found that the campus ecology in Beijing facilitated the transmission of dissident ideas and information about movement activities. It squeezed students into many small dormitory-based student networks which sustained a high level of student participation, encouraged interuniversity competition for activism, and upheld many ecology-dependent strategies of collective action. I will discuss these in turn in this section. In the next section, I will present a case study of the April 27 student demonstration, to show how ecology-based mobilization mechanisms manifested themselves in one of the most important events of the 1989 Movement.[19]

DISSIDENT IDEAS AND THE TRANSMISSION
OF INFORMATION REGARDING THE MOVEMENT

Most students live in campus dormitories. With six to eight students living in each dormitory room, a few dozen classmates of the same sex living in several closely situated dormitory rooms, and several hundred students in each building, a dormitory area of a university in Beijing can accommodate up to ten thousand students. Many informants reported that they usually chatted in the dormitory room from one to several hours each day. Although politics and political grievances were not always the topic, they did constitute a major theme when the socioeconomic situation in China was worsening. As I discussed in chapter 4, when the student political control system in universities greatly declined during the late 1980s, dormitory rooms became the primary locations in which nonconforming ideologies spread and achieved dominance.

The communication of dissident ideas was also facilitated by the ecology of the Haidian District. The distance between most universities in Beijing is less than half an hour by bicycle. Such short distances made interuniversity communication extremely easy. Before the 1989 Movement, famous dissidents and liberal intellectuals were often invited to give talks in various universities. If a talk was given by someone famous, students from the other universities would go there by bicycle. As soon as the movement started, the very first action of many activists was to go to other universities (especially the major ones) to see

---

19. In the following, I will take the impact of homogeneity as an established fact and focus only on how design factors of Beijing universities shaped the density, distribution, and spatial movement of Beijing students in a way that facilitated student mobilization.

what was happening. They went there to read big-character posters, listen to speeches, and establish connections. Thus, from the very beginning, campus ecology gave a largely spontaneous movement the appearance of a coordinated action.

SANCTIONS AGAINST FREE RIDERS

During the 1989 Movement, students would often march together in a demonstration by school, class, and often major. This form of collective action has been explained as a manifestation of Chinese culture, which encourages solidarity, loyalty, and friendship.[20] However, to explain a sign of group solidarity in terms of a group culture is tautological. More importantly, this line of reasoning neglects the structural basis of this solidarity and thus runs the danger of assuming that all the students participated in the movement for the same reason. In my study, I found that students not only often marched together by school, class, and major, but also by dormitory room. However, they did this not just out of a sense of group solidarity but because the campus ecology and dormitory-based student networks were the bases of mutual influence, persuasion, and even coercion among students.

The key here is the dense living environment on campus, especially dormitory rooms. With six to eight students living in the same dormitory room for a period of four years, it is as if every student was forced to play an Axelrodian game in which cooperation is the only optimum long-term solution.[21] Therefore, once movement participation was regarded by most students as a morally desirable action, avoiding participation became very difficult for those who actually did not intend to participate in the beginning. Among fifty-six student informants, fourteen reported open attacks by active participants on less active ones in dormitories. Students in the same or nearby dormitory rooms often checked each other's behavior. One student commented:

> All students joined the movement after several demonstrations. Students who did not go would feel isolated and hated. For example, when the government asked us

20. Calhoun (1994, 170).

21. In the language of game theory, this is a prisoners' dilemma game involving a small number of people and with a large number of iterations. As Axelrod (1984) has nicely demonstrated, repeated encounters between two players in a game will make cooperation the only robust and optimum long-term solution. In other words, it is actually unnecessary to introduce Chinese culture at this point because sense of solidarity or friendship will at most only function as an initial condition of the Axelrodian game to speed up the rise and dominance of conformist behavior.

to resume class, only one student went to class. As a result, that student was accused of being a renegade. (no. 4)

Another student described what happened in his dormitory room on the evening of April 26, which made him eventually join the April 27 student demonstration:

[When the April 26 *People's Daily* editorial was broadcast,] students in our dormitory room were very angry. Many of them decided to go to demonstrate. They asked me. I said I did not want to go. . . . They were mad at me. . . . They quarreled with me angrily. I found this unbearable and thought, we are fellow students, why should you talk to me like this? . . . There was a party member in our dormitory room who did not want to go either. . . . He told us that they had just had a meeting. It was explained in the meeting that there would be a lot of policemen on the way the next day. He asked the other students not to go. . . . Then people poured out their anger toward him. (no. 42)

Because of the high student density in dormitory buildings, coercion among students could sometimes go beyond a dormitory room. Feigon, for example, mentions how a TOEFL teacher at People's University was accused by his friends of being a traitor because he had held a TOEFL class during the class boycott.[22] However, no one has given an account as vivid as one of my informants (no. 62):

During the whole process of the movement, one event left me with a very deep impression. In the Law Department, there were quite a few graduate students of the 1989 class who did not care about the movement at all and played mah-jongg in their dormitory rooms every day. I knew this from a notice board in no. 46 building. It read: "Since the hunger strike, several scoundrels on the fifth floor have not cared about the movement at all, and have lost all their conscience. They have been locking themselves in their dorms and playing mah-jongg every day. We are disgusted with their behavior." . . . I also remember a line on a big-character poster. It said: "Those red noses and black hearts are playing mah-jongg even when the other students are on a hunger strike. Beware of your dog noses!"

However, most pressure was subtler. When a follow-up question was asked ("What did you think of those students who did not participate in the movement at all?"), the following was a rather typical answer: "We did not care

22. Feigon (1990, 148).

about those students. Because these people did not interact with classmates even at regular times, no one paid much attention to them" (no. 37). In other words, nonparticipating students were labeled as deviants by their classmates. Obviously, such mutual checking could effectively sustain movement participation largely because of the particularities of the relevant living conditions.

INTERUNIVERSITY COMPETITION FOR ACTIVISM

Most of the 67 universities in Beijing are located close to one another. The close proximity of universities facilitated mutual imitation and interuniversity competition for activism, which also sustained student participation.[23] In the interviews, I found that some students from People's University were proud of being the leading troop in the April 27 demonstration, which was considered a highly risky action. Students from the University of Political Science and Law were proud of the numerous firsts that they earned during the movement, despite being a small university:

> Later, we calculated that our university owned thirteen firsts. We were the first university that went to demonstrate on the street and that went on a class boycott. The first chairman of The Autonomous Student Union was our student. The headquarters of the Dialogue Delegation was located in our university, and many others. . . . We were very proud of that. The fame of our university has grown thereafter. (no. 59)

Finally, when students from Beijing University talked about their activities during the 1989 Movement, they talked as if they were the unquestioned leaders of the movement. Their most eloquent slogan was: "The whole nation does not fall asleep as long as Beijing University is still awake" (no. 51). One student leader in the University of Political Science and Law commented on Beijing University this way:

> When our university demonstrated on the street on April 17, Beijing University rushed to Tiananmen the same evening. . . . Students at Beijing University always feel that they are different from the rest of the universities. Therefore, when they felt they might lose the leadership [as in early May] they came out with the radical tactic of a hunger strike. (no. 60)

23. Interuniversity competition was also encouraged by the fact that, as the ideological legitimacy of the state declined, some students took activism as a point of honor and equated the level of activism with the prestige of their university.

Such comments should not be taken too literally. However, they do reveal intense interuniversity competition during the 1989 Movement. It was the ecology of the Haidian District—the concentration of so many universities in such a small area—that made such competition extensive, instantaneous, and interactive.

THE DEVELOPMENT OF ECOLOGY-DEPENDENT
STRATEGIES OF MOBILIZATION

So far, I have shown how campus ecology facilitated student mobilization and why patterns of student mobilization during the 1989 Movement cannot be properly understood without a knowledge of campus ecology. At this level, my analysis still points to student solidarity and therefore supports resource mobilization theories, and especially Gould's analysis of mobilization during the Paris Commune.[24] In the following, however, I will present another set of findings which are equally important to the student mobilization but which are nevertheless not clearly related to student networks.

Most universities in Beijing have similar spatial layouts, which regulate the daily life and spatial routine of students on campus. During the 1898 Movement these layouts facilitated the formation of many ecology-dependent strategies of student mobilization. For example, at each university big-character posters and announcements were concentrated, and mobilization was initiated, only in specific places. These places emerged because they were central to students' daily lives. The famous Triangle at Beijing University, the third student dining hall at People's University, and the tenth dining hall at Qinghua University are such places. For example, the Triangle is located between student dormitories, the library, classrooms, and several dining halls (figure 8.1). The post office, the bookstore, and several other shops are also in the vicinity. Whenever students go to the classroom, library, dining hall, post office, or back to their dormitories, they have to pass the Triangle.

The most important student movement organization to emerge during the 1989 Movement—the Beijing Students' Autonomous Union—was actually a very weak organization with neither a prior history nor grassroots membership (chapter 6). However, it was able to organize several large-scale demonstrations that challenged the state. How could it organize demonstrations so effectively? Apart from the dormitory factors, the campus layout also greatly enhanced its ability to carry out its role effectively. At Beijing University, for example, when

24. Roger V. Gould (1991, 1993, 1995).

student activists wanted to organize a demonstration, all they needed to do was just "put several posters at the Triangle, write down the time and location of the gathering, the purposes of the demonstration, and the slogans to be used, and then wait in the place and bring students out on that day" (no. 69). If not enough students showed up, the activists usually marched inside the campus along the avenues between dormitory buildings. In my study, I found that marching along the avenues between dormitories before demonstrations on the street was a standard way for Beijing students to achieve a high level of mobilization; this is another example of an ecology-dependent strategy. For instance, on the evening of April 17, 1989, a few hundred students were milling around the Beijing University Triangle area, looking at big-character posters and making speeches. At this point, someone just back from downtown informed them that people from the University of Political Science and Law had already taken to the street. Some students became very excited and wanted to stage a demonstration at Tiananmen Square as well. Only around two hundred students followed them. These students marched inside the dormitory area first, however. As they shouted and made noise, more and more students were attracted and came out of their dormitories. The size of the formation gradually swelled from a few hundred to between five and six thousand, and eventually they marched out of the campus. This was the first student demonstration by the students of Beijing University.

Now, to what extent can we understand this type of mobilization process in terms of networks and solidarity? The closest network explanation of this event holds that Beijing University had two types of network during the 1989 Movement; an activist-based movement network and many structurally equivalent dormitory-based networks of friends. Strong ties existed in each type of network. Within each dormitory-based network, some students were exposed to dissident ideas earlier and were sympathetic to the movement. Thus, when they saw the demonstration outside, they persuaded and even coerced their fellow roommates to join in. Here, campus ecology was important only to the extent that it connected a social movement network with all the dormitory-based networks simultaneously. If one is preoccupied with modeling movement mobilization as a networking process, one may consider the ecological linkage as "structural holes,"[25] or weak ties.[26]

This type of explanation is not totally unreasonable. Even with the size of Beijing University, it could still be argued that all students might be in the same

25. Burt (1992).
26. Granovetter (1973).

network through either chains of friends or a certain structural equivalence. However, this network explanation has two problems. First, it is very difficult to conceive of shouting and making noise in a place as a network mode of communication extending to all those who can hear it. Social networks are commonly defined as a finite set of nodes (actors) linked by lines (social relations).[27] To make network analysis a meaningful tool in sociology, those lines are usually confined to social relations that are relatively stable and that can be specified prior to a study. They are also restricted to exchanges of privileged and specific information and resources or to boundary overlapping among actors.[28] For example, if there is a loud clap of thunder in the middle of the night which wakes up many people, we cannot say that these people acquire information about the storm through social networks. However, if someone is not awakened by the thunder and does not know about the storm until informed by a friend, we can comfortably say that such a person acquires this piece of information through a network relation.[29] Obviously, those students who shouted outside targeted everyone and anyone who lived in the dormitories rather than a specific group of people. In other words, information about the demonstration was passed not through prior existing ties but through nearly simultaneous direct contact with all who lived on campus. The mode of information transmission was thus diffused and nonprivileged. Network analysis loses its analytical power if we interpret information transmission of this kind as networked.

Second, the role of networks for movement mobilization is not just to provide a means of communication but to evoke an already existing sense of solidarity. In other words, if we argue that students were mobilized that evening through networks, we should expect that students who came out of their dormitories would sort roughly into two categories: those that emerged out of a sense of solidarity, and those who came out because they were persuaded or coerced by their roommates. However, this was not the case on that evening. This was still April 17, only two days after Hu Yaobang' sudden death. At this stage, as it is described in chapter 6, most students in Beijing had not been mobilized politically. Therefore, while some joined the march on that evening out of various grievances or a sense of solidarity, most followed the march without a political reason. In fact, according to one of my informants (no. 63), more than half of the students came out of dormitories and followed the march wearing

---

27. See Laumann and Pappi (1976) or Wasserman and Faust (1997) for similar definitions.

28. Laumann and Pappi (1976) and Laumann and Knoke (1987, 12–13).

29. In reality, the distinction is not always that clear. A general rule is that the more privileged and specific the linkages among the nodes, the more such linkages are subject to meaningful sociological analysis.

slippers and gradually left the march before it arrived at Tiananmen Square. He and many of his friends in fact followed the demonstration simply because they wanted to *kanrenao* (literally, "watch the fun").[30] In short, there was no clear evidence of persuasion and coercion among students that evening. No common grievances, identity, or network-based mobilization can be reconstructed.

What about the intensive persuasion and coercion inside the dormitory which I have discussed earlier? There was a threshold: the majority of students only acted as sympathetic audiences most of the time during the movement and did not care about their fellow roommates' decisions about participating in the movement. However, on some occasions the state's reaction to the movement was deemed unreasonable by most students. At that point, students started to share their anger in dormitories, and more committed students started to persuade and even coerce the less active ones to join protest activities.[31] Students' reaction to the April 26 *People's Daily* editorial, to which I will now turn, represents one such occasion.

The April 27 Demonstration

On April 26, the *People's Daily* published an editorial that labeled the movement as a planned conspiracy and antigovernment turmoil (chapter 7). The contents of the editorial were broadcast on the April 25 evening news. The students were deeply alienated by the outdated language that the editorial used. They decided to defy the editorial by a demonstration on April 27.

I choose the April 27 student demonstration as a case study to illustrate the importance of campus ecology in the process of mobilization. This demonstration was one of the most important events of the 1989 Movement. It marked the first large-scale open defiance of the Chinese state since the communists took power. The success of the demonstration in many ways shaped the subsequent dynamics of the movement, leading finally to the crackdown. Equally important, the demonstration was perceived by many students as an extremely risky event, perhaps even more so than the night of June 3. Some students even wrote wills before joining the demonstration. Though the demonstration was not suppressed, the state did set up many police lines to try to stop the students from entering Tiananmen Square. (The major police lines that the

---

30. When they arrived at Tiananmen Square, the size of demonstration was only around 2,000, including many students from other universities who joined along their way to the Square.

31. The distinction made here bears similarities to Tilly's (1978, 73) distinction between defensive and offensive styles of mobilization.

demonstrators encountered are marked in figure 8.4.) The existence of state force and the perceived danger pushed students to utilize any possible resources, including ecological conditions, to make the demonstration successful.

After hearing the editorial and the news of the proposed demonstration, students as well as activists gathered in dormitory rooms to express their anger and to discuss what would happen if they went out. Most expected a harsh crackdown, but many still decided to participate. The feeling of injustice was too strong for students to succumb to threats. However, most students were also extremely worried. Here, except for the coercion that I have discussed earlier, more determined roommates also acted as counselors to the less committed ones. One student (no. 59) recalled:

> Several of my roommates were very worried about the possible consequences of the next day's demonstration. I had to comfort them. They said that I was very persuasive and should share my ideas with other students in the university. They suggested that I use the intercom in the porter's room. The intercom was installed for the porter to get a particular student when there was a phone call for her/him. . . . We turned on all the switches so that people in every dormitory room could hear but no one outside would know.

Meanwhile, the broadcasting stations of the Students' Autonomous Unions in many universities repeatedly aired speeches from student activists, young teachers, and famous dissidents denouncing the editorial and the government and seeking to boost the morale of students. Places like the Triangle in Beijing University were crowded with people for the whole day of April 26. They made speeches, shouted slogans, and sang songs. Activists' emotions were kept high.

The demonstration took three routes to Tiananmen Square. Students from Beijing University, People's University, Qinghua University, Northern Communication, Beijing Agriculture, and other schools took the western route. The assemblies from the eight big institutions of higher learning, the University of Political Science and Law, and Beijing Normal University were among those that took the middle route. Finally, a few other universities took the eastern route.[32] Figure 8.4 also illustrates the paths of the western and middle routes.

However, the students did not march to Tiananmen Square directly. They zigzagged. In what follows, by centering on the path of the demonstrators from

32. Wu Ren (1990b).

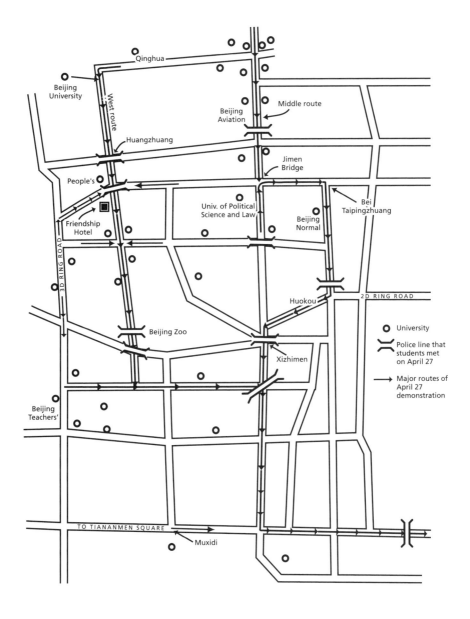

FIGURE 8.4. The west and middle routes of student protest and police lines during the April 27 demonstration.

People's University and the University of Political Science and Law, I will explain how and why students marched this way, as well as other ecology-related issues.

On the morning of April 27, some students appeared at People's University. Among them quite a few were from Beijing Agriculture University. Yet, under enormous pressure, no one dared to march out of the campus as planned. One informant (no. 39) even saw a student leader with a red microphone announcing that the demonstration was canceled, but many students remained. After quite some time, one student came out and suggested marching inside the university. Many followed. After they had marched and shouted for five or six circuits of the university, more and more people had been attracted and had joined in. The students became increasingly excited and eventually rushed out of the gate. However, when they were out, they did not march directly to Tiananmen Square. Intimidated by a police line at the Friendship Hotel intersection, not far away from People's University, the students marched in the opposite direction to try to meet the students from Beijing University and Qinghua University.

Here, many liaison men (most were male students) played an important role. The liaison men coordinated the demonstrators by informing the demonstrators of the sizes and locations of different police lines as well as of the activities of students in other universities. While some liaison men were assigned the task by movement activists, others were simply students who rode bicycles from place to place in order to see more of the demonstration. On the way, they passed the news. Now, as soon as the students of People's University marched out of the campus, some liaison men rushed to Beijing University and shouted in front of the gate of Beijing University: "People's University has come out. What are you waiting for?" Students in Beijing University then came out.

There was a police line at the Huangzhuang intersection. However, with students from Beijing University, Qinghua University, and People's University on either side of it, the police line collapsed. The students joined up and marched back to the Friendship Hotel intersection. The Northern Communication students and students from some other universities also arrived at the southern side of the intersection, without yet daring to push away the police line. Now, with students from Beijing University and Qinghua University at its rear and students from many other universities at the other side of the police line, the students headed by People's University easily pushed the police away from the Friendship Hotel intersection.

This was a historic breakthrough for students of the west as well as the middle routes. Many students who had stayed outside the formation joined in.[33] Liaison men spread in different directions to inform the students of their own universities. The size of the formation expanded enormously. An informant (no. 70) vividly described what was happening at the Friendship Hotel intersection:

> When students of People's University met the police lines, they dared not march forward and asked students from Beijing University to go first. But students of Beijing University did not want to go either. . . . At the moment, quite a few self-appointed organizers from the outside stepped in and commanded demonstrators to line up well, to keep a good order and so on. As the intersection became more and more crowded, people from the outside repeatedly shouted: "Go . . . go . . . Let's go together!" Finally students of People's University started to move forward. When they confronted the police lines, students talked to policemen about constitutional rights. The policemen had no reaction. Then students started to push. The police lines collapsed soon after. On seeing this, organizers and students from different universities rushed back to get their own students. I heard a student from Beijing Industrial University say that we lost face today and rushed back quickly.[34] Students from those universities then waited at different intersections. The scale of the demonstration expanded enormously.

That morning many students rode bicycles from one university to another. On their way, they also passed news and therefore consciously or unconsciously coordinated the movement. One of my informants (no. 57) acted as a liaison man on that day:

> When I got up in the morning, I saw that students in Beijing Teachers' University were already marching at the campus stadium. I wanted to know what was happening at People's University. I went there by bicycle. By the time that I arrived, People's University students had gone north to meet students from Beijing University. I then followed. By the time that I met with the students of People's University they had already joined with students from Beijing University and moved back again. I then rode back to the Friendship Hotel intersection and watched. There were police lines there and students from Northern Communication had been stopped by them on the south side. When the big troops arrived, with efforts from both sides the police line soon collapsed. . . . As soon as students pushed policemen aside, I rode back to Beijing Teachers to see what they were doing there. I saw that

33. The student demonstration was separated from urban residents by picket lines on each side. See the next chapter for discussion of the reason behind this strategy.

34. Here, the student said his university lost face because students in his university did not participate in the Friendship Hotel incident, perceiving it as too dangerous. See the earlier section on interuniversity competition for more discussion of this issue.

students were sitting on the sidewalk outside their university. I passed the message: go quickly in the direction of Chegongzhuang, students from other universities are coming.

The University of Political Science and Law took the middle route. Initially, students in that university were not able to get out, for the president and a few other university authorities were standing in front of the gate claiming that it was too dangerous to go outside. They requested that the students confine their activities to the campus for their own safety. The president even begged the students not to join the demonstration. Facing a senior and respected president, most students hesitated. However, a few students had already gone to other universities to see what was happening there. When the news came back that students of Beijing Aviation University had broken one police line and were marching in their direction, the students in the University of Political Science and Law rushed out and moved south in the direction of Tiananmen Square. Meanwhile, picket lines were formed outside the demonstrators. Only about two hundred students were inside the picket lines. Including followers, the formation comprised no more than six to seven hundred people.

When they marched to Mingguangcun intersection, a police line stopped them. The students dared not march further. They withdrew and moved north to the University of Posts and Telecommunications. As one student (no. 60) recalled:

When we arrived at the University of Posts and Telecommunication, we shouted loudly outside their campus. I saw a lot of students who had been stopped inside their gate by some teachers. Many students were waving to us from the windows of their dormitory rooms. We shouted: "Come down! Come down!" Then more and more students jumped over the campus wall. Eventually students inside the University of Posts and Telecommunications pushed their way out of the gate.

Meanwhile, more students from the University of Political Science and Law came over from the campus and more and more students outside the picket lines joined in. Students within the picket lines increased to some seven to eight hundred. Some other universities from the south, such as Central Finance, also joined. They then continued to march north. At Jimen Bridge they met with students from Beijing Aviation, Beijing Medical, and many other universities. The above-quoted informant recalled that he was already unable to see the two ends of the student formation after the two groups merged. Together they moved east to the Taipingzhuang intersection, then south to meet with students of Beijing Normal University.

During this entire time, liaison men continuously passed news of what had happened along the western route, a route taken by several of the most prestigious universities. As they arrived at Beijing Normal University, news came from the west that students of Beijing University and People's University had broken the Friendship Hotel police line. Students in the middle route cheered. They decided to join the western route. So they marched southwest, pushed away a police line at Huokou and eventually met the western route after the Xizhimen intersection.

Several witnesses recalled the moment as unforgettable. By the time the two groups met, all the intersections were filled with students and Beijing residents. People who stood on the Xizhimen overpass could not see where the crowds ended. A renowned leader (no. 69) told me with emotion that he had never seen such a magnificent scene in his life. At this point, most students were no longer worried about their safety. But it was not until they broke the last police line at Liubukou and entered Tiananmen Square that they realized that the government was totally defeated. Their joy was fully expressed on their way back to their universities as they cried, shouted, and sang songs. Many students walked back. By the time they got back it was already midnight. They had walked for nearly twenty hours!

What had made the April 27 demonstration so successful? High levels of grievances and government restraint did play a role here. However, the dormitory factors, the campus environment, and most importantly students' successful use of ecology-dependent strategies were also crucial. Often, students did not march directly out of the campus. Were they to have done so, not many students would have followed. The crowd size was still not large enough, people were not yet excited, and the students were too afraid. Instead, they first marched inside the campus. By marching and shouting, not only did they attract more and more students but they also created an atmosphere of excitement and heightened the pitch of their anger. Finally, they built up enough courage to march out.

Although full of anger, the students felt deadly afraid once on the street. They avoided confronting the police when they did not feel strong enough. Therefore, they tried to bypass the police line and get more students from other universities. With so many universities around, they were always able to do so. When they had to confront the policemen, the police lines were already dwarfed or overwhelmed by the masses of students coming from all over.

Finally, the instantaneous interactions among universities were also very important. Students in many universities would have never demonstrated out-side the campus if liaison men had not passed the news that other universities were already on the street. On the other hand, students who were already out-side of their campuses might not go very far if students from other universities did not join in. These ecology-dependent strategies were highly effective ex-actly because of the physical environment of the campuses and the whole uni-versity district.

Others Issues concerning the Ecology of Movement Mobilization

While I was writing this chapter, colleagues and friends raised questions con-cerning the validity of this approach. Some of the questions are so important that they deserve special attention. We know that the Haidian university dis-trict was formed during Mao's era. Why, however, did the same university en-vironment which contributed to the rise of student movements in the 1980s not lead to any sizable student uprising during Mao's era?[35] Here, I believe the key lies in the weakening of the student control system in the universities. As I argued in chapter 4, during Mao's era many students turned in classmates who expressed independent thinking because they more or less believed in commu-nism and felt it was moral to do so. Moreover, during that time the state as-signed jobs to students upon graduation, and students who were politically more active (including checking upon other students' political conduct) usu-ally got better positions. Therefore, the high student density and other spatial characteristics of the campus actually extended the effectiveness of student control. After the economic reform, however, the ideological legitimation of the communist state greatly declined, while other avenues of status attainment outside the realm of state control opened up. Participating actively in mutual supervision seemed neither moral nor profitable. Therefore, the campus envi-ronment, which once had facilitated political control over students, became conducive to student mobilization.

Some resource mobilization theorists have also emphasized the importance of the density, homogeneity, and spatial distribution of a population for so-cial movement mobilization.[36] Marx also argued in his "Manifesto" that the concentration of workers into a small number of factories would enhance the

35. I exclude the Red Guard Movement during the 1960s because that was to a great extent a state-sponsored mobilization.

36. See, especially, Tilly (1976, 1978) and Tilly and Schweitzer (1982).

political capacity of the proletariat.[37] However, my emphasis on the importance of the ecological environment still provides additional insights. First, although great theoretical variations exist among scholars of resource mobilization, a key insight of resource mobilization theory is that the density and the homogeneity of a population matters to movement mobilization only to the extent that they facilitate group solidarity. This is understandable because what is implied in the theory is that high density and homogeneity actually lead to a low mobilization potential if a population is assembled simply as "a sack of potatoes," as Marx characterized nineteenth-century French peasants.[38]

I am by no means trying to undermine the importance of organizations and networks in the mobilization process. However, this chapter shows that the design factors of Beijing universities, the accompanying density and distribution of a population, and its patterned spatial movement had great importance for the formation of student networks on campus. This importance cannot be properly understood without a knowledge of the campus ecology. Therefore, the analysis at this level bears similarities to one of Simmel's insights: that when certain social relationships are ordered around an immobile artifact, the artifact will become a socially important pivot of human interaction.[39] This Simmelian idea is the basis for research scattered in urban studies,[40] human geography,[41] small group ecology,[42] and environmental psychology.[43] However, with a few exceptions,[44] it has not been adopted to explain political processes as complex as large-scale social movements.

Moreover, my study suggests that some ecology-dependent processes of mobilization cannot be reduced to networks and organizations. The zigzag route of the demonstrations, the specific places where students put their big-character posters and made speeches, and the marches inside the dormitory

---

37. Marx (1985a, 227–28).

38. Marx (1985b, 317).

39. Spykman (1964, ch. 4).

40. Beckham (1973), Burgess (1925), Duncan and Duncan (1955), Fischer (1977), Krupat (1985), McKenzie (1924), Park (1915, 1936), and Warner (1963).

41. Garling and Evans (1991), Gold (1980), Gollege and Timmermans (1988), and Werlen (1993).

42. See Baldassare (1975, 1977), Case (1981), Festinger, Schachter, and Back (1950), and Sommer (1967, 1969). Here, Festinger, Schachter and Back's (1950) work is particularly interesting. They found that people tend to make friends with immediate neighbors. Moreover, the design factors of a housing project—such as the location of mail boxes and stairways, the position of an apartment in a court or a building, and the door that an apartment faces—would determine people's daily spatial movement, friend-making, and group formation in a community.

43. Barker (1968), Loo (1972), Osmond (1957), Saegert and Winkel (1990), and Schoggen (1989).

44. For example, Roger V. Gould (1995) and Tilly and Schweitzer (1982).

areas had much more to do with the spatial layout of the campuses and the university district than with the organizations and networks of the movement. Trying to explain these kinds of mobilizing strategies in terms of networks and solidarity would not only blur our sensitivity toward variations behind the seemingly similar process of movement mobilization but would also stretch the common definition of social networks to such an extent that every kind of social relation becomes a network relation and every kind of knowledge transmission must be network-based communication.[45]

The importance of ecology to movement mobilization lies in the fact that, other factors being equal, the potential for mobilizing a population will be different if the same population is spatially arranged in a different way. Now, the issue is that, beyond telling a convincing story, how could we tell whether campus ecology really made a significant contribution to student mobilization during the 1989 Movement? Fortunately, although this is a case study, several pieces of evidence that I gathered during my research can provide comparative evidence for my argument. First, during the 1980s, student mobilization in Beijing had two rather consistent patterns. Students who were from outside Beijing had a higher participation rate and graduate students had a lower participation rate than undergraduates from the city.[46] The pattern can be interpreted in a few ways, yet they both can be simply explained in terms of the spatial positions of these different categories of students: Beijing students were able to go home after the April 22 class boycott, so they were not exposed as much to movement activities as were students who remained in their dormitories. On the other hand, each graduate student dormitory room housed only two to four students. As some were married and lived off campus, the real occupancy was often lower

45. Roger V. Gould (1991, 1995) has a series of publications which essentially argue that, because of Haussmann's projects, the new Paris residential areas were no longer class based. Consequently, the mobilizing base of the Paris Commune was no longer working-class consciousness, as was the case of the June rising of 1848, but neighborhood solidarity. My work shares similarities with Gould's work because both of us are interested in how spatial arrangement of the people contributed to movement mobilization. However, we also have different focuses. While Gould focuses on the impact of the macro-design factors of Haussmann's projects on movement mobilization, I study ecological impact not only at the level of the university district but also at the level of campuses and even dormitories. Furthermore, Gould intends to let networks speak for an ecologically embedded social structure. His idea is thus tied to the "group solidarity" wisdom. My strategy is to let the ecology speak for the mobilization, and I have shown that the mobilization during the 1989 Movement was assisted not only by ecology-based student networks but also directly by the campus ecology itself.

46. A study conducted in Beijing University also indicated that the participation rate in the 1986 Student Movement was for city students 49.6 percent, for rural students 58.9 percent, and for small town students 68.2 percent (Liu and Huang 1989). The same paper also reported that graduate students participated considerably less than undergraduates.

than the official capacity. Therefore, it was more difficult, if not impossible, to form any kind of majority in a room.

Interestingly, I also found that when a university had two campuses, one inside and another outside the Haidian District, the one outside the district had a lower rate of movement participation. For example, Beijing Normal University had two campuses, and the one outside had a much lower rate of participation than the one located inside the university district. In the course of his narrative, a student of that university said: "My first year of university life was spent on the campus near Beihai. We did not join in the class boycott. We also participated in very few demonstrations. We did not go to the main campus very often. We knew little about what was going on over there" (no. 33). In other words, to participate in the movement, one has to be at least exposed to the environment in which it is taking place. This is a very good controlled case. Since different degrees of participation occurred at the same university, it is very difficult to imagine factors other than the spatial location of campuses affecting the level of student participation.

Conclusion

In the late 1980s, the state-society relationship in China was such that intermediate social organizations outside the control of the state were illegal and dissident networks were limited by the state to a very small circle. Consequently, the 1989 Movement had a poor organizational resource. Nevertheless, the 1989 Movement achieved a very successful student mobilization. This chapter argues that campus ecology played a decisive role in student mobilization especially during the early period of the movement.

During Mao's era, the Chinese state had designed universities in such a way that by the late 1980s Beijing had sixty-seven universities, most of which are located in Haidian District. The space inside a campus is divided into a student living quarter, teaching quarter, recreational quarter, commercial quarter, and so on. Most university students in Beijing also lived on campus. With six to eight undergraduate students living in a single dormitory room, and several hundred students in each building, a dormitory area in a university could accommodate up to ten thousand students. In my research, I found that the campus environment nurtured many close-knit student networks and shaped the spatial routine of student life. During the 1989 Movement, this campus ecology directly exposed Beijing students to an environment that was conducive to collective action. It also gave rise to some central locations for participant mobilization, encouraged dormitory-based communication and coercion, facilitated interuniversity competition for activism, and shaped the routes of student demonstrations both on and off campus. As illustrated by the April 27 demonstration, students actively made use of the campus ecology in such a way that it encouraged movement participation and invalidated the state control measures. In addition, the campus ecology also facilitated the formation of a rather stable set of ecology-dependent strategies of collective action, which lent many unique characteristics to, and to some extent patterned the dynamics of, the 1989 Movement.

nine

STATE-SOCIETY RELATIONS
AND THE DISCOURSES AND
ACTIVITIES OF A MOVEMENT

Why did Chinese students take Hu Yaobang's sudden death and his memorial service as opportunities for political action? Why did Chinese students frequently cut their own fingers and use the blood to write slogans? Why did three students kneel in front of the Great Hall of the People to hand in a petition? In short, why did the 1989 Beijing Student Movement have a particular pattern of activities and what was the impact of those activities on the dynamics of the movement? So far, scholars have approached this type of question from a cultural perspective.[1] For example, to prevent other Beijing populations from joining the demonstration, students often set up picket lines and made anyone who wanted to join a march show his or her student identity card. This type of activity is commonly interpreted as a reflection of the students' sense of elitism, an ethos

---

1. Since the 1980s, we have seen the rise of an approach that views people as largely emotional creatures and the rhetoric and activity patterns of social movements as determined by either current "texts" (ideology) or past "scripts" (culture) (e.g., Baker 1990; Hunt 1984; Sewell 1985). Wasserstrom (1991), Esherick and Wasserstrom (1990), and Pye's (1990) works on the 1989 Movement have closely followed this approach.

which in turn is seen as rooted in Chinese culture.[2] This explanation, which attributes a cultural manifestation simply to culture itself, can be misleading.

For instance, in studying protest activities in China during the twentieth century, I found that the rhetoric and activities of the 1989 Movement were actually truer to traditional Chinese culture than those of earlier student movements. In relation to the above example of student elitism, for instance, I found that the students of the May 4th Movement of 1919 had actually praised workers as sacred (*laogong shensheng*), tried to earn their own living through labor (*bangong bandu*), and mobilized workers and merchants to form a broad coalition. I also found that during the December 9th Movement of 1935–36 students launched a rural crusade in the south to mobilize China's peasantry into an anti-Japanese coalition.[3] Yet if we believe that the patterns of a social movement are determined by culture, the 1989 Movement should appear less, not more, traditional than those two earlier movements, since Chinese culture has only become more modern over the course of the twentieth century. Therefore, the finding poses a puzzle.

These findings pushed me to conduct a more systematic comparison between the 1989 Movement and the two earlier student movements, a comparison that eventually led to a structural analysis centered on state-society relations. In the study, I found that the 1989 Movement was developed under a state-society relationship different from those that pertained during the two earlier student movements. Unlike the eras of the earlier movements, the 1980s found China with a unitary state, weak independent organizations, and state legitimacy based on moral and economic performance. The major argument of this chapter is that because this unitary state had allowed state authoritarianism to penetrate deeply into society, students in the 1980s feared repression more than students during the earlier movements had. Some culturally interpretable patterns of movement activity, such as the picket lines, were strategies intended to avoid immediate repression. Moreover, because of the weakness of associational life, many activities during the 1989 Movement emerged spontaneously, and often simultaneously, in a given time and space. These activities might be rooted in Chinese culture, in a communist style of mobilization, or in Western influences. The people also acted from any of a number of motives. However, the simultaneous occurrence of several activities in the same location made the psychology of sympathetic bystanders an important factor in shaping the patterns of the movement. One of the central arguments of this chapter is that

2. Chan and Unger (1990), Macartney (1990), and Perry and Fuller (1991).
3. See Israel (1966, 134–38) for more details about the event.

people's views regarding the proper behavior of movement activists and the government are shaped by their understanding of state legitimation. During the late 1980s, most urban Chinese's notion of what legitimates a state had changed from communist ideology to economic and moral performance, a notion more in accordance with the ideas found in an earlier, more traditional China.[4] Those who watched the movement were thus more receptive to culturally and morally charged rhetoric and activities, and they became highly emotional when the state reacted harshly to morally charged acts. This further intensified the traditionalism expressed during the 1989 Movement.

Over ten years ago, Snow and his associates published an influential article that depicts the activities of a social movement as rational strategies deployed by organizers to mobilize those individuals or groups who had not been persuaded by a movement's ideological agenda.[5] They call the process "frame alignment."[6] Since then, the idea of framing has been used to refer to dominant ideologies (master frames), rhetorical strategies, the symbolic meaning of a collective action, and government and media responses to movements.[7] The perspective adopted in this chapter shares similarities with frame analysis because I am also interested in the symbolic aspect of social movements. However, as a major frame analysis scholar has commented on the work of his own field,[8] most publications on social movement framing tend to be either efforts to further develop the concept theoretically or case studies that tell us frame stories.[9] They have been "written as though participant mobilization were simply a matter of movement activists pushing the appropriate rhetorical button," and their reasoning "tend(s) to work backward from successful mobilization to the framings activists proffered and then posit a casual linkage between the two." Few empirical studies on frame analysis have focused, as this chapter does, on the objective existence of a common "schemata of interpretation" in society (in my case, a common sense of state legitimation) and its impact on the frame process, or have linked the popular interpretation template to a set of particular social structures.

4. See chapters 1 and 7.

5. Snow et al. (1986).

6. However, the idea of injustice or of an injustice frame was already the focus of some earlier studies (Gamson, Fireman and Rytina 1982; Moore 1978).

7. See, for example, Benford (1993), Gamson and Wolfsfeld (1993), McCarthy, Smith, and Zald (1996), Snow and Benford (1988, 1992), Tarrow (1994), and Zald (1996).

8. Benford (1997, 421, 412).

9. For example, Evans (1997), Hank (1995), Ryan (1991), Snow et al. (1986), Snow and Benford (1988, 1992), Williams and Williams (1995), and Zou and Benford (1995).

Scholars have recently tried to establish a linkage between a social movement's framing strategies and its political opportunity structures.[10] Both the strategic framing and political opportunity structure approaches center on the actors in social movements. Under the new, hybrid opportunity-framing approach, social movement framing remains largely a strategic process, and social structures enter the analytic picture only because the frame matters to social movement actors' "expectations for success or failure."[11] However, structures are not just cognitive cues or instruments that assist well-organized social movement actors to implement the best strategies. Social structures are also about habits, sentiments, and rather fixed notions of right and wrong. In my view, the opportunity-framing approach assumes a model of human agency that privileges the making of rational choices. In contrast, I take social movement actors to be real humans with capacities both for performing rational calculations and for expressing emotional responses. In certain critical situations, actors in the 1989 Movement made deliberate, strategic choices. In other such situations, they were more moved by their emotions. Methodologically, it is difficult to determine at the micro-level whether a particular political action during a movement is driven by rationality or by emotion. Nevertheless, we are able to examine the structural conditions under which rational behaviors or emotional actions achieve domination. Therefore, this chapter focuses less on the motivations of movement actors than on the macro-structural conditions that facilitated the dominance of certain traditional and often highly emotional activities during the 1989 Movement. While the opportunity-frame perspective tries to link social structure with activity patterns and social movement dynamics through opportunities and strategies, I link them through people's common sentiments about state power.[12]

Participants in social movements usually adopt forms of rhetoric and activity that are already familiar to them in a cultural setting. Tilly defined the sum total of the available forms of collective action as repertoires of collective action. He also convincingly explained the changes in these repertoires in Western Europe in the past 500 years.[13] However, the forms of action that comprise a repertoire are more extensive than the specific forms of action that

10. Diani (1996), Evans (1997), Gamson and Meyer (1996), and Oberschall (1996).

11. Tarrow (1994, 85).

12. Although frame scholars acknowledge the existence of a popular interpretation template by such phrases as "schemata of interpretation," "experiential commensurability," and "narrative fidelity," their empirical focus is always on the strategy of movement actors rather than on the psychology of the people who watch a movement. See, for example, Snow and Benford (1988) and Benford (1997) for these concepts.

13. Tilly (1978, 1986).

are adopted in a particular social movement. Therefore, simply to point out the importance of culture in a social movement does not explain much; we also need to ask why movement participants adopt certain forms of rhetoric and action and not others. This chapter is an attempt to move in the direction of answering that question.

This chapter proceeds in the following manner. First, after a short introduction of the two earlier student movements, I delineate the patterns of movement rhetoric and activities during the 1989 Movement (the variations of dependent factors). Second, I describe the different state-society relationships underlying the May 4th, December 9th, and 1989 Movements (the variations of independent factors). In the last two sections, I analyze how the different state-society relationships discussed in the previous section shaped movement rhetoric and activities as well as the development of movements (the causal relations between the dependent and independent factors). For those not familiar with the comparative-historical approach, I have indicated the logic of each section by quantitative analogies in the parentheses above. These remain just analogies, however, because the structural dimensions that I have adopted are impure constructions rather than fully operationalized variables.

Historical Backgrounds of the Two Earlier Student Movements

The May 4th Movement of 1919, the December 9th Movement of 1935–36, and the 1989 Movement are the three largest student movements in the history of twentieth-century China. They all started in Beijing and spread across the nation. Here, I only briefly introduce the May 4th and December 9th Movements, since other information on these two movements will be presented in the later comparative sections.[14] The May 4th Movement was the first major student movement in modern China. After 1917, China's new intellectuals and students had initiated a vast modernization drive that aimed to strengthen the country through science and democracy. This modernization drive to a great extent paved the way for the rise of the movement. The movement, however, was named after the May 4th incident in 1919: on that day, over three thousand Beijing students marched in the streets in an anti-Japanese demonstration protesting the Shandong resolution of the Versailles Peace Conference. As merchants, workers, and other urban residents joined the students, anti-Japanese

14. Interested readers may consult Chow (1967), Israel (1966), Israel and Klein (1976), and Yeh (1996) for the May 4th and December 9th Movements.

protests soon spread to many other Chinese cities. Eventually the government of Northern China had to dismiss three pro-Japanese officers and refuse to sign the Versailles Peace Treaty. The impact of the May 4th Movement was profound. Politically, it contributed to the rise of the CCP and the reorganization of the Nationalist Party (Guomindang). Culturally it facilitated the rise and dominance of vernacular literature and mass education and the decline of Confucianism and traditional ethics.

While the May 4th Movement was at once prodemocratic and nationalistic, the December 9th Movement was mainly a nationalistic reaction to Japanese aggression. By 1935, Japan had occupied the whole Dongbei region and a large part of Hebei province. Beijing was virtually encircled by Japanese troops. On December 9, 1935, thousands of Beijing students marched to urge the government to resist the Japanese invasion. The movement spread to most of urban China in 1936. The impact of this movement was also monumental. It helped the CCP rebuild its urban base, which had been destroyed by the Guomindang. It also split the governing elites and led to the Xi'an Incident.[15] A series of chain reactions during and after the movement led to the establishment of a united front between the Guomindang and CCP to fight against the Japanese invasion, paving the way for the communist victory in China.[16]

Patterns of Activity during the 1989 Movement

While this study investigates the impact of state-society relations on the patterns of social movement activity, I do not claim that social movement activities are completely shaped by state-society relations. In comparison with the May 4th Movement of 1919 and the December 9th Movement of 1935–36, the 1989 Movement has three distinctive features. The movement was much more pro-Western in appearance; it bore the strong imprint of the Cultural Revolution and of the communist style of mass mobilization more generally; and finally, culturally embedded rhetoric and movement activities figured much more centrally in the 1989 Movement than in the two earlier student movements. In what follows, I will briefly introduce each of these patterns, relating the last to state-society relations in China during the 1980s.

---

15. On December 12, 1936, General Zhang Xueliang detained Jiang Jieshi, the generalissimo, to try to force him to stop the war with the communists and lead all of China to resist the Japanese invasion. This is known as the Xi'an Incident.

16. Johnson (1962).

PRO-WESTERN CHARACTERISTICS OF THE MOVEMENT

During the 1989 Movement, Chinese students flashed the V-sign to indicate victory, built a Statue of Liberty turned "Goddess of Democracy" in Tiananmen Square, held countless press conferences to attract Western attention, provided Western and Hong Kong journalists with easy access to their headquarters, and routinely listened to foreign broadcasts for news and feedback.[17] This list of pro-Western attributes can be expanded. The movement's pro-Western nature was also reflected in its language. English banners such as "For the People, By the People," "Absolute Power, Absolute Corruption,"[18] "Give me Democracy or Give me Death", "Glasnost," and "People Power" appeared everywhere. This pro-Western attitude was new to China. Although the two earlier student movements were anti-Japanese, students also expressed their grievances with other foreigners. For example, during the May 4th Movement, when Shanghai students demonstrated around Waitan Park in the British Concession, several students smashed a board in front of the park which read "No Chinese and Dogs."[19] During the May 4th Movement, Guomindang elites had to take steps to keep the movement from becoming explicitly anti-Western.[20]

Both the May 4th and the December 9th Movements took place between the world wars, during a time when colonialism still dominated international politics. Weak nations such as China were constantly bullied by big powers acting on their conflicting geopolitical interests. Given this situation, nationalism became a major feature of the movements. The May 4th students advocated Westernization only because they believed that democracy could save China from foreign aggression. By the time of the 1989 Movement, however, colonialism was seen as part of the distant past; intellectuals and students were no longer so concerned with saving China. Instead they felt great pain as a consequence of the strong state that their predecessors had dreamed of and fought for. They had also witnessed the decline of the Soviet Union and a new wave of worldwide democratization. State socialism was no longer treated as a viable model; capitalism and democracy had again become the twin engines of the

---

17. According to Macartney, "Access to inner sanctums [at Tiananmen Square] was granted only to the Western and Hong Kong press" (1990, 9–10). Moreover, student leader Wang Dan visited Hong Kong reporters almost daily "to feel out their attitude to the students, to find out whether the outside world was interested in the movement."

18. See the photos in *Xuese de Limin* (1989, 48, 68).

19. Xu Deheng (1987, 76).

20. Liu Yongming (1990).

world system. The pro-Western nature of the movement revealed fundamental changes in the international environment and in the mood of Chinese intellectuals and students.

THE IMPRINT OF COMMUNIST MASS MOBILIZATION

Communist education had imprinted a set of habits and iconic images on students. For example, during the 1989 Movement students sang "L'Internationale" whenever they felt that their action was heroic and tragic. Although "L'Internationale" is part of a legitimate set of symbols under the regime, students sang the song frequently because the song is rebellious in spirit and singing it was a standard way to express this type of emotion, one that students had learned through revolutionary dramas and films.

Certain tactics popularized during the Cultural Revolution had an even greater impact on the 1989 Movement. The hunger strike was arguably the single most important form of protest during the 1989 Movement. The strike led to the success of the movement, both in terms of the scale of mobilization it achieved and of the worldwide attention it generated. It also sowed the seeds for martial law and the final military crackdown. Significantly, the tactic was not used during the May 4th and the December 9th Movements but was popularized only during the Cultural Revolution.[21] The impact of the Cultural Revolution on the 1989 Movement can be seen from Zheng Yi's account of his involvement in the movement.[22] In his book, Zheng describes organizing a large-scale hunger strike during the Cultural Revolution. He also depicts how he passed on his experiences in that regard to activists at Beijing University, suggesting to students there that they stage a hunger strike as early as April 22. Zheng Yi's fascinating story certainly had its impact on young listeners such as Wang Dan, Chai Ling, and Zhang Boli, all of whom were key figures in the hunger strike.

Between May 16 and 26, 1989, around 172,000 students from various provinces went to Beijing by train.[23] Students also went by other means of transportation. Thus, in late May Tiananmen Square was filled by energetic newcomers who were reluctant to leave. These students went to Beijing not just to support the movement but to take advantage of the opportunity to get a free

21. For instance, in the early 1980s, in order to return to cities, the sent-down youth in Yunnan province staged a hunger strike that involved over a thousand individuals. The action pushed the Chinese government to deal with them immediately and led to the success of the protest (Deng Xian 1992).

22. Zheng Yi (1993, 62–68).

23. Wu et al. (1989, 474).

trip to visit the capital. This phenomenon, which had a tremendous impact on the development of the movement, is called "linking up" (*chuanlian*). The practice of traveling long distances as a part of the petition process started during the earlier student movements,[24] yet it is the Cultural Revolution that gave *chuanlian* a new meaning—*chuanlian* as massive free tourism. By 1989, most old Red Guards regarded the Cultural Revolution as a personal as well as a collective tragedy. Nevertheless, most of them had good memories of *chuanlian*.[25] In the interviews, all the students whom I asked about *chuanlian* knew very well about the Red Guards' exciting travel experiences during the Cultural Revolution. Past novelties became this movement's routine.

THE TRADITIONALISM OF THE 1989 MOVEMENT

What is most stunning and hard to explain about the 1989 Movement is that its language and activities were actually more traditional and moralistic than those of the May 4th and the December 9th Movements. This is not to suggest that China's traditional culture had no impact on the two earlier movements, or that there are no similarities among the three movements. For example, in premodern China kneeling in a public place was a major way by which the Chinese proclaimed their discontents and appealed to the public for support. Indeed, we see that during the May 4th Movement students knelt in front of workers and merchants to try to mobilize them. Nevertheless, kneeling had never been as significant a movement tactic as it became during Hu Yaobang's funeral on April 22, 1989. Never before had kneeling brought out the emotions of hundreds of thousand of students and triggered a Beijing-wide class boycott. The same was true of staging protests during funerals. During the May 4th Movement, the funeral protests at Tianjin and Shanghai were only minor activities.[26] During the December 9th Movement, Beijing students did hold a memorial service and demonstrate on the street for Guo Qing, a high school student who had died in prison. However, when the government suppressed this activity, no further radical actions followed.[27] The 1989 Movement, by contrast, started after Hu Yaobang's sudden death and for its first week centered on mourning activities.

Students of the 1980s also brought back some of the rhetoric that their predecessors during the May 4th era had vehemently attacked, and which had

24. Wasserstrom (1991, 88).
25. Jin Yucheng (1996).
26. Chow (1967, 129, 143).
27. Han Xuchang (1986, 103–108); Israel (1966, 145).

gradually disappeared from China's political discourse. Traditional Chinese virtues such as loyalty, filial piety, and images of extended family were under severe attack during the May 4th Movement;[28] yet during the 1989 Movement, students and Beijing residents frequently used language drawing on these elements to mobilize emotions. One frequently encountered slogans that centered on extended family relations, such as: "Mama, we are not wrong!" "Mama: I am hungry, but I won't eat!" "Grandpa Zhao, uncle Li, come save our big brothers and sisters!" and "Your big brothers have been very anxious!" In addition, one also encountered language that emphasized very traditional Chinese values: "Fasting to the death is only a small deed!"[29] "Loyalty [to the country] and filial piety cannot be obtained at the same time," and "It is not because there is no retribution, it is because the time has not yet come! When the time comes, retribution will definitely come from the people!" (*Bushibubao, Shijianweidao! Shijianyidao, Renminbibao*).[30]

The adoption of traditional language was not just an individual initiative. For example, the "Hunger Strike Declaration," arguably one of the most important student declarations of the 1989 Movement, was filled with traditional rhetoric and with elitist sentiment such as "When a person is about to pass away, he speaks kindly and wisely; when a bird is about to die, it cries sadly" and "Please forgive us. Your children cannot be loyal and show filial piety at the same time." Few declarations during the May 4th and the December 9th Movements bore traits of this sort; such language (and the values embedded in it) was in fact a target of attack in some student manifestos during the May 4th Movement.

No wonder that China scholars have been so committed to explaining the 1989 Movement by one or another facet of traditional Chinese culture. Yet while it is not difficult to find strong empirical support for such connections, these explanations do not provide any clue as to why the 1989 Movement was more traditional and more culturally driven than the May 4th and the December 9th Movements.[31]

28. See, for example, Chow (1967, 58–59).

29. This is a slightly modified version of half of a traditional Chinese couplet, the other half of which goes: "Keeping one's chastity is the most important matter." The couplet was used to exhort a widow in traditional China to remain faithful to her dead husband.

30. This is the slogan shouted by Chai Ling during early May 1989 (Hinton and Gordon 1997, 109). It expresses the Buddhist notion of reincarnation, that life is circular and one's status in the next life depends on one's deeds in the current life. It is part of folk wisdom in China.

31. One may simply view the traditionalism of the 1989 Movement as a nostalgic cultural revival. While it is true that people are nostalgic, this is not enough to explain the revival of a major cultural tradition. Major cultural revival must be accompanied by certain structural changes that either make that culture more

It is quite tempting to explain this difference in terms of the core issues of each of the three movements. This works partially for the May 4th Movement. There is no doubt that the iconoclastic nature of the movement delegitimized the use of traditional rhetoric and tactics. However, this explanation does not work for the December 9th Movement, because it was almost purely nationalistic, and there is little reason to expect a nationalistic movement in the 1930s to be less traditional than a prodemocratic movement in the 1980s.

One might also argue that the activity patterns of the 1989 Movement point to the resilience of culture. Yet, it is illogical to assume that youths of the 1980s were more exposed to traditional culture than the May 4th and the December 9th youths. In the twentieth century, China has arguably undergone the most dramatic social change in its long history. A considerable portion of the May 4th youths were brought up in large extended families. In comparison, modern students were mostly brought up in urban nuclear families and were subject to much more liberal child-rearing practices. During the May 4th era, female students had to fight to wear modern hairstyles and to attend the same schools as males. By contrast, students in the 1980s could date rather freely. Moreover, many of the May 4th and December 9th students were educated with a blend of traditional and modern curricula, while the students in the 1980s were educated with more Westernized curricula. Finally, modern students lived in the age of information. They were much more exposed, albeit superficially, to the Western lifestyle and mentality than earlier students had been. Therefore, we need other explanations.

State-Society Relations in the Three Student Movements

In this book's introduction, I defined the three major dimensions of state-society relations as being the nature of the state, the nature of society, and the links between the state and society. Now, I will follow these dimensions in giving a brief historical account of the different state-society relationships operating during the May 4th Movement of 1919, the December 9th Movement of 1935–36, and the 1989 Movement. I begin with the May 4th Movement.

At first glance, we see that all three movements broke out under authoritarian governments. Yet their underlying state-society relationships were qualitatively different. The May 4th Movement started eight years after the 1911

---

relevant or facilitate the development of certain cultural institutions that will fight for that culture. In a way, this chapter can be seen as an analysis of the structural conditions that revived some traditional cultural elements in China during the 1980s.

Republican Revolution. When it began, China consisted of two rival states, with the north controlled by warlords and the south by a coalition of the Guomindang and some southern warlords. The movement was aimed against some pro-Japanese elements in the northern government. China at that time had two major political parties, the Guomindang and Jinbudang (the Progressive Party). While they were otherwise in political competition, both parties urged the northern government not to sign the Versailles Peace Treaty. The Progressive Party was generally conservative and often a supporter of the warlord government in the northern parliament. During the May 4th Movement, however, some members of the party, especially Liang Qichao, supported the students. Before the movement, the Guomindang had split into a southern revolutionary and a northern parliamentarian faction, neither of which really initiated the movement. But individual Guomindang members, such as Cai Yuanpei, Wu Zhihui, Zhang Ji, Ye Chucang, Dai Jitao, and Shao Lizi, were behind the movement from the very beginning. Moreover, more Guomindang members from both the northern parliamentary and southern revolutionary factions came to support the movement after it started. In fact, when the center of the movement shifted to Shanghai, for all practical purposes the Guomindang almost led the movement.[32] But support for the movement was not limited to political parties. Some powerful warlords associated with the northern government, such as Wu Peifu and Zhang Jingyao, also publicly expressed their sympathy for the students. Thus, the students were actually backed by a politically powerful and organizationally resourceful coalition. Still, if the northern government during the May 4th era was no less authoritarian and repressive than the communist government of the 1980s would be, its state elites were certainly more fragmented.

The northern government's weakness was reflected in the limited degree to which its authoritarianism penetrated Chinese society. Between 1912 and 1914, that government, then still representing the whole of China, passed a series of laws to restrict people's rights to free speech, assembly, association, and the press. However, such laws could not extend to provinces and cities controlled by local warlords, or to foreign concessions, where publication and association were not regulated by Chinese law. Even within its own sphere of political influence, the northern government had proved unable to eliminate organizations not under its control. Therefore, commercial organizations, labor unions, and other nongovernmental organizations were in place long before the May 4th Movement. Some of these organizations, such as the Chamber of Commerce

32. Liu Yongming (1990).

of China in Beijing and Shanghai, the Citizens' Diplomatic Association, and the Chinese Industry Association,[33] played important roles during the May 4th Movement. After Yuan Shikai's failure to restore a monarchy and his subsequent death in 1916, the Beijing government's capacity for control deteriorated even further. Newspapers, magazines, and student organizations controlled by the new intellectuals mushroomed in Beijing. At Beijing University, for example, over twenty new associations were formed long before the rise of the May 4th Movement. The Association of Personal Ethics (Jindehui), with a membership of over five hundred (over 25 percent of the university's population), had organized virtually all the new intellectuals in the university. Organizations such as the New Tide Society, the Citizens' Magazine Society, and the Mass Media Research Society provided the leadership for the movement.[34]

Immediately before the rise of the December 9th Movement, by way of contrast, China seemed more tightly controlled by a repressive government. In 1927 the Guomindang broke with the CCP and started to kill CCP members. By 1935, the Guomindang had unified most parts of China and pushed the CCP to abandon its southern bases and retreat to the Shanbei area. In the meantime the Guomindang also tried to eliminate the CCP in the cities. Hundreds of thousands of communists and their supporters were captured and killed, and most underground communist organizations in the cities were destroyed. This "white terror" also extended to Chinese society at large. After 1927, pro-communist labor unions, student societies, and left-wing organizations were banned, and other social organizations were placed under governmental control.[35] In Beijing, for example, the universities, with the exception of Yanjing and Qinghua,[36] were very quiet politically before 1935.

However, although the Guomindang regime was very repressive, a highly divided governing elite on the top and the existence of a professional Leninist

33. The predecessor of the Chinese Industry Association was the so-called Chinese Workers' Party established in 1912. It declined after a failed uprising against Yuan Shikai in 1913 but gradually regained its influence in Shanghai after 1916. The Guomindang was behind both the early Chinese Workers' Party and the later Chinese Industry Association.

34. Zhang Yunhou et al. (1979).

35. For example, whereas before 1927 Shanghai had been a heartland of left-wing working-class politics, in the years between 1927 and 1937 left-wing workers' movements were so repressed that workers' unions in Shanghai became controlled by local gangsters (Perry 1993, ch. 5).

36. Yanjing was an American private university, and Qinghua was established and funded by war reparations that China paid to the United States in the aftermath of the Boxer Rebellion. The reparations were imposed in 1901 in a treaty China signed with the Western powers and Japan. In 1908, the U.S. Congress passed a bill that returned part of the reparation money to China, to be used to establish Qinghua University and to provide scholarships for Chinese students to study in the United States. In both universities the Guomindang's influence was relatively weak and free association was more tolerated.

communist party at the bottom strongly affected the government's capacity to penetrate society. When China was unified in the late 1920s, most warlords were not militarily eliminated but politically co-opted. Thus many warlords still controlled their own bases and troops. Some of them, such as Feng Yuxiang and Zhang Xueliang, had great sympathy for the December 9th Movement because of their nationalism and because of the fact that their northern power bases were being undermined by the Japanese.[37] Furthermore, the Guomindang had a revolutionary tradition rooted in its history and in its ideological underpinnings. Jiang Jieshi was able to repress the communists but could do very little to highly influential left-wing party members. During the December 9th Movement, left-wing and liberal Guomindang leaders, led by Song Qingling and He Xiangning, the widows of Sun Zhongshan and Liao Zhongkai, vehemently supported the students' actions. Therefore the governing elite's attitude toward the movement was highly divided.[38]

Meanwhile, although the communists were driven to Shanbei, the Guomindang was unable to defeat them completely. Even before they arrived in Shanbei, the communists advocated a united front with the Guomindang against the Japanese invasion. At the time, most government troops stationed near Shanbei were part of Zhang Xueliang's Army, which had retreated from Dongbei in 1931. Thus the communists' proposal strongly resonated among Dongbei army officers who were homesick and deeply humiliated by their peaceful retreat from their home province. For a period, a truce existed between local Guomindang troops and the Red Army.

By the end of 1934 the CCP in Beijing had been completely destroyed as an organization. However, in early 1935 the CCP started to reestablish its underground organs through a peripheral organization called the Chinese Association of Military Defense. The members of the association used Yanjing and Qinghua Universities as bases to expand their influence. By the time the December 9th Movement broke out, the CCP had reestablished its Beijing branch

---

37. This was especially true of Zhang Xueliang, who had come under a lot of public pressure since he followed Jiang Jieshi's orders and withdrew his troops from Dongbei in 1931 without offering any resistance to the Japanese invasion.

38. Here is an example of how students benefited from divisions among the elites. On February 23, 1936, forty-four Dongbei University students were arrested in Beijing. Student leader Song Li went to Zhang Xueliang for help. Zhang wrote a letter to the chief of the military police in Beijing and requested that he release the students. He also asked Song Li to act as his secretary and to deliver the letter. When Song was in Beijing, he was recognized by local authorities as one of the students on the arrest list, yet nobody dared to arrest him. Instead, Song was well treated, and all of the forty-four arrested students were released as Zhang requested (Song Li 1982). This kind of politics would have been unimaginable during the 1989 Movement.

and controlled radical student networks.[39] Most of these students turned out to be crucial leaders in the movement and later revolutionary veterans. Thus, even though the CCP headquarters at Shanbei was not aware of it, the CCP local in Beijing played a role in facilitating the December 9th Movement.[40] Moreover, soon after the movement began, the CCP strengthened its presence in it. The CCP gradually gained control over the movement in several major cities, particularly Beijing and Tianjin. Thus the December 9th Movement was increasingly supervised by the CCP.

One point that I need to bring out is that the principal basis of state legitimation during both the May 4th and December 9th periods was nationalism. Since the Opium War in 1840, foreign aggression had become an increasingly urgent problem for China. In the wake of foreign aggression, nationalist consciousness rose, first among intellectuals and then among other urban populations. China's defeat in the Sino-Japanese War in 1894 was a crucial catalyst for radicalism. Afterwards, having a strong state capable of defending China became a dream of the Chinese (chapter 2). It was in this atmosphere that China's political elites staged the reforms and rebellions that eventually overthrew the Manchu government and established the Republic in 1912. The same radical atmosphere still prevailed when Chinese intellectuals and students staged the May 4th and December 9th Movements.

The 1989 Movement also broke out in an authoritarian regime, but the state-society relations behind it were qualitatively different from the two earlier student movements.[41] During the late 1980s, the state still claimed its legitimacy in the ideological terms of the Four Cardinal Principles written in the preamble of the Chinese Constitution. However, after the reform in 1978, China's urban population increasingly knew more about the outside world. Comparing their nation's development to that of the West, and especially to that of their

39. Chen Qiwu (1982); Yao (1987).

40. Edgar Snow (1966) insists that the December 9th Movement was largely spontaneous and that the early leaders of the movement were "mostly Christian or Christian-trained youths . . . not a Communist among them." Snow seems to have underestimated the communists' role in initiating the movement. In fact, many leaders of the movement had joined the CCP before the movement began. Some of them, such as Yu Qiwei (Huang Jing), Yao Keguang (Yao Yilin), Wang Rumei (Huang Hua), and Song Li, were also among the frequent guests of Snow's family. See Liao, Zhang, and Liu (1993) for the political careers of these December 9th Movement leaders.

41. In comparison with the states in the two earlier movements, the Chinese state in the 1980s was closer to a "post-totalitarian regime" as defined by Linz and Stepan (1996). According to them, this kind of regime is a decayed form of a totalitarian regime. It emphasizes rational decision making but is still officially committed to an elaborate ideology. It tolerates a certain level of economic and social pluralism but a very limited political pluralism, due to the state's still-overwhelming presence.

newly rising East Asian neighbors, urban Chinese found that their government had delivered far less to them than had been promised. This shortfall, coupled with bitter memories of the disastrous Cultural Revolution and with the new international wave of democratization, led the younger generation of intellectuals and students to become increasingly critical of the regime's ideological stance. This does not mean that most people during the 1980s perceived the state as illegitimate, however. What happened in China was a shifting of public perception of the basis of state legitimation from leftist ideology back to performance.[42] Particularly relevant in the context of this chapter was the moral dimension of state legitimation. As was mentioned in chapters 1 and 7, after the ideological legitimation of the state declined, moral and ritual performance once again became a popular criterion by which the people would judge their government.

Nevertheless, although a crisis of ideological legitimacy could be widely felt in urban China during the 1980s, no rival political organizations or parties existed then, as had been the case during the earlier student movements. Moreover, in the late 1980s most of the top-level government offices were still controlled by CCP veterans who had joined the party long before the communists took power. These veterans were aware of China's economic backwardness and its other problems. However, they also believed that these problems did not result from communism or authoritarianism but rather from inexperience. They realized that reform was an absolute necessity, but they never intended to give up what millions of their comrades had died for. They were confident because they had an armed force controlled by veteran senior officers, most of whom were veterans themselves (chapter 7). Thus, the legitimation crisis actually had no catastrophic impact on the higher echelons of the state leadership. Western analysts have highlighted the factional nature of Chinese government during the 1989 Movement. But the crucial fact is that no top state leaders really supported the students during the movement. Their differences were more over strategies to calm down the movement. This contrasts sharply with what happened during the May 4th and the December 9th Movements, when powerful governing elites openly supported the students.

China in the 1980s was much freer than it had been during Mao's era. This created an opening for the rise of the 1989 Movement. However, this openness should not be exaggerated. In the early years after the communists took over power, the state had wiped out independent social organizations and replaced them with party-controlled workers', women's, youth, and vocational organi-

---

42. See chapters 4 and 7 for more details.

zations. More independent forms of organizations emerged during the 1980s as China's reform deepened (chapter 1). However, the new associations were still at a very rudimentary stage of development and not comparable to organizations during the republican era. Most of these organizations also had a semi-official status and were never intended to mobilize against the state.[43] During the 1980s, truly dissident activities often led to punishment ranging from job loss to imprisonment. Therefore, during the 1989 Movement, all the movement organizations emerged with no prior history, and student mobilization was facilitated more by the ecology of the campuses and Tiananmen Square than by the strength of organizations.

State-Society Relations and Patterns of Movement Activity

In the last section, I argued that China during both the May 4th Movement of 1919 and the December 9th Movement of 1935–36 had a fragmented state, divided elites, strong opposition parties or intermediate associations, and a state legitimized primarily by its capacity for national defense, while communist China during the 1980s had a relatively unitary governing elite that held much tighter control over society, despite the fact that a large proportion of the urban population judged it by its moral and economic performance, not by its ideology. Now, I will analyze how these differences shaped the rhetoric and activities of the 1989 Movement.

Because China in the 1980s had a less fragmented state and weaker intermediate associations than had existed during the May 4th and the December 9th Movements, the 1989 Movement was unable to organize so freely and raise demands so directly. In this setting, the students sought to avoid head-on repression by twisting or hiding their real demands and goals behind legitimate forms of collective action. Many activities during the 1989 Movement can be straightforwardly explained as strategies that aimed to create a "safe space" to lower the possibility of repression.[44]

Let us recall the picket line example which I gave at the beginning of this chapter. In the past, the communist government had treated student activism relatively leniently but had severely sanctioned worker activism or any attempt to build an alliance between students and workers. Moreover, when a student demonstration did not employ pickets, urban youths, some of them

43. Wang, Zhe, and Sun (1993).
44. Evans and Boyte (1992), Gurr (1986), Lichbach (1995), Opp and Roehl (1990), and James C. Scott (1985).

hooligans, had tended to mingle with demonstrators, making the demonstration less orderly and threatening to turn it into a riot. To avoid allowing the government to justify repression with such side effects, the students over time developed the picket line strategy to ensure that a demonstration went on in an orderly fashion.[45]

The same logic also explains why funeral protests, which were only marginally used during the May 4th and the December 9th Movements, became so important for the 1989 Movement. Before the December 9th demonstration, student activists explicitly rejected Helen Snow's (a foreigner) suggestion that students start their demonstration with a mock funeral by carrying a "corpse of North China" through the streets of Beijing.[46] Why was a tactic that was rejected by "traditional students" heavily used by "modern students?" In fact, as is illustrated in both chapters 5 and 6, a few student activists in Beijing had begun preparing for the 1989 Movement long before Hu Yaobang's sudden death. They would have started this movement anyway, regardless of Hu's physical condition. Yet Hu's sudden death provided then with an excellent opportunity. At the time of his death, Hu was still a member of the CCP Politburo and therefore a top statesman. Since to mourn a government leader is a legitimate action, to start a collective action by centering on Hu Yaobang's funeral shielded the intention of movement activists and made immediate repression impossible.

The students' fear of repression also manifested itself in other activities. On April 26, the government published the *People's Daily* editorial that labeled the movement as antirevolutionary turmoil. When students demonstrated on April 27 in defiance of the editorial, however, the slogans that students shouted the most were "Long live the Communist Party!" and "Support socialism!"[47] They also shouted slogans centered on issues of official corruption and high inflation. The slogans were not radical, even from the perspective of conservative communist leaders. This led many observers to conclude that the students were loyal to the system and that their movement was in many ways similar to the remonstration of China's traditional intellectuals before an emperor. I do not deny that China's traditional political culture assigns

45. For example, riots broke out in both Changsha and Xi'an during and after student demonstrations on April 22. Massive looting occurred in both cities. Ten vehicles and about twenty houses were burned during the Xi'an riot. In the April 26 *People's Daily* editorial, the government claimed that student demonstrations had facilitated these riots. Student leader Cheng Zhen (1990, 175) has given exactly the same account of why they tried to keep other sections of the Beijing population from joining the demonstrations during the early stage of the movement.

46. Israel (1966, 115–16).

47. Wu et al. (1989, 62).

particular social roles to intellectuals and that modern Chinese students were influenced by these scripts. However, the rhetoric that students used during the April 27 demonstration makes for a somewhat misleading example. As early as April 18, student activists had unveiled seven demands at Tiananmen Square, at the center of which were calls for freedom of speech, the press, and association (chapter 6). These demands guided the movement from that point onward. That the slogans which students used during the April 27 demonstration were strikingly different from the earlier ones is best explained by considerations of strategy. By demonstrating on the street after the *People's Daily* editorial, the students challenged the regime's authority. However, by restricting their rhetoric to conformist slogans and to a few major social problems of common concern, the movement activists were able to mobilize more students from within and public sympathy from without, while denying the government an excuse for repression.

Thus far I have explained how the state's repressive and unitary nature pushed social movement actors during the 1989 Movement to use conformist strategies to expand the potential for mobilization and to lessen the possibility of immediate repression. However, strategy cannot be the only explanation. During the movement, many students bit their fingers to write slogans in blood; one of my informants reported that he had hit and smashed his own face in anger; a student leader (no. 69) recalled that in late May he saw a woman with tears falling down her cheeks and hair all over her face kneeling outside the student headquarters in the Square crying, chanting, and begging the students not to leave.[48] In fact, emotional displays constituted a major part of movement activities. If I were a social psychologist, I would certainly attribute the domination of cultural activities during the 1989 Movement to the emotional nature of the movement. The logic is straightforward: when people act emotionally they tend to act out what they are most familiar with, to act according to those behavioral codes that have already been imprinted in their minds and to which they have become habituated.[49]

However, such an explanation could not constitute the whole story either. We know that a huge number of people participated in the 1989 Movement in an increasingly unorganized fashion.[50] Also, most movement activities were carried out in a few places, such as Tiananmen Square, the Triangle at Beijing

48. In my interview with this student leader, he insisted that during the martial law period Tiananmen Square was like a mental hospital. He usually had a clear mind. However, each time he returned to the Square and saw many people acting this way he became emotional and confused.

49. Kitayama and Markus (1994); Triandis (1989).

50. Chen Xiaoya (1996).

University, or the Third Student Dining Hall at People's University (chapters 6 and 8). During the movement, people frequently visited these places after work, after dinner, or any time as they wanted. Most of them simply acted as sympathetic bystanders. When so moved, a few of them would stage actions of their own. The relatively unorganized and place-centered nature of these activities made the relationship between movement actors and bystanders very much like that between "street theater actors" at a fair and the people who visit that fair. Someone who had visited Tiananmen Square during the movement was likely to encounter several independent protest activities either simultaneously or sequentially, and a huge crowd of sympathetic bystanders mingling inside and looking for something interesting. Those who acted on the stage might follow traditional, modern, or foreign scripts of social movements. They might also act out of impulse, calculation, or a combination of both. For the most part, their forms of action and motivations did not matter at this level because most of these activities came and went without having a substantial impact on the movement. Yet some activities, like the three students kneeling and the hunger strike, touched the hearts of hundreds of thousands of sympathetic observers and shaped the dynamics of the movement. I found that it was at this level that movement activities during the 1989 Movement appeared to be more traditional than those during the May 4th or the December 9th Movements. Obviously, what mattered here was the psychology of those who were watching the protests.

In their study of the "Zoot-Suit" riot, Turner and Surace found that a symbol would not evoke uniform group action and unrestricted hostile behavior unless its presence aroused uniformly and exclusively unfavorable feelings toward an object under attack.[51] If we consider movement rhetoric and activities as symbols and the sources of state legitimation as such an object, the logic which Turner and Surace uncovered is certainly applicable to my case. I argue that people's acceptance of particular forms of movement rhetoric or activity is shaped by their perception of state legitimation. During the 1980s, moral performance was a major source of state legitimation. Therefore, people were more receptive to morally (culturally) charged activities and got angry when the government reacted improperly to these activities. Thus when on April 22 three students knelt on the steps of the Great Hall of the People, Li Peng's failure to come out to receive their petition immediately triggered a citywide class boycott (chapter 6). In fact, many other activities took place around the same time,

---

51. Turner and Surace (1956).

but none of them were able to capture the hearts of students and shape the future of the movement. An informant (no. 60) recalled what happened when Li Peng did not come out to receive the three kneeling students:

> I never trusted the Communist Party. I did not believe that they would really do any thing good. I knew that nothing would be accomplished even if Li Peng came out to meet us, yet I still wished that Li Peng would come out to say a few words. But he did not come out. We felt extremely sad and many of us burst out crying. . . . At one point, I even punched my own face several times and blood gushed out of my face. Then I was pulled away by several friends. . . . On my way out, I saw that students were crying everywhere. I also saw that a journalist was crying like a baby and chanting: "This is a bastard government. This is a shit government. This is a useless government." I also heard some students shout: "Down with Li Peng!"

This informant was a very radical student leader, and yet he wished that Li Peng would come out and meet them. As Pye has noted, coming out and receiving a petition in such a circumstance was a ritual that even a mandarin of imperial China had to fulfil.[52] Contrary to most students' expectations, Li Peng did not come out. On that day, what my informant and the journalist acted and cried out was actually a general sentiment—a sentiment of total disappointment in the government. They had this sentiment not because the government was not democratic (even though some of them were fighting for democratization) but because a leader of the government failed to perform a proper ritual, a ritual upon which the state was now basing its legitimacy. It was out of this sentiment that most Beijing students participated in a general class boycott the following day.

In an informal interview, student leader Zhou Fengsuo told me that during the April 27 demonstration Beijing residents on the sidewalks responded enthusiastically when students shouted slogans against official corruption and high inflation. However, slogans such as "Free press," "Free association," and "Democracy" were poorly received. Consequently, he observed a gradual drift of the slogans shouted during the demonstration from the issue of freedom and democracy to that of official corruption and inflation. The reason for the differentiated response from the people on the sidewalks was clear. By the late 1980s, the major sources of state legitimacy were economic and moral performance;

52. Pye (1990, 168).

most students and Beijing residents did not really care about how the government was formed, but they did care whether the government was moral and whether it could bring order and economic prosperity. Slogans centered on official corruption and inflation attracted a wide audience because they resonated with most people's expectations of the government.

Many other examples can be given of how people responded differently to various movement activities. During the hunger strike mobilization between May 11 and 13, radical students tried to mobilize students to join the strike by using different claims. At the University of Political Science and Law, the major reason was: "The government has not yet rehabilitated our movement, but Dongchang starts to spread rumors again." [53] This was not successful. By noon of May 13, only seven or eight students had volunteered for the hunger strike. Beijing Normal University's major claim was: "In order to advance China's democratization, we voluntarily participate in a hunger strike." This was not convincing either. Very few students signed up. At the more radical Beijing University, activists had made different speeches to try to mobilize students. However, by the evening of May 12, only about forty students had signed up to be hunger strikers. At this point, student activist Chai Ling made an emotional speech to give her reason for a hunger strike. In her speech, she did not capitalize on the democratic aspect of the movement. Rather she emphasized that "my hunger strike is for the purpose of seeing just what the true face of the government is, to see whether it intends to suppress the movement or to ignore it, to see whether the people have a conscience or not, to see if China still has a conscience or not, if it has hope or not." [54] Shen Tong was among the majority who were initially against the idea of a hunger strike. He recalled his impression after Chai's speech:

> Chai Ling's speech was so personal and direct, yet it touched me as no other speech had. I had been trying all day to come to terms with the idea of the hunger strike, and no one had said anything that satisfied me. Chai Ling made me understand why students would want to make such a sacrifice. We were asking the government for dialogue and recognition. Were these two things worth dying for? I didn't think so. But Chai Ling's speech made me and many others realize that the hunger strike was about much more than those two demands. [55]

53. The slogan was a response to He Dongchang's rather harsh comments about the movement made several days earlier.

54. The excerpt is from Han and Hua (1990, 198).

55. Shen Tong (1990, 237).

After Chai's speech, the number of students signed up for the hunger strike at Beijing University immediately went from around forty to nearly three hundred. Rhetoric centered on the democratic goals of the movement was not effective, but a call for the students to use their own lives to test the government's morality received an enthusiastic response.

The above analysis explains why the 1989 Movement focused on moral issues even though the goal of the movement was democracy. Since moral performance was the basis of state legitimacy, activities that morally discredited the government posed a more fundamental challenge to the state and thus were able to mobilize more people. Therefore, during the hunger strike, almost all the people in Beijing, even those working in state institutions, eventually supported the students. Most Beijing residents also joined the mass resistance to the army after martial law was imposed. Most of them, especially those from peripheral government institutions, did not stand up to fight for a democratic China. Instead they protested a central government that kept silent while students were dying of hunger and that tried to use troops to repress students. In short, many people participated in the movement because they were angry; they were angry because the government's actions violated the people's common notion of how a good government should act.

Now I want to return to the issue of why traditional languages and activities were less manifest during the two earlier student movements. The difference seems to be attributable to two factors. First, early in this century foreign aggression was the most urgent problem, and how to stop it was the focus of the Chinese political elites. As stated before, the principal foundation of state legitimacy then lay in the state's capacity to resist foreign aggression rather than in its moral conduct and its ability to regulate the economy. In other words, while the nationalist goals of both the May 4th and December 9th Movements had actually challenged the regime's legitimacy, simple moral issues were at those moments less able to move people if they were not directly related to nationalism.

Secondly, in contrast to the 1989 Movement, social and political organizations played significant roles in the two earlier movements. All three student movements were spontaneously initiated. Emotional displays were also widespread during the May 4th and the December 9th Movements. However, in the two earlier movements, organized forces moved in to exploit the situation, whereas during the 1989 Movement no such political forces existed. The strategic activities of political organizations also freed the two earlier student movements from emotion-ridden rhetoric and activities. In the next section, I elaborate this point.

Strength of Movement Organizations and Patterns of Movement Dynamics

Now I will examine the role of organizations in each of the three student movements to see how they shaped the activities and development of the three movements. To reduce the length of the discussion, I will focus on the key political players behind each of the three student movements: the Guomindang during the May 4th Movement of 1919, the CCP in the December 9th Movement of 1935–36, and China's leading liberal intellectuals in the 1989 Movement. My discussion will also be limited to one crucial instance for each of the three student movements. I start with the May 4th Movement.

We know that most of the organizations involved in the May 4th Movement had a history prior to the movement. These organizations had independent resources, political expertise, and clear interests. Many of these organizations were anchored by senior Guomindang members or their close associates, most of whom actively participated in the movement as soon as it started. These Guomindang members, who had political credentials that derived from their own prior revolutionary activities, were crucial in the movement's leadership and coordination. During the May 4th Movement, an organization such as the Federation of All Organizations of China was able to coordinate and lead the movement mainly because it was comprised of a group of associations that each had independent organizational resources and experienced leaders with unsurpassed credentials.[56]

During the May 4th Movement, the senior Guomindang members supported the movement and yet on the other hand successfully manipulated it for their own interests. The Guomindang supported the nationalistic goals of the movement and wanted to use the movement to expand its political influence. However, the Guomindang did not want to see the movement develop into an anti-Western riot as the Boxer Rebellion had, nor did it intend to see the movement hurt China's economy. Finally, the Guomindang was not interested in provoking a revolution. This was clearly shown by the activity patterns of the movement. By June 1919 the center of the movement had moved to Shanghai. On June 5, Shanghai industries and businesses, as well as Shanghai workers, all

---

56. The Federation of All Organizations in China was composed of the Student Union of the Republic of China, the Society of Women Comrades for Patriotism, the Christian National Salvation Society, the National Chamber of Commerce, the All-China Journalists' Union, and representatives from other social groups, including labor, gentry, and religious. It was established on June 5, 1919 in Shanghai at a meeting held at the invitation of the Student Union of Shanghai. Famous Guomindang members such as Huang Yanpei, Ye Chucang, and Zhang Menglin, among others, presided over the meeting.

joined a general strike to support the students. At the time of the strike, the Guomindang controlled most labor unions in Shanghai. Yet the Guomindang was still cautiously trying to avoid the possible unintended consequences of a large-scale workers' strike. As soon as the strike started, the Guomindang's official newspaper, the *Republican Daily*, published an editorial that appealed to the workers "to keep order and not get involved in any insurrections."[57] Over the following days, through the *Republican Daily* and other major newspapers, the Guomindang reiterated its idea of the goals and proper strategies of the strike. The Guomindang stressed that the strike was aimed not at Chinese business owners and Westerners but only at the Japanese and a few traitors in the northern government. It even demanded that service workers in the foreign concessions not join the strike so that the lives of the Westerners would not be seriously affected. Finally, when the news reached Shanghai that the northern government had dismissed Cao Rulin, Zhang Zongxiang, and Lu Zongyu, the three publicly identified pro-Japanese traitors, the Guomindang-controlled labor unions immediately called off their strike. At the time, student leaders in Shanghai had different ideas. Thus Sun Zhongshan immediately called major student leaders to his Shanghai home.[58] In the meeting, he convinced the students that it was time to restore order and demanded that students actively try to persuade Shanghai businessmen to end the commercial strike.[59] Students did as Sun Zhongshan asked. The next day, June 12, the Shanghai students organized a demonstration to celebrate their "victory" and used the occasion to persuade shop owners to end the commercial strike. Such a dramatic transition would not have occurred without the support and intervention of the Guomindang.

In comparison with those of the May 4th era, the intermediate organizations during the December 9th Movement were relatively weak. In fact, with the exception of Yanjing University and Qinghua University, where America and American liberalism still had some influence, political organizations in most Beijing universities were kept very small and ineffective by the government

57. *Republican Daily* (June 6, 1919).

58. During the May 4th Movement Sun Zhongshan several times summoned the student leaders in order to present to them his own strategic recommendations. For example, Shanghai students had started the class boycott on May 26. Yet, student leaders in Shanghai had no plan for what to do next. Thus on May 29 Sun Zhongshan asked his people to meet with the student leaders and pass on his message. Sun suggested that the students initiate bold and radical actions in order to ignite and fan the flames of popular outrage (Zhu Zhonghua 1982). Two days later, students in Shanghai organized a memorial demonstration for a student who had died in Beijing. Thirty thousand people reportedly participated in the demonstration.

59. Liu Yongming (1990, 188). At the time, many shop owners had made a commitment that their stores would not open without the permission of the students.

before the rise of the December 9th Movement. Thus the movement started much more spontaneously. Nevertheless, many students who played crucial roles in initiating the movement, and consequently captured its leadership, were left-wing students or underground members of the CCP. Moreover, before the December 9th Movement, active students were also being organized by a communist-controlled organization called the Chinese Association of Military Defense. By the time of the December 9th Movement, this organization had branches in quite a few universities and high schools in Beijing. Finally, by 1935 the CCP had developed into a highly disciplined Leninist party, which means that all its members followed the decisions of the higher-level leadership. These factors helped the CCP gradually take over the movement in several crucial cities, especially Beijing and Tianjin.

Like the Guomindang during the May 4th Movement, the CCP leadership supported the movement out of a sense of nationalism. They also saw the movement as an opportunity to gain back their political influence in cities and as an occasion to establish a united front with the Guomindang and other political forces against Japanese aggression. Obviously, the CCP was not interested in radical actions at this point.

The CCP headquarters in Shanbei was not aware of the movement at the time it started. However, the CCP immediately recognized the importance of the occasion. Soon after the movement began, the CCP headquarters sent a senior member, Liu Shaoqi, to Tianjin to take charge of the CCP North China Bureau; his immediate task was to take over control of the movement. Here the turning point was occasioned by Guo Qing's death. Guo Qing, a high school student, was beaten and later died in jail. The students in Beijing became very angry and organized a memorial service at Beijing University in protest. Local authorities banned the meeting and deployed a huge number of policemen outside the university. The students were very emotional. When a student rushed onto the stage and suggested carrying a coffin and demonstrating outside the university, most students followed. However, the demonstrator were met head-on with repression. Only six to seven hundred students eventually managed to demonstrate outside the campus, where about a hundred were wounded and fifty-three were arrested, including several major student leaders. The action was immediately criticized by Liu Shaoqi as ultra-leftist.[60] Liu then reorganized the CCP Beijing Committee and dismissed those whose ideas were not congenial to the policy of the CCP Central Committee. He wrote a letter to students

---

60. Liu was the president of the People's Republic of China before the Cultural Revolution, and he died during the Cultural Revolution after being purged from the party.

and requested them not to continue to act radically. He also demanded that they resume classes and respect their teachers and parents.[61] Moreover, Liu asked students to differentiate between the Nanjing government and that of the local military leader, Song Zheyuan. He promptly coined the slogans: "Support the Chief of the Committee Song to lead the anti-Japanese resistance!" and "Support the 29th Army to fight against the Japanese!" He also contacted hundreds of Guomindang elites to gain their sympathy. Liu's efforts were successful. From then on, Beijing students no longer acted radically and the local military leader Song Zheyuan relented and released the arrested students. The movement changed its course after the CCP Central Committee gained control.

This example shows that Chinese students were indeed more likely to follow culturally embedded forms of collective action, such as the funeral ritual, during the movement. Yet, it also suggests that the impact of culture was not as deterministic as some cultural theorists have claimed. The students during the December 9th Movement initiated a funeral demonstration in anger, but once it was suppressed, no more radical actions followed. On the contrary, the funeral demonstration was labeled as ultra-leftist and the movement took a different course. The movement was able to drastically change its orientation because the student organizations were controlled either by CCP members or by left-wing students who, closely associated with the communists, unconditionally followed the CCP's lead.

In comparison with the two earlier student movements, the 1989 Movement broke out in an organizational near vacuum. Resourceful and politically experienced opposition parties, like the Guomindang in the May 4th and the CCP in the December 9th eras, did not exist during the 1980s. All the social movement organizations that emerged during the 1989 Movement had no prior history. These organizations were formed in haste. As a result, the leaders of student organizations were not elected by significant numbers of people with reasonable procedures, nor did they have reputable past movement experiences (chapter 6). The development of the movement brought to the fore not only many newly formed organizations but also numerous politically ambitious students with different ideas. These students, regardless of whether they were in or outside the leadership of the movement organizations, tended to act on their own during the movement. Since a large number of students at that time had one or another kind of grievance, any type of radical activity during the 1989

---

61. The article was reprinted in 1987 with a title "Close-Doorism and Adventurism" (Liu Shaoqi 1987).

Movement was able to attract some followers. During the May 4th and the December 9th Movements, movement organizations gained authority as the movement proceeded. By contrast, during the 1989 Movement major movement organizations were increasingly fragmented and marginalized and the movement became more and more dominated by spontaneous mass activities.

At the time, China's leading liberal intellectuals comprised the only political force that could have had an impact on the course of the movement comparable to that of the Guomindang in the May 4th era and the CCP in the December 9th era. These intellectuals, through their books, their speeches at campus conferences, and other activities, had prepared the way for the movement and had won respect among some students (chapter 2). Yet those students who were closest to the leading intellectuals and therefore had a more refined understanding of China's problems and of the goals of the movement were continuously marginalized by those who had gained their credentials through dedicated radical actions. Moreover, out of fear of repression, leading liberal intellectuals had deliberately distanced themselves from the movement in its early stages (chapters 6 and 7). By the time that they became collectively involved in the movement, it was already May 14, one day after the start of the hunger strike. Moreover, they first participated in the movement as mediators between the government and radical students, seeking to bring the hunger strike to an end. Not only did their efforts prove to be futile, but also the ambiguity of their stance further undermined their already weak standing within the movement. During late May, liberal intellectuals were more and more concerned about the future of the movement. A reflection of this concern was the establishment of the Joint Federation, which claimed to incorporate all the political forces in Beijing. Yet this organization failed to harness the tide of the movement and help it avert a tragic ending. This happened because, unlike the Guomindang and the CCP during the May 4th and the December 9th Movements, the liberal intellectuals in the 1980s had neither substantial organizational resources nor adequate political experience.[62] Under these conditions, credentials became their only resource; but compared with the Guomindang and the CCP leaders, liberal intellectuals in the 1980s lacked past revolutionary experience as necessary credentials for leadership. In contrast to the newly emergent radical students in the 1989 Movement, the liberal intellectuals joined the movement later and did not participate in the hunger strike, which was generally considered to

---

62. As it is shown in chapter 6, China's leading liberal intellectuals in fact often acted as naively and radically as the young students when faced with a crisis situation.

be the action which showed the greatest amount of dedication.[63] Therefore, all the discussions and decisions made by the Joint Federation turned out to be useless empty talk. As it proceeded, the movement was increasingly driven by emotion and radical action. This finally led the movement into a head-on confrontation with the government—and a tragic outcome.

Conclusion

This chapter compares the 1989 Movement's patterns of activity with those of the May 4th and the December 9th Movements. I found that movement activities during the 1989 Movement had three distinctive patterns: they were more pro-Western in appearance, they bore a strong imprint of the communist styles of mass mobilization, especially those popularized during the Cultural Revolution, and perhaps most strikingly, they had a more traditional outlook than the two earlier student movements. While the first two distinctions can be explained by changes in the international environment, differences in the goals of the movements, and experiences of past collective action, the last has to be explained as a factor of the different state-society relations behind the three student movements.

Three entwined features characterized state-society relations in China during the late 1980s: a unitary state, performance legitimation, and the weak development of social organizations outside the realm of the state. This chapter argues that because of the weakness of independent social organizations, spontaneity actually increased after the 1989 Movement passed beyond its initial phase. When many spontaneous activities occur simultaneously at the same time and place, the psychology of audiences becomes important. Cultural forms of activity dominated the 1989 Movement because students and Beijing residents at the time judged their government by its moral performance. They became very angry when the government reacted improperly to culturally and morally charged movement activities.

---

63. This feeling was clearly revealed in Wuer Kaixi's comment on the actions of the twelve leading intellectuals at the beginning of the hunger strike (Hinton and Gordon 1997, 121–23): "The problem with intellectuals was that they played the wrong role. They were acting as mediators between the students and government. We forced the government to the negotiation table. This was the first time in forty years and we accomplished it. We, students, acted as an independent political force. And then, we invited intellectuals to join us. They came to the Square to address us as children. The message we got is that we had gone too far and everything had to go gradually. *What have they done to have the right to criticize us?*" (emphasis mine).

In social movement studies, the focus has shifted from social psychology to resource mobilization and political processes. While theorists previously treated social movements as crowd-ridden activities driven by emotional displays, resource mobilization and political process scholars treat movement activities as the rational strategies of movement organizers. In reality, both spontaneity and organized behavior figure importantly in most social movements.[64] This chapter shows that, other factors being equal, the role of organizations in a social movement is a function of state-society relations. The May 4th and the December 9th Movements became more and more strategy-driven because of the existence of fragmented states and strong organized forces outside the realm of the state. Yet, the 1989 Movement became emotion-ridden due to the absence of organized forces to fill in the political vacuum created by the movement itself. Seen in this light, the transition from social psychological to resource mobilization and political process perspectives in social movement studies in the West might have reflected the reality that, because of the poor development of intermediate organizations, the early social movements in Western countries also tended to be more spontaneous and emotionally driven than more recent ones that have operated under a "multi-organizational field."

This study shows that the dynamics of a social movement may be determined not only by strategies of movement organizations but also by norms and symbols that emerge in a series of interactions between the state and the movement participants, as well as by interactions of active participants with sympathetic audiences. Therefore, the analysis also has similarities with classic social psychological perspectives that emphasize emotion and the formation of emotional activities through symbolic interactions.[65] The difference is that classic theories were not so interested in the structural bases from which symbols are interpreted and norms emerge. By showing that in a social movement norms or "schemata of interpretation" often emerge around certain legitimate symbols defined by a particular state-society relationship, this chapter links not only micro-level strategic processes but also emotional processes with macro social structures.

64. Killian (1984), McPhail (1991), and Oliver (1989).
65. For example, Blumer (1946) and Turner and Killian (1987).

ten

THE STATE, MOVEMENT COMMUNICATION, AND THE CONSTRUCTION OF PUBLIC OPINION

A social movement is a public event. Those who happen to encounter a particular social movement will have their own views of it.[1] Media coverage of a social movement, and the way it is covered, have been crucial to the public awareness, support, and development of social movements.[2] Although there are significant differences among the positions taken by media scholars, most see both the media and public opinion in the West as relatively conformist institutions. It has been demonstrated that the media generally reproduce the agendas of journalists' sources.[3] When a news story is about the government, reports generally reflect official views.[4] Since many social movements are

1. See Turner (1969) for discussion of the public perception of social movements.
2. Kielbowicz and Scherer (1986); Ryan (1991).
3. Gans (1979).
4. See, for example, Sigal (1973). This is particularly true in international news stories (Ball-Rokeach and DeFleur 1976; Dickson 1992). In America, while the Soviet downing of a Korean jet was portrayed by the media as a moral outrage, the U.S. downing of an Iranian plane was depicted as a technical problem (Entman 1991). During the Gulf War U.S. news stories focused mainly on promoting American military and

anti-establishment, the media tend to neglect them.[5] Even when the media report on a social movement, they tend to marginalize, trivialize, and distort the scale and the goals of the movement.[6] Such distortions are also characteristic of public opinion. In the West, public opinion generally follows the lead of the media, especially as it concerns issues with which people do not have daily experience.[7] Therefore, Gamson and Modigliani are able to find a close correlation between the public's view of nuclear power in the United States and the way the U.S. media portray it.[8] In cases where people do have daily experience of an event on which the media have reported, the public interpretation is more likely to be plural and contested.[9]

During my research, I found that Chinese journalists tried from the very beginning to escape from government control and report positively on the 1989 Beijing Student Movement, and furthermore that when the media reported negatively on the movement, China's public opinion followed not the media but rumors. However, as soon as the government's control over the media weakened, positive accounts of the movement dominated news coverage, public opinion followed the media, and rumors no longer played a major role in shaping public opinion. This kind of relationship between the media and public opinion, itself part of the dynamics of the movement, greatly contributed to the tragic outcome of the 1989 Movement. In this chapter I describe and analyze this pattern of interactions between the media and public opinion and its impact on the 1989 Movement.

---

technological superiority and neglected other aspects of the war, particularly the civilian deaths on the Iraqi side (Griffin and Lee 1995). Thus, the Gulf War appeared like "Nintendo warfare" in U.S. news reports (Kellner 1992).

5. Some studies have painted a pluralist picture of the Western media's reporting on social movements (e.g., Goldenberg 1975; Greenberg 1985; Szasz 1994). These studies, however, only concentrate on the interest group politics type of social movements, which aim at minor reformist issues, or on the "loyal opposition" type of social movements organized or supported by resourceful elites.

6. Gitlin (1980); Molotch (1979).

7. Lang and Lang (1981); Pride (1995).

8. Gamson and Modigliani (1989).

9. The relationship between media discourse and public opinion has been heavily debated. While earlier studies generally argue that the public would have a pluralist response to the same message (e.g., Hastorf and Cantril 1954), more recent studies tend to argue or imply that the public in the West generally follow the media's lead (e.g., Connell 1980; Hall et al. 1978; Herman and Chomsky 1988). Between them, researchers assign different degrees of autonomy to the public perception of the media's message, depending on issues, audiences, and personal relevance (Ball-Rokeach and DeFleur 1982; McNair 1988). However, no studies have reported a case where the public opinion in the West has gone totally against the media's message. For more discussion of the issue, see Curran (1990).

This chapter starts with an analysis of the range of news coverage in China before the rise of the 1989 Movement. Since the 1989 Movement was publicized through multiple communication channels, including domestic media, international media, student controlled broadcasting centers, and word of mouth, in the second section I try to gauge which channels were most important to the dynamics of the movement, and therefore which should be the focus of the analysis. The main body of the chapter is a narrative of the behavior of the Chinese media and of public opinion during the 1989 Movement. To keep the narrative uninterrupted, I leave my interpretation of their behavior and their impact on the development of the movement to the last section. Since the analytical tools of my interpretation draw primarily on the state-society relations model that I developed in earlier chapters, this chapter will not deal with the theoretical issues separately.

News Coverage in the Chinese Media Before the 1989 Movement

According to some, the media and public opinion in China were easily radicalized because China's media coverage had been so artificially narrow in comparison with that in the West. This is a popular interpretation shared by scholars who study the Chinese media[10] and by the Chinese intellectuals who have pushed the government for more openness. Certainly, narrow media coverage accurately describes the Chinese media during Mao's era. Yet during that era such narrow coverage was achieved through the cooperation of a majority of Chinese journalists. When China's media underwent reform in the 1980s, Chinese journalists started to introduce such Western journalistic principles as timeliness, objectivity, and readability. The editors of major media outlets obtained more freedom to decide on the news themselves. At this point, in a manner associated with the general intellectual trend toward liberalization that I discussed in chapter 2, Chinese journalists started to question the CCP's monopoly of the media and to push for press freedom.[11] The combined result of both the state-led reform and the journalists' push for openness drastically broadened the scope of news coverage in China. To give readers a more concrete sense of the Chinese media at this juncture, this section examines the news content of one major Chinese medium just before the 1989 Movement.

10. Lee (1994), Ma, Liu, and Chen (1989), and Zhao and Shen (1993).

11. See Zhao Yuezhi (1998b) for a more detailed overview on the general media liberalization in China after the mid-1980s.

To allow the analysis to achieve a certain depth within a limited space, I focus on the contents of domestic news stories that appeared in the March 15, 1989 *People's Daily*.[12]

During the late 1980s, the *People's Daily* was published in editions of eight pages.[13] The first page was for important domestic and international news, the second for general domestic news, the third for general international news, and pages seven and eight were for human interest stories, poetry, and prose from China and abroad, in-depth analysis of international politics and economics, and advertisements. The contents of pages four, five and six changed on a daily basis. Page four always featured "Sports," but its other column alternated between "Social Life" and "Cultural Life." More negative stories were expected when "Social Life" was featured. Page five alternated three columns in a weekly cycle: "Economy," "Politics and Law," and "Education, Science, and Humanity." In early 1989 a major theme of the "Education and Humanity" column, featured every Wednesday and Saturday, was the declining status of intellectuals and the educational crisis. Page six was for literature, literary criticism, social theory, memoirs, and other cultural matters; every Wednesday and Saturday the page featured "Letters from Readers." During 1988 and 1989 negative stories dominated this column.

On March 15, 1989, the paper carried a total of sixty domestic news stories. The front page had 10, the second 21, the fourth 11, the fifth 5, and the sixth 13. Among the 60 stories, 28 (46.7%) are coded as negative (table 10.1).[14] The percentage of negative news increases in later pages. While 10 percent of the news on the first page was negative, the percentage rises to 92.3 percent for the sixth page. This is understandable since the first two pages of the daily gave priority to stories on government activities, items over which editors had little control. When it came to the fourth page, editors had the power to decide what to cover, and most news stories became negative.

Let me start with the news on the fourth page. This page's "Social Life" column covered seven stories, organized under the theme of crimes and social disorder; six of these were negative. Here are two examples: One article is en-

12. I chose the *People's Daily* because it is the premier Chinese official newspaper. March 15 was a Wednesday; no major political events were happening. Initially I chose the day because it was exactly one month before the beginning of the 1989 Movement. Later, I found that every Wednesday and Saturday the percentage of negative news tended to be higher in that paper (I will explain why in the following). Since the bias is systematic and my purpose is to explore the extent of negative news coverage, this selection is ideal.

13. See Chang Won Ho (1989, ch. 3) for a similar discussion of page arrangement in the *People's Daily*.

14. They code as negative not because they report news such as traffic accidents or murder cases, but because they point out social problems related to China's economic and political systems.

TABLE 10.1   The Range of Domestic News Coverage in the March 15, 1989, *People's Daily*

	Page Number				
	1	2	4	5	6
Total stories on page	10	21	11	5	13
Negative stories	1	5	7	3	12
Percentage of negative stories	10.0	23.8	63.6	60.0	92.3

Note: People's Daily is the largest official newspaper in China.

titled "The Fact That a Large Number of People Used Public Cars to Visit Prisoners Is a Matter of Great Concern." It reports that many Beijing residents used cars belonging to public institutes or the government to go to the prison to visit convicted family members. It ends with a list of 32 plate numbers that a reporter had copied down while in front of a juvenile prison in Beijing on March 8. The story depicts widespread official corruption, a major theme of the coming student movement (chapter 5). It also allows people to infer that the children of government officials (those who had cars assigned by the government for work) had a disproportionately high crime rate. Another article, "Serious Problems of Unlawful Marriage in Some Villages," warns of the extent of social disorder in rural China. In just one county of Guangdong province, investigators found 14,700 couples who had never legally registered their unions.

The fifth page featured the "Education, Science, and Humanity" column. All five stories were negative news. For my purposes, however, I code only three of them as negative, since the other two, about spoiled children, are not overtly political. The three stories center on the educational crisis in China, another theme of the coming student movement (chapters 3 and 5). The first is a commentary entitled "A Place for the Ivory Tower." It complains about the then-current wave of commercialism, stating that "Not all scholastic and artistic work can be converted into money. If every activity is evaluated by market value, a large number of intellectuals will have to change their jobs or go into business." [15] Another article reports a discussion held in a local normal college about the value of schooling. Most students thought that schooling was important, but they all complained that one did not need to be educated to get rich and that those who had more education tended to live a poorer life.

15. See chapter 3 for the 1988 commercial fever and its impact on intellectuals.

In the "Letters from the Readers" column on the sixth page, thirteen articles treated managerial problems in state or collective enterprises, reflecting people's concern about the economic crisis and high inflation, a popular source of discontent during 1989 (chapter 5). The page is anchored by an investigative report by a *People's Daily* journalist entitled "Under Constant Distress from Robbery." It describes how local residents near a big steel factory used trolleys, trucks, and even tractors to steal the factory's products. This had developed to such an extent that sometimes dozens of people would carry away steel in the presence of policemen. Hundreds of stores had been opened around the factory area to purchase "steel and iron waste," profiteering from the thefts.

As can be seen, even before the 1989 Movement, such sources of major public discontent as official corruption, the economic crisis, and the lower status of intellectuals had been major themes of China's most orthodox official newspaper. Based on this extensive negative news coverage, as well as on the way that the negative news was depicted in the media, it could be argued that at least during the late 1980s the range of news coverage in the Chinese media was in some aspects no narrower than that in the West. This is not to say that China's journalists enjoyed more freedom than their Western colleagues did. Rather, while Western journalists in theory enjoy a high level of legally guaranteed freedom, they use only a small portion of their rights. On the other hand, during the late 1980s, Chinese journalists faced possible government sanctions and enjoyed less freedom but made full use of all of the latitude available to them, adopting the potential freedom of Western journalists as an ideal goal and continuously pushing in that direction.[16]

Crucial Channels of Mass Communication during the Movement

Unlike in the West, where most individuals get to know a social movement through formal domestic media, in China the international media, such as the VOA and the BBC, are a major source of news for the urban population. Informal communication channels, such as word of mouth, big-character posters, handbills, and student broadcasts also figured importantly in transmitting movement ideas to the public at large.[17] Thus we need to specify the roles that

16. The strategy that journalists adopted has been vividly called "hitting line balls" *(Dacabianqiu)*, which means to hit the ball to the very edge of a Ping-Pong table (Hsiao and Yang 1990).

17. By formal communication, I refer to television, international and domestic radio broadcasts, and regularly circulated newspapers. By informal communication, I mean big-character posters, handbills, public speeches, broadcasting stations and newspapers controlled by the students, and word of mouth. Regarding student-controlled broadcasting stations, see chapter 4, note 34.

different forms of communication played during the 1989 Movement before we can have a meaningful analysis of the media as a whole. Scholars who have studied the communication aspect of the movement emphasize the importance of international media.[18] I therefore start with an evaluation of the importance of the international media for the 1989 Movement in Beijing, focused mainly on He and Zhu's study of the VOA during the 1989 Movement.[19] (I cover only this monograph because it has greater depth than the other writings.)

He and Zhu's study is based on interviews with seventy-one Chinese students who are now in North America but were in China during 1989. In their report, they claim that the VOA delivered news to millions of Chinese who could not otherwise obtain it, provided the movement with a master frame (that of a "prodemocracy movement"), reinforced people's antigovernment attitudes, and coordinated the movement. While it was true that most Beijing students and much of the general urban population listened to the VOA or the BBC during the movement, He and Zhu have certainly exaggerated and misunderstood the importance of the foreign media. For instance, it was not the VOA that put democracy forward as a movement master frame; before the movement started, liberal intellectuals and radical students had already organized numerous seminars and conferences to spread nonconformist ideas on Beijing campuses.[20] The Democracy Salon at Beijing University, for example, had been formed long before the movement started and had no direct link to the VOA's reporting, and yet its ideas about political reform and democratization became the movement's master frame. In short, the prodemocratic nature of the 1989 Movement was directly related to intellectual discourse during the late 1980s, to which foreign media made only a secondary contribution.

Moreover, in my study I asked thirty-six informants the question "What were the means by which you and your classmates came to know about the movement?"[21] In the process of probing, I gave a list of possibilities including Western media (such as the VOA and the BBC), domestic media, direct observation, word of mouth, big-character posters, student broadcasts, and speeches. I asked them to list their sources in order of importance. Fifteen informants (or 16.5 percent out of the total selections) chose foreign media as *one* of their

18. See He and Zhu (1994) and Mark (1991). Note that the Chinese government also accused the VOA of being an "external cause" of the movement and a rumor center (Chen Xitong 1989). In June 1989 alone, the *People's Daily* published five articles and news reports attacking VOA's reporting on the movement.

19. He and Zhu (1994).

20. See chapters 2 and 5.

21. When I designed this question, I expected to discover that the foreign media had a huge impact on the 1989 Movement, but as the interviews went on I found this was not the case. Thus, the question was gradually not used in the interviews, which is, I think, a mistake.

TABLE 10.2   My Informants' Major Sources of Information during the 1989 Movement

	Semiformal Channels		Informal Channels		Formal Channels	
	Big-Character Posters	Student Broadcast	Personal Observation	Word of Mouth	Official Media	Foreign Media
N	20	15	18	13	10	15
mean	1.17	1.73	1.44	2.08	2.00	3.00
s.e.	0.08	0.20	0.20	0.23	0.20	0.19

Note: N is the number of informants who made a particular selection, and s.e. is the standard error of the sample mean. Thirty-six informants were asked this question (see the text for details). The total number of selections made by all the thirty-six informants is ninety-one. Mean is the average order of importance that informants assigned to a particular medium.

sources (table 10.2). In comparison, 27 percent of He and Zhou's respondents listed foreign media as a major source of information. Many factors might lead to such a difference; here, I identify two major ones.

First, our population and questions are different. My thirty-six informants were all from Beijing, but thirty of He and Zhu's seventy-one respondents were not from Beijing. The question which He and Zhu asked was: "Which of the following channels did you rely on for information about the June 4 event?" Although using "June 4 event" to refer to the whole movement was quite common among the Chinese, the wording might have led some informants to focus only on the military crackdown around June 4. Most official media in China kept silent during the military crackdown. Students, especially those not from Beijing, had to rely on foreign media for news about it.

Second, He and Zhou gave respondents three choices: Chinese media, foreign media, and personal sources (personal observations and word of mouth). Yet most of my informants listed what I also define as semiformal communication channels—such as the big-character posters and student-controlled broadcasting stations—as an important source of information, a category missing from He and Zhu's questionnaire. Logically, the omission of important categories will force respondents to make other choices. Assuming the omission spread people's attention evenly to other categories, then a deletion of semiformal media categories would reduce the total number of selections made by my 36 informants from 91 to 56. The percentage of informants who report foreign media as an important source would thus be inflated to 26.8 percent, surprisingly close to He and Zhu's finding.

A more important issue concerns not how many people selected foreign media as one of their information sources, but how important this source was to their daily interpretation of the movement. Thus I asked informants to order the importance of the sources that they were relying on to make sense of the movement. Their rankings were coded numerically, with one representing the most important and six the least (most of them only made three or four choices). Now, the importance of big-character posters (mean = 1.30, s.e. = 0.12), student broadcasting centers (mean = 1.73, s.e. = 0.20), and direct observation (mean = 1.44, s.e. = 0.20) is truly striking in comparison with that of foreign media (mean = 3.00, s.e. = 0.19). In fact, none of my informants listed foreign media, namely the VOA and the BBC, as their most important sources, but three of them commented without probing that foreign news did not have a strong impact on them because their stories were not very rich in comparison with those from other channels. Western journalists' general lack of a deep cultural knowledge of China led their coverage to center more on iconic symbols and slogans, stars of the movement, unconfirmed rumors, and human interest stories than on the movement's internal dynamics. Overall, it was the unofficial communication channels that reached the hearts and minds of the majority of Beijing students.

The foreign media's impact also differed with respect to different populations. Gorbachev's state visit had attracted about 1,200 foreign journalists to Beijing.[22] Yet when they arrived in Beijing those journalists focused instead on the 1989 Movement. Their interest in the movement and frequent interviews with student activists certainly gave the demonstrators a feeling that "the whole world is watching," greatly enhancing their confidence. Moreover, the foreign media's reports also mobilized overseas Chinese. After mid-May, a huge number of overseas donations flooded into Beijing (chapter 6). The foreign media's attention also encouraged students to adopt many foreign media-oriented strategies such as flashing V-signs, writing English banners, and holding press conferences. The impact of the foreign media is a very complicated issue; yet overall, they did not play as significant a role in shaping Beijing students and residents' interpretation of and participation in the movement as did other communication channels.

Ten of my informants also chose China's official media as one of their sources of information; thus it is the channel least chosen by my informants. However, those who made the choice tended to believe that the official media were an important source of information (mean = 2.00, s.e. = 0.20), much more important than the foreign media. This result can be explained in a

22. Mark (1991, 268).

number of ways. My interviews have led me to the conclusion that during the movement no particular communication channel had a constant impact on public opinion. Most of the time, China's official media kept silent, so that people had to rely on unofficial channels for information. There was however a period when the state lost control over the official media. In that period, the official media reported on the movement in a positive manner, and people relied on them for the news. Since my questions about the media's impact did not probe into temporal and spatial variations, informants had to answer them in terms of their overall impression. Fewer people chose the official media in my interviews possibly because this highly positive coverage occurred only in a short period during the entire movement.

The Media, Public Opinion, and the Dynamics of the 1989 Movement

I have argued that Beijing students and residents tended to interpret the 1989 Movement by relying on an alternation between China's official media and other less formal channels of communication. Focusing on the official media, I will now present an empirical account of how the official media and the less formal communication channels alternatively shaped Beijing students and residents' views of the movement and consequently influenced the nature and degree of their participation in it.

AN OVERVIEW ON THE BEHAVIOR
OF THE OFFICIAL MEDIA DURING THE MOVEMENT

The analysis here focuses on movement-related news in the *People's Daily* and *Guangming Daily*, arguably two of China's most important official newspapers.[23] Table 10.3 lists the number of movement-related articles and news reports in the two dailies and the results of content analyses of these articles.[24] I code an article as "negative" vis-à-vis the student movement if the title or key sentences of the article include such or similar phrases as "turmoil," "antirevolutionary rebellion," "against the Four Cardinal Principles," "bourgeois liberalization," "order the arrest of," or "support the decision of the Central Committee." I code

23. China's central TV station, the CCTV, also behaved similarly during the movement. See Friedland and Zhong (1996).

24. There is a rich tradition of using media's coverage of movements to study social movements (Franzosi 1987; Mueller 1997; Olzak 1989; Shapiro and Markoff 1998). Although my study has a different focus, it certainly bears an influence of this tradition.

TABLE 10.3   China's Two Major Official Newspapers' Patterns of Coverage
of the 1989 Movement

	No. of Articles						
	Before Apr. 27	Apr. 28– May 4	May 5– May 13	May 14– May 19	May 20– May 24	May 25– May 31	June 1– June 4
People's Daily:							
Negative	10	6	0	0	10	30	20
Neutral	0	8	10	15	10	8	4
Positive	0	0	0	17	6	3	1
Guangming Daily:							
Negative	10	2	0	0	12	48	24
Neutral	0	9	7	11	10	7	0
Positive	0	0	2	30	5	0	0
Total	20	25	19	73	53	96	49
Degree of state control of the media	State in control	State starting to lose its control		State control collapsed	State struggling to gain back its control		State in control again

a report as "positive" if the title or key sentences of an article contain phrases such as "patriotic action," "moved to tears," "express support for [students]," "Democracy [is good]," "[The movement] is rational, peaceful and orderly," or "We salute students." Finally, a report is coded as "neutral" when its main focus is on the process of an event. In an authoritarian regime, the official media usually do not give "objective" accounts of oppositional activities. Therefore, many articles that I have coded as neutral are actually relatively positive toward the movement. The difference between a neutral and a positive account is one of degree. While neutral accounts still tried to balance the students' side of the story with government views, positive accounts totally supported the students.[25]

The two newspapers in question had slightly different patterns of coverage of the movement (table 10.3). The *People's Daily* moved more slowly than did the *Guangming Daily* toward positive coverage. Before May 13, while the *Guangming Daily* had started to report on the movement positively, *People's Daily*'s accounts

25. Many ambiguous articles are also put in this category. For example, in the May 7 *People's Daily*, there was a piece entitled "A Peaceful Ending of the May 4 Student Demonstration in Beijing: Hong Kong's Stock Market Rising," which links the movement with Hong Kong's economic confidence. The report can be interpreted as a reminder to the government that their treatment of the movement would have an international impact. However, it could also be understood as an appraisal of the government's more conciliatory strategy toward the movement. Therefore, I code this report "neutral."

were still between neutral and negative. However, when martial law began, the *Guangming Daily* acted more compliantly than did the *People's Daily*. After May 25, the *Guangming Daily* no longer carried positive reports on the movement, but the *People's Daily* managed to publish positive news as late as June 2.[26] In fact, as I will discuss later, even on June 4—the day of the military crackdown—the *People's Daily* still published articles and news that used innuendo and an allegorical style of writing to express indignation at the military repression.

Otherwise, these two newspapers' styles of covering the 1989 Movement can be categorized into five periods. In the first period, between April 15 and 27, the two newspapers carried twenty related articles, all of which depicted the movement as a turmoil-inducing illegal activity. The second period, between April 28 and May 13, saw a gradual opening of the official media. More movement-related articles appeared, and more and more news articles carried neutral or even positive tones. Within this period there was a clear dividing line: between April 28 and May 4, negative and neutral coverage coexisted, whereas after May 5 negative depictions of the movement totally disappeared while positive accounts emerged. The state had started to lose control over the media.

The third period, between May 14 and 19, roughly covers the period of the hunger strike. A total of seventy-three news articles on the movement appeared in the two papers during this time, many of which were lengthy front-page reports. Most of these articles were very positive about the movement, and none of them were negative. The state's control over the media collapsed. The fourth period, from May 20 to 31, was a period of contestation. Every kind of report, ranging from positive to neutral to negative, appeared in the newspapers. This showed the government's attempt to regain control and the journalists' resistance. Gradually the government gained the upper hand. Thus early in this period, that is, between May 20 and 24, one still saw positive and neutral accounts; by May 25 the number of positive reports had declined, while negative reports had skyrocketed.

The last period started on June 1. Among the forty-nine articles from this period that focused on the issue, only five treated the movement neutrally or

26. On June 2, a short, flower-framed report entitled "June First: A Glance at Tiananmen Square" appeared on the front page of the *People's Daily*. June 1 is China's national Children's Day and many children were brought to Tiananmen Square by parents. The report portrayed a picture of great harmony at the Square, where the students occupying the Square welcomed, presented gifts to, and took photos with the children as well as entertained them with some theatricals. The report claimed that a parent actually felt unhappy not about the Tiananmen Square occupation but about the fact that two parks around Tiananmen Square were not open to the public because of martial law. The message was very clear: the students had not created turmoil, but martial law had brought inconvenience to Beijing residents.

positively. While journalists' resistance was obvious, the state gained back control over them. Still centering my attention on the official media, I will now discuss in more detail how during each of these five stages Beijing students and residents' movement activities were alternatively shaped by official accounts of the movement and by rumors circulated through unofficial channels of communication.

APRIL 15 TO 27: THE MEDIA PUSH, GOVERNMENT
RESISTANCE, AND A RUMOR-DRIVEN MOBILIZATION

Before April 27, although the official media had neglected or negatively depicted the movement, many journalists, especially the younger ones who had graduated during the 1980s, had already gone to observe it firsthand. When they returned, they wrote about the movement positively and often urged the editors-in-chief of their newspapers to publish their accounts. During this period, the chief editors of major newspapers, whether or not sympathetic to the movement, successfully resisted the pressure.[27] However, there was one noticeable exception. On April 23, the *Science and Technology Daily (Keji Ribao)*, a small newspaper with a largely intellectual audience, published a story entitled "Wind and Rain: A Farewell with Solemn Songs." The article positively described students' activities during Hu Yaobang's state funeral on April 22. The government tried to stop the distribution of the edition, but editors and reporters carried the papers in person to post offices to make sure that they were delivered. This article was later posted on many Beijing campuses and cheered by students.[28] This was a small breach in the dike, but it encouraged journalists from other newspapers to try to broaden it. In the following days, articles carrying neutral and even positive descriptions of the movement appeared in some more widely circulated newspapers, among them the *Workers' Daily, Farmers' Daily, Beijing Youth Daily*, and *Chinese Women's Daily*.

In this period, conflict broke out between the *World Economic Herald* (the *Herald*) and the Shanghai Municipal Party Committee. The conflict was significant because both students and journalists used it to push forward their vision of

---

27. According to Faison (1990), only a few days after the movement started, two young journalists at the *People's Daily* brought a story about a student demonstration to their editor-in-chief, Tan Wenrui, seeking its publication. However, their efforts were not successful.

28. Lin Zexin, the newspaper's editor-in-chief, actually did not want to publish this article (Faison 1990, 148–49). However, Lin eventually backed off because the young journalists at the paper persuaded the majority of the staff to threaten to resign if the article was not printed.

press freedom. The *Herald* was a Shanghai-based tabloid-sized weekly with circulation of about 300,000.[29] It was published under the jurisdiction of the Shanghai Academy of Social Sciences; the editor-in-chief, Qin Benli, was appointed by the government. Yet the newspaper paid salaries, costs, and taxes out of the revenue generated from sales and advertisements. It was therefore considered a semi-official newspaper—a hybrid form that had emerged during China's reform.

In the late 1980s, the *Herald* became one of the most outspoken newspapers in China, often serving as a mouthpiece for liberal intellectuals.[30] The incident began on April 19, when the *Herald's* Beijing bureau and the *New Observer* magazine held a joint forum in memory of Hu Yaobang. Outspoken intellectuals such as Dai Qing, Ren Wanding, Hu Jiwei, Yan Jiaqi, Chen Ziming, and Su Shaozhi were invited. They discussed two issues: rehabilitating Hu Yaobang and reevaluating the Anti–Bourgeois Liberalization Campaign. They saw Hu's dismissal from the CCP's General Secretary position in 1987 as an "illegal change of leadership." Yan Jiaqi even claimed: "The main problem China has had to this day has been a lack of democracy. A handful of people can just talk among themselves, put aside people's interests, and reach an unpopular decision."

The *Herald* then prepared a lengthy six-full-page report on the forum, to be published on April 24. When the Shanghai authorities heard the news, they asked for a preview.[31] After the preview, the authorities requested that Qin Benli delete a few hundred characters—the most provocative sentences. The reason given was bad timing: since the seventieth anniversary of the May 4th Movement was approaching and students in Beijing had already been on the street, such content would agitate students and put too much pressure on the government. Qin Benli rejected the request, however. On April 21, Shanghai party boss Jiang Zemin in person persuaded Qin Benli to agree to make changes; but actually Qin had already ordered that the paper be printed before his meeting with Jiang. By the time that Shanghai authorities found this out,

---

29. The following narrative regarding the *Herald*, unless otherwise specified, follows Shen Jinguo (1995), Faison (1990), Hsiao and Yang (1990), and Wu et al. (1989).

30. See chapter 2 for the *Herald's* activities during 1988.

31. In China, news control was implemented through a preview system. Before the reform, news stories in all official media were supposedly previewed by different-level party committees. When an important news story was going to appear in the *People's Daily*, it would be reviewed by the highest officials in charge of propaganda. During the 1980s, the preview system was never abolished, but news selection became mainly the responsibility of chief editors and most news items that appeared in the media were no longer previewed. This later system was called the editor responsibility system. See Hong and Cuthbert (1991, 144) for discussion of the preview system.

160,000 copies of the paper had been printed, and some had already found their way to Beijing. On April 23, Jiang Zemin ordered the paper to stop printing this edition (edition A) and discussed with Qin Benli the preparation of a modified version (edition B). Qin Benli agreed to follow Jiang's demand, but he did not order workers to print the new edition. On April 24, not a single copy of the *Herald* came out. This made Jiang Zemin very angry. On April 26, Jiang, on behalf of the Shanghai Municipal Party, dismissed Qin Benli from his position as editor-in-chief and sent a work committee to reorganize the newspaper. Jiang's decision immediately put the government on the defensive. Afterwards, journalists, students, and liberal intellectuals both in Shanghai and in Beijing seized the opportunity to demonstrate for a free press.

Yet, despite such rumblings, the major official media in this period remained pretty much under the control of the state. During this period, students depended for the most part on big-character posters, student-controlled broadcasting stations, and word of mouth for information. As a result, their interpretation of the movement and consequently their participation in it was largely shaped by rumors. The major rumors of this period, such as the "Xinhua Gate Bloody Incident" and Li Peng's supposed promise to meet students after Hu Yaobang's state funeral on April 22, which I have discussed in chapter 6, aroused a widespread sense of injustice that encouraged participation in the movement.

APRIL 28 TO MAY 13: THE MEDIA PUSH
AND THE GOVERNMENT'S CONCESSION

After the April 27 student demonstration, the government adopted a strategy of limited compromise. Government officials started to hold dialogues with students, and objective accounts of the movement appeared in major official media. When Zhao Ziyang came back from North Korea on April 30, he went further along this direction. State concessions took a toll on the movement. Since most Beijing students were satisfied with the state's concessive measures, more and more universities resumed classes and the movement went into decline. In this period, the protests initiated by journalists were crucial in sustaining the movement.

Many journalists supported Qin Benli after he was dismissed as editor-in-chief. On April 28, eighteen journalists and editors of *Chinese Youth Daily* telegraphed the *Herald*, saying "We salute our respected *World Economic Herald* and comrade Qin Benli! Long live the undistorted news!" Seventy-five journalists

and editors from *China Daily* also sent a telegram, which said: "Stand upright—
editor-in-chief Qin is the exemplar of journalism; truth is eternal—the *Herald*
has been the pioneer during ten years of reform!"[32] Meanwhile, journalists from
the *People's Daily, Guangming Daily, Chinese Women's Daily, Workers' Daily, Farmers'
Daily,* and some other newspapers and magazines also sent letters and telegrams
in support of Qin Benli. In the following days, liberal intellectuals and journalists tried to challenge the Shanghai Municipal Party Committee's decision
through legal means, claiming that the party had no right to dismiss Qin Benli
because his appointment came through the Shanghai Academy of Social Sciences and the Chinese World Economy Association. Therefore, the dismissal
had violated the norm of "separation of the party and state" which the CCP
had advocated since the reform. In fact, the *Herald's* Beijing bureau, supported
by Beijing lawyers, even vowed to file a libel suit against Jiang Zemin for the
damage that he had caused to Qin Benli.[33]

The protests were quite effective. After April 27, objective accounts of the
movement appeared in major official newspapers. On May 5, Zhao Ziyang told
Hu Qili and Rui Xingwen—the two top leaders in charge of media control
and propaganda—that there was "no big risk in opening up a bit by reporting
on the demonstrations and increasing the openness of news."[34] Zhao's assessment obviously echoed the view of Hu Jiwei and many of his advisors that the
free press is actually a buffer to distract people from their grievances and a lever
to minimize the state's mistakes.[35] The next day, a lengthy and objective account of the May 4 student demonstration appeared on the front page of the
People's Daily. The article was accompanied by a photograph of the student demonstration with a flag of the Beijing Students' Autonomous Union in the front.

The journalists continued to push forward. The biggest event in this period
was that 1,013 journalists from over thirty news agencies and newspapers signed
a petition that demanded an open dialogue with the leaders of the CCP Central
Committee. On May 9 about two hundred journalists marched to the Chinese
Association of Journalism to deliver the petition. The government responded
swiftly. From May 11 to May 13, Hu Qili, Rui Xingwen, Yan Mingfu, and Wang
Renzhi went to the Xinhua News Agency, *People's Daily, Guangming Daily,* and
Chinese Youth Daily respectively to talk with editors and journalists. During Hu

32. Wu Ren (1990b, 47).

33. Wu et al. (1989, 138).

34. Faison (1990, 156).

35. Hu Jiwei, editor-in-chief of the *People's Daily* until 1983, was a member of the Standing Committee
of the National People's Congress, chairman of the Chinese Association of Journalism, and a chief advocate of press freedom until he was deposed from his positions after the student movement.

Qili's dialogue with journalists of the *China Youth Daily*, the director of the Journalism Department of the newspaper, Guo Jiakuan, told Hu that "the biased media accounts were a major factor that escalated the movement."[36] Hu Qili responded by saying: "News reform has become an absolute necessity." On May 15 this sentence was quoted as a big headline on the *People's Daily*'s front page. Such a response from a high-level government leader encouraged further rebellious activities among journalists.

A final note: while rumors had played a crucial role in shaping public opinion and the development of the movement in the first period, this was not the case during the second period. While rumors still existed, they no longer had an explosive effect, as the major media were becoming increasingly open.

MAY 14 TO 19: THE HUNGER STRIKE, THE COLLAPSE
OF MEDIA CONTROL, AND MASS PARTICIPATION

During the hunger strike period, the official media reported on the movement in an extremely positive manner. Between May 14 and 19, a total of seventy-four movement-related news articles appeared in the *People's Daily* and *Guangming Daily*, none of which were negative about the movement (table 10.3). The peak was reached on May 18. On that day the *Guangming Daily* featured ten articles on the movement and the *People's Daily* nine. They almost covered the first and second pages of the two newspapers and squeezed the news of Gorbachev's state visit into a small corner. The following excerpt from a report in the May 17 *Guangming Daily* illustrates the tone of the Chinese media then and its mobilizational effect:[37]

> Beginning in the early morning, demonstrators shouted slogans, held banners, and marched on Changan Avenue to show their support to students. . . .
>
> Compared with yesterday, more workers and middle school students joined in the march. Workers from factories came with their own banners. Our reporters saw that one of the banners read "Democracy and rule of law!" Middle school students also had their own banners, some of which read: "Brothers and sisters, please drink a bowl of sweet juice!" and "Grandpa, please come to support our fasting brothers and sisters!"
>
> The demonstrators held different banners and shouted various slogans. The major ones included: "Students love our country. We love students!" "Eradicate official profiteering and corruption!" "Save the students, save China!" "The tides of

36. Wu et al. (1989, 181).
37. Ibid., 235–37.

democracy are irresistible!" People from religious communities in the capital held the banner "Have mercy, be loving!" The banner from the Bank of China is "We object to being the cashiers of official profiteers!"

Today, some streets in the capital were jammed, but students and people of different communities were well under control and maintained good order. The pickets organized by students from Qinghua University and Beijing University of Science and Technology maintained the order from east of Tiananmen Square and the Xinhua Gate; many lifelines allowed ambulances to drive through. The march was orderly, with no incidents. . . .

Today, Beijing residents also came to see their family members and to express their sympathy to the hunger strikers. Grouped under street committee, neighborhood compound, or dormitory, they brought the hearts of mothers. "My children, where are you?" Mother and son cry on each other's shoulder once they have found each other; no people were left untouched. Those mothers unable to find their children were crying all the way, calling for their children, appealing to our consciences.

In today's Beijing, the heart-catching siren could be heard everywhere. When our reporters talked to demonstrators, many of them had only one thought: students' lives are on the verge of destruction or death. This is the most critical moment. The situation should no longer last. A sea of supporters has cried out with the strongest possible voice that the party and the government should show the strongest possible sincerity and come out with practical measures.

To our knowledge, the Hunger Strike Headquarters had only two demands. The first is to ask the government to recognize the student movement as a patriotic democratic movement; the second is to have an immediate dialogue with the highest-level leaders on an equal basis. A cadre from a government institution told our reporter that these two conditions are not excessive. I do not know why the government has not so far taken any action. A worker said: "It is perfectly justified that 'masters' should demand to have dialogues with 'public servants.' What are our leaders afraid of, seeing the people?" A university professor said: "A hundred hours of hunger strike in itself is a great victory. The people have now sided with students and the people are forever right."

The official media delivered a uniform message: that the movement was patriotic and democratic, the students reasonable and orderly, the government uncompromising, indecisive, and unreasonable, and the people all supportive and sympathetic toward the movement.

When China's journalists fought for "press freedom," their slogan was: "We want to tell the truth, please don't force us to lie!" [38] It seemed that they wanted

38. This is one of the slogans raised during the May 4 demonstration by Beijing's journalists, quoted from Liang et al. (1989, 331).

to be able to write Western objective-style reports. However, as soon as state control over the media collapsed, journalists wrote stories that were one hundred percent in favor of the students. Some even took the students' opinion as the criterion for news reports. A hunger striker (no. 60) recalled:

> In this period, the [official] media played an extremely important role. At that time, newspapers were free. As soon as the paper was printed, the journalists carried it to Tiananmen Square themselves. They itched to give every student a bundle of newspapers. Therefore, during the hunger strike we were able to read many newspapers such as the *Economic Daily*, *Guangming Daily*, and *People's Daily*. Because of the picket system, journalists had difficulties entering the hunger strike camp. Even so, when they wrote reports, they came to us for comments. When they published their articles, they also asked us for our opinions of them.

We know that the government did try to negotiate with the students as soon as the hunger strike started. The government also provided crucial aid to keep the hunger strikers alive (chapter 6). Such governmental activities, properly framed and reported, would surely have enhanced the government's public image; yet no official media touched on any of these activities. Moreover, the students did not behave as well as the media portrayed them to have. If the journalists did not know of the vicious power struggles among student leaders, they must at least have seen the widespread waste in the Square that others witnessed.[39] Most likely the journalists knew of this but chose not to cover it. The media coverage of the dialogue between the students and the government on May 14 provides another example (chapter 6). As one of my informants (no. 58) recalled, the dialogue ended in chaos; journalists who attended the meeting were very disappointed by the students' performance. Many journalists in the meeting complained to the students about their bad performance and told them that they did not want to cover the story because of this. As a result, no major newspapers in Beijing covered the dialogue in detail. This certainly added to people's impression that the government had no sincere desire to talk with the students. I must stress that there was no consideration of state censorship here; it had momentarily broken down. All that existed was self-censorship in terms of what should and should not be reported.[40]

When the hunger strike had just begun on May 13, most Beijing students and

39. Liu Xiaobo (1992, 142).

40. Berlin (1993, 264) also noticed that at the height of press freedom in mid-May, news stories from the official media often distorted the movement in a way that favored the students. He found that although chants of "Down with Deng Xiaoping!" and "Down with the Communist Party!" echoed through the early

residents neither understood nor supported the action. By May 17 and 18, however, millions of supporters jammed inside the Square. Many factors contributed to this quick change of public opinion, but the way that the official media reported on the movement was certainly an important factor. This was what a farmer told a reporter from the *People's Daily* about why he joined a demonstration: "In the past few days I have been watching television and have seen how the students are suffering. I am very sympathetic to them; I have to come out." During my extensive informal interviews with people of various occupations, I have tried to make sense of movement participation during the hunger strike period. A rather frequent response has been: "At that time, even the *People's Daily* supported the students. We had nothing to worry about."

MAY 20 TO JUNE 4: GOVERNMENT CONTROL,
MEDIA RESISTANCE, AND THE REVIVAL OF RUMORS

The government declared martial law on the evening of May 19. Between May 20 and June 4, the government tried to gain back control over the media. Although China's official media were eventually forced into silence after the military repression, the journalists' courage was remarkable. This section mainly focuses on the *People's Daily* because journalists at that newspaper put up very strong resistance to the government's efforts.[41]

When martial law had just started, a major concern of state leaders was consolidating the government. Major newspapers and TV stations were asked to cover the government's side of the story about martial law by publishing, for example, Li Peng's speech before the meeting of political, administrative, and military cadres in the capital. Beyond that, the media were pretty much left alone. Therefore, negative and positive stories appeared on the same page of a newspaper. While negative stories were usually those required by the top government, neutral or positive accounts of the movement were prepared by journalists themselves.

Things started to change on May 25, when martial law troops occupied major media outlets in Beijing.[42] After that, while negative accounts of the movement skyrocketed, the number of positive and neutral accounts first greatly declined and then, after June 4, disappeared (table 10.3). This does not mean that

---

stage of the movement, many news articles claimed that the students had never carried banners or slogans calling for the downfall of the Communist Party or its leaders.

41. For the resistance at other newspapers, see Wu et al. (1989, 381–82).

42. This does not mean soldiers had a role here. The soldiers never intervened in the daily work of the media, but their presence signaled that the government had consolidated power.

journalists started to cooperate with the regime. As early as May 21, the *People's Daily* started to use innuendo, allegory, and other modes of indirect communication rooted in Chinese literary tradition to express their objection to martial law.[43] For example, on May 21 the *People's Daily* ran a dispatch on the front page on the resignation of the Italian prime minister after the conflict between the Italian Socialist Party and the Christian Democratic Party had intensified. The message was that Li Peng, China's own prime minister, should also step down to ease the current conflict. The next day, also on the front page, the *People's Daily* ran a small story about Hungary's potential political instability. However, the headline was a quote from a speech by Hungary's prime minister: "Using troops to solve domestic conflicts is not allowed."

Such innuendo appeared on and off in the *People's Daily* during martial law. It peaked again on June 4, the day after the military repression. For example, in the domestic news section that day (page 4), there was a story about a handicapped person winning an athletics medal. Yet, the story was accompanied by the incongruous headline: "The People's Hearts Will Never Be Conquered." Also, for the international news column (page 3), the editors selected a cluster of three stories with the titles: "Students in Seoul Staging a Hunger Strike to Protest the Government's Killing of Students"; "Israeli Army Invades South Lebanon: Again They use Airplanes and Tanks to Deal with Civilians"; and "The Leader of Poland Says that Election is a Great Try-out for Conflict Resolution: One Must not Play with Fire!" Here, the title of the last story was printed in a small font, but its subtitle "One Must not Play with Fire!" was in big and bold characters and was not particularly related to the news. An old proverb in China says that those who play with fire will eventually burn themselves; the implication was that the government was playing with fire.[44]

In addition to expressing their indignation indirectly, the editors of the *People's Daily* also opened a small flower-framed box on the front page in which a neutral matter-of-fact style of writing was used to provide updates on the movement and martial law.[45] Between May 21 and May 30, the stories were always entitled "The *Nth* Day of Martial Law in Beijing." After the government put a stop to this, the *People's Daily* still managed to publish basically the same type of story in roughly the same size flower-framed box in the May 31, June 2,

43. For more discussion of the topic, see Frank Tan (1993, 287).

44. The same story about Poland also appeared on the CCTV evening news on June 5. During the report, the CCTV very unusually posted "One Must Not Play with Fire!" on the screen with no other background shown (Ma, Liu, and Chen 1989, 326).

45. In Chinese newspapers, short human-interest stories are often published by adding a flower frame outside a story.

and June 4 editions of the paper. In footnote 26 above, I discussed the June 2 story. Here, I will focus on how the June 4 report, "Last Night in Beijing," appeared on the front page of the paper.

As a former *People's Daily* journalist recalled, the journalists who were on the street and who saw the conflicts and the deaths felt very angry and cried while telling their colleagues what they had seen.[46] Meanwhile, calls came in from various Beijing hospitals to report the number of wounded people that they had received, from people outside Beijing asking whether the VOA's report of the massacre was true, and from Beijing residents telling what they had seen and asking whether the *People's Daily* was going to report the event. All the people who worked that night were emotionally distraught. Many were in tears while carrying out their duties.

Some journalists asked Lu Chaoqi—the first deputy editor-in-chief of the paper who was in charge that night—to permit them to write a report on what was happening. Lu was also crying at the time and agreed with their request. Eventually, they came out with a report about six hundred Chinese characters in length. Then Lu asked the page editor to prepare a flower-framed space on the front page. At this moment, someone representing the CCP Central Committee called Lu and demanded that the daily not report the repression. Lu Chaoqi replied: "All the people in the world know this. It will be very awkward if we do not report it at all." The conversation ended unhappily.

Lu Chaoqi discussed the telephone conversation with colleagues. They decided to make some changes but insisted on keeping the story. Lu further shortened the story to about two hundred characters. Since the space was already prepared, this small news had to be sparsely situated in a larger space, with a larger title "Last Night in Beijing." It reads as follows:

> "Since the early morning of June 3, a serious antirevolutionary turmoil has broken out in the Capital," claimed the June 4 editorial of *Liberation Army Daily.* Around 10:00 P.M. on June 3, gun cracks were heard around the Military Museum area, and martial law troops started to advance on the city.
>
> Since midnight, Friendship Hospital, Fuwai Hospital, Beijing Center for Emergency Care, Railway Hospital, Fuxing Hospital, Xiehe Hospital, Guanganmen Hospital, and others have continuously called us to report the deaths of those hospitalized. At the time this news was written, martial law troops have forced their way into Tiananmen Square.

---

46. Zi Ye (1993).

Thus did the *People's Daily* report the military repression and the resulting deaths while the repression was still going on.[47]

Under martial law, while the Chinese media carried fewer and fewer positive accounts of the movement, people turned once more to less formal communication channels for information. Rumors again took on a prominent position, as they had during the early stage of the movement. The following are examples of some widely circulated rumors that appeared during martial law: "Marshal Nie Rongzhen told Deng Xiaoping that martial law was against the people's will." "Marshal Xu Xiangqian opposes martial law and said that he would shoot anyone who dared to open fire on students." "Wan Li has established a provisional government in Canada." "All Beijing jails are preparing space to house the soon-to-be arrested students." "The Ministry of Foreign Affairs and the other seven ministries oppose martial law and refuse to acknowledge the leadership of Li Peng's government." "The All China Federation of Trade Unions is going to organize a countrywide strike to oppose martial law." "Hundreds of retired veterans appealed to the CCP Central Committee, demanding that the movement not be repressed by military means." "The vice commander of the 38th Army committed suicide, and 75 percent of the regimental and above ranking officers of the Army have either been dismissed or placed under house arrest because they refused to carry out martial law."

Here are some of the rumors that circulated immediately before, during, and after the military repression: "A martial law soldier driving a military jeep ran over and killed three people." "Thousands of students were killed at Tiananmen Square." "Over twenty thousand civilians died in the massacre." "The martial law army placed military inmates at the front of their formation to let them kill civilians." "The 38th and 28th Armies are fighting with the 27th Army."

---

47. Along with the *People's Daily*, a few other media institutions in Beijing also reported on the repression. Most noticeably, on the noon of June 4, Li Dan, the announcer of Radio Beijing's English Station, broadcast a very emotional statement:

Remember June 3, 1989. A most tragic event happened in the Chinese capital, Beijing. Thousands of people, most of them innocent civilians, were killed by fully armed soldiers when they forced their way into the city. Among the killed are our colleagues at Radio Beijing. The soldiers were riding on armored vehicles and used machine guns against thousands of local residents and students who tried to block their way. When the army convoy made a breakthrough, soldiers continued to spray their bullets indiscriminately at crowds in the street. Eyewitnesses say some armored vehicles even crushed soldiers who hesitated in front of the civilians.

Radio Beijing's English Department deeply mourns those who died in the tragic incident and appeals to all its listeners to join our protest for this gross violation of human rights and the most barbarous suppression of the people. Because of the abnormal situation here in Beijing, there is no other news we could bring to you. We sincerely ask for your understanding and thank you for staying with us at this most tragic moment.

"Martial law troops entered Beijing University, killed over twenty students, and arrested many others." "Li Peng was shot and wounded by a policeman." "Deng Xiaoping has fled to a foreign country." "Deng Xiaoping is dead."

The Chinese government tried to clear up the rumors. For example, on May 22, the *People's Daily* reported that marshals Nie Rongzhen and Xu Xiangqian requested that students not believe rumors. Their appearances belied the rumor that they opposed martial law. On May 22, 23, and 24, the *People's Daily* (and other major official newspapers) published loyalty letters from almost every provincial government and state institution in part to clear up the rumors. Yet, all these efforts were in vain. People were on the street everywhere, in small groups, exchanging rumors and opinions. For every one rumor that was refuted, hundreds more were created. The government could do very little about this.

Rumors were not spread just by word of mouth; big-character posters and student-controlled broadcasting stations were also important. A student activist mentioned in his May 21 diary that a van belonging to the hunger strike group drove back and forth at Tiananmen Square broadcasting through its loudspeakers that the Ministry of Foreign Affairs and many other government functionaries had announced their separation from the government, that the Shanghai government had announced its independence, and so forth.[48] As Liu Xiaobo complained during a Joint Federation meeting:

> Nowadays, Tiananmen Square has almost become a rumor center. Regardless of sources and authenticity, anybody can bring in a story and broadcast it through the student broadcasting center. The more sensational the news, the higher its value. If things go on like this, what is the difference between our news and communist propaganda?[49]

In this period, rumors consisted of roughly two types; those concerning the internal division of the government and those concerning government brutality. Rumors about governmental divisions gave people hope and encouraged

---

48. *China News Digest* (1994, 8).

49. Liu Xiaobo (1992, 187). This does not mean that all the activists taking charge of the broadcasting centers deliberately spread rumors. In fact, some of them tried hard to stop them. An activist recalled his personal experiences while in charge of Qinghua University broadcasting center thus: "Today, some people reported that Deng Xiaoping is dead. I thought it hard to believe, and therefore did not let them announce it. . . . Later, a middle-aged person around forty came to the center. He told us that the news was absolutely reliable and almost forced us to broadcast it. Again, I insisted on not broadcasting it. I sat him down in a chair and told him that if Deng was really dead, the situation would change very soon. Announcing it or not would not matter" (*China News Digest*, 1994, 12).

them to continue fighting,[50] while rumors about government brutality made people angry and encouraged them to risk themselves in seeking revenge. Had people known that most of the information around them was unfounded rumor and that the top state elites had consolidated even before martial law had begun, they would have thought that any efforts at resistance were risky and futile. In this sense, rumors formed the basis of the public interpretation of the movement and contributed to its tragic outcome.[51]

State-Society Relations and Media Behavior

The above section shows that during the 1989 Movement the Chinese media persistently fought to report the movement in an extremely positive manner, and that the public did not follow the frames presented by the domestic media until it portrayed the movement positively. Therefore, both the media and the public acted radically. Now, I will interpret this pattern in terms of China's state-society relations during the 1980s. Scholars generally agree that in the West news tends to conform to the dominant culture and the public on the whole does so as well. In other words, in the West both the media and public opinion are conformist institutions. It therefore might be helpful to discuss the issue by focusing on the forces that led to the differences.

MARKET VERSUS ADMINISTRATIVE CONTROL

A notable difference is that Western media operate under the market while the Chinese media up to the 1980s were mainly administratively controlled. This is not to say that Western governments never interfere with the media. In fact, much of British media history in the nineteenth century was about how the state intervened against radical presses.[52] In the United States during the Vietnam War both Johnson and Nixon interfered with media routines by

50. Other rumors also added uncertainty and encouraged people to fight. For example, during the movement there were rumors that according to "international law" a government would have to step down if it failed to respond to a hunger strike within seven days, and that martial law would be invalid if it could not be enforced in two days. See Calhoun (1994, 77, 94) for discussion of these rumors.

51. The foreign and Hong Kong media also played a certain role in spreading rumors; they did not create rumors themselves, but they were eager to report them (Lee and Chan 1990). For example, as several Hong Kong journalists recalled (Lu et al. 1989, 336–44), in order to generate sales, some newspaper owners in Hong Kong bypassed their journalists stationed in Beijing to push their papers to cover unconfirmed rumors. These newspapers often circulated back to Beijing, where they lent great authenticity to the rumors that they reported.

52. Cranfield (1978); Curran and Seaton (1985).

leaning on their friends among the wealthy network owners and by intimidating reporters.[53] However, the state in the West usually does not intervene in the daily routines of the media. Therefore, before examining how political forces shape the nature of media and public opinion, I will first briefly discuss whether the difference in their relations to economic and administrative control might be a major factor that accounts for the different nature of the Chinese and Western media.

It has been argued that in the West profit concerns make all news corporations face a systematic shortage of staff. Reporters have to rely on routine news provided or even partially written by the government,[54] and on "expert opinions" that save them from time-consuming investigations and from possible libel suits.[55] It is also argued that under the market the media have to follow the dominant culture and the majority view because otherwise punitive actions from the masses will lower viewing or subscription rates and thus advertising revenues.[56] A more crucial market bias is that the amount of advertising revenue is not just determined by the size of audiences or subscribers but by their buying power. Newspapers that can reach wealthy people can generate a larger profit and thus sell their papers well below cost, enabling them to further expand their subscriber base.[57] Because of this, mainstream media editors often overtly push reporters to produce stories that will enlarge audiences, especially among populations with great purchasing power.[58]

These features of market control of the media resemble the prime characteristics of the market itself: both are diffused and impersonal. No one invented the market, yet everyone and every institution has to follow market principles. Thus the radical media and radical ideas can be marginalized and constrained without generating grievances against the state. In comparison, in China during the 1980s, media control was carried out by persons in the name of the government, control criteria changed with state policy, and if something went wrong, the state was perceived to be at fault.

53. Gitlin (1980).

54. Epstein (1973), Fishman (1980), and Ryan (1991).

55. Soley (1992); Tuchman (1972).

56. Gans (1979, ch. 8) argues that reporters do not feel much pressure from viewers and advertisers in the production of news. This could be true. However, it is also possible that the networks and reporters that he studied had become conformist long before Gans started his project. Therefore, reporters could work within the system without feeling any overt pressure.

57. Herman and Chomsky (1988). For example, Curran (1978) has demonstrated how after World War II newspapers oriented toward the lower classes in Britain declined and then were eliminated by middle-class oriented newspapers as a result of the latter's rising advertising revenue.

58. Ryan (1991, 121–22).

The market regulation theory certainly has explanatory power in the Chinese case. Yet, it cannot be the only crucial factor. First, China's official media did not begin as anti-establishment. During Mao's era, the media were among the most loyal elements of the CCP. For most Chinese journalists, the major problem during Mao's era was not how to escape from administrative control but how best to actively cooperate with the system (chapter 2). Second, the media was not born under a market economy as a conformist institution. In Britain, for example, it was not until the rise of the "entertainment" press in the mid-nineteenth century that the radical press started to decline. This decline was due to a combination of two factors: the successful repression of Chartism and the rise of the middle classes. While this repression gave the radical media a heavy blow, the rise of the middle classes (not just in politics, but also in numbers) made it possible for "entertainment" publications to be sold below cost, thus destroying the radical press.[59] Finally, when things became really bad, journalists in the West could also be radicalized. In the 1960s in the United States, for example, when the United States troops could not win the Vietnam War, both the media and public opinion became rebellious.[60]

Therefore, the market and the media do not have a definite relationship. The market contributes to media conformism in the West mainly because capitalism has been functioning reasonably well. The news cannot always tell stories that are fundamentally different from reality. Consent can be manufactured, but only within limits. Otherwise, the burdens of conscience of newsmakers and audiences will generate frustration and resistance. This brings us to people's consciousness, and more fundamentally to the legitimacy of state power.

STATE-SOCIETY RELATIONS AND MEDIA BEHAVIOR

The central argument of this chapter is that the radical nature of the media and of public opinion during the 1989 Movement was primarily shaped by state-society relations in China during the 1980s. In the following, I try to provide an interpretation of the radical nature of the Chinese media and of public opinion and their impact on the development of the 1989 Movement. The interpretation is based on several dimensions of state-society relations already developed in the earlier chapters. These are the method of media control, the source of state legitimation, the strength of intermediate organizations, and the

59. Cranfield (1978) shows that readers of the earlier "entertainment" papers and magazines were mainly middle class.

60. Gitlin (1980).

public psychology resulting from past state behavior. At the center of the analysis lies people's consciousness, that is, whether the people, including journalists,
are satisfied with reality, trust the government, and view state power as ideologically legitimate.[61] I keep state-society relations in Western democratic
countries as the background for comparison.

One difference between China and the West is their different methods of
media control. In the West, elite pluralism and a long-standing legal tradition
allow indirect and impersonal control of the media. Although restraints on the
press are common, they are carried out by a combination of the government,
corporate owners, editors, and readers through market mechanisms and legal
measures, and only occasionally through direct intervention. Therefore, even if
journalists are unhappy about restraints, their grievances lack a single target. In
China, media control is carried out directly by the state. During Mao's era,
news restraints were extensive but journalists were cooperative; the combination yielded very narrow media coverage without much resistance. In the 1980s,
editors had more and more autonomy to decide what to publish, and media
control was not always effective. At this point, however, journalists increasingly
felt restricted by the system, treating it as a hurdle to a free press. Thus even a
comparatively minor effort of government censorship such as the *Herald* incident could ignite widespread state-centered discontent and rebellion.

During the 1980s, the communist state experienced a crisis of ideological
legitimation among intellectuals (including journalists). However, during the
early 1980s most journalists still tried to work within the system, even though
they thought that China's political system needed to be improved; they believed that allowing the media to criticize the government's wrongdoing would
be an important way to prevent the government from making mistakes (chapter 2). But why did such a loyal opposition end in rebellion? We know that legal-
electoral legitimacy is the basis of Western democracy. Since almost every adult
can vote and the government is elected by the majority, the election itself becomes the basis of state legitimacy. This political system is not as volatile;
government scandals and mistakes lead only to governmental changes, not to a
legitimacy crisis. In this system, the majority is apolitical, and radicals are iso-

---

61. Gramscian theorists also emphasize the importance of people's consciousness (Gitlin 1980; Gramsci 1971). My argument differs from a Gramscian approach in at least three respects. First, Gramscian culture hegemony theory emphasizes class power, whereas I focus on state power. Second, for Gramscian theorists class domination is a process of "manufacturing consent," but they seldom specify the limitations of
this process. In my view, consent can only be manufactured within limits. Most importantly, Gramscians
tend not to specify the basis of "culture hegemony" and why its capacity differs in different countries. In
my argument, conflict resolving capacity (or the capacity to sustain hegemony) differs in different countries as a function of state-society relations.

lated and hopeless. A profit-oriented media institution will only cover scandals or make minor criticisms of state policies or their implementation; it will not attack the system itself.

In China, however, the state based its power on communist ideology during Mao's era and then, in the 1980s, on economic and moral performance. When a government relates its legitimacy to concrete promises, it also takes responsibility for them. Thus government mistakes and political scandals will often lead to a legitimacy crisis. With regard to the media, this type of government faces a dilemma. If it heavily controls information and restricts the media, its economy and society will lose their vigor. However, if it gives the media freedom, even friendly criticisms will sometimes endanger state power. Such a threat to the state's legitimacy will therefore elicit sanctions against the media. Such sanctions, however, will only generate further state-centered grievances. This was exactly the relationship between the Chinese media and the state during the 1980s. To improve its performance, the government had to endorse reform and open its door to the world, but such policies required a relatively open media that the government could not tolerate. The so-called Anti–Spiritual Pollution Campaign in 1983 and the Anti–Bourgeois Liberalization Campaign in 1987 were both aimed at curtailing the flow of information. However, the spirit of the economic reform and the open-door policies contradicted these campaigns. Thus during the 1980s the Chinese media was becoming both more free and more oppositional. The Chinese media's path of development was thus different from that of the media in nineteenth-century Britain: while the British government eventually incorporated the media into the establishment, the Chinese government could not institutionalize an originally loyal opposition. Even though most journalists only intended to help the government to reform the system, their actual relationship with the state produced dissidents and their sympathizers. As a result, the media radicalized.

In the West public opinion tends to follow the media constructively, becoming plural and divided over controversies of common concern, but forgetting an issue when the media stops reporting on it. During 1989, by contrast, when the official media did not report or covered the movement negatively, China's public opinion followed rumors instead; when the media reported positively on the movement, however, it began to follow them again.[62] Several factors may have contributed to this difference, but I confine my discussion to issues that were related to the media and communication.

---

62. To be more precise, when the movement just began, public opinion was mainly the opinion of students, but it expanded to all Beijing residents as the movement developed.

During the 1989 Movement, most Chinese felt discontent regarding social problems such as official corruption, inflation, and the declining status of intellectuals (chapters 3 and 5). Later, when the hunger strike and martial law started, the public was greatly concerned about the health of hunger strikers and felt angry that the government had used troops to repress students. Now that the public was concerned about and sympathetic to the movement and dissatisfied with the news in the official media, the public turned to other communication channels. Much of the news in these channels turned out to be unfounded rumors and deliberate fabrications. Yet because the public was unhappy about the situation and distrustful of the government, rumors that could create an image of an unreasonable government gave it great pleasure and tended to be believed and passed on regardless of their truth value. Also, because the public was sympathetic to the students, rumors about internal government power struggles, the death of a government leader, or anything that could create uncertainties and thus encourage movement mobilization were also widely circulated and hailed.[63] Therefore during the 1989 Movement major rumors often galvanized the emotions of hundreds of thousands of Beijing residents and drove the momentum of the movement.

Why were the people attracted by these rebellious messages? To this Tocquevillian question, we have to give his classic answer—the weaknesses of intermediate associations. We know that independent associations were just emerging in China during the 1980s (chapter 1). The majority of the Chinese were still organized around their workplaces, and their sectional interests never entered national politics. Nevertheless, because most people had been affected in similar ways by past large-scale, state-orchestrated attempts at social engineering, they shared common feelings of grievance and distrust towards the state and a correspondingly high interest in national politics. Therefore, unlike in the West, where people are sectionally and sectorially organized and public opinion is conformist and highly diffused on most issues, public opinion in China tended to be uniform and biased against the state.

I have explained why millions of Beijing residents could be mobilized by rumors; but why was the public then suddenly swayed and mobilized by the official media during the hunger strike? This had much to do with the public image of the official media during the late 1980s. The Chinese media had acted as the voice of the CCP since the party came to power. During the 1980s, the

---

63. According to Turner and Killian (1987, 54), the intellectual and emotional context existing in the listeners' minds governs what kind of rumors listeners will accept or reject, or modify as they are passed on. Moreover, the speed of a rumor's transmission is determined by the level of concern that people have on issues related to that rumor (Festinger, Schachter, and Back 1950).

media gained more freedom. It was not yet free from government censorship, however, especially in regard to sensitive political issues (such as freedom to report a social movement). Thus by the late 1980s the public still treated major official media coverage of sensitive political issues as the voice of the government. Because the public did not trust the government, it refused to follow the media when the movement was covered negatively. However, when the media reported on the movement positively, public opinion immediately followed the media's construction. This was more than the media frame resonating with public opinion. Equally importantly, since in the past the media had always acted as the government's voice, positive media coverage led most people to believe that the government or at least some major leaders in the government had decided to acknowledge the movement. To most Beijing residents who were sympathetic to the movement, this message removed all their concerns about any negative consequences of joining the movement. The positive media coverage also encouraged movement mobilization in another way. In China, the daily control of the people was exercised by leaders of work-units, such as factories, department stores, schools and other public institutions. After the official media reported positively on the movement, leaders of such public institutions had two choices. They could go against the tide of mobilization by exercising control in workplaces; but by doing this they would not only be making themselves very unpopular but also would possibly be going against the top echelons of the government. Therefore, they had every reason to choose to tolerate and even support the mobilization in their work-units, since the latter action won them popularity and involved no political risks. Thus, regardless of their personal political views, most leaders in workplaces tolerated or even supported the mass mobilizations, granted paid leave, and supplied necessary resources to the workers who participated in demonstrations and other protest activities. Some of them even organized demonstrations themselves. This was why many Beijing residents were semi-officially mobilized during the hunger strike period (chapter 6). This style of mobilization reflected a particular state-society relationship.

This also in part explains why Beijing residents poured onto the streets by the millions to stop soldiers under martial law, when the official media no longer explicitly supported the students. The people's consciousness, once turned on, cannot be turned off right away. Despite the facts that the state had tightened control over the media and that lower-level government leaders no longer openly supported the movement, the momentum that the movement had acquired during the hunger strike carried over into the martial law period.

In this chapter, I have also indicated that most rumors circulated during the movement could have been fabricated by individual movement activists. This certainly went against the popular notion that most rumors came from the government. In fact, it is easy for an organization as complex as the state to justify its actions politically, but it is difficult to deny the existence of a large event that occurs in a public place. When a government does not want the public to know about a large public event, it needs the cooperation of many insiders who know the facts. For example, if the Chinese government wanted to claim that the martial law troops did not kill any people on the night of June 3, they would need cooperation from police, soldiers, and journalists who all knew of the killings firsthand. Otherwise, those who opposed the military crackdown would be further alienated, and those who supported the repression would feel insulted. That is why, despite enormous embarrassment, the Chinese government had to report the number of people killed during the repression. Top state leaders also have difficulty spreading rumors by themselves. For example, if Deng Xiaoping were interested in spreading rumors about various power struggles within the government, it would be unlikely that he would do so himself. He would have to instruct his associates to instruct further lower-ranking officers to carry out the order. This could involve many people, and his personal image could be hurt in front of his associates. He might also invite public and collegial attack should something get out of his control. Thus, when a government spreads rumors, it is usually lower-level bureaucrats or specific government institutions that engage independently or semi-independently in the activity. This is possible only when lower-level officers are actively cooperating with the state. During the 1989 Movement, however, most lower-ranking government cadres were sympathetic to the students.

On the other hand, for individuals, creating a rumor is a private choice that is easy to carry out. Moreover, active participants in a social movement usually believe in what they are fighting for. Therefore, the fabrication of rumors may not be considered as immoral in itself so long as the participants believe that this will increase the chances of obtaining the collective goods for which they are fighting.[64] Thus, rumors will be supplied during a movement as long as

---

64. A big-character poster that appeared in Beijing University on April 22, entitled "It is Actually a Plot," suggested that some student activists actually thought of inciting police brutality: "I want to tell you something to prevent other students from becoming the victim of conspirators. On April 19, when I talked excitedly with my classmates about what we were doing at Tiananmen Square and the Xinhua Gate, a student who was not my classmate, but a key movement activist that many of you know, jumped in: 'The best thing is to let the police beat us. We then can have a good excuse to mobilize students.' I asked: 'Are you guys going to deliberately induce policemen to beat you?' He replied: 'You should not put it that way, but this is very effective to mobilize students.'" (Leng and Miao 1989, 37). During the movement, stu-

information is controlled and the state lacks ideological legitimation among a large section of the population. In this sense, rumor fabrication is also related to state-society relations, particularly to the sources of state legitimation.

Conclusion

In this chapter, I have presented the following relationships between the media and public opinion during the 1989 Movement. When the movement had just begun, the media neglected or negatively reported on the movement because of state control. However, the public (the would-be student participants) did not follow the media frame and instead based their interpretation of the movement on rumors circulated via informal communication channels. Between early and mid-May, the government's control over the media declined, and positive accounts of the movement mushroomed in the media. During the hunger strike the government's control over media collapsed, and the media reported on the movement in an extremely positive manner. In this period public opinion closely followed the media frame, and rumors played only a minor role. After martial law, the government regained its control over the media, less positive accounts of the movement appeared, people again decoupled their interpretation of the movement from the official media frame, and rumors reemerged to shape public opinion. In a sense, both the official media and public opinion during the 1989 Movement were radical institutions.

This chapter argues that the radical nature of China's media and public opinion during the 1989 Movement was primarily shaped by the state-society relationship that pertained during the late 1980s. During the reform, the Chinese government had to open up the media in part for the economy. However, China's political system, which linked legitimation to ideology and performance, was susceptible even to friendly media criticism and tended to produce dissidents. Moreover, during the late 1980s most Chinese were unhappy about their situation, did not trust the government, and still believed that the Chinese media spoke only for the state. Thus during the 1989 Movement journalists in China tried hard to free themselves from state control and positively report on the movement, and the public relied on rumors for news when the media reported on the movement negatively. However, once the official media escaped

---

dents usually regarded this type of big-character poster as having been written by someone working for the government.

from state control and positively reported on the movement, the public still treated the media as the voice of the government. Thus, positive coverage not only called all the people's attention to the movement but also removed the fear of repression and confused the work-unit-level government officials. The consequence was that millions of people poured out to support the movement.

CONCLUSION

This conclusion focuses on three issues. First, in sharp contrast to its repeated political upheavals during the 1980s, China exhibited a prolonged period of political stability in the 1990s. Thus we need to know what contributed to this political stability. Second, I also suggest that although China has experienced many positive changes in the 1990s, the state-society relationship that led to the rise and shaped the development of the 1989 Movement has not been fundamentally altered. Therefore, another large-scale social movement is still possible in China in the future, and, once it begins, it may also follow a dynamic similar to that of the 1989 Movement. To avoid having such a movement happen again, the current Chinese leaders need to place political reform at the top of their agenda. Finally, I am going to highlight some major theoretical goals that I have struggled to achieve as well as the basic characteristics of state-society relations theory.

Before moving on, it might be useful to point out that most analyses presented in this chapter are based not on formal interviews but on insights derived from my readings and my informal interviews with various members of the urban population, which I conducted during my field trips in China. To limit its length, I also confine my analysis to a minimum.

Political Stability in the 1990s

Except for the recent student demonstrations triggered by the NATO bombing of the Chinese embassy in Yugoslavia, there have been virtually no large-
scale protest activities in China in the 1990s. In sharp contrast to its repeated
political upheavals during the 1980s, China experienced a prolonged period of
political stability: an outcome that surprised many observers, especially dissidents who fled China after the 1989 Movement. Here, I argue that the stability
was brought about by a series of changes in state-society relations in China after the 1989 Movement.

THE CHANGING NATURE OF STATE LEADERSHIP

After the military repression, many China experts believed that conservatives
would dominate the Chinese leadership and China's reform would stop. In fact,
as I have analyzed in chapter 7, most top Chinese state leaders in the 1980s had
two basic convictions. Because of the disastrous Maoist past, a general sense of
the failure of the state-socialist model, and massive grievances in society, the
top state elites believed that a reform was the only way for the regime to survive. Moreover, most top leaders of that time joined the communist revolution
long before the communists took power, and they maintained a high degree of
loyalty to the CCP. These two characteristics were reflected in Deng Xiaoping's
core political wisdom—*liangshou douying*—which can be translated as being firm
in sticking both to economic reform and to political stability. These basic
convictions among top state leaders were also reflected in their selection of the
next generation of state leaders after the 1989 Movement.

The three top leaders ousted in the later 1980s, Hu Yaobang, Zhao Ziyang,
and Hu Qili, had one thing in common: they tended to be idealistic about
the student movement and did not seem to know how to deal with crisis politics. When a student movement started in 1986–87, Hu Yaobang took almost
no action. During the 1989 Movement, when the Chinese media tried to free
itself from state control to report the movement positively, Zhao Ziyang and
Hu Qili, having the notion that media openness contributes to political stability, ordered censorship lifted. As a result, China's media were soon out of the
state's control. Subsequently, the extremely positive official media reports on
the movement during the hunger strike period greatly assisted its mobilization
(chapter 10).

When these leaders were ousted, they were replaced by Jiang Zemin, Li Ruihuan, and later Zhu Rongji. These new generation leaders shared two qualities: they had been major leaders of the reform in big cities during the 1980s, and they appeared to have keener intuitions of how to deal with crisis politics. Let us look at how the two new leaders from Shanghai had dealt with the student unrest during the 1980s.[1] In 1986, when Jiang Zemin was informed that students at Jiaotong University were going to stage a demonstration, he immediately went to meet the students at the university's auditorium. During the meeting, in order to show to the students that he might actually have a better understanding than they did of the issue of democracy, he even recited the whole text of Lincoln's Gettysburg Address in English. Although to some his action might have looked showy and shallow, it did make a good impression among the students and forestalled the attempted demonstration.[2] If this example shows that Jiang had a good sense of the tactics needed in dealing with crisis politics, his dismissal of Qin Benli (chapter 10), after Qin refused to make a change in a provocative report that was to appear in the April 24 *World Economic Herald*, certainly demonstrates that he was also able to confront a crisis with an iron hand.

The same is true for Zhu Rongji. Zhu was in charge of Shanghai after Jiang Zemin left for Beijing in late May 1989. During that period he showed no romanticism about the movement, as Zhao Ziyang had, nor was he afraid of meeting the people, as Li Peng appeared to have been. Zhu went to many places to meet and talk with people, and he made two televised speeches on May 22 and June 8.[3] To avoid antagonizing the people, he seldom used phrases such as "antirevolutionary turmoil" to refer to the movement. He even avoided a direct focus on the nature of this movement in his talks. Instead, he emphasized the negative consequences of the movement, such as the paralysis of the public transportation and policing systems, the problems of food supply in the city, and the rising crime rate—all of which were becoming increasingly pronounced by late May. Zhu emphasized that political stability was in everybody's interest and pleaded for the cooperation of Shanghai people for the sake of their common interest. Zhu did win some support from the people. While hundreds and thousands of Beijing residents were fighting street battles, Shanghai's workers organized by hundreds and thousands to clear roadblocks and maintain public order.

1. Li Ruihuan was mayor of Tianjin. He also dealt with the local student movements very skillfully.
2. Gao Gao (1994, 318–19); He and Gao (1993, 97).
3. Zhu Rongji (1989).

In comparison with the top leaders during the 1980s, the current leadership has shown much more sophistication in their management of the affairs of state. First, the current leaders have adopted different strategies for dealing with dissidents. In the 1980s, the government often published articles and books criticizing the ideas of dissidents and had people study these articles; such actions publicized dissident ideas otherwise unknown to most people. Many public heroes during that period, including Wei Jingsheng and Fang Lizhi, were actually created by the government itself. In the 1990s, the top state leaders seldom did that. Instead, they used professional police to control dissidents and periodically sent some dissidents out of the country. By sending the dissidents out to the Western countries, the state not only freed itself from many "troublemakers" but also used the dissidents as bargaining chips in international negotiations. As a result, dissident activity lost much of its public profile in the 1990s.

Second, while there must be many power struggles among the current top leaders, there has been no indication that any of them exploited the 1989 Movement for personal political gain. Their political instincts may have told them that the event was such a great national trauma that its emotional forces, if again invoked, would blow them away altogether. The strategy they adopted in dealing with the issue was called *waisong neijin*, that is, to treat any events related to the 1989 Movement seriously yet quietly so that the problem might be controlled without public attention. For example, they must be aware that "anti-revolutionary turmoil" was a label for the movement that very few Chinese would accept. Over time, they started to label the movement as a "turmoil" or simply as an "event." They also emphasized the illegal aspect of the movement and possible "instabilities" that the movement could have brought about if the students had succeeded. (Many Chinese who experienced the Cultural Revolution accept this claim to a great degree.) Each year around June 4, the day that the military repression was carried out, the government deploys many plainclothes police around Tiananmen Square and other sensitive locations. Any sign of protest activities would be immediately stopped. In 1999, partly to prevent any possible protests on the movement's tenth anniversary, the state even blocked Tiananmen Square and started a renovation.

The most significant improvement of their statesmanship, however, was in their handling of the economy. During the 1980s, most top leaders did not seem to have much experience with the market economy. They also did not take very seriously the public tolerance of uncertainties associated with the reform. They even tried to implement price reform and other radical reform measures in the late 1980s when people's confidence in reform was at a very low ebb, which in part contributed to the crisis before the 1989 Movement (chapters 2 and 3). By contrast, the leaders in the 1990s were much more cautious about public tolerance of reform. The best example is the economic adjustment between 1994 and 1996. In 1992, the Chinese economy was again in a quick ascent. Associated with this, however, was overspending, overinvestment, and high inflation. In late 1993, the state decided to adjust the economy. However, unlike the earlier economic adjustments, this adjustment was unique in two ways. The earlier economic adjustments usually started at a time when the economy was already in a very bad shape, and the adjustment was drastic, like slamming on the brakes of a speeding vehicle. Therefore, the entire society was painfully affected. This time, the adjustment was initiated while the economy was still in a good shape. Therefore, the state was able to carry it through more patiently and to target only problems that contributed to the overheated economy. Also, by the early 1990s, market mechanisms had already penetrated the Chinese economy. Unlike the earlier economic adjustments, this time the state used administrative measures as well as market mechanisms such as adjustments in interest rates, lending, and taxation to direct the economy.

The state brought the economic growth rate down from 14.2 percent in 1992 to 9.7 percent in 1996. Meanwhile, the inflation rate dropped from 21.7 percent in 1994 to 6 percent in 1996. The adjustment was achieved by slowing down the rate of growth by 4.5 percent in four years. This was the first time in communist China that an overheated economy was controlled without leading to a serious recession.[4] Many Chinese economists called the whole process a "soft landing."[5] In the next few years, although the Chinese economy was still full of problems, it maintained a reasonable growth rate and low inflation. By the late 1990s, a not really very healthy but relatively well-managed Chinese economy had become an important stabilizing factor during the East Asian financial crisis. The success of the economic adjustment contributed to the regime's stability.

In summary, the 1989 Movement had actually functioned as a selective mechanism that eliminated idealistic politicians and selected a leadership group who could not be simply classified as reformers or conservatives but who had a Machiavellian sense of politics and a better understanding of economic issues. The behavior of this new state leadership contributed to the regime's stability.

4. Liu and Liu (1997).
5. Gao and Wang (1997), Kuang (1998), Liu and Liu (1997), and Zhao Yining (1995).

Also contributing to China's political stability were the great changes that took place in society during the 1990s. While most of these changes were the results of state policy shifts and of the further development of the market economy and civil society, others were unintended consequences of the 1989 Movement. For example, after the 1989 repression, the government paradoxically gained "trust" among Chinese. This is not to suggest that the people approved of the bloody military repression. Rather, during the 1980s, a major worry among the Chinese had been whether state policy was going to return to that current in Mao's era. Therefore, people habitually associated many state policy adjustments with leftist revival and became panicked by them (chapters 2 and 5). However, the reform continued in the 1990s. The fact that even after military repression the state still maintained the reform policy brought more and more Chinese to the realization that reform was the only way out for the state. In my trips to China, I found that 1993 was the last year that Chinese were still very interested in rumors related to the struggles between conservatives and reformers in the government. After that, the rhetoric of factionalism was confined to the Hong Kong media and to Western analysts. Therefore, although social changes were no less great in the 1990s, the changes no longer exerted the kind of psychological impact on the people as they had during the 1980s, because few Chinese now doubted the general direction of social change. It was in this sense that a change in public psychology contributed to the regime's stability.

Intellectual elites, rank-and-file intellectuals and students, and urban residents were the major populations that played important roles during the 1989 Movement. In the following, I will discuss how changes in each population contributed to political stability in the 1990s.

Intellectual Elites. I have argued earlier that because of long-time repression and isolation, intellectual elites during the 1980s did not have much trust in the state or good knowledge of the West. Moreover, they had been indoctrinated in Maoist radicalism and idealism, even though they no longer believed in Marxism. Consequently, China's intellectual discourse was dominated by idealism, opportunism, and radicalism. These all facilitated the rise of the 1989 Movement (chapter 2).

The mood of intellectual elites, however, changed in the 1990s. First, after the military repression, the most vocal and radical intellectual elites and radical students fled to the West and the lesser ones were forced into silence. Yet, in the 1990s, while the state still kept a lid on activities that directly challenged the regime, it adopted a more laissez-faire attitude toward general cultural production. Much of the focus of the Anti–Spiritual Pollution Campaign in 1983 and the Anti–Bourgeois Liberalization Campaign in 1986–87 was aimed at attacking the cultural products that orthodox Marxists considered as bourgeois. Such campaigns antagonized many intellectuals and pushed them toward radicalism. In the 1990s, however, no such campaigns were initiated.[6] Equally importantly, after 1992 China experienced another economic boom. The boom induced a swift change of attitude and attention among Chinese intellectuals. In the 1980s, intellectual elites had generally viewed communism as a central problem and a market economy and Western democracy as the solution. Therefore, they frequently challenged the ideological base of the regime and created crisis discourses by centering on grand and abstract issues such as "world citizenship" and the "demise of yellow civilization" (chapter 2). By contrast, intellectual elites in the 1990s were more commercially motivated. They were generally not interested in directly challenging the regime and were more focused on activities that could increase pluralism in society yet meanwhile bring them immediate economic benefits.[7]

Second, during the 1980s "new" ideas often had an explosive effect in society, as in successive social fevers such as Sartre fever, Nietzsche fever, *River Elegy* fever, and reportage novel fever (chapter 1). Hundreds or even thousands of students would jam into a university auditorium to listen to a talk by a member of the intellectual elite (chapter 2). After over a decade of reform and open door policies, the flow of information was rising rapidly in China: in the newspaper industry, for example, even at its peak the whole of China had only a little more than two hundred newspapers before the reform started.[8] However, the number increased to 1,534 in 1991 and to 2,200 by 1995. By the end of 1995, a total of 72 million copies were sold daily.[9] With more and more books and

6. In fact, as Wang Meng and Zhao (1994, 15) mention, in the 1990s the activities of intellectuals "would no longer be so interfered with as long as they were not intended to overthrow the government." As a result, intellectuals of different interests and tastes started to form their own circles and spaces.

7. In 1997, I informally interviewed a young journalist. He earned between 5,000 and 7,000 yuan per month. The main task of his job was to translate foreign movies for a TV station. During the interview, he expressed great satisfaction with his job. He also mentioned the caution he took in the TV station to avoid touchy topics that would challenge the regime directly. However, he told me that beyond a few political taboos that he had no interest in touching, he was basically free to choose any foreign movies to translate and that one of the criteria for him to choose a particular movie was to promote pluralism and tolerance in society. For example, he told me how he had translated movies with homosexual themes, hoping that the audience could gradually accept homosexuality as a way of life.

8. At its lowest point, which was in 1967, the whole of China had only 43 regular newspapers (Zhao Yuezhi 1998, 17).

9. Zhao Yuezhi (1998, 57).

newspapers carrying different ideas floating around in society, ideas no longer had the explosive effect that they had had during the 1980s.

Third, if a pro-Western mentality characterized the general intellectual mood of the 1980s, the 1990s saw a surge of nationalism among Chinese intellectuals.[10] This trend was certainly reflected by several bestsellers in China, including *China Can Say No* and *Behind the Scenes of a Demonized China*, and by the student demonstrations after the NATO bombing of the Chinese Embassy in Belgrade.[11] What is striking is that many of the intellectual elites who promoted nationalism were Western-trained and were promoters of Western ideas during the 1980s. Therefore the rise of nationalism was not simply a product of government propaganda, even though the state has so far enjoyed its stabilizing effect. At the surface level, events such as the *Yinhe* (Milky Way) ship incident several years ago and the recent NATO bombing have all played important roles in the rise of nationalistic sentiment in China.[12] However, at a deeper level, at least among many intellectuals that I have talked to, their sense of nationalism was triggered by two persistent facts. During the 1980s, most of them were very excited about the former Soviet Union's path of political development and despised Deng Xiaoping's "crossing the river by touching the stone" style of reform, but now they were disappointed by Russia's chaotic internal politics and poor economic performance and by the fact that Western countries were actually less interested in assisting Russia in its painful democratic transition than in weakening its international positions. Moreover, although the intellectuals that I talked to were aware of many problems in China, they were also pleased by many positive changes since 1992. Therefore, they were very disappointed by the U.S. media's generally negative coverage of China. Many fighters for press freedom in China during the 1980s now found that the bias in the U.S. media was probably more persistent because of the existence of stronger cultural hegemony.[13] In other words, the cold war mentality that persisted among some U.S. politicians and international news reporters may ironically have stabilized the Chinese regime.

10. Zhao Suisheng (1997).

11. Li and Liu (1996); Song, Zhang, and Qiao (1996).

12. The *Yinhe* Incident started when United States warships stopped a Chinese cargo ship on the open sea, because the United States suspected that China was using the ship to secretly send chemical weapons to Iran. Eventually, as the Chinese source claimed, United States naval officers boarded the ship to inspect it but found nothing. The United States never apologized for the action. The news that the United States navy could stop a Chinese cargo ship on the open sea to make a search created an outburst of public opinion in China. As for the Embassy bombing, with five missiles fired at the Embassy from different directions, most Chinese believed that it was not a simple mistake.

13. Chen Jie (1999); Li and Liu (1996).

Rank-and-File Intellectuals and Students. There was a huge improvement in the economic well-being of intellectuals and intellectuals-in-making (students) during the 1990s. Both a change in mentality and a further transformation of social structures contributed to this economic improvement. During the 1980s most intellectuals and students did not have much understanding of the market economy and despised commercial activities. They also believed that the reform would bring them more political and economic benefits. Therefore when they saw that the emerging market economy actually degraded some of their prestige and economic benefits, their grievances became pronounced (chapter 3).

However, as reform continued, the intellectuals and students, especially after jealously observing other people become rich day by day, gained an understanding of the market economy. In the 1990s, especially during the second commercial wave of 1992–93, more and more intellectuals and students detached themselves from traditional intellectual mentalities and became involved in commercial activities or found much better paying jobs in the private or foreign sectors.[14] In universities, during the first commercial wave around 1988, only a few students ventured to do some business on campus. Moreover, their activities were censured by teachers and generally despised by fellow students. By 1992, doing business or working for others to get some extra money had become very common among students.[15] In fact, when I interviewed Beijing students in 1993, I saw that several of my student informants carried pagers. At that time, this was pretty much an indication that these students were involved in quite serious moneymaking activities. Such commercialism had transformed many people who had formerly considered themselves as intellectuals into a professional class.

Changes in mentality were not the only factor. Other structural changes in society also contributed to the transformation. During the 1980s, China's market economy was still at a very early stage of development. Collective industries employed only petty technologies, private businesses were run by people with little or no education, and very few large-scale, high-tech joint ventures and foreign firms existed. The society simply could not provide enough opportunities for the educated class (chapter 3). In the 1990s, by contrast, many medium- and large-scale collective and private businesses emerged. Large-scale foreign firms were also mushrooming. High-income white-collar jobs became common in major cities. The economic boom after 1992 also brought enormous wealth. As

14. For example, in 1993 alone, over 300,000 intellectuals quit state-sector jobs and started their own businesses (Li Qiang 1996).

15. Xie (1993).

the whole society became richer, the Chinese were willing to pay more money to receive an education and to consume various cultural products. Moreover, with more big private businesses emerging and more and more private companies now controlled by educated people,[16] a huge amount of money flowed into the hands of intellectuals and students through donations, sponsorships, and foundations.[17] In sum, while most intellectuals and students considered themselves economic losers during the 1980s, they were unquestionably winners in the 1990s. Therefore, they became more interested in making money than in directly challenging the state.

The Urban Residents. On an absolute scale, the living standards of this population also improved in the 1990s. However, in comparison with the educated population, this population benefited significantly less from the economic boom of the 1990s.[18] Moreover, China started to reform the large state-owned companies. For several reasons, more and more state-owned businesses started to lose money and had to lay off workers or even to file for bankruptcy. The uncertainties associated with bankruptcy, layoffs, forced early retirement, and underemployment were enormous. If one were to make a prediction concerning the possible rebellious forces in urban China in the 1990s, urban workers would certainly be the candidates. However, for several reasons, although small-scale strikes and riots broke out very frequently in many cities,[19] no large-scale movements occurred.

What is immediately noticeable is the fact that Chinese workers were organizationally and especially ideologically impoverished. After intellectuals became a rich class, few of them were interested in organizing workers or providing them with movement ideologies. Without grand reasons to rebel, the dislocated population could only discharge its grievances by small-scale riots and strikes focusing on immediate economic problems.[20]

Beyond this, several structural changes also undermined the potential of

16. While private businessmen were the least educated population in urban society in the 1980s (chapter 3), in the 1990s more and more large businesses were run by people who had formerly considered themselves to be intellectuals.

17. Li Qiang (1996).

18. Ibid.

19. Li Xiaolin and Fu (1998), Mu (1996), and *World Journal* (1999b).

20. For example, almost all white-collar workers working in large joint ventures and foreign firms had a higher educational background, which meant they were regarded as intellectuals in China. In my conversations with several of them, I was surprised to find that they frequently referred to the workers who demonstrated on the streets after being laid off as *diaomin*, which can be literally translated as cunning and wicked rascals.

large-scale working-class movements. The first is that even though serious problems existed in the state-owned enterprises, the whole economy was developing. Therefore, except in a few rust-belt industrial cities such as Anshan and Datong, in most places the younger and more able workers in the state sector could, if laid off, find new jobs in the private sector. The layoffs hit really hard only those workers who were already at the margins of society and therefore had the least capacity to rebel.[21] Moreover, even for this population, the situation was not as bad as their monthly income figures suggested. This was because in China to financially support one's parents and to find jobs for immediate family members is a norm rather than an exception. As long as someone in a family was doing well, other family members would benefit. Therefore, many social problems were resolved at the family level.

The increasing domination of social life by market mechanisms also contributed to the absence of working-class movements. In the 1980s, Chinese society was relatively uniform and the state still mainly relied on administrative measures for policy implementation. Therefore a change of state policy often hit a large population, and when things went wrong, millions of people were affected.[22] In the 1990s, as society became more complicated and market mechanisms came to dominate social life, most people's economic well-being was determined less by the state than by the economic performance of specific companies. Consequently, many grievances of the Chinese urban population were now aimed at leaders of a particular factory or firm. This marks a sharp contrast to the situation during the 1980s, when most economic grievances were state-centered. In the 1990s, in many local economic conflicts, the state could actually act as a mediator rather than be a target of the aggrieved population. When the state dealt with the issues carefully, local strikes sometimes even increased the legitimacy of the regime.[23]

China's Political Future in the Early Twenty-first Century

A discussion of how the changes of state-society relations contributed to China's political stability in the 1990s raises the question of whether these

21. Seniors and women were highly over-represented in this population.

22. Zhou Xueguang (1993).

23. For example, early this year the Changsha municipal government used the police force to repress a riot, which resulted in one death and over one hundred injuries. Local people became outraged. In response, the state immediately criticized the repression and dismissed the city's CCP general secretary (*World Journal* 1999a). This kind of state action generally discharged people's grievances.

developments will lead to long-term political stability. My answer to this question is not so positive. Although the Chinese economy has performed reasonably well, serious socioeconomic problems still exist and will perhaps worsen in the near future. China's state industry is continuously losing money, and China's banking system is in great disarray. These have become the two biggest hurdles for China's further reform. Because of the vast scale of these enterprises and the significance of the vested interests involved, the challenges of reforming the state sector and the banking system are tremendous. Should things go wrong, the released tensions could easily shake the regime. Urban China may also face an even bigger labor surplus in the near future, as farmers migrate to the cities looking for opportunities, as unemployment resulting from layoffs in unprofitable state industries mounts, and as renewed population growth sends more and more youth into the job market.[24] Since most of these new laborers will be employed in the burgeoning private, joint venture, and foreign sectors, government control over urban residents will further decline. Without a good social security system, managing this population could also pose a profound challenge to the regime in an economic downturn. In addition, in the past few years the Chinese government has greatly expanded university enrollments. If this expansion leads to large numbers of students facing the prospect of unemployment upon graduation, the situation would be similar to that of the 1980s (chapter 4), and the stage could again be set for another student movement.

Listing the problems faced by a changing society with a population as large as China's is not a difficult task. What I want to stress here is that although China's state-society relations have greatly improved over the past ten years, the political conditions that underwrote the rise and shaped the development of the 1989 Movement have not been fundamentally eliminated. Without political reform, not only is another large-scale social movement or other political disturbance possible, but should such a movement start, it could well follow a trajectory similar to that of the 1989 Movement.

Many reasons for this could be given. I will restrict the discussion here to issues concerning the basis of the regime's legitimation. In the last section, I argued that after the 1989 Movement state-society relations in China had developed in such a way as to minimize the problems that prevailed during the early Chinese reform and to contribute instead to the regime's political stability. However, the problem is that many of these changes were brought about by improvements in "ruling methods" rather than by fundamental changes in the

24. Youth in the 15 to 24 age cohort will grow from 96 million in 2000 to 114 million in 2010 (Jack Goldstone, pers. comm.).

nature of the regime. Until now, the state has been dominated by a party that clenches onto a communist ideology that fewer and fewer Chinese take seriously, while the top government leaders, all belonging to that party, are still not freely elected through a commonly accepted procedure. Since very few Chinese really believe in communism, the state in reality has to base its legitimacy on moral and economic performance (and occasionally on nationalism). A regime basing its legitimacy only on performance, however, is intrinsically unstable. No economy can always be maintained at a high rate of development. Even if China's current economic growth rate could be maintained for several decades, the regime's political stability would still not be secured. Currently, the regime enjoys a high level of performance legitimation in part because most Chinese still have a vivid memory of the chaotic politics and miserable life they experienced during Mao's era, and they thus greatly treasure the more regulated politics and much better life they have now. Therefore, the regime's call for political stability in the name of economic development has resonated with many Chinese. What will happen after another twenty years or so, when the people who have firsthand experience of the Cultural Revolution have grown old? The Chinese by then may take affluence and stability for granted, and the state will no longer be able to use stability and development to justify its rule. In any event, when a state bases its legitimacy on performance, it will be held responsible for it. This will be a great burden for any performance-based regime.

It could be argued that people will blame the government anyway when social problems become very serious. Nevertheless, for a political system that contains multiple political forces (such as a multiparty democracy),[25] such grievances can be to a great extent discharged by a change of government through elections or other routine procedures. Since the system contains an alternative, it is very difficult for the people to unite and fight the system itself. However, the Chinese state, at least in its current form, contains no such alternatives. Moreover, because of the state's performance-based nature, any challenge to the performance of some top state leaders or specific state policies also implies a head-on challenge to the regime's legitimacy. As my discussion of the interactions between the state and people during the 1989 Movement has shown (chapter 7), the nature of such opposition offers extremely limited opportunities for compromise between the people and the government.

Regardless of its political nature, a state can always deal with social movements through repression. When a state is based on legal-electoral legitimation,

25. Here, I assume that all the political forces accept the same rules of the game and compete only for the office and not on the basis of ideology.

repression—or even a threat of repression—usually carries a very clear message that movement participants can scarcely ignore. Moreover, as long as acts of repression are based on law, even if they are very brutal, the acts can be perceived as legitimate by the governing elites and by the members of the public who watch the movement from the sidelines.[26] However, in a country where the state is based on moral legitimation, people base their judgments of political issues on morality (chapters 7, 9). As the development of the 1989 Movement shows, legal codes convey little meaning in a morally based political system.[27] The situation will be even worse when a social movement challenges a morally based regime on moral terms. In such a situation, any state control measures will be seen as immoral and will automatically undermine the regime's basis of legitimation.

During the 1990s, we saw the emergence of nationalism in urban China. The Chinese government also initiated several patriotic campaigns to boost its legitimacy.[28] But although, as I have argued earlier, the Chinese government has so far enjoyed the stabilizing effect of this emergence of nationalism, nationalism cannot be a stable base for the regime's long-term stability. Excessive nationalism will destabilize the peaceful international environment vital for China's current economic development. Nationalistic aims once expressed need to be reached. The agitated nationalistic sentiment will put great pressure on the government. Most crucially, nationalism emerges with the rise of nation-states. One of the political bases of nation-states is citizenship, which requires civil rights, political rights, and social rights[29]—rights that the current Chinese government is unable to fully grant to its people. The authoritarian nature of the regime was not a problem during Mao's era, when the state enjoyed a high level of ideological legitimation and people saw the CCP as the vanguard of the nation. Beginning in the 1980s, however, fewer and fewer Chinese viewed the CCP and the government as the only representative of national interests.

26. For example, in the United States, the elites and the majority of the population seldom questioned the legitimacy of government repression during the early stages of the labor and civil rights movements.

27. I observed, in contrast, a large demonstration in front of the Chinese Embassy in Ottawa after the 1989 military repression. Some students decided to lead others in a rush into the embassy. There were only a few policemen in front of the embassy, walking back and forth to create a space between the demonstrators and the building. However, each time these students ran toward the embassy, the policemen stopped them by just raising their hands to show disapproval. I was surprised by the effectiveness of the gesture here, since in Beijing, before the repression, hundreds of warnings from the state were unable to move the students out of Tiananmen Square. I was impressed by the effectiveness of a state control measure when it is backed by a respect for the law itself, independent of the government.

28. See Zheng (1999) for recent literature on the rise of nationalism in China during the 1990s.

29. Barbalet (1988); Marshall (1950).

The meaning of nationalism became contested.[30] Thus, the Chinese government during the 1990s frequently restricted spontaneous nationalistic collective actions by the masses. One example is the government's rejection of students' application to stage a demonstration in 1998 after the news that many ethnic Chinese women had been raped during the riots in Indonesia reached Beijing. The restriction not only led to conflicts between students and the government but also changed some students' views of the government. I argue that the contradiction between mass-based nationalism (which requires full citizenship) and authoritarianism (which denies citizenship) will pose a great challenge to the Chinese regime if nationalism comes to dominate China's political life.

In the above analysis, I have only used the idea of state legitimation. However, as I have shown in this book, when a large-scale social movement emerges in the context of the type of state-society relationship that is current in China, the movement will be likely to be structured on an ecological basis (chapter 8), be dominated by emotions, traditions, and rumors (chapters 7, 9, and 10), and be encouraged by a rebellious media and by sympathetic expressions of public opinion (chapter 10). Therefore, once such a large-scale social movement gains momentum, a state such as the current China actually has few means of conflict resolution. Often, the state is left with only two choices: surrender or repression. As events in the former Soviet Union and other Eastern European countries have clearly shown, when confronted with this alternative, a generation with no revolutionary experience may not defend a regime by way of bloody military repression. Even if some leaders were to decide on repression, the more professionally trained soldiers may no longer follow their orders. A sudden surrender, instead of gradual change, made the transition to democracy in the former Soviet Union very painful.

That a performance-based regime is intrinsically unstable, and that such a regime, once it faces political challenges, has great difficulty containing them, is indeed bad news for the current Chinese leaders. Therefore, the current Chinese leaders should place political reform at the top of their agenda. This is not to suggest that China should copy any particular Western political system. However, such a political reform has to aim at changing the foundation of state power from ideology and performance legitimation to legal-electoral legitimation. It should minimally include formally abandoning Marxism as a state ideology, renaming the Communist Party as a socialist party, establishing an independent legal system, and gradually instituting competitive elections with

---

30. Guo (1998).

candidates competing only for the office rather than for mutually incompatible ideologies.

In the report by Jiang Zemin to the Fifteenth Congress of the CCP Central Committee delivered in September 1997, there is a section on political reform. Although much of the section is limited to legal and administrative reform (that is, reform of the organizations and functions of government and public institutions), the report triggered a surge of democratic discourse in China.[31] In recent publications, Chinese scholars have examined such problems in China as bad credit, overinvestment in the housing market, capital outflows, increasing income disparities, abuse of law, and the violation of basic human rights. They believe that most of these problems are related to official corruption and to the lack of checks and balances of government power through legal, public opinion, and electoral channels. They argue that China's economic reform has developed to a stage where democratization has become an absolute necessity. Right now, most of these books are written as friendly recommendations to the state. However, as has been repeatedly demonstrated in the history of China in the twentieth century, such a loyal opposition can easily be radicalized when these intellectual elites are frustrated either by a hardline state reaction or by emerging social problems.

Fortunately, these publications are still openly circulated in China, indicating that the government has at least been tolerating such discussion. In fact, the top state leaders themselves may be well aware of the problems confronting Chinese society. However, because of their experience of the 1989 Movement, they may perceive great danger in political reform—the danger of a sudden and total collapse of the government in the face of a rising disloyal opposition. Therefore, the government has so far relied mainly on legal and administrative reforms as a solution to the existing problems. Legal and administrative reforms certainly combat some social problems. The reforms will also prepare modern institutions—such as a more robust legal system, a professional bureaucracy, and interest-based civil associations—crucial to a successful democratic transition.[32] Nevertheless, I cannot foresee how legal and administrative reforms could lead to independent courts and elected legislatures becoming the foundation of state legitimation, in place of ideology and performance. I suspect that the success of legal and administrative reforms will actually make communist ideology and authoritarianism even more irrelevant to Chinese

31. See Dong and Shi (1998), Ling and Ma (1999), Liu Zhifeng (1999), Liu Zuoxiang (1999), Rong et al. (1998), and Wu Daying and Yang (1999).

32. Linz and Stepan (1978, 1996); Przeworski (1991).

society, which may further undermine the regime's legitimacy in the long run. Therefore, while legal and administrative reforms are absolutely necessary, they are not substitutes for more fundamental political reforms.

No top state leaders are willing to instigate a political reform of which they themselves would be among the first victims. Therefore, timing is extremely important. The democratic transition in both South Korea and Taiwan started in the late 1980s.[33] The democratic transition in South Korea was initiated by large-scale student demonstrations that toppled the regime, while Taiwan's transition started when the economy was in a good shape and dissident forces were still well contained. Consequently, the Guomindang in Taiwan was able to control and benefit from the initial democratization process. For a country with China's size, regional diversities, and scale of problems, if a political reform starts in the middle of an economic crisis and social upheaval, oppositions may not only blow away the existing political forces but also unleash separative nationalisms and other traditional forces which would bring disaster not only to China but also possibly to the whole world. A successful political reform has to be timed so that, when it comes, it is not "too little, too late."

Theoretical Remarks

As sociologists, we need to have a sense of what history is. To put it into one sentence, I would argue that while history is a longitudinally patterned mess,[34] it can be seen cross-sectionally as a highly complex jigsaw puzzle made up of poorly interlocked pieces. The latter idea came to me when I bought my then three-year-old daughter a two-hundred-piece puzzle with pieces that were not fully interlocked. Jigsaw puzzles with fully interlocked pieces can be assembled in only one way. Lower-quality puzzles that are not fully interlocked have been cut into pieces that can be physically assembled in more than one way, although only one such assembly will result in the picture on the box. I was surprised to find that my daughter succeeded in fitting the pieces together—and in producing a new picture that was quite different from the one printed on the cover. This analogy is valid when we consider that historians do not have the puzzle box at hand and thus do not have an exact picture of the completed puzzle. It is worth noting in this regard that my daughter seldom looked at the pictures on jigsaw puzzle boxes before turning four. Apparently, the cognitive processes of three-year-olds are in this respect different from older children and adults—

33. Friedman (1994); Wachman (1994).
34. The idea that history is a patterned mess is from Mann (1993).

and in a way similar to those of people who strive to fit together the poorly interlocked pieces of the puzzles of history.

This incident illustrated for me why so many descriptions and analyses, some of which are far removed from the actual event, can be constructed for a complex historical process. Nevertheless, we should not be defeated by the fact and retreat into a totally subjective understanding of history. Although complete reconstruction of a complex historical process is neither possible nor necessary, some constructions do capture historical logic better than others. In this book, in presenting the historical factors to be explained, I have acted as a serious historian in constructing micro-level facts and have struggled to achieve contextually rich descriptions that also celebrate the complexity of human actions and experiences, as humanists do. At the same time, when it comes to providing explanations, I have striven for analytical depth and rigor.

Since my intention has been to explain the origins and patterns of the 1989 Beijing Student Movement, my task has been to find a model (with a set of explanatory factors and related mechanisms) that can account for the important variations associated with the movement's origin and dynamics. I believe that such a model should contain three qualities of scientific explanation.

First, it should be parsimonious. The model contains only the minimum number of explanatory factors, and yet it explains all the important variations in the rise and development of the 1989 Movement. On the patterns of development of the movement, for instance, I intended to achieve a simultaneous understanding of several important aspects, including the role of the state in the movement, the movement's mobilization structure, the linguistic dimension of the movement, and the impact of media and public opinion. Yet this is hardly an ambitious undertaking within the heavily theorized field of the study of social movements and revolutions. For example, political process models and state-centered theories focus on the impact of state structures and behaviors on the rise and development of social movements and revolutions. The resource mobilization model explains the dynamics of a social movement in terms of the resources available to social movement entrepreneurs. In cultural explanations, a social movement is driven by the internal logic of a cultural text. None of the theories explains all the important characteristics of the rise and development of the 1989 Movement.

In this book, each empirical chapter analyzes an important feature associated with the rise and development of the 1989 Movement. Although most theories of social movements and revolutions are not made to explain the whole range of topics that this book covers, some of them do offer competing explanations of some of the topics covered in the empirical chapters. When that is the case,

I have provided a short review of the competing theories in that empirical chapter. Thus, unlike a typical case study, which only has a theoretical discussion in the introduction, this book introduces new literatures in many empirical chapters. Those theories are not the focus of the introduction because they do not compete with the theories that inform the entire book, and to include them would be a distraction to the theme of the introduction.

Second, the model must to be falsifiable; others should be able to propose alternative models to explain the same phenomena. Unfalsifiable models are very popular in sociology. The political opportunity structure model in social movement research is an example.[35] This is not to deny the importance of opportunity for social movements. The problem is that one cannot form alternative hypotheses to test the theory's validity. Structural concepts such as ideology, state, caste, class, demography, community, family, gender, and ethnicity not only carry specific mechanisms but can also be so defined that they exclude other such structural concepts as factors. Therefore, theories employing such concepts are falsifiable. However, phrases like "political opportunity" refer not to any particular macro-structural mechanism but to rational choice assumptions. The subjective nature of the concept allows all movement-inducing factors to be labeled as one or another kind of structured opportunity. Since any facilitating factor can be labeled as an opportunity, what can be disputed is only the relative importance of specific dimensions of political opportunities, not the theory itself.[36] Therefore, I did not follow this theoretical approach.[37]

Third, the model must be based on high-quality empirical evidence. A complex historical event can be presented in so many ways and at so many different levels of detail that scholars often have different criteria for the validity of qualitative analyses. Nevertheless, one can certainly hope to increase the validity of qualitative analyses and thus the theoretical understanding by truthfully reconstructing micro-level facts and their contexts. To this end, I have adopted

35. Costain and McFarland (1998), Eisinger (1973), Gamson and Meyer (1996), Jenkins and Klandermans (1995), Kitschelt (1986), Kriesi (1996), Kriesi et al. (1995), McAdam (1996), Meyer and Staggenborg (1996), Meyer and Tarrow (1998), Rucht (1990, 1996), and Tarrow (1992, 1994, 1996).

36. It may be argued that political opportunity structure theorists also analyze the role of objective structures in social movement dynamics. Yet once we define an objective social structure as an opportunity, we immediately assign a subjective quality to that social structure. That is why Tarrow (1994, 85) has to define political opportunity structures in terms of their role in providing "incentives for people to undertake collective action by affecting their expectations for success or failure."

37. Currently some scholars have tried to deal with the problem by classifying dimensions of political opportunity structures (Gamson and Meyer 1996; McAdam 1996; Tarrow 1992, 1994, 1996). For example, Gamson and Meyer have put all kinds of political opportunities into a 2-by-2-classification table along stable-versus-volatile and cultural-versus-institutional axes. However, attempts of this sort only cut the big conceptual sponge into small pieces without changing the theory's all-inclusive nature.

a "detective" style of research in reconstructing crucial events in the rise and development of the 1989 Movement. (I omit a more detailed description of the
research since the introduction has given an example on how a crucial event in
this book is typically reconstructed.)

The state-society relations model was constructed after a back-and-forth
dialogue between the empirical findings and the criteria discussed above. Although "state-society relations" has been a frequently used concept in political
science and sociology, this book attempts to turn this interpretative concept
into an analytic tool with measurable dimensions and mechanisms. In addition,
very few case studies have tried to explain the characteristics of a social movement as large as the one covered in this book.

Early efforts at structural analysis tended to predict the rise and outcome
of social movements or revolutions from categorical differences in structural
factors.[38] However, structures manifest themselves in continuous interactions
among social actors.[39] Complex social processes are usually path dependent;
earlier events, even if they are accidents, qualify the temporal and causal construction of the later events.[40] Few outcomes of social movements or revolutions are predetermined by categorical social structures or individual intentions. This book follows a relational analysis. I model the development of the
1989 Movement as a "structured contingency."[41] I emphasize how social structures patterned people's activities and how their activities pushed the movement in a way that gradually shut the doors to other possible outcomes and that
made the final head-on conflict between the people and the state increasingly
inevitable. Therefore, when the 1989 Movement began, even its initiators were
not clear about the goals that they intended to accomplish. In other types of
state-society relations, similar protest activities are more likely to turn into reformist drives than into a bloody revolution-like confrontation. I also analyzed,
on the one hand, how the activities of some students such as Chai Ling, Li Lu,
and Zhang Boli shaped the dynamics of the movement (chapter 6), and, on the
other hand, how structural forces allowed some students and movement activities to dominate and shape the development of the movement, eventually turning every other possibility into an "inaccessible alternative."[42]

38. For example, Paige (1975), Skocpol (1979), Stinchcombe (1961), and, to a less extent, Moore (1966).

39. Relational sociology is currently advocated by a number of scholars, especially Tilly (1986), Alexander (1988), and Emirbayer (1997), but few systematic empirical studies have been done in that direction.

40. Gocek (1990, 112).

41. Karl and Schmitter (1991).

42. Tsou (1991, 295).

In short, my research shows that the dynamic of contentious collective actions, while it is shaped by the structure of state-society relations, develops through the continuous interactions of agents, with outcomes that become certain only very late. While I also see social movements as political processes, what distinguishes the state-society relations theory from some other political process models is that it traces the origins and outcomes of a social movement at the intersections in the continuous meso- and micro-level interactions among different social actors including the state. The state-society relations model is also an intersection model.

Contained in the intersection model is also the idea that social orders and social outcomes are results of the aggregation of the actions and interactions of individuals.[43] Yet, once we decide to "bring men back in" to a structural analysis,[44] we immediately face ontological questions concerning what is human and what constitutes human agency. For example, different assumptions regarding human nature lead to different versions of what people need to accomplish, in order to form a just and peaceful society. Scholars whose intellectual lineage descends from Hobbes or Rousseau, Locke or Marx, advocate an elitist or mass politics, procedural or popular democracy.

In sociology, there are three schools of thought with distinctive approaches to the question of how to relate the actions of human individuals to macro structures.[45] According to the first, social structures and culture mainly function to provide the criteria by which people make rational choices. This notion of context-bound rationality is currently very popular in sociology thanks to the rise of new institutionalism in organizational studies and of political opportunity models in social movement research.[46] The second school considers human activities as meaning-driven discursive processes. According to this approach, social structures mainly function as meaning systems and people's actions are "text-driven."[47] Much research, including some works on the French Revolution and on the 1989 Movement, has followed this tradition.[48] Related to the discourse analysis approach is another line of research that views social

43. This perspective is commonly called methodological individualism. See Boudon (1987), Brinton and Nee (1998), and Oberschall (1993).

44. Homans (1964).

45. This is called the micro-macro link problem (Alexander, Giesen, Munch, and Smelser 1987).

46. For the new institutionalism, see Adams (1996), Brinton and Nee (1998), Czada, Heritier, and Keman (1996), DiMaggio (1988), and Granovetter (1985).

47. Geertz (1983), Jabri (1996), Steinberg (1994), and Terdiman (1986).

48. See Hunt (1984), Baker (1990), Furet (1981), and Sewell (1985) for works on the French Revolution, and Wasserstrom (1991), Esherick and Wasserstrom (1990), and Pye (1990) for the 1989 Movement.

interactions as norm-driven, emotion-ridden processes. With this tradition, the impact of structures on human behavior can operate at a subconscious level, and structures regulate feelings rather than rational minds. Recently, a new wave of emotion studies of social movements and revolutions attest to the potency of this century-old tradition.[49]

In this book, I have freely borrowed from all three approaches. Although history is not just a text, people are often moved by cultural symbols and ideas, and social processes usually have an important linguistic dimension. I have treated the ideational and discursive dimensions of the struggle between the state and people as an interactive process. What I am interested in are the impact of social structures on the experiences of the people, and consequently on the patterns of their meaning-creation and production, rather than on the exact mental processes of the actors. My analysis of the ideologies of intellectual elites (chapter 2), of the sources of state legitimation and the patterns of movement-state interactions (chapter 7), of movement rhetoric (chapter 8), and of media discourse and public opinion (chapter 10) are clearly influenced by this tradition.

I also assume that many activities before and during the movement were strategic or at least partially so. My analysis throughout the book benefits from game theory approaches, especially works by scholars including Mancur Olson, Robert Axelrod, and Thomas Schelling.[50] However, in an epistemological sense I do not argue that all of a movement's activities result from strategic calculations. I am hesitant about the more ambitious version of rational choice theory that tries to incorporate structures and culture as "selective incentives,"[51] "tool kits,"[52] or "opportunity structures" that assist people in selection of the best strategies. The rational choice model has been criticized in so many ways that I see no need to repeat the criticisms here.[53] Rather, I want to add two related comments. First, for scholars who study culture, it is an indisputable fact that cultural forces also operate at a subconscious level as habits and instincts. Second, social structures are not opportunities that become meaningful only when actors have a clear understanding of them. Social structures exercise influences on actors whether the actors are aware of their ex-

---

49. Goodwin (1997), Jasper (1997, 1998), Lindholm (1990), and Scheff (1994).
50. Olson (1965), Axelrod (1984), and Schelling (1962).
51. See Fireman and Gamson (1979), Friedman and McAdam (1992), Gamson (1975), and Wilson (1973) for the idea of selective incentives.
52. Laitin (1988), Swidler (1986), Tarrow (1994, 122), and Zald (1996).
53. Collins (1981), Turner and Killian (1987), Jasper (1997), and Lindholm (1990).

istence or not. In the book, social structures have both an objective and a sub-jective quality.

Although I do not regard social movements as purely emotional activities, the strongest micro-level influence on the book's narrative style is from the broad microsociological tradition that views social processes as norm- or value-driven interactions. Most chapters of this book follow a time order, and the events are contextualized as interactive processes between the state and people or among the people themselves. Readers may find, for example, that my analy-sis of why the confrontations between the students and the state continuously escalated (chapter 7), of why students tended to be moved by languages and activities more in keeping with traditional Chinese culture (chapter 8), and of why Chinese media coverage and public opinion toward the movement exhib-ited a particular pattern of interactions (chapter 10) bears the strong imprint of Garfinkel's ethnomethodology, Collins's concept of "interaction ritual chains," and some of Turner's studies.[54] For example, in chapter 7 I argue that people's micro-level actions and perceptions largely followed their respective notions of state legitimacy. Because China's top state elites and the people had different understandings of state legitimation, their behaviors and perceptions during the 1989 Movement were governed by different cognitive models. Thus, each side continuously made moves that violated the other player's understanding of the nature of the "game" and irritated the other player.

Few works on social movements and revolutions have relied on the con-cept of legitimation as much as this book. The book defines three dimensions of state legitimation and measures different social groups' understanding of legitimation along these dimensions. Then, it shows how this macrostructure of state legitimation provided basic norms that patterned the longitudinal meso- and micro-level interactions between the government and the people and among the people themselves, which contributed to the tragic ending of the movement.

In this book, I have tried to be as truthful as possible in identifying struc-tural forces and patterns of interaction between the state and the people and among the people during the movement. To make human agents real, I have been deliberately vague about models of human action and have borrowed freely from all three above-mentioned approaches. In other words, I have adopted so-ciological approaches that others may view as contradictory. Is it possible and

---

54. Blumer (1969), Collins (1981, 1990), Garfinkel (1967), Turner and Killian (1987), and Turner and Surace (1956).

beneficial to incorporate several contradictory sociological theories in a single paradigm? A short answer is that it is possible because the state-society relations model developed in this book is an *empirical* rather than a *formal* model. Since some readers may not be familiar with the concepts, I shall elaborate on them a little more here.

In general, I see formal and empirical modeling as two basic scientific approaches, each having its own values. In sociology, for example, if we closely follow mode-of-production Marxism in an analysis, we are interested in a formal question concerning the amount of variation that we can explain if the mode of production is assumed to be the structural basis of social actions. If we follow the new institutionalism, we link macro structures with a model of rational humans, and we are interested in the amount of variation that the theory can explain when we assume that "bounded rationality" is the basis of social actions. However, the purpose of this study is not to develop sociology as a formal science but to explain the rise and development of the 1989 Movement in a way that is as close to reality as possible. This is what I call an empirical approach. To incorporate contradictory theories in an empirical approach is not only possible but also beneficial. This is because most contradictory sociological theories actually capture different facets of a complex social reality that is itself contradictory. They are contradictory only in a formal sense, not in an empirical sense.

Let me provide some examples from other disciplines to further illustrate the point. Physics is almost completely dominated by formal approaches because in physics models such as Newton's laws of motion and Maxwell's equations can describe reality so well that no other approaches are necessary. In population biology, however, the situation becomes more complicated. For example, Malthus's equation captures the exponential nature of population growth. Yet few populations grow exponentially, given population-specific constraints such as food, density-dependent diseases, inter- and intra-population competition, predators, and climate. Therefore, population biologists have developed two modeling strategies. While formal models (most start with Malthus) aim to capture essences of population dynamics, empirical models (usually the extension of life table methods) incorporate as many empirical complexities as possible to describe population dynamics in the closest possible manner. Again, since my purpose is not to develop a formal theory but to gain an empirical understanding of the causes and development of the 1989 Movement, I link empirically determined social structures with real humans who are both strategic and emotional. Although sociologists have a tendency to misunderstand the nature of the two methods, empirical modeling has existed in sociology for a long time. Indeed, as Stinchcombe has commented, the secret to the success of George Herbert Mead and Max Weber lies in "the fact that they make both people and structures real." [55]

I ague that an empirically motivated structural analysis of social movements should not be linked to a specific model of human activity, but to real humans. This does not mean that structural analyses are not able to deal with the issue of rationality and emotions in social movements. Rational strategies and emotions are inseparable constituents of most of human behaviors. Since it is very hard to determine whether a specific activity is a purely emotional display or a strategic choice, micro-level debates of their relative importance will not bring us very far. Therefore, instead of treating rational strategies, culture, or emotions as some sort of "exogenous variables" to social movements, I have tried to understand the structural conditions that regulated their respective degrees of dominance in a particular movement. The 1989 Movement tended to be driven by emotions, rumors, and traditional cultural elements exactly because it developed under an authoritarian state with higher state unity and the capacity to penetrate society, a society with very weak development of intermediate organizations, and a state legitimation based on moral and economic performance. Seen in this light, even the fact that many scholars opt for sociological theories that stress rational choices may itself reflect a set of structural transformations in the West. That is, when the market dominates the economy, national politics centers on regular elections, and well-defined legal codes penetrate almost every sphere of human life, the most important dimensions of human activity fit into accounting books. Consequently, rationality dominates social life, and Western sociological theories also increasingly rely on rationalistic assumptions about humans. Yet, what the resurgence of traditionalism during the 1989 Movement teaches us is that cultural and emotional claims might gain new purchase, at least in the political sphere, under certain other structural transformations.

55. Stinchcombe (1975, 27).

APPENDIX I *A Methodological Note*

This study relies on information obtained through interviews with informants who participated in or witnessed the 1989 Beijing Student Movement,[1] as well as on secondary sources, including news reports, witness accounts, archives, factual and statistical data from both Chinese and English sources, and many memoirs published by student activists exiled to Western countries. Most secondary data was obtained from the McGill, Harvard, Princeton, University of Chicago, and Chinese University of Hong Kong libraries. I have also done research in the Shanghai Library, the Beijing Library, the Library of the Shanghai Academy of Social Sciences, the Fudan University Library, the Beijing Archives, and the Shanghai Archives to collect data not available outside of China. In the introduction, I gave an example of how I have typically integrated these various sources of data in writing this book. Here I will discuss a few other issues related to the data collection.

Based on my knowledge of the uneven quality of Chinese surveys, research, and publications, I established four guidelines for collection of the secondary data: (1) I sought to use raw data or simple descriptive statistics rather than data already subjected to more sophisticated statistical procedures. (2) I relied more on data appearing in scientific journals and internal government documents meant for limited domestic audiences, since data from such sources are less likely to be tailored for propaganda purposes than those published in official newspapers or for larger audiences. (3) When possible, I used the results from straightforward, value-free survey questions. For example, I would prefer the results from the second of the following two questions: "Do you still support the reform, even if your living standard may be temporarily affected?" and

1. Here I describe only the major methodologies of this book. In some chapters I also used other methods, such as small-scale samples (chapters 3 and 5) and content analyses of newspapers (chapter 10). I explained these methods in the relevant chapters.

"Has your living standard declined in recent years?" [2] (4) I used data published for general purposes, especially those that are not directly linked to any research questions of this study, since they are less likely to be systematically biased. For example, there is little reason to suspect such data as the percentage of social science students enrolled in Chinese universities or the increase in TOEFL testing centers in Beijing, but they may have great sociological significance for this analysis.

My interviews were of two kinds: formal and informal. By formal interviews, I mean interviews that were guided by a set of prepared questions (see the appended interview questions) and almost always taped. By informal interviews, I refer to interviews that did not follow a specific list of questions and that most of the time were not taped. The informal interviews have been conducted ever since I started my research, but most intensively in 1993 and 1997 during my two research trips to China. They were conducted for several purposes, at different times. At the outset of my research, informal interviews helped me make sense of the movement so as to construct questions for formal interviews. During the research, I came across some people who were not in the population category that I had decided to interview formally but who nevertheless were important for my understanding of the movement, and I interviewed them informally. For example, in 1993 I interviewed Ding Zilin and her husband Jiang Peikun, both former professors of the People's University. Their experiences of the 1989 Movement and their insights into it constituted a valuable source because they have been China's most devoted human rights activists since their son's tragic death on the night of June 3. Finally, I also use informal interviews to clear up some specific questions concerning the dynamics of the movement. For example, to understand the role of Beijing workers during the 1989 Movement, I supplemented the other data that I had collected by interviewing nine workers from various Beijing factories in 1997.

Although I have conducted extensive informal interviews with people of various occupations, most interview material that appears in this book comes from formal interviews. Seventy people were formally interviewed: thirty in Montreal and forty in Beijing. The Canadian interviews were carried out between December 1992 and March 1993. The Beijing interviews were conducted in April and May 1993. The study's main focus was the 1989 Movement in Beijing; hence most informants were students or teachers in Beijing at that time. How-

---

2. The first question has at least three problems. The concept of reform is abstract, and very positively valued in the media; Chinese culture strongly favors individual sacrifice for the public good; and finally, "living standard may be temporarily affected" is put too hypothetically. Therefore, the result constructed from this question is not very meaningful.

ever, there were six informants from outside the capital—two from Guangzhou, two from Tianjin, one from Sichuan, and one from Jilin. These six informants were interviewed in order to obtain some sense of local diversities and of the relationship between local student movements and those in Beijing.

Before an interview started, I always chatted with an informant until the conversation became natural. I explained the purpose of the study, specified the time period that I wanted them to talk about, and assured them of the anonymity of the interview material. I also told them that they could refuse to answer a question if it made them uncomfortable for whatever reason. In fact, very few informants refused to answer any question, and the Beijing informants showed no more restraint than the Montreal informants did. The interviews were semistructured. Two sets of questions were prepared, one for students and another for political workers (mainly political instructors and class directors). Over the course of the first several interviews a few questions were added or dropped. The two sets of questions in Appendix 2 were the final versions stabilized after the sixteenth informant. The questions were used only as a base from which to probe further. Thus they only served as a guideline, with some questions added and some left out during each interview. They were strictly followed only if an informant was very passive. Most informants would elaborate without prompting after a few minutes of conversation. In a few cases, especially in interviews with activists of the movement, the prepared questions were not followed in order to give the respondents the maximum freedom to describe their experiences and activities. Nevertheless, their narratives still addressed most of the basic interview questions. Most interviews lasted between thirty and ninety minutes, with the longest lasting about five hours. Since different types of informants were asked different sets of questions, and otherwise similar informants may have been probed differently, the sample size for the statistics extracted from the interviews is normally smaller than the number of informants being interviewed.

The refusal rate for interviews in Canada was 33 percent; that is, of the forty-five people asked, fifteen refused to be interviewed. The most common reason for a refusal was that the potential informants were afraid of the possible consequences to them or their relatives in China, even though the purpose of the study and the anonymity of the interviews was clearly explained. Most of those who refused to be interviewed were not active participants in the 1989 Movement. This reaction was discouraging, since I planned to interview in Beijing, where the danger for interviewees could be real and where I had only several friends of friends with whom to start. To my surprise, among the forty-two people that I contacted in Beijing, only two refused to be interviewed—a refusal rate of 5 percent. At first, the declared purpose of the study for the Beijing interviews was not "to study the 1989 Movement" but "to study youth culture in the late 1980s," even though I was asking the same questions. After several interviews, when I sensed that the Beijing informants were actually more open than those in Canada were, I began to declare the real purpose in my contact with informants.

A tape recorder was always available for the interviews, although each time I specifically asked for permission to use it. There were four informants who refused to be recorded, two in Canada and another two in Beijing.

The interviews were conducted in late 1992 and early 1993, while the movement took place in 1989. So there is the possibility of distortion and forgetting on the part of informants. To avoid just obtaining superficial historical memories, I encouraged the informants to talk about their personal experiences and activities rather than to make general comments on events of which they did not have direct experience. To avoid memory bias, I also did not probe into impressions or experiences of a short-term nature. After the interview, I cross-checked the precision of an informant's narrative by the other informants' descriptions of the same event. Sometimes, when an informant's description was part of a major event, the published accounts were also used to check reliability. Possibly because the period before and during the 1989 Movement was such a dramatic one, the narratives of my informants showed a strong consistency.

Informants were recruited through a snowball method: after each interview, an informant was asked to suggest friends who might be willing to participate. The 1989 Movement has been a politically sensitive topic to most Chinese. This method was thus appropriate because Chinese tend to put a lot of trust in friends. However, to ensure the representativeness of informants and to maintain efficiency in data collection, I made some decisions as to whether or not a suggested candidate should be interviewed. For example, to minimize redundant information, I tried not to recruit two informants who were roommates at the time of the 1989 Movement. Prior to the interview, I was also aware that undergraduates, students in key universities, and students of the social sciences and humanities were more active in the movement. I decided that my informants should reflect this fact. As the following profiles show, the sample turned out to be reasonably representative.

Of the seventy informants, social science and humanity majors made up 44 percent ($n = 31$), compared to an 18.5 percent national average. In 1989, thirty-seven of the informants were undergraduate students, eleven were graduate students, sixteen were political control cadres and teachers, and six worked in various cultural and academic institutions. The informants were from eigh-

TABLE AI.I   Years in Which Undergraduate and Graduate Informants Entered University

Year	1984	1985	1986	1987	1988	1989
No. of informants	2	10	9	19	6	2

TABLE AI.2   Level of Activism among Informants in the Canadian and Beijing Samples

	Level of Activism				
	0	1	2	3	4
Canadian sample	1	10	11	8	0
Beijing sample	5	10	6	13	6
Total	6	20	17	21	6

teen universities and four cultural and academic institutions. Most of them were from Beijing University ($n = 12$), People's University ($n = 12$), Qinghua University ($n = 10$), Beijing Normal University ($n = 8$), the University of Political Sciences and Law ($n = 4$), and Beijing Chemical University ($n = 4$). Except for Beijing Chemical, these were the most active universities during the 1989 Movement. No attempt was made to control the gender of informants, of whom fifty-three were males and seventeen females. This ratio should be reasonably representative since female students were less active in the movement than their male counterparts.

Most informants entered university between 1985 and 1988 (table AI.1). This was ideal because students enrolled in 1984 and 1985 were preparing to graduate, while students beginning their studies in early 1989 were still orienting themselves. In my research, I found that the most active students were those who entered the universities between 1986 and 1987.

In terms of their level of movement participation, my seventy informants ranged from movement leaders to those who barely participated in any movement activities (table AI.2). Table AI.2 also indicates that the Canadian and Beijing informants were not that different with respect to their levels of participation in the 1989 Movement, except that all the student leaders were from the Beijing interviews. Here, the level of movement participation is defined as follows: nonparticipants (0) were those who, at most, only observed marches and other activities from the outside. Low-level participants (1) were those who participated in only a few demonstrations, but no other activities. Median-level participants (2) were those who participated in the major demonstrations during the 1989 Movement, such as the April 27 demonstration. However, their level of participation could change over time, with some withdrawing totally after a certain period. The activists (3) were those who participated in almost all the major demonstrations and were active throughout the 1989 Movement. Some might have even initiated other activities such as making speeches, writing big-character posters, and joining in hunger strikes. The organizers (4) were those students who had held leadership positions in one or more of the following organizations: The Students' Autonomous Union at either city or university level, the Beijing University Students' Dialogue Delegation, and the Hunger Strike Headquarters.

In the book, I have occasionally used statistics to test whether relationships existed between the factors under consideration. Almost all the statistical methods require a probability sample, a condition that is not met by a typical snowball sample. What I want to point out is that the interviews were conducted about three years after the 1989 Movement. During that period, as I found in the interviews, many informants' circles of friends had changed. The changes in these circles, in addition to uncertainties involved in a snowball sample, may have, to a certain extent, remedied the problems of a nonrandom sample.

The interviews were carried out in Chinese. All the quotations in this book are my translations. The quotations were labeled by numbers to mark the source of information while maintaining anonymity.

APPENDIX 2 *Interview Questions*

Translation of the Interview Guide for Student Informants

BACKGROUND INFORMATION: AGE _____; UNIVERSITY STUDIED _____;
FROM (YEAR) _____ TO (YEAR) _____; MAJOR _____; ACADEMIC
LEVEL IN 1989 _____.

1. Could you briefly describe your activities on a typical school day when you were at the university? (Questions 2 through 18 may not be followed if the response to question 1 opened interesting themes for further probing, or if some of the following questions were spontaneously answered.)

2. On average, how many hours a day did you spend on course-related activities?

3. How would you describe your level of diligence compared with that of your classmates? (above average, average, or below average)

4. What were your major after-class activities?

5. Did you often read novels and reportage novels? (if yes:)
    5a. Had you read reportage novels written by authors such as Liu Binyan, Su Xiaokang, and Jia Lusheng before 1989?

6. At that time, did you have some particular impressions of these reportage novels?

7. Did you watch the TV series *River Elegy* at the time when it was broadcast? (What did you think of the series when you watched it?)

8. In 1988 and 1989, a popular saying was that university students constituted four factions—the mah-jongg faction, the TOEFL faction, the xuan faction, and the yuanyang faction. Does this well describe student life at your university?

9. How many students were there in your class? Among them, how many had taken the TOEFL examination and how many have gone abroad? (If respondents had already gone abroad, or had taken or were preparing for the TOEFL test before 1990:)
   9a. What were your main purposes in going abroad back then?
   9b. When did you learn that one could go abroad by taking the TOEFL examination and applying to foreign universities, language schools, etc.?

10. I have seen many reports on the "commercial fever" among university students during 1988 and 1989. Were commercial activities common among your classmates during this period?

11. Did you try to make some money during your university life?

12. Were some students (including yourself) very successful at making money?

13. How did your classmates, teachers, and the university authorities feel about those students who were involved in commercial activities?

14. Did you often chat with your classmates during your time in university?

15. What were the major topics?

16. When your conversation touched upon politically sensitive issues, did you and your classmates feel a kind of hesitation? In other words, were you afraid that other students might report the contents of the conversation to the authorities?

17. In 1988, the Chinese state implemented the economic adjustment policy. Did you and your classmates have some particular comments on the new policy at the time?

18. In private conversations among your classmates, did you have some shared grievances about society and the university? (Did you talk about them frequently?)

19. Could you describe your personal experiences and activities during the 1989 Movement? (Here again, questions 20 through 29 may not be followed if informants had opened interesting themes for further probing or if they had already answered some of the questions.)

20. When was the first time that you joined a movement activity—for example, a march?
    20a. To your knowledge, how were marches and other movement activities organized? (For example, how did you know that there would be a march on a particular day?)

21. Did you join demonstrations frequently? (Do you remember how often you joined marches?)
    21a. Besides marches, did you participate in other movement activities?

22. Were there some students in your class who did not participate in any movement activities and/or who showed little concern about the movement?
    22a. What did you think of those students who did not participate in the movement at all? (If respondent did not participate in any movement activities: Did you feel any pressure because you did not take part in the movement?)

23. Before the movement began, there were some voluntary student organizations such as the Democratic Salon and the Olympic Institute in Beijing University. Were these kinds of organizations common in your university?

24. Did you ever join one of those organizations?

25. In 1988 and 1989, a "conference fever" emerged at Beijing universities. Were these political conferences really very popular in your university?

26. How often did you go to these conferences?

27. During the movement, how did students communicate with each other?

28. What were the means by which you and your classmates got to know about the movement (probe: Western media, domestic media, direct observation, informal communication [big-character posters, speeches, handbills, student broadcasts, word of mouth])?

29. In your view, who constituted the main population at Tiananmen Square after May 20? The Beijing students or students from other cities? (What led you to this conclusion?)

30. What did you think about the Four Cardinal Principles before the 1989 Movement?

31. Do you have any comments on the current situation in the former Soviet Union?

32. If another large-scale movement broke out tomorrow, would you join a movement again? (Could you elaborate?)

33. What do you think about the movement now?

34. Were your parents worried about you when you participated in the movement?

35. Do you know of *chuanlian* that occurred during the Cultural Revolution? (How did you know that?)

Translation of the Interview Guide for Political Workers

BACKGROUND INFORMATION: AGE _____; UNIVERSITY STUDIED _____;
FROM (YEAR) _____ TO (YEAR) _____; MAJOR _____; HIGHEST
DEGREE HELD _____.

1. Could you briefly describe your daily activities on a typical school day when you were a student. (Questions 2 to 6 may not be followed if an informant covered these questions or opened interesting themes for further probing.)

2. When you were a student, how many hours did you spend on class-related activities on an average day?

3. How did you consider your level of diligence compared with your classmates? (above average, average, or below average)

4. What were your major after-class activities?

5. Did you often read novels and reportage novels? (if yes:)
5a. Had you read reportage novels written by authors such as Liu Binyan, Su Xiaokang, and Jia Lusheng before 1989?

6. At that time, did you have some particular impressions of these reportage novels?

7. Did you watch the TV series *River Elegy* when it was broadcast? (What did you think of the series when you watched it?)

8. Could you describe your job as a class director (or a political instructor)? (Questions 9 to 25 may not be followed if responses to question 8 opened interesting themes for further probing or if some of these questions had been already answered.)

9. Could you describe the structure and function of the ideological-political control system in your university?

10. What were/are the major responsibilities of a class director (or political instructor)?

11. What did/do you think about these tasks?

12. Was/Is your attitude common among class directors and political instructors?

13. When you were assigned the job as a class director (or a political instructor), did you plan to work in this position for long?

14. (If yes, but the respondent has changed jobs:) What made you change your job?

15. (If no:) What made you treat the job as a temporary one?

16. What about other class directors (or political instructors) whom you know? Did they feel the same as you did?

17. In your class, how many students were assigned jobs as class directors or political instructors after graduation? How many are still in your university?

18. In 1988 and 1989, a popular saying was that university students constituted four factions, that is, the mah-jongg faction, the TOEFL faction, the xuan faction, and the yuanyang faction. Did this well describe student life in your university?

19. Did the students in your class feel free to discuss political and other issues with you?

20. Were there any students who ever tried to report the improper behavior of other students to you?

21. (If yes:) What were the major subjects of those reports?

22. If the secret report was about political matters, how did you deal with the informer as well as the reported students?

23. Would students who frequently reported others to you get good jobs after graduation?

24. I have seen many reports on the "commercial fever" among university students during 1988 and 1989. Was this common in your university?

25. What did you and your colleagues think about students who were involved in moneymaking activities?

26. Could you describe your personal experiences and activities during the 1989 Movement? (Again, questions 27 through 32 may not be followed if an informant opened interesting themes for further probing or already answered some of the questions.)

27. When was the first time that you joined a movement activity—for example, a march?

28. How would you know there would be a march?

29. Did you join demonstrations frequently? Do you remember how many times you joined demonstrations?

30. Besides marches, did you participate in other movement activities?

31. Are there any class directors (or political instructors) that you know of who did not participate in any movement activities and showed little concern about the movement?

32. Before the movement began, there were some voluntary student organizations such as the Democratic Salon and the Olympic Institute in Beijing University. Were those organizations common in your university?

33. In 1988 and 1989, a "conference fever" emerged in many universities. Were those political conferences popular at your university?

34. What did you think of the Four Cardinal Principles before the 1989 Movement?

35. Do you have any comments on the current situation in the former Soviet Union?

36. If another large-scale movement broke out tomorrow, would you participate in a movement again? (Could you elaborate?)

37. What do you think about the movement now?

38. Do you know of *chuanlian* that occurred during the Cultural Revolution? (How did you know that?)

39. How many students were in your undergraduate class? How many of them have been abroad?

References

Adams, Julia. 1996. "Principals and Agents, Colonialists and Company Men: The Decay of Colonial Control in the Dutch East Indies." *American Sociological Review* 61:12–28.

Adams, Walter, ed. 1968. *The Brain Drain.* New York: Macmillan Company.

Agarwal, Vinod B., and Donald R. Winkler. 1985. "Foreign Demand for United States Higher Education: A Study of Developing Countries in the Eastern Hemisphere." *Economic Development and Cultural Change* 33:623–44.

Alexander, Jeffrey C. 1988. *Action and its Environments.* New York: Columbia University Press.

Alexander, Jeffrey C., Bernhard Giesen, Richard Munch, and Neil J. Smelser, eds. 1987. *The Micro-Macro Link.* Berkeley: University of California Press.

Alford, Robert R., and Roger Friedland. 1985. *Powers of Theory: Capitalism, the State, and Democracy.* Cambridge: Cambridge University Press.

Altbach, Philip G. 1968a. "Student Politics and Higher Education in India." In *Turmoil and Transition: Higher Education and Student Politics in India,* edited by Philip G. Altbach, 17–73. New York: Basic Books.

———. 1968b. *Student Politics in Bombay.* Bombay: Asia Publishing House.

———. 1974. "Student Politics: Historical Perspective and the Changing Scene." In *The Higher Learning in India,* edited by Amrik Singh and Philip G. Altbach, 139–66. Delhi: Vikas Publishing House.

———. 1991. "Impact and Adjustment: Foreign Students in Comparative Perspective." *Higher Education* 21:305–23.

———, ed. 1981. *Student Politics: Perspectives for the Eighties.* Metuchen, N.J.: Scarecrow Press.

———, ed. 1989. *Student Political Activism: An International Reference Handbook.* New York: Greenwood Press.

Altbach, Philip G., and Wang Jing. 1989. *Foreign Students and International Study: Bibliography and Analysis, 1984–1989.* Washington, D.C.: University Press of America.

Aminzade, Ronald. 1993. *Ballots and Barricades: Class Formation and Republican Politics in France, 1830–1871.* Princeton, N.J.: Princeton University Press.

Amsden, Alice. 1989. *Asia's Next Giant: South Korea and Late Industrialization.* New York: Oxford University Press.

Anderson, Benedict R. 1983. *Imagined Communities: Reflections on the Origin and Spread of Nationalism.* London: Verso.

Anderson, Lisa. 1986. *The State and Social Transformation in Tunisia and Libya, 1830–1890.* Princeton, N.J.: Princeton University Press.

Arendt, Hannah. 1951. *Totalitarianism.* New York: Harcourt, Brace & World.

Arjomand, Said Amir. 1988. *The Turban for the Crown: The Islamic Revolution in Iran.* New York: Oxford University Press.

Axelrod, Robert M. 1984. *The Evolution of Cooperation.* New York: Basic Books.

Ba Jin. 1986. "Wenge bowuguan" (On the Cultural Revolution museum). *Xinmin wanbao,* August 26, 1986.

Bai Nanfeng. 1987. "Young People's Attitudes: Will They Welcome Reforms?" In *Reform in China: Challenges and Choices,* edited by Bruce L. Reynolds, 161–87. New York: Sharpe.

Bajiu zhongguo minyun ziliaoce. 1991. Hong Kong Chinese University Student Union.

Baker, Keith Michael. 1990. *Inventing the French Revolution: Essays on French Political Culture in the Eighteenth Century.* Cambridge: Cambridge University Press.

Baldassare, Mark. 1975. "The Effects of Density on Social Behavior and Attitudes." *American Behavioral Science* 18:15–25.

———. 1977. "Residential Density, Household Crowding, and Social Networks." In *Networks and Places,* edited by Claude S. Fischer, 101–15. New York: Free Press.

Baldwin, John W., and Richard A. Goldthwaite. 1972. Universities in Politics: Case Studies from the Late Middle Ages and Early Modern Period. Baltimore: Johns Hopkins University Press.

Ball-Rokeach, Sandra J., and Melvin L. DeFleur. 1976. "A Dependency Model of Mass- Media Effects." *Communication Research* 3:3–20.

———. 1982. *Theories of Mass Communication.* 4th ed. New York: Longman.

Barbalet, J. M. 1988. *Citizenship: Rights, Struggle and Class Inequality.* Minneapolis: University of Minnesota Press.

Barker, Roger G. 1968. *Ecological Psychology.* Stanford, Calif.: Stanford University Press.

Barnett, A. Doak, and Ralph N. Clough, eds. 1986. *Modernizing China: Post-Mao Reform and Development.* Boulder, Colo.: Westview Press.

Barrow, Clyde W. 1993. *Critical Theories of the State: Marxist, Neo-Marxist, Post-Marxist.* Madison: University of Wisconsin Press.

Bashiriyeh, Hossein 1984. *The State and Revolution in Iran, 1962–1982.* New York: St. Martin's Press.

Bastid, Marianne. 1988. *Educational Reform in Early Twentieth-Century China.* Translated by Paul J. Bailey. Ann Arbor: Center for Chinese Studies, University of Michigan.

Bates, Robert H. 1981. *Markets and States in Tropical Africa.* Berkeley: University of California Press.

Baum, Richard. 1993. "The Road to Tiananmen: Chinese Politics in the 1980s." In *The Politics of China: 1949–1989*, edited by Roderick MacFarquhar, 340–471. Cambridge: Cambridge University Press.

———. 1994. *Burying Mao: Chinese Politics in the Age of Deng Xiaoping.* Princeton, N.J.: Princeton University Press.

Bayat, Asef. 1997. *Street Politics: Poor People's Movements in Iran.* New York: Columbia University Press.

Beckham, Barry. 1973. "Some Temporal and Spatial Aspects of Interurban Industrial Differentiation." *Social Forces* 51:462–70

Beijing jiusanluntan. 1989. "Beijing jiusan sheyuan wenjuan diaocha jieguo xuanzai" (Some results of a survey in the jiusan xueshe Beijing branch). No. 1:29–33.

Bendix, Reinhard. 1962. *Max Weber: An Intellectual Portrait.* Garden City: Anchor Books, Doubleday and Company.

———. 1968. *State and Society: A Reader in Comparative Political Sociology.* Boston: Little Brown.

Benford, Robert. D. 1993. "Frame Disputes within the Disarmament Movement." *Social Forces* 71:677–701.

———. 1997. "An Insider's Critique of the Social Movement Framing Perspective." *Sociological Inquiry* 67:409–30.

Berk, Richard A. 1974. "A Gaming Approach to Crowd Behavior." *American Sociological Review* 39:355–73.

Berlin, Michael J. 1993. "The Performance of the Chinese Media During the Beijing Spring." In *Chinese Democracy and the Crisis of 1989*, edited by Roger V. Des Forges, Luo Ning, and Wu Yen-bo, 263–75. Albany: State University of New York Press.

Bernstein, Thomas. 1977. *Up to the Mountains and Down to the Villages: The Transfer of Youth from Urban to Rural China.* New Haven: Yale University Press.

Bezucha, Robert J. 1974. *The Lyon Uprising of 1834: Social and Political Conflict in the Early July Monarchy.* Cambridge, Mass.: Harvard University Press.

Black, George, and Robin Munro. 1993. *Black Hands of Beijing: Lives of Defiance in China's Democracy Movement.* New York: John Wiley and Sons.

Blau, Peter M. 1963. "Critical Remarks on Weber's Theory of Authority." *American Political Science Review* 57:305–16.

Blelloch, David Habershon. 1969. *State and Society in a Developing World.* London: C. A. Watts.

Blumer, Herbert. 1946. "Elementary Collective Behavior." In *New Outline of the Principles of Sociology*, edited by Alfred McClung Lee, 170–78. New York: Barnes and Noble.

Boudon, Raymond. 1987. "The Individualistic Tradition in Sociology." In *The Micro-Macro Link*, edited by Jeffrey C. Alexander, Bernhard Giesen, Richard Munch, and Neil J. Smelser, 45–70. Berkeley: University of California Press.

Brake, Wayne te. 1998. *Shaping History: Ordinary People in European Politics, 1500–1700.* Berkeley: University of California Press.

Braungart, Richard G., and Margaret M. Braungart. 1992. "From Protest to Terrorism: The Case of SDS and the Weathermen." *International Social Movement Research* 4:45–78.

Bright, Charles, and Susan Harding, eds. 1984. *Statemaking and Social Movements: Essays in History and Theory.* Ann Arbor: University of Michigan Press.

Brinton, Mary C., and Victor Nee, eds. 1998. *The New Institutionalism in Sociology.* New York: Russell Sage Foundation.

Brook, Timothy. 1992. *Quelling the People.* New York: Oxford University Press.

Burgess, Earnest W. 1925. "The Growth of the City: An Introduction to a Research Project." In *The City,* edited by Robert E. Park, Earnest W. Burgess, and Roderick D. McKenzie, 47–62. Chicago: University of Chicago Press.

Burns, John P. 1989. "China's Governance: Turbulent Environment." *China Quarterly,* no. 119:481–518.

Burt, Ronald. 1992. *Structural Holes: The Social Structure of Competition.* Cambridge, Mass.: Harvard University Press.

Byrd, William A. 1992. *Chinese Industrial Firms under Reform.* A World Bank Publication. London: Oxford University Press.

Byrd, William A., and Qingsong Lin. 1990. *China's Rural Industry: Structure, Development, and Reform.* A World Bank Publication. London: Oxford University Press.

Calhoun, Craig J. 1983. "The Radicalism of Tradition: Community Strength or Venerable Disguise and Borrowed Language?" *American Journal of Sociology* 88:886–914.

———. 1991. "The Problem of Identity in Collective Action." In *Macro-Micro-Linkages in Sociology,* edited by Joan Huber, 51–75. Newbury Park, Calif.: Sage.

———. 1994. *Neither Gods nor Emperors: Students and the Struggle for Democracy in China.* Berkeley: University of California Press.

Cang Lixin, ed. 1990. *Dui bashi niandai shoudu daxuesheng zongxiang yanjiu* (A longitudinal study on university students in Beijing during the 1980s), (Internal circulation only). Beijing: Beijing Shifan Xueyuan Chubanshe.

Cao Fang. 1989. "Shilun dangdai qingnian de weiji yishi" (Analyses on the crisis consciousness of current younger generation). *Qingnian yanjiu,* no. 6:9–12.

Cao Rida. 1989. "Ershijiufen zhenduanshu: dangdai daxuesheng xintai yipie" (Twenty-nine diagnoses: a glance at the psychology of contemporary university students). *Shehui,* no. 7:29–31.

Case, F. Duncan. 1981. "Dormitory Architecture Influences." *Environment and Behavior* 13:23–41.

Casper, Gretchen, and Michelle M. Taylor. 1996. *Negotiating Democracy: Transitions from Authoritarian Rule.* Pittsburgh, Penn.: University of Pittsburgh Press.

Chai Xiaowu. 1988. "Yanjiusheng jiaoyu chuxianle weiji" (The crisis of the graduate educational system). *Shehui,* no. 12:17–19.

Chamberlain, Heath B. 1993. "On the Search for Civil Society in China." *Modern China* 19:199–215.

Chan, Anita, and Jonathan Unger. 1990. "China after Tiananmen." *The Nation,* January 22.

Chang Hao. 1971. *Liang Ch'i-ch'ao and Intellectual Transition in China, 1890–1907.* Cambridge, Mass.: Harvard University Press.

———. 1987. *Chinese Intellectuals in Crisis: Search for Order and Meaning (1890–1911).* Berkeley: University of California Press.

Chang Jung. 1991. *Wild Swans: Three Daughters of China.* New York: Simon & Schuster.

Chang Won Ho. 1989. *Mass Media in China.* Ames: Iowa State University Press.

Cheek, Timothy. 1997. *Propaganda and Culture in Mao's China: Deng Tuo and the Intelligentsia.* Oxford: Oxford University Press.

Chehabi, H. E., and Alfred Stepan, eds. 1995. *Politics, Society, and Democracy.* Boulder, Colo.: Westview Press.

Chen Guishui. 1989. "Xiang shoudu zhongyao jingwei mubiao kaijin" (Moving toward the important guardian targets in the capital). In *Jieyan yiri,* 1:11–13. Beijing: Jiefangjun Wenyi Chubanshe.

Chen Jie. 1999. "Meiguo meiti jiu yiding gongzheng ma?" (Is the American media really impartial?) *People's Daily Online,* June 5.

Chen Juqi and Yang Shuixiao. 1989. "Jingren de liushi" (The astonishing run–off). *Liaowang,* no. 5:18–19.

Chen Qiwu. 1982. "Guanyu yaoerjiu yundong de yixie qingkuang" (On the December 9th Movement). In *Yaoerjiu yundong huiyilu* (A memoir of the December 9th Movement), 60–171. Beijing: Renmin Chubanshe.

Chen Xiaoya. 1996. *The Democratic Movement on Tian-an-men Square, 1989.* Taibei: Fengyunshidai Publishing Company.

Chen Xitong. 1989. "Guanyu zhizhi dongluan he pingxi fangeming baoluan de qingkuang baogao" (A report on the suppression of turmoil and antirevolutionary rebellion). In *Bajiu Zhongguo Minyun Jishi* (Daily reports on the movement for democracy in China), edited by Wu Mouren et al., 959–87. N.p.

Chen Yizi. 1990. *Zhongguo, shinian gaige yu bajiu minyun: Beijing liusi tusha de beihou* (China's ten years of reform and 1989 democratic movement: Behind the June 4 massacre). Taibei: Lianjing Chuban Gongsi.

Chen Yun. 1990. "Speech to CCP Central Advisory Commission Standing Committee." In *Beijing Spring, 1989: Confrontation and Conflict,* edited by Michel Oksenberg, Lawrence R. Sullivan, and Marc Lambert, 331–33. Armonk, N.Y.: Sharpe.

Cheng Chu-yuan. 1990. *Behind the Tiananmen Massacre.* Boulder, Colo.: Westview Press.

Cheng Zhen. 1990. "Gongyun yu Xueyun, Minyun" (On the worker movement, student movement and democracy dovement). In *Gongren Qilaile* (Workers are standing up). Hong Kong: Hong Kong Workers' Union Education Publishing House.

Cherrington, Ruth. 1991. *China's Students: The Struggle for Democracy.* London: Routledge.

Chesneaux, Jean. 1972. *Popular Movements and Secret Societies in China, 1840–1950.* Stanford, Calif.: Stanford University Press.

China News Digest. 1994. "Bajiu xueyun de riri yeye—yiwei qinghua xuezi de jingli, jianwen" (The days and nights of the 1989 student movement—The experiences of a student of Qinghua University). Supplementary, no. 39 (vols. 1–4).

China International Examinations Coordination Bureau. 1990. *TOEFL, TSE, GRE, MAT, MELAB: Kaosheng xuzhi* (Examiners' handbook). (Internal circulation only).

China Statistical Yearbook. 1990. New York: Praeger.

Chirot, Daniel, ed. 1991. "What Happened in Eastern Europe in 1989?" In *The Crisis of Leninism and the Decline of the Left: The Revolutions of 1989,* 3–32. Seattle: University of Washington Press.

Chow Tse-tsung. 1967. *The May Fourth Movement: Intellectual Revolution in Modern China.* Stanford, Calif.: Stanford University Press.

Cobban, Alan B. 1975. *The Medieval Universities: Their Development and Organization.* London: Methuen.

Collins, Randall. 1979. *The Credential Society: An Historical Sociology of Education and Stratification.* New York: Academic.

———. 1981. "On the Microfoundations of Macrosociology." *American Journal of Sociology* 86:984–1014.

———. 1990. "Stratification, Emotional Energy, and the Transient Emotions." In *Research Agendas in the Sociology of Emotions,* edited by Theodore D. Kemper, 27–57. Albany, N.Y.: SUNY Press.

———. 1995. "Prediction in Macrosociology: The Case of the Soviet Collapse." *American Journal of Sociology* 100:1552–93.

Connell, Ian. 1980. "Television News and the Social Contract." In *Culture, Media, Language,* edited by Stuart Hall, Dorothy Hobson, Andrew Lowe, and Paul Willis, 139–56. London: Hutchinson.

Converse, Philip. 1964. "The Nature of Belief Systems in Mass Publics." In *Ideology and Discontent,* edited by David Ernest Apter, 206–61. New York: Free Press.

Corney, Frederick C. 1988. "Rethinking a Great Event: The October Revolution as Memory Project." *Social Science History* 22:389–414.

Costain, Anne N., and Andrew S. McFarland, eds. 1998. *Social Movements and American Political Institutions.* Lanham, Md.: Rowman and Littlefield.

Cranfield, G. A. 1978. *The Press and Society from Caxton to Northcliffe.* London: Longman.

Creel, Herrlee Glessner. 1953. *Chinese Thought from Confucius to Mao Tse-tung.* Chicago: University of Chicago Press.

Curran, James. 1978. "Advertising and the Press." In *The British Press: A Manifesto,* edited by James Curran, 252–55. London: Macmillan.

——— 1990. "The New Revisionism in Mass Communication Research: A Reappraisal." *European Journal of Communication* 5:135–64.

Curran, James, and Jean Seaton. 1985. *Power Without Responsibility: The Press and Broadcasting in Britain.* 2d ed. London: Methuen.

Curtis, Russell, and Louis A. Zurcher. 1973. "Stable Resources of Protest Movements: The Multiorganizational Field." *Social Forces* 52:53–61.

Czada, Roland, Adrienne Heritier, and Hans Keman, eds. 1996. *Institutions and Political Choice: On the Limits of Rationality.* Amsterdam: VU University Press.

Dai Qing. 1993. "Yetan chunxia zhijiao" (My experiences in spring 1989). *China News Digest,* no. 12:2–24.

Dan Ding. 1989. "Xidan lukou: junhuo! junhuo!" (Rescuing arms and ammunition at Xidan intersection). In *Jieyan yiri,* 1:120–46. Beijing: Jiefangjun Wenyi Chubanshe.

Das, Man S. 1972. *Brain Drain Controversy and International Students.* Lucknow: Lucknow Publishing House.

Davis, Deborah, and Ezra F. Vogel, eds. 1990. *Chinese Society on the Eve of Tiananmen.* Cambridge, Mass.: Harvard University Press.

Delgado, Gary. 1986. *Organizing the Movement: The Roots and Growth of Acorn.* Philadelphia: Temple University Press.

Deng Fang. 1997. "Information Gaps and Unintended Outcomes of Social Movements: The 1989 Chinese Student Movement." *American Journal of Sociology* 102:1085–112.

Deng Xian. 1992. "Zhongguo zhiqingmeng" (The dream of the Chinese sent-down youth). *Dangdai,* no. 5:4–117.

Deng Xiaoping. 1983. *Deng xiaoping wenxuan* (The selected works of Deng Xiaoping), vol. 2. Beijing: Renmin Chubanshe.

Deyo, Frederic C., ed. 1987. *The Political Economy of the New Asian Industrialism.* Ithaca, N.Y.: Cornell University Press.

Di Palma, Giuseppe. 1991. "Legitimation from the Top to Civil Society." *World Politics* 44:49–80.

Diamond, Larry, Juan J. Linz, and Seymour Martin Lipset, eds. 1988. *Democracy in Developing Countries: Latin America.* Boulder, Colo.: Lynne Rienner Publishers.

Diamond, Larry, and Marc F. Plattner, eds. 1996. *The Global Resurgence of Democracy.* 2d edition. Baltimore: Johns Hopkins University Press.

Diani, Mario. 1996. "Linking Mobilization Frames and Political Opportunities: Insights from Regional Populism in Italy." *American Sociological Review* 61:1053–69.

DiBona, Joseph. 1968. "Introduction: Students, Politics, and Universities in India." In *Turmoil and Transition: Higher Education and Student Politics in India,* edited by Philip G. Altbach, 131–71. New York: Basic Books.

Dickson, Sandra H. 1992. "Press and U.S. Policy Toward Nicaragua, 1983–1987: A Study of the New York Times and Washington Post." *Journalism and Mass Communication* 69:562–71.

DiMaggio, Paul J. 1988. "Interest and Agency in Institutional Theory." In *Institutional Patterns and Organizations: Culture and Environment,* edited by Lynne G. Zucker, 3–21. Cambridge, Mass.: Ballinger.

Ding Xueliang. 1994. *The Decline of Communism in China: Legitimacy Crisis, 1977–1989.* Cambridge: Cambridge University Press.

Ding Zilin. 1994. *Liusi shounanzhe mingce* (The June 4 death list). Hong Kong: The Nineties Monthly.

Dittmer, Lowell. 1989. "The Tiananmen Massacre." *Problems of Communism* 38:2–15.

———. 1990a. "Patterns of Elite Strife and Succession in Chinese Politics." *China Quarterly*, no. 123:405–30.

———. 1990b. "China in 1989: The Crisis of Incomplete Reform." *Asian Survey* 30:25–41.

Dogan, Mattei. 1995. "Testing the Concepts of Legitimacy and Trust." In *Politics, Society, and Democracy*, edited by H. E. Chehabi, and Alfred Stepan, 57–71. Boulder, Colo.: Westview Press.

Dong Lei. 1990. "Zhongguo jiaoyu beiwanglu" (A memorandum on Chinese education). *Shuguang*, no. 1:125–32.

Dong Yuyu and Shi Binhai, eds. 1998. *Zhengzhi zhongguo* (Political China). Beijing: Jinri Zhongguo Chubanshe.

Douglas, William A. 1971. "Korean Students and Politics." In *Student Activism: Town and Gown in Historical Perspective*, edited by Alexander DeConde, 221–24. New York: Charles Scribner's Sons.

Du Ruiqing. 1992. *Chinese Higher Education: A Decade of Reform and Development (1978–1988)*. New York: St. Martin's Press.

Duncan, Otis Dudley, and Beverly Duncan. 1955. "Residential Distribution and Occupational Stratification." *American Journal of Sociology* 60:493–503.

Durkheim, Emile. 1933. *The Division of Labor in Society.* New York: Free Press.

Eastman, Lloyd E. 1988. *Family, Fields, and Ancestors.* New York: Oxford University Press.

Eckstein, Harry, and Ted R. Gurr. 1975. *Patterns of Authority: A Structural Basis for Political Inquiry.* New York: John Wiley & Sons.

Educational Statistics Yearbook of China. 1989. Beijing: Renmin Chubanshe.

Eisinger, Peter K. 1973. "The Conditions of Protest Behavior in American Cities." *American Political Science Review* 67:11–28.

Emirbayer, Mustafa. 1997. "Manifesto for a Relational Sociology." *American Journal of Sociology* 103:281–317.

Entelis, John P., and Phillip C. Naylor, eds. 1992. *State and Society in Algeria.* Boulder, Colo.: Westview Press.

Entman, Robert M. 1991. "Framing U.S. Coverage of International News: Contrasts in Narratives of the KAL and Iran Air Incidents." *Journal of Communication* 41:6–27.

Epstein, Edward Jay. 1973. *News from Nowhere: Television and the News.* New York: Random House.

Esherick, Joseph W. 1987. *The Origins of the Boxer Uprising.* Berkeley: University of California Press.

Esherick, Joseph W., and Jeffrey N. Wasserstrom. 1990. "Acting Out Democracy: Political Theatre in Modern China." *Journal of Asian Studies* 49:835–65.

Etzioni, Amitai. 1964. *Modern Organizations.* Englewood Cliffs, N.J.: Prentice Hall.

Evans, John H. 1997. "Multi-Organizational Fields and Social Movement Organization Frame Content: The Religious Pro-Choice Movement." *Sociological Inquiry* 67:451–69.

Evans, Peter. 1979. *Dependent Development: The Alliance of Multinational, State, and Local Capital in Brazil.* Princeton, N.J.: Princeton University Press.

———. 1995. *Embedded Autonomy: States and Industrial Transformation.* Princeton, N.J.: Princeton University Press.

Evans, Sara M., and Harry C. Boyte. 1992. *Free Space: The Sources of Democratic Change in America.* Chicago: University of Chicago Press.

Fairbank, John K., and Edwin O. Reischauer. 1978. *China: Tradition and Transformation.* Boston, Mass.: Houghton Mifflin Press.

Faison, Seth. 1990. "The Changing Role of the Chinese Media." In *The Chinese People's Movement: Perspectives on Spring 1989,* edited by Tony Saich, 145–63. Armonk, N.Y.: Sharpe.

Fang Linian. 1989. "Women yao haohao huozhe huilai zuozheng" (We must stay alive to testify). In *Lishi de chuangshang,* vol. 1, edited by Han Shanbi, 241–51. Hong Kong: Dongxi Wenhua Shiye Chuban Gongsi.

Fang Lizhi. 1990. *Bring Down the Great Wall: Writings on Science, Culture, and Democracy in China.* New York: Knopf.

Fang Ming, Chen Sha, and Yu Yichi. 1988. "Congshure sanrentan" (Three people's discussion of the book series fever). *Xinhua wenzhai,* no. 10:202–7.

Farhi, Farideh. 1990. *States and Urban-Based Revolutions: Iran and Nicaragua.* Urbana, Ill.: University of Illinois Press.

Feagin, Joe R., and Harlan Hahn. 1973. *Ghetto Revolts: The Politics of Violence in American Cities.* New York: Macmillan Company.

Fei Hsiao-tung. 1939. *Peasant Life in China: A Field Study of Country Life in the Yangtze Valley.* London: Paul, Trench, Trubner.

———. 1986. "Wenzhouxing" (A visit to Wenzhou). *Xinhua wenzhai,* no. 8:55–62.

Fei Hsiao-tung and Chang Chih-I. 1945. *Earthbound China: A Study of Rural Economy in Yunnan.* Chicago: University of Chicago Press.

Fei Xiaotong (Hsiao-tung) et al. 1984. *Shehuixue gailun* (An introduction to sociology). Tianjin: Tianjin Renmin Chubanshe.

Feigon, Lee. 1990. *China Rising: The Meaning of Tiananmen.* Chicago: Ivan R. Dee.

Fernandez, Roberto, and Doug McAdam. 1989. "Multiorganizational Fields and Recruitment to Social Movements." In *Organizing for Change: Social Movement Organizations in Europe and the United States,* edited by Bert Klandermans, 315–43. Greenwich, Conn.: JAI.

Festinger, Leon, Stanley Schachter, and Kurt Back. 1950. *Social Pressures in Informal Groups.* Stanford, Calif.: Stanford University Press.

Fewsmith, Joseph. 1994. *Dilemmas of Reform in China: Political Conflict and Economic Debate.* Armonk, N.Y.: M. E. Sharpe.

Finer, Samuel E. 1997. *The History of Government from the Earliest Times.* Vol. 1. Oxford: Oxford University Press.

Fireman, Bruce, and William A. Gamson. 1979. "Utilitarian Logic in the Resource Mobilization Perspective." In *The Dynamics of Social Movements*, edited by Mayer N. Zald and John D. McCarthy, 8–44. Cambridge, Mass.: Winthrop.

Fischer, Claude S. 1977. *Network and Places: Social Relations in the Urban Setting.* New York: Free Press.

Fishman, Mark. 1980. *Manufacturing the News.* Austin: University of Texas Press.

Fogelson, Robert M. 1971. *Violence as Protest: A Study of Riots and Ghettos.* Garden City: Anchor Books.

Foran, John, ed. 1997. *Theorizing Revolutions.* London: Routledge.

Francis, Corinna-Barbara. 1991. "The Institutional Roots of Student Political Culture: Official Student Politics at Beijing University." In *Chinese Education: Problems, Politics and Prospects*, edited by Irving Epstein, 394–415. New York: Garland.

Franzosi, Roberto. 1987. "The Press as a Source of Socio-Historical Data." *Historical Methods* 20:5–16.

Friedland, Lewis A., and Zhong Mengbai. 1996. "International Television Coverage of Beijing Spring 1989: A Comparative Approach." *Journalism Monographs*, no. 156.

Friedman, Debra, and Doug McAdam. 1992. "Collective Identity and Activism: Networks, Choices, and the Life of a Social Movement." In *Frontiers in Social Movement Theory*, edited by Aldon D. Morris and Carol McClurg Mueller, 156–73. New Haven: Yale University Press.

Friedman, Edward, ed. 1994. *The Politics of Democratization: Generalizing East Asian Experiences.* Boulder, Colo.: Westview Press.

Friedman, Edward, Paul G. Pickowicz, and Mark Selden. 1991. *Chinese Village, Socialist State.* New Haven: Yale University Press.

Friedrich, Carl J., and Zbigniew K. Brzezinski. 1965. *Totalitarian Dictatorship and Autocracy.* Cambridge, Mass.: Harvard University Press.

Fu Peirong. 1992. "Criticism and Originality." *Chinese Sociology and Anthropology* 24, no. 2:54–57.

Furet, Francois. 1981. *Interpreting the French Revolution.* Cambridge: Cambridge University Press.

Gabaccia, Donna R. 1988. *Militants and Migrants: Rural Sicilians Become American Workers.* New Brunswick, N.J.: Rutgers University Press.

Gamson, William A. 1975. *The Strategy of Social Protest.* Homewood, Ill.: The Dorsey Press.

Gamson, William A., Bruce Fireman, and Steven Rytina. 1982. *Encounters with Unjust Authority.* Homewood, Ill.: Dorsey Press.

Gamson, William A., and David S. Meyer. 1996. "Framing Political Opportunity." In *Comparative Perspectives on Social Movements*, edited by Doug McAdam, John D. McCarthy, and Mayer N. Zald, 275–90. New York: Cambridge University Press.

Gamson, William A., and Andre Modigliani. 1989. "Media Discourse and Public

Opinion on Nuclear Power: A Constructionist Approach." *American Journal of Sociology* 95:1–37.

Gamson William A., and Gadi Wolfsfeld. 1993. "Movements and Media as Interacting Systems." In *Citizens, Protest, and Democracy,* edited by Russell Dalton, 114–25. Newbury Park, Calif.: Sage.

Gans, Herbert J. 1979. *Deciding What's News.* New York: Vintage Books.

Garfinkel, Harold. 1967. *Studies in Ethnomethodology.* Englewood Cliffs, N.J.: Prentice Hall.

Gao Gao. 1994. *Hou wengeshi* (The post Cultural Revolution Chinese history), vol. 2. Taibei: Lianjing Chubanshiye Gongsi.

Gao Qinglin and Wang Xiaoguang. 1997. "Yici kongqian de chenggong zhizuo" (An unprecedented successful operation). *Outlook Weekly,* no. 34:4–6.

Gao Xin. 1990. *Beiwei yu huihuang* (The modest and the glorious). Taibei: Lianjing Chuban Gongsi.

———. 1995. "Dangnei kaimingpai zai 'liusi' zhong de ganga juese" (The awkward position of the communist party enlightened faction during "June fourth"). *China Spring,* no. 4:19–22; no. 5:14–21.

Gao Zi. 1990. "Dui dangqian gaoxiao shizi duiwu jianshezhong yixie wenti de sikao" (Reflections on some problems in current college teacher resource construction). *Zhongguo gaodeng jiaoyu,* no. 11:17–19.

Gao Zirong. 1989. "Yipian xinwengao" (A news manuscript). In *Jieyan yiri,* 2:6–9. Beijing: Jiefangjun Wenyi Chubanshe.

Garling, Tommy, and Gary W. Evans. 1991. *Environment, Cognition and Action.* New York: Oxford University Press.

Ge Chengyong and Ren Dayuan. 1992. "Dangdai qingnian shixue gongzuozhe shixue yanjiu zhi wojian" (My view on current researches in history by young historians). *Tansuo yu zhengming,* no. 10:41–45.

Geertz, Clifford 1973. *The Interpretation of Culture: Selected Essays.* New York: Basic Books.

———. 1983. "Blurred Genres: The Refiguration of Social Thought." In *Local Knowledge: Further Essays in Interpretative Anthropology,* 19–35. New York: Basic Books.

Geertz, Hildred. 1991. *State and Society in Bali: Historical, Textual and Anthropological Approaches.* Leiden: Kitlv Press.

Gellner, Ernest. 1988. *State and Society in Soviet Thought.* Oxford: Basil Blackwell.

———. 1994. *Conditions of Liberty: Civil Society and its Rivals.* London: Penguin Books.

Gernet, Jacques. 1987. "Introduction." In *Foundations and Limits of State Power in China,* edited by Stuart R. Schram, xv–xxvii. Hong Kong: The Chinese University Press.

Gershenkron, Alexander. 1952. "Economic Backwardness in Historical Perspective." In *The Progress of Underdeveloped Areas,* edited by Berthold Hoselitz, 3–29. Chicago: Chicago University Press.

Gitlin, Todd. 1980. *The Whole World is Watching: Mass Media in the Making and Unmaking of the New Left.* Berkeley: University of California Press.

———. 1987. *The Sixties: Years of Hope, Days of Rage.* New York: Bantam.

Giugni, Marco G., Doug McAdam, and Charles Tilly, eds. 1998. *From Contention to Democracy.* Lanham, Md.: Rowman & Littlefield.

Gocek, Fatma Muge. 1995. "Whither Historical Sociology: A Review Essay." *Historical Methods.* 28:107–16.

Gold, Hohn R. 1980. *An Introduction to Behavioral Geography.* New York: Oxford University Press.

Gold, Tom. 1986. *State and Society in the Taiwan Miracle.* Armonk, N.Y.: Sharpe.

Goldenberg, Edie N. 1975. *Making the Papers.* Lexington, Mass: Lexington Books.

Goldman, Merle. 1994. *Sowing the Seeds of Democracy.* Cambridge, Mass.: Harvard University Press.

Goldstone, Jack A. 1991. *Revolution and Rebellion in the Early Modern World.* Berkeley: University of California Press.

———. 1998. "Social Movements or Revolution?" In *From Contention to Democracy,* edited by Marco G. Giugni, Doug McAdam, and Charles Tilly, 125–45. Lanham, Md.: Rowman & Littlefield.

Goldstone, Jack. A., and Bert Useem. 1999. "Prison Riots as Microrevolutions: An Extension of State-Centered Theories of Revolution." *American Journal of Sociology* 104:985–1029.

Gollege, Reginald G., and Harry Timmermans. 1988. *Behavioral Modeling in Geography and Planning.* London: Croom Helm.

Gong Liu. 1986. "Yeshuo wenge bowuguan" (My view on the Cultural Revolution museum). *Xinhua wenzhai,* no. 11: 125–26.

Goodwin, C., and M. Nacht. 1986. *Decline and Renewal: Causes and Cures of Decay among Foreign Trained Intellectuals and Professionals in the Third World.* New York: Institute of International Education.

Goodwin, Jeff. 1989. "Colonialism and Revolution in Southeast Asia: A Comparative Analysis." In *Revolution in the World-System,* edited by Terry Boswell, 59–78. New York: Greenwood Press.

———. 1997. "The Libidinal Constitution of a High-risk Social Movement: Affectual Ties and Solidarity in the Huk Rebellion." *American Sociological Review* 62:53–69.

Goodwin, Jeff, and Theda Skocpol. 1989. "Explaining Revolutions in the Contemporary Third World. *Politics and Society* 17:489–509.

Gould, Roger V. 1991. "Multiple Networks and Mobilization in the Paris Commune, 1871." *American Sociological Review* 56:716–29.

———. 1993. "Collective Action and Network Structure." *American Sociological Review* 58:182–96.

———. 1995. *Insurgent Identities: Class, Community, and Protest in Paris From 1848 to the Commune.* Chicago: University of Chicago Press.

Gould, Stephen Jay. 1981. *The Mismeasure of Man.* New York: Norton & Company.

Gramsci, Antonio. 1971. *Selections from the Prison Notebooks.* Edited and translated by Quintin Hoare and Geoffrey Nowell Smith. New York: International Publishers.

Granovetter, Mark S. 1973. "The Strength of Weak Ties." *American Journal of Sociology* 78:1360–80.

———. 1985. "Economic Action and Social Structure: The Problem of Embeddedness." *American Journal of Sociology* 91:481–510.

Greenberg, Donald W. 1985. "Staging Media Events to Achieve Legitimacy: A Case Study of Britain's Friends of the Earth." *Political Communication and Persuasion* 2:347–62.

Griffin, Michael, and Lee Jongsoo. 1995. "Picturing the Gulf War: Constructing an Image of War in Time, Newsweek, and U.S. News and World Report." *Journalism and Mass Communication Quarterly* 72:813–25.

Guangming Daily. 1987. "Beijing diqu gaoxiao jinnian 600 duoming biyesheng bei tuihui de shishi shuoming gaojiao gaige mianlin tiaozhan, biyesheng dao jiceng qu shizaibixing" (The fact that over 600 university graduates were returned by employers challenges our educational system and tells us that assigning university graduates to the basic work-units is a must). Oct. 30.

———. 1989. "Tongji Wang Dan deng 21 ming 'gaozilian' toutou he gugan fenzi" (Order the arrest of Wang Dan and other twenty leaders and core members of the autonomous university student association). June 14.

Guo Yingjie. 1998. "Patriotic Villains and Patriotic Heroes: Chinese Literary Nationalism in the 1990s." In *Nationalism and Ethnoregional Identities in China*, edited by William Safran, 163–88. London: Frank Cass.

Gurr, Ted R. 1986. "Persisting Patterns of Repression and Rebellion: Foundations for a General Theory of Political Coercion." In *Persistent Patterns and Emergent Structures in a Waning Century*, edited by Margaret P. Karns, 149–68. New York: Praeger.

Habermas, Jürgen. 1975. *Legitimation Crisis.* Boston: Beacon Press.

Haggard, Stephen. 1990. *Pathways from the Periphery: The Politics of Growth in the Newly Industrializing Countries.* Ithaca, N.Y.: Cornell University Press.

Halebsky, Sandor. 1976. *Mass Society and Political Conflict: Toward a Reconstruction of Theory.* Cambridge: Cambridge University Press.

Hall, John A. 1985a. *Powers and Liberties.* London: Penguin Books.

———. 1985b. "The Intellectuals as a New Class: Reflections on Britain." *Culture, Education and Society* 39, no. 3:206–20.

———. 1995. *Civil Society: Theory, History, Comparison.* Cambridge: Polity Press.

Hall, Stuart, Chas Critcher, Tony Jefferson, and Brian Robert. 1978. *Policing the Crisis.* London: Macmillan.

Han Xuchang. 1986. *Yaoerjiu yundong shiyao* (A history of the December 9th Movement). Beijing: The College of the CCP Central Committee.

Han Minzhu and Hua Sheng. 1990. *Cries for Democracy: Writings and Speeches from the 1989 Chinese Democracy Movement.* Princeton, N.J.: Princeton University Press.

Hanagan, Michael P., Leslie Page Moch, and Wayne te Brake. 1998. *Challenging Authority: The Historical Study of Contentious Politics.* Minneapolis: University of Minnesota Press.

Hank, Johnston. 1995. "A Methodology for Frame Analysis: From Discourse to Cognitive Schemata." In *Social Movements and Culture,* edited by Hank Johnston and Bert Klandermans, 217–46. Minneapolis: University of Minnesota Press.

Harding, Harry. 1987. *China's Second Revolution: Reform after Mao.* Washington, D.C.: Brookings Institution.

Haskins, Charles H. 1957. *The Rise of Universities.* Ithaca, N.Y.: Cornell University Press.

———. 1971. "The Earliest Universities." In *Student Activism: Town and Gown in Historical Perspective,* edited by Alexander DeConde, 19–32. New York: Charles Scribner's Sons.

Hastorf, Albert, and Hadley Cantril. 1954. "They Saw a Game: A Case Study." *Journal of Abnormal and Social Psychology* 49:129–34.

Hayhoe, Ruth. 1988. "China's Intellectuals in the World Community." *Higher Education* 17:121–38.

———. 1989. *China's Universities and the Open Door.* Armonk, N.Y.: Sharpe.

———. 1990. "China's Returned Scholars and the Democracy Movement." *China Quarterly,* no. 122:293–302.

———. 1992. *Education and Modernization: The Chinese Experience.* Oxford: Pergamon Press.

———, ed. 1987. *Chinese Educators on Chinese Education.* Canadian and International Education.

Hayhoe, Ruth, and Marianne Bastid, eds. 1987. *China's Education and the Industrialized World: Studies in Cultural Transfer.* Armonk, N.Y.: Sharpe.

He Ping. 1993. "Xin geren suodeshuifa shishi yihou" (After the implementation of the new law on individual income taxes). *People's Daily* (overseas edition), Dec. 25.

He Pin and Gao Xin. 1993. *Zhonggong xinquangui* (The new communist party elites in China). Hong Kong: Lizhi Chubanshe.

He Sha. 1992. "Qingnian jiaoshi: Jiushiniandai gaoxiao sixiang zhengzhi jiaoyu de guanjian yu nandian" (Young teachers: the key and the problem of university political education in the 1990s). *Qingnianchao,* no. 2:18–20.

He Xilai. 1989. "Lun dangdai baogao wenxue dachao zhongde lixing jingshen" (On the rationalistic spirit of the current reportage novel wave). *Guangming Daily,* June 20.

He Xingan. 1988. "Shenchen de yousi—Su Xiaokang baogao wenxue manyi" (Thoughtful concerns—A general discussion on Su Xiaokang's reportage novels). *People's Daily,* March 18.

He Zhizhou, ed. 1989. "Tucheng sishiba xiaoshi shilu." In *Xuewo zhonghua,* 205–11. Hong Kong: Xinyidai Wenhua Xiehui.

He Zhou and Zhu Jianhua. 1994. "The Voice of America and China." *Journalism Monographs,* no. 143.

Heirich, Max. 1971. *The Spiral of Conflict: Berkeley 1964.* New York: Columbia University Press.

Henze, Jurgen. 1992. "The Formal Education System and Modernization: An Analysis of Developments Since 1978." In *Education and Modernization: The Chinese Experience,* edited by Ruth Hayhoe, 103–39. Oxford: Pergamon Press.

Herman, Edward S., and Noam Chomsky. 1988. *Manufacturing Consent: The Political Economy of the Mass Media.* New York: Pantheon Books.

Hinton, Carma, and Richard Gordon. 1997. *The Gate of Heavenly Peace.* Hong Kong: Mirror Books.

Hirschman, Albert. 1970. *Exit, Voice, and Loyalty.* Cambridge, Mass.: Harvard University Press.

Ho, Samuel P. S., and Ralph W. Huenemann. 1984. *China's Open Door Policy: The Quest for Foreign Technology and Capital.* Vancouver: University of British Columbia Press.

Homans, George C. 1964. "Bringing Men Back In." *American Sociological Review* 29:809–18.

Hong Junhao and Marlene Cuthbert. 1991. "Media Reform in China Since 1978: Background Factors, Problems, and Future Trends." *Gazette* 47:141–58.

Horowitz, Helen Lefkowitz. 1987. *Campus Life: Undergraduate Cultures from the End of the Eighteen Century to the Present.* New York: Alfred A. Knopf.

Howland, H. 1967. *Brain Drain: How it Affects the Philippines.* Washington, D.C.: Foreign Service Institute, U.S. Department of State.

Hou Dejian. 1989. "Liuyue siri cheli Tiananmen guangchang shi wode qinshen jingguo" (My personal experiences during the June 4 Tiananmen Square evacuation). *Hong Kong Economic Daily,* August 24.

Hsiao Ching-Chang and Yang Mei-Rong. 1990. "Don't Force Us to Lie: The Case of the World Economic Herald." In *Voice of China,* edited by Lee Chin-Chuan, 111–21. New York: Guilford Press.

Hsieh Pao Chao. 1978. *The Government of China (1644–1911).* New York: Octagon Books.

Hua Guofeng. 1978. "To Build a Modern, Powerful Socialist Country." In *The People's Republic of China: A Documentary History of Revolutionary Change,* edited by Mark Selden and Patti Eggleston, 695–701. New York: Monthly Review Press.

Hua Ying and Cao Shuzhen. 1988. "Over Three Hundred People Apply for Jobs with the Hilton Hotel." *Chinese Economic Studies* 21:26–28.

Huan Guocang. 1989. "The Roots of the Political Crisis." *World Policy Journal* 6: 609–20.

Huan Xiaoping. 1989. "Huxue lixianji" (An adventure in tiger's den). In *Jieyan yiri,* 2:42–47. Beijing: Jiefangjun Wenyi Chubanshe.

Huang Jie and Mou Xiaoguang. 1990. "Zhongguo qingnian sichao beiwanglu" (A memorandum on the ideological trends among Chinese youth). *Qingnian yanjiu,* no. 9:20–27.

Huang, Philip C. 1972. *Liang Ch'i-ch'ao and Modern Chinese Liberalism.* Seattle: University of Washington Press.

———. 1993. "Public Sphere/Civil Society in China?" *Modern China* 19:216–40.

Huang, Ray. 1981. *1587: A Year of No Significance.* New Haven: Yale University Press.

Huigu yu fansi (Retrospection and introspection). 1993. Germany: Rhine Forum.

Hunt, Lynn. 1984. *Politics, Culture and Class in the French Revolution.* Berkeley: University of California Press.

Huntington, Samuel P. 1968. *Political Order in Changing Societies.* New Haven: Yale University Press.

———. 1991. *The Third Wave: Democratization in the Late Twentieth Century.* Norman: University of Oklahoma Press.

Israel, John. 1966. *Student Nationalism in China: 1927–1937.* Stanford, Calif.: Stanford University Press.

Israel, John, and Donald W. Klein. 1976. *Rebels and Bureaucrats: China's December 9ers.* Berkeley: University of California Press.

Jabri, Vivienne. 1996. *Discourses on Violence.* Manchester: Manchester University Press.

Janos, Andrew C. 1986. *Politics and Paradigms: Changing Theories of Change in Social Science.* Stanford, Calif.: Stanford University Press.

Jasper, James M. 1997. *The Art of Moral Protest: Culture, Biography and Creativity in Social Movements.* Chicago: University of Chicago Press.

———. 1998. "The Emotions of Protest: Affective and Reactive Emotions in Social Movements." *Sociological Forum* 13:397–424.

Jenkins, J. Craig, and Bert Klandermans, eds. 1995. *The Politics of Social Protest.* Minneapolis: University of Minnesota Press.

Ji Xinguo. 1989. "Qingchangqian de tanpan" (The negotiation before the Tiananmen Square evacuation). In *Jieyan yiri*, 1:263–68. Beijing: Jiefangjun Wenyi Chubanshe.

Jia Lusheng. 1988a. "Gaibang piaoliuji" (A band of wandering beggars). In *Shensheng yousi—dangdai zhongguo xinchao qishilu* (Holy concerns—Inspirations from new thinking in contemporary China), vol. 2, edited by Chao Si, 97–148. Beijing: Zhongyang Minzuxueyuan Chubanshe.

———. 1988b. "Dier qudao (Jiexuan)." (The second channel [abbreviated]). *People's Daily*, overseas edition, Nov. 14.

Jin Dalu. 1993. "Tan chuguochao—dangdai zhongxuesheng" (On the tide of going abroad—contemporary middle school students). *Zhongguo qingnian yanjiu*, no. 1:24–29.

Jin Guantao et al. 1992. "Let us come together with the people to think" (Selections of remarks made at a forum on *River Elegy*). *Chinese Sociology and Anthropology* 24, no. 4:16–28.

Jin Ren. 1989. "Zhao Ziyang tongzhi de jierushuo yu 'heshang' de 'xinjiyuan'" (From the engaging theory of comrade Zhao Ziyang to the "new era" of the *River Elegy*). *Guangming Daily*, August 14.

Jin Yucheng, ed. 1996. *Piaopo de honghaiyang: wode dachuanlian* (A waving red sea: my involvement in the great chuanlian). Taibei: China Times Publishing Company.

Johnson, Chalmers A. 1962. *Peasant Nationalism and Communist Power: The Emergence of Revolutionary China, 1937–1945.* Stanford, Calif.: Stanford University Press.

———. 1982. *Revolutionary Change.* 2d ed. Stanford, Calif.: Stanford University Press.

Jowitt, Kenneth. 1983. "Soviet Neotraditionalism: The Political Corruption of a Leninist Regime. *Soviet Studies* 35:275–97.

Karl, Terry Lynn, and Philippe C. Schmitter. 1991. "Modes of Transition in Latin America." *International Social Science Journal* 128:269–84.

Kassow, Samuel D. 1989. *Students, Professors, and the State in Tsarist Russia.* Berkeley: University of California Press.

Katznelson, Ira. 1985. "Working-class Formation and the State: Nineteenth-Century England in American Perspective." In *Bringing the State Back In,* edited by Peter Evans, Dietrich Rueschemeyer, and Theda Skocpol, 257–84. Cambridge: Cambridge University Press.

Katznelson, Ira, and Aristide R. Zolberg, eds. 1986. *Working Class Formation.* Princeton, N.J.: Princeton University Press.

Keane, John. 1988. *Democracy and Civil Society.* London: Verso.

Kellner, Douglas. 1992. *The Persian Gulf War.* Boulder, Colo.: Westview Press.

Kielbowicz, Richard B., and Clifford Scherer. 1986. "The Role of the Press in the Dynamics of Social Movements." *Research in Social Movements, Conflicts and Change* 9:71–96.

Killian, Lewis M. 1984. "Organization, Rationality and Spontaneity in the Civil Rights Movement." *American Sociological Review* 19:770–83.

Kim Shinil. 1989. "South Korea." In *Student Political Activism: An International Reference Handbook,* edited by Philip G. Altbach, 173–82. New York: Greenwood Press.

Kitayama, Shinobu, and Hazel Rose Markus. 1994. *Emotion and Culture.* Washington, D.C.: American Psychological Association.

Kitschelt, Herbert. 1986. "Political Opportunity Structures and Political Protest: Anti-Nuclear Movements in Four Democracies." *British Journal of Political Science* 16:57–85.

Kong Xianjin. 1989. "Zhijiu gongan juzhang" (Rescuing a director of the public security bureau). In *Jieyan Yiri,* 2:48–53. Beijing: Jiefangjun Wenyi Chubanshe.

Kornai, Janos. 1959. *Overcentralization in Economic Administration: A Critical Analysis Based on Experience in Hungarian Light Industry.* Oxford: Oxford University Press.

———. 1989. *The Socialist System: The Political Economy of Communism.* Princeton, N.J.: Princeton University Press.

Kornhauser, William. 1959. *The Politics of Mass Society.* New York: Free Press.

Kraus, Richard. 1989. "The Lament of Astrophysicist Fang Lizhi: China's Intellectuals in a Global Context." In *Marxism and the Chinese Experience: Issues in Contemporary Chinese Socialism,* edited by Arif Dirlik and Maurice Meisner, 294–351. Armonk, N.Y.: East Gate Books.

Kriesi, Hanspeter. 1996. "The Organizational Structure of New Social Movements in a Political Context." In *Comparative Perspectives on Social Movements*, edited by Doug McAdam, John D. McCarthy, and Mayer N. Zald, 152–84. Cambridge: Cambridge University Press.

Kriesi, Hanspeter, Ruud Koopmans, Jan Willem Duyvendak, and Marco G. Giugni. 1995. *The Politics of New Social Movements in Western Europe, A Comparative Analysis*. Minneapolis: University of Minnesota Press.

Kristof, Nicholas D. 1990a. "How the Hardliners Won." In *Tiananmen: China's Struggle for Democracy*, edited by Winston L. Y. Yang and Marsha L. Wagner, 171–84. Baltimore: Contemporary Asian Studies Series, University of Maryland.

———. 1990b. "Prelude to Tiananmen—The Reason Why China Erupts." In *Tiananmen: China's Struggle for Democracy*, edited by Winston L. Y. Yang and Marsha L. Wagner, 33–42. Baltimore: Contemporary Asian Studies Series, University of Maryland.

Krupat, Edward. 1985. *People in Cities: The Urban Environment and its Effects*. Cambridge: Cambridge University Press.

Kuang Zhihong. 1998. *Zhongguo jingji de ruanzhaolu* (The soft landing of the Chinese economy). Shanghai: Shanghai Yuandong Chubanshe.

Kumar, Krishan. 1993. "Civil Society: An Inquiry into the Usefulness of a Historical term." *British Journal of Sociology* 44:375–95.

Kwong, Julia. 1979. *Chinese Education in Transition: Prelude to the Cultural Revolution*. Montreal: McGill-Queen's University Press.

Laba, Roman. 1991. *The Roots of Solidarity*. Princeton, N.J.: Princeton University Press.

Laitin, David D. 1988. "Political Culture and Political Preferences." *American Political Science Review* 82:589–97.

Lang, Gladys Engel, and Kurt Lang. 1981. "Mass Communications and Public Opinion: Strategies for Research." In *Social Psychology: Sociological Perspectives*, edited by Morris Rosenberg and Ralph H. Turner, 653–82. New York: Basic Books.

Laumann, Edward O., and Franz U. Pappi. 1976. *Networks of Collective Action: A Perspective on Community Influence Systems*. New York: Academic Press.

Laumann, Edward O., and David Knoke. 1987. *The Organizational State: Social Choice in National Policy Domains*. Madison: University of Wisconsin Press.

Lawson, John, and Harold Silver. 1973. *A Social History of Education in England*. London: Methuen.

Lee Chin-Chuan, ed. 1994. *China's Media, Media's China*. Boulder, Colo.: Westview Press.

Lee Chin-Chuan and Joseph Man Chan. 1990. "The Hong Kong Press Coverage of the Tiananmen Protests." *Gazette* 46:175–95.

Leng Quanqing and Miao Sufei, eds. 1989. *Jingxin dongpo de 56 tian—1989 nian 4 yue 15 ri zhi 6 yue 9 ri meiri jishi* (The soul-stirring 56 Days—A daily account on the events between April 15 and June 9, 1989), (Internal circulation only). Beijing: Dadi Chubanshe.

Levi-Strauss, Claude. 1966. *The Savage Mind.* Chicago: The University of Chicago Press.

Li Guanghua. 1992. "Daxuesheng sushe wenhua de bianyi" (Changes and variations in dormitory culture among university students). *Zhongguo qingnian yanjiu,* no. 2:23–25.

Li Guoqing. 1988. "Dangdai daxuesheng de ziwo tongyixing weiji" (The crisis of contemporary university students). *Qingnian yanjiu,* no. 7:1–5.

Li Honglin. 1986. "Xiandaihua yu minzhu" (Modernization and democracy). *World Economic Herald,* June 2.

Li Huxiang. 1989. "Yige shenqiangshou de zishu" (A sharpshooter's account). In *Jieyan yiri,* 2:136–43. Beijing: Jiefangjun Wenyi Chubanshe.

Li Jinmin. 1988. "Daxuesheng zhong de 'nicaire' jiqi jiexi" (An analysis of the 'Nietzsche fever' among university students). *Qingnian yanjiu,* no. 12:30–35.

Li Lu. 1990. *Moving the Mountain.* London: Macmillan.

Li Peier. 1989. "Shexia heitaiyang—Wuer Kaixi" (Shooting down the black sun—Wuer Kaixi). In *Renmin buhui wangji* (People won't forget), edited by sixty-four Hong Kong journalists, 207–11. Hong Kong: Hong Kong Journalist Association.

Li Peng. 1989. "Li Peng huijian yahang nianhui keren" (Li Peng met with the delegates of Asian development bank annual meeting). *People's Daily,* May 6.

Li Qiang. 1996. "Naoti daogua yu woguo shichang fazhan de liangge jieduan" (A reversed income scale between intellectuals and workers and the two-stage development of China's market economy). *Shehuixue yanjiu,* no. 6:5–12.

Li Rui. 1994. *Lushan huiyi shilu* (A protocol of the Lushan meeting). Zhengzhou: Henan Renmin Chubanshe.

Li Shaojun. 1989. "Linghao xingdong" (Number zero action). In *Jieyan yiri,* 2:27–29. Beijing: Jiefangjun Wenyi Chubanshe.

Li Shengtang. 1989. "Liubuko jiu junhuo" (Rescuing arms and ammunition at Liubuko intersection). In *Jieyan yiri,* 1:147–54 Beijing: Jiefangjun Wenyi Chubanshe.

Li Tieying. 1990. "Guanyu woguo jiaoyu gongzuo ruogan wenti de huibao (zhaiyao)." (A report on several educational issues in our country [abstract]). *People's Daily* (overseas edition), January 3.

Li Wu. 1988. "'Zhu Hong xianxiang' de huhuan" (A cry for "Zhu Hong phenomenon"). *Outlook Weekly,* nos. 8, 9:40–41.

Li Xiaolin and Fu Xinyu. 1998. "Chengqi Zaijiuye de baohusan" (Expanding the reemployment mechanism). *Outlook Weekly,* no. 19:9–11.

Li Xiguang and Liu Kang. 1996. *Yaomohua zhongguo de beihou* (Behind the scenes of a demonized China). Beijing: Zhongguo Shehui Kexue Chubanshe.

Li Xinhua. 1988. "Xifang sichao yu zhongguo xuechao" (Western social thoughts and Chinese student movements). *Dangdai qingnian yanjiu,* nos. 11, 12:7–18.

Li Zehou. 1989. *Dangdai sichao yu zhongguo zhihui* (Contemporary thoughts and Chinese wisdom). Taibei: Dahong Tushu Youxian Gongsi.

Liang Heng. 1984. *Son of the Revolution.* New York: Vintage Books.

Liang Meifen, Tan Weier, Liu Ruishao, Chen Tianquan, and Ma Miaohua. 1989. "Dangbao Jizhe menghuitou" (The rebellion of journalists in party newspapers). In *Renmin Buhui Wangji* (People won't forget), edited by sixty-four Hong Kong journalists, 328–33. Hong Kong: Hong Kong Journalist Association.

Liao Gailong, Zhang Pinxing, and Liu Yousheng. 1993. *Xiandai zhongguo zhengjie yaoren zhuanlue daquan* (Biographies of eminent contemporary Chinese politicians). Beijing: China Broadcasting and Television Publishing Company.

Lichbach, Mark Irving. 1995. *The Rebel's Dilemma.* Ann Arbor: University of Michigan Press.

Lin Jiayou. 1990. *Xinhai geming yundongshi* (A history of the xinhai revolution). Guangzhou: Zhongshan University Publishing House.

Lin Nan. 1992. *The Struggle for Tiananmen: Anatomy of the 1989 Mass Movement.* Westport, Conn.: Praeger.

Lin Nan and Xie Wen. 1989. "Occupational Prestige in Urban China." *American Journal of Sociology* 93:793–832.

Lindholm, Charles. 1990. *Charisma.* Oxford: Blackwell.

Ling Zhijun and Ma Licheng. 1999. *Five Voices in Present China.* Guangzhou: Guangzhou Chubanshe.

Linz, Juan J. 1988. "Legitimacy of Democracy and Socioeconomic Systems." In *Comparing Pluralist Democracies: Strains on Legitimacy,* edited by Mattei Dogan, 65–113. Boulder, Colo.: Westview Press.

Linz, Juan, and Alfred Stepan. 1996. *Problems of Democratic Transition and Consolidation: Southern Europe, South America, and Post-Communist Europe.* Baltimore: Johns Hopkins University Press.

———, eds. 1978. *The Breakdown of Democratic Regimes.* Baltimore: Johns Hopkins University Press.

Lipset, Seymour Martin. 1972. *Rebellion in the University.* Boston: Little Brown.

———. 1981. *Political Man: The Social Bases of Politics.* Baltimore: Johns Hopkins University Press.

———. 1983. "Radicalism or Reformism: The Sources of Working-Class Politics." *American Political Science Review* 77:1–18.

———, ed. 1967. "University Students and Politics in Underdeveloped Countries." In *Student Politics,* 3–53. New York: Basic Books.

Liu, Alan P. L. 1990. "Aspects of Beijing's Crisis Management: The Tiananmen Square Demonstration." *Asian Survey* 30:505–21.

———. 1996. *Mass Politics in the People's Republic: State and Society in Contemporary China.* Boulder, Colo.: Westview Press.

Liu Dehuan and Huang Dongyou. 1989. "1986 niandi de xuechao yuanyin tanxi" (An analysis of the causes of the student-uprising at the end of 1986). *Qingnian yanjiu,* no. 5:27–32.

Liu Guoguang and Liu Shucheng. 1997. "Lun Ruanzhaolu" (On Soft-landing). *Xinhua wenzhai,* no. 3:48–50.

Liu Qinglong. 1990. "Shehui yingxiang yu xuexiao sixiang zhengzhi jiaoyu diaocha yu shiyan de sikao" (My investigation and thoughts on social influence and university political education). In *Dui bashi niandai shoudu daxuesheng zongxiang yanjiu* (Longitudinal studies on university students in Beijing during the 1980s), edited by Cang Lixin, 52−61. Beijing: Beijing Shifan Xueyuan Chubanshe.

Liu Shaoqi. 1987. "Guanmenzhuyi yu Maoxianzhuyi" (Close-doorism and adventurism). In *Yaoerjiu yundong* (December 9th Movement), edited by Zhonggong Beijing shiwei dangshi ziliao zhengji weiyuanhui (The party history council of the CCP Beijing Committee), 62−65. Beijing: Zhonggong Dangshi Ziliao Chubanshe.

Liu Xiangyang. 1989. "Disanci langchao: wenpingre" (The third wave: the diploma fever). In *Wuci langchao* (Five waves), edited by Xiao Qinfu, 98−137. Beijing: Zhongguo Renmin Daxue Chubanshe.

Liu Xiaobo. 1992. *Mori xingcunzhe de dubai.* (A soliloquy by a survivor of the doomsday). Taibei: Shibao Chuban Gongsi.

Liu Xinli. 1989. "Bachuang sanyuanqiao" (Eight times, we finally passed the sanyuan bridge). In *Jieyan yiri*, 1:224−32. Beijing: Jiefangjun Wenyi Chubanshe.

Liu Yongming. 1990. *Guomindangren yu wusi yundong* (Guomindang and the May 4th Movement). Beijing: Zhongguo Shehuikexue Chubanshe.

Liu Zhifeng. 1999. *Zhongguo zhengzhi tizhi gaige wenti baogao* (On the issues of China's political reform). Beijing: Zhongguo Dianying Chubanshe.

Liu Zhongyi. 1989. "Xuechao: guangdong weihe xiangdui pingjing?" (The student unrest: why is it relatively calm in Guangdong province). *Chinese Women's Daily*, May 10.

Liu Zuoxiang. 1999. *Maixiang minzhu yu fazhi de guodu* (China: marching toward democracy and the rule of law). Jinan: Shandong Renmin Chubanshe.

Lofland, John. 1970. "The Youth Ghetto." In *The Logic of Social Hierarchies*, edited by Edward Laumann, Paul M. Siegel, and Robert W. Hodge, 756−78. Chicago: Marrham Publishing Company.

Loo, C. 1972. "The Effects of Spatial Density on the Social Behavior of Children." *Journal of Applied Social Psychology* 2:372−381.

Lu Jianhua. 1991. "Dangdai qingnian de zhengzhi jiazhiguan" (Political orientations of the contemporary youth). *Qingnian yanjiu*, no. 1:1−7.

Lu Yongxiong, Huang Hanjun, Chen Tianquan, Fan Zhuoyun, and Li Peier. 1989. "Xianggang xinwenjie huihuangzhong de wudian" (Blemishes on the glory of Hong Kong press). In *Renmin buhui wangji* (People won't forget), edited by sixty-four Hong Kong journalists, 336−44. Hong Kong: Hong Kong Journalist Association.

Lull, James. 1991. *China Turned On: Television, Reform and Resistance.* London: Routledge.

Lytle, Guy Fitch. 1974. "Patronage Patterns and Oxford Colleges, 1300−1530." In *The University in Society*, vol. 1., edited by Lawrence Stone, 111−49. Princeton, N.J.: Princeton University Press.

————. 1984. "The Careers of Oxford Students in the Later Middle Ages." In *Rebirth, Reform and Resilience: Universities in Transition, 1300–1700*, edited by James M. Kittelson and Pamela J. Transue, 213–53. Columbus: Ohio State University Press.

Ma Miaohua, Liu Ruishao, and Chen Tianquan. 1989. "You zhibi zhi qubi" (From direct to innuendo style of report). In *Renmin buhui wangji* (People won't forget), edited by sixty-four Hong Kong journalists, 322–28. Hong Kong: Hong Kong Journalist Association.

Ma Qianli. 1987. "Management of the 'Stupid Melon Seed Dealer' and Its Evasion of Taxes and other Tax Problems." *Chinese Economic Studies* 21, no. 1:76–83.

Macartney, Jane. 1990. "The Students: Heroes, Pawns or Power-Brokers?" In *The Broken Mirror: China After Tiananmen*, edited by George Hicks, 3–23. Essex: Longman.

MacFarquhar, Roderick. 1974. *The Origin of the Cultural Revolution*, vol. 1: *Contradictions among the People 1956–1957*. London: Oxford University Press.

————. 1983. *The Origin of the Cultural Revolution*, vol. 2: *The Great Leap Forward 1958–1960*. London: Oxford University Press.

————. 1993. *The Politics of China: 1949–1989*. Cambridge: Cambridge University Press.

MacInnis, Donald E. 1989. *Religion in China Today: Policy and Practice*. Maryknoll: Orbis Books.

Madsen, Richard. 1990. "The Spiritual Crisis of China's Intellectuals." In *Chinese Society on the Eve of Tiananmen: The Impact of Reform*, edited by Deborah Davis and Ezra F. Vogel, 243–60. Cambridge, Mass.: Harvard University Press.

Malani, Mohsen M. 1994. *The Making of Iran's Islamic Revolution*. Boulder, Colo.: Westview Press.

Mann, Michael. 1975. "The Ideology of Intellectuals and Other People in the Development of Capitalism." In *Stress and Contradiction in Modern Capitalism*, edited by Leon N. Lindberg, 275–307. Lexington, Mass.: Lexington Books.

————. 1986. *The Sources of Social Power*, vol. 1: *A History of Power from the Beginning to A.D. 1760*. Cambridge: Cambridge University Press.

————. 1988. *State, Wars and Capitalism: Studies in Political Sociology*. Oxford: Basil Blackwell.

————. 1993. *The Sources of Social Power*, vol. 2: *The Rise of Classes and Nation-states, 1760–1914*. Cambridge: Cambridge University Press.

Mark, Steven. 1991. "Observing the Observers at Tiananmen Square: Freedom, Democracy, and the News Media in China's Student Movement." In *Culture and Politics in China*, edited by Peter Li, Steven Mark, and Marjorie H. Li, 259–84. New Brunswick, N.J.: Transaction Publishers.

Marks, Gary Wolfe. 1989. *Unions in Politics: Britain, Germany, and the United States in the Nineteenth and Early Twentieth Centuries*. Princeton, N.J.: Princeton University Press.

Marshall, Thomas Humphrey. 1950. *Citizenship and Social Class*. Cambridge: Cambridge University Press.

Marx, Karl. 1985a. "The Communist Manifesto." In *Karl Marx, Selected Writings*, edited by David McLellan, 221–47. New York: Oxford University Press.

———. 1985b. "The Eighteenth Brumaire of Louis Bonaparte." In *Karl Marx, Selected Writings*, edited by David McLellan, 300–325. New York: Oxford University Press.

McAdam, Doug. 1982. *Political Process and the Development of Black Insurgency, 1930–1970.* Chicago: University of Chicago Press.

———. 1986. "Recruitment to High-Risk Activism: The Case of Freedom Summer." *American Journal of Sociology* 92:64–90.

———. 1996. "Conceptual Origins, Current Problems, Future Directions." In *Comparative Perspectives on Social Movements*, edited by Doug McAdam, John D. McCarthy, and Mayer N. Zald, 23–40. New York: Cambridge University Press.

McAdam, Doug, John D. McCarthy, and Mayer N. Zald, eds. 1996. *Comparative Perspectives on Social Movements.* New York: Cambridge University Press.

McAdam, Doug, and Ronnelle Paulsen. 1993. "Specifying the Relationship between Social Ties and Activism." *American Journal of Sociology* 99:640–67.

McAdam, Doug, Sidney Tarrow, and Charles Tilly. 1996. "To Map Contentious Politics." *Mobilization* 1:17–34.

McCarthy, John D. 1987. "Pro-life and Pro-choice Mobilization: Infrastructure Deficits and New Technologies." In *Social Movements in an Organizational Society*, edited by Mayer N. Zald and John D. McCarthy, 49–66. New Brunswick, N.J.: Transaction Publishers.

McCarthy, John, D., Jackie Smith, and Mayer N. Zald. 1996. "Accessing Public, Media, Electoral, and Government Agendas." In *Comparative Perspectives on Social Movements*, edited by Doug McAdam, John D. McCarthy, and Mayer N. Zald, 291–311. New York: Cambridge University Press.

McCarthy, John D., and Mayer N. Zald. 1973. *The Trend of Social Movements in America: Professionalization and Resource Mobilization.* Morristown, N.J: General Learning Corporation.

———. 1977. "Resource Mobilization and Social Movements: A Partial Theory." *American Journal of Sociology* 82:1212–41.

McDaniel, Tim. 1988. *Autocracy, Capitalism and Revolution in Russia.* Berkeley: University of California Press.

———. 1991. *Autocracy, Modernization and Revolution in Russia and Iran.* Princeton, N.J.: Princeton University Press.

McKenzie, Roderick D. 1924. "The Ecological Approach to the Study of the Human Community." *American Journal of Sociology* 30:287–301.

McNair, Brian. 1988. *Images of the Enemy.* London: Routledge.

McPhail, Clark. 1991. *The Myth of the Madding Crowd.* New York: Aldine de Gruyter.

Meisner, Maurice. 1967. *Li Ta-chao and the Origins of Chinese Marxism.* Cambridge, Mass.: Harvard University Press.

———. 1986. *Mao's China and After: A History of the People's Republic.* New York: Free Press.

Meyer, David, and Suzanne Staggenborg. 1996. "Movements, Countermovements, and the Structure of Political Opportunity." *American Journal of Sociology* 101:1628–60.

Meyer, David S., and Sidney Tarrow. 1998. *The Social Movement Society.* Lanham, Md.: Rowman and Littlefield.

Michels, Robert. 1962. *Political Parties.* New York: Collier Books.

Migdal, Joel S. 1988. *Strong Societies and Weak States: State-Society Relations and State Capacities in the Third World.* Princeton, N.J.: Princeton University Press.

———. 1994. "The State in Society: An Approach to Struggles for Domination." In *State Power and Social Forces,* edited by Joel s. Migdal, Atul Kohli, and Vivienne Shue, 7–34. Cambridge: Cambridge University Press.

Min Weifang. 1991. "Higher Education Finance in China: Current Constraints and Strategies for the 1990s." *Higher Education* 21:151–61.

Molotch, Harvey. 1979. "Media and Movements." In *The Dynamics of Social Movements,* edited by Mayer N. Zald, and John D. McCarthy, 71–93. Cambridge, Mass.: Winthrop.

Moore, Barrington. 1966. *Social Origins of Dictatorship and Democracy.* Boston: Beacon Press.

———. 1978. *Injustice: The Social Bases of Obedience and Revolt.* White Plain, N.Y.: Sharpe.

Morley, Felix. 1949. *The Power in the People.* Toronto: D. Van. Nostrand Company.

Mu Wenjian. 1996. "Jianshao laodong tufa shijian de guanjian zainali?" (What are the keys to minimize worker protests?) *Outlook Weekly,* no. 30:21.

Mueller, Carol. 1997. "International Press Coverage of East German Protest Events, 1989." *American Sociological Review* 62:820–32.

Nasatir, David. 1967. "University Experience and Political Unrest of Students in Buenos Aires." In *Student Politics,* edited by Seymour Martin Lipset, 318–31. New York: Basic Books.

Nathan, Andrew J. 1986. *Chinese Democracy.* Berkeley: University of California Press.

———. 1990. *China's Crisis: Dilemmas of Reform and Prospects for Democracy.* New York: Columbia University Press.

———. 1997. *China's Transition.* New York: Columbia University Press.

National Center for Education Statistics, Digest of Education Statistics. 1989, 1993. U.S. Department of Education. Office of Educational Research and Improvement, NCES 93–292.

Nee, Victor, and David Mozingo, eds. 1983. *State and Society in Contemporary China.* Ithaca, N.Y.: Cornell University Press.

Ni Futian. 1989. "Shouwei dahuitang" (Defending the National People's Congress). In *Jieyan yiri,* 1:64–70. Beijing: Jiefangjun Wenyi Chubanshe.

Nian Yan. 1988. "Zhonggong xuezhe youguan 'qiuji' wenti de taolun" (The 'world citizenship' discussion by scholars of communist China). *Zhongyang ribao* (Taiwan), August 29.

Oberschall, Anthony. 1973. *Social Conflict and Social Movements.* Englewood Cliffs, N.J.: Prentice Hall.

————. 1993. *Social Movements: Ideologies, Interests, and Identities.* New Brunswick, N.J.: Transaction Publishers.

————. 1996. "Opportunities and Framing in the Eastern European Revolts of 1989." In *Comparative Perspectives on Social Movements,* edited by Doug McAdam, John D. McCarthy, and Mayer N. Zald, 93–121. New York: Cambridge University Press.

O'Donnell, Guillermo, Philippe C. Schmitter, and Laurence Whitehead, eds. 1986. *Transitions from Authoritarian Rule: Comparative Perspectives.* Baltimore: Johns Hopkins University Press.

Offe, Claus. 1973. "The Abolition of Market Control and the Problem of Legitimacy (I)." *Kapitalistate* 1:109–16.

Oksenberg, Michel, Lawrence R. Sullivan, and Mark Lambert, eds. 1990. *Beijing Spring: Confrontation and Conflict, The Basic Documents.* Armonk, N.Y.: Sharpe.

Oliver, Pamela E. 1989. "Bringing the Crowd Back In: The Nonorganizational Elements of Social Movements. *Research in Social Movements, Conflict and Change* 11:1–30.

Olson, Mancur. 1965. *The Logic of Collective Action.* Cambridge, Mass.: Harvard University Press.

————. 1990. "The Logic of Collective Action in Soviet-type Societies." *Journal of Soviet Nationalities* 1:8–27.

Olzak, Susan. 1989. "Analysis of Events in the Study of Collective Action." *Annual Review of Sociology* 15:119–41.

Opp, Karl-Dieter, and Christiane Gern. 1993. "Dissident Groups, Personal Networks, and Spontaneous Cooperation: The East German Revolution of 1989." *American Sociological Review* 58:659–80.

Opp, Karl-Dieter, and Wolfgang Roehl. 1990. "Repression, Micromobilization, and Political Protest." *Social Forces* 69:521–47.

Osmond, Humphry. 1957. "The Relationship between Architect and Psychiatrist." In *Psychiatric Architecture,* edited by Charles E. Goshen, 16–20. Washington, D.C.: American Psychiatric Association.

Ost, David. 1990. *Solidarity and the Politics of Anti-Politics.* Philadelphia: Temple University Press.

Paige, Jeffrey M. 1975. *Agrarian Revolution: Social Movements and Export Agriculture in the Underdeveloped World.* New York: Free Press.

Park, Robert E. 1915. "The City: Suggestions for the Investigation of Human Behavior in the City Environment." *American Journal of Sociology* 20:557–612.

————. 1936. "Human Ecology." *American Journal of Sociology* 42:3–49.

Parish, William L., and Martin King Whyte. 1978. *Village and Family in Contemporary China.* Chicago: University of Chicago Press.

Peng Hu. 1989. "Tuiche tingjin guangchang" (Pushing our truck and marching into the Square). In *Jieyan yiri*, 1:216–23. Beijing: Jiefangjun Wenyi Chubanshe.

Pepper, Suzanne. 1984. *China's Universities: Post-Mao Enrollment Policies and Their Impact on the Structure of Secondary Education.* Ann Arbor: Center for Chinese Studies, University of Michigan.

———. 1990. *China's Education Reform in the 1980's: Policies, Issues, and Historical Perspectives.* Berkeley: Institute of East Asian Studies, University of California at Berkeley.

Perry, Elizabeth J. 1991. "Intellectuals and Tiananmen: Historical Perspectives on an Aborted Revolution," In *The Crisis of Leninism and the Decline of the Left*, edited by Daniel Chirot, 129–46. Seattle: University of Washington Press.

———. 1992. "Casting a Chinese 'Democracy' Movement: The Roles of Students, Workers and Entrepreneurs." In *Popular Protest and Political Culture in Modern China*, edited by Jeffrey N. Wasserstrom and Elizabeth J. Perry, 146–64. Boulder: Westview Press.

———. 1993. *Shanghai on Strike: The Politics of Chinese Labor.* Stanford, Calif.: Stanford University Press.

Perry, Elizabeth J., and Ellen V. Fuller. 1991. "China's Long March to Democracy." *World Policy Journal* 8:663–85.

Perry, Ronald, David F. Gillespie, and Howard A. Parker. 1976. *Social Movements and the Local Community.* Beverly Hills, Calif. Sage.

Pinard, Maurice. 1975. *The Rise of a Third Party: A Study in Crisis Politics.* Montreal: McGill-Queen's University Press.

Poggi, Gianfranco. 1990. *The State: Its Nature, Development and Prospects.* Oxford: Polity Press.

Polletta, Francesca. 1998. "Legacies and Liabilities of an Insurgent Past." *Science History* 22:479–512.

Poznanski, Kazimiersz. 1992. *Constructing Capitalism: The Reemergence of Civil Society and Liberal Economy in the Post-Communist World.* Boulder, Colo.: Westview Press.

Pride, Richard A. 1995. "How Activists and Media Frame Social Problems: Critical Events versus Performance Trends for Schools." *Political Communication* 12:5–26.

Przeworski, Adam. 1991. *Democracy and Market: Political and Economic Reforms in Eastern Europe and Latin America.* Cambridge: Cambridge University Press.

Pusey, James Reeve. 1983. *China and Charles Darwin.* Cambridge, Mass.: Harvard University Press.

Pye, Lucian W. 1990. "The Escalation of Confrontation." In *The Broken Mirror: China after Tiananmen*, edited by George Hicks, 162–79. Essex, England: Longman.

Qin Jiwei. 1996. *Qin Jiwei huiyilu* (A memoir of Qin Jiwei). Beijing: Jiefangjun Chubanshe.

Quan Jinglian. 1990. "Dui Beijing gaoxiao xuesheng sixiang zhengzhi jiaoyu de kaocha yu fenxi" (An analysis of the political education of university students in Beijing). *Qingnian yanjiu*, no. 3:15–18.

Rait, Robert S. 1971. "The Earliest Universities." In *Student Activism: Town and Gown in Historical Perspective*, edited by Alexander DeConde, 33–38. New York: Charles Scribner's Sons.

Rao, L. G. 1979. *Brain Drain and Foreign Students*. New York: St. Martin's Press.

Rashdall, Hastings. 1936. *The Universities of Europe in the Middle Ages*. 2d ed. London: Oxford University Press.

Ren Bin. 1989. "Jieyanzhong de diyici liuxue" (The first blood during martial law). In *Jieyan yiri*, 1:32–37. Beijing: Jiefangjun Wenyi Chubanshe.

Ren Jiayu. 1991. "Daxuesheng 'wotan' wenhua tanxi" (An analysis of the "wotan" culture among university students). *Dangdai qingnian yanjiu*, no. 6:10–13.

Ren Yanshen. 1990. "Shoudu wusuo gaoxiao xuesheng zhengzhi sixiang zhuangkuang de diaocha baogao" (A report on an investigation of students' political attitudes in five Beijing universities). In *Dui bashi niandai shoudu daxuesheng zongxiang yanjiu* (Longitudinal studies on university students in Beijing during the 1980s), edited by Lixin Cang, 112–27. Beijing: Beijing Shifan Xueyuan Chubanshe.

Reynolds, Bruce L., ed. 1987. *Reform in China: Challenges and Choices: A Summary and Analysis of the CESRRI Survey*. New York: Sharpe.

Riddle, Phyllis. 1993. "Political Authority and University Formation in Europe, 1200–1800." *Sociological Perspectives* 36:45–62.

Rigby, Thomas H., and Ferenc Fehér, eds. 1982. *Political Legitimation in Communist States*. New York: St. Martin's Press.

Ringer, Fritz K. 1979. *Education and Society in Modern Europe*. Bloomington: Indiana University Press.

Rong Jingben et al. 1998. *Transformation from the Pressurized System to the Democratic System of Cooperation*. Beijing: Central Compilation and Translation Press.

Rosen, Stanley. 1985. "Prosperity, Privatization, and China's Youth." *Problems of Communism* 34:1–28.

———. 1987. "The Private Economy." *Chinese Economic Studies* 21:3–9.

———. 1990. "The Impact of Reform Politics on Youth Attitudes." In *Chinese Society on the Eve of Tiananmen: The Impact of Reform*, edited by Deborah Davis and Ezra F. Vogel, 283–305. Cambridge: Harvard University Press.

———. 1991a. "Political Education and Student Response: Some Background Factors Behind the 1989 Beijing Demonstrations." In *Chinese Education: Problems, Policies, and Prospects*, edited by Irving Epstein, 416–48. New York: Garland Publishing.

———. 1991b. "The Role of Chinese Students at Home and Abroad as a Factor in Sino-American Relations." In *Building Sino-American Relations*, edited by William T. Tow, 162–202. New York: Paragon House.

Rosen, Stanley, and Gary Zou, eds. 1990–91. "The Chinese Debate on the New Authoritarianism." *Chinese Sociology and Anthropology* 23: nos. 2, 3, 4; and 24, no. 1.

————. 1991–92. "The Chinese Television Documentary *River Elegy* (Part 1 to 3)." *Chinese Sociology and Anthropology* 24, nos. 2, 4; and 25, no. 1.

Rosenbaum, Arthur Lewis, ed. 1992. *State and Society in China: The Consequences of Reform.* Boulder, Colo.: Westview Press.

Rosenberg, Michael M., William B. Shaffir, Allan Turowetz, and Morton Weinfeld, eds. 1987. *An Introduction to Sociology.* 2d. edition. Toronto: Methuen.

Rosenthal, Naomi, Meryl Fingrutd, Michele Ethier, Roberta Karant, and David MacDonald. 1985. "Social Movements and Network Analysis: A Case of Nineteenth-Century Woman's Reform in New York State." *American Journal of Sociology* 90:1022–54.

Rucht, Dieter. 1990. "Campaigns, Skirmishes, and Battles: Anti-Nuclear Movements in the USA, France, and West Germany." *Industrial Crisis Quarterly* 4:193–222.

————. 1996. "The Impact of National Contexts on Social Movement Structure: A Cross-movement and Cross-national Comparison." In *Comparative Perspectives on Social Movements,* edited by Doug McAdam, John D. McCarthy, and Mayer N. Zald, 185–204. Cambridge: Cambridge University Press.

Rueschemeyer, Dietrich, Evelyne H. Stephens, and John D. Stephens. 1992. *Capitalist Development and Democracy.* Chicago: University of Chicago Press.

Ryan, Charlotte. 1991. *Prime Time Activism.* Boston: South End Press.

Saegert, Susan, and G. Winkel. 1990. "Environmental Psychology." *Annual Review of Psychology* 41:441–77.

Samudavanija, Chai-Anan. 1989. "Thailand." In *Student Political Activism: An International Reference Handbook,* edited by Philip G. Altbach, 183–96. New York: Greenwood Press.

Sanshibajun Junshi (A history of the 38th army). 1994. Beijing: Jiefangjun Wenyi Chubanshe.

Scheff, Thomas J. 1994. *Bloody Revenge: Emotions, Nationalism, and War.* Boulder, Colo.: Westview Press.

Schell, Orville. 1988. *Discos and Democracy: China in the Throes of Reform.* New York: Pantheon Books.

————. 1994. *Mandate of Heaven.* New York: Simon & Schuster.

Schelling, Thomas C. 1962. *The Strategy of Conflict.* Cambridge, Mass.: Harvard University Press.

Schmitter, Philippe C. 1993. *Some Propositions about Civil Society and the Consolidation of Democracy.* Wien: Institut für Höhere Studien.

Schneider, David M. 1976. "Notes toward a Theory of Culture." In *Meaning in Anthropology,* edited by Keith H. Basso and Henry A. Selby, 197–220. Albuquerque: University of New Mexico Press.

Schoggen, Phil. 1989. *Behavior Settings.* Stanford, Calif.: Stanford University Press.

Schram, Stuart R. 1988. "China After the 13th Congress." *China Quarterly,* no. 114: 177–97.

Schurmann, Franz. 1968. *Ideology and Organization in Communist China.* Berkeley: University of California Press.

Schwartz, Benjamin I. 1964. *In Search of Wealth and Power: Yan Fu and the West.* Cambridge, Mass.: Harvard University Press.

———. 1987. "The Primacy of the Political Order in East Asian Societies: Some Preliminary Generalizations." In *Foundations and Limits of State Power in China,* edited by Stuart R. Schram, 1–10. Hong Kong: The Chinese University Press.

Scott, James C. 1985. *Weapons of the Weak: Everyday Forms of Peasant Resistance.* New Haven: Yale University Press.

Scott, Joseph W., and Mohamed El-assal. 1969. "Multiversity, University Size, University Quality, and Student Protest: An Empirical Study." *American Sociological Review* 34:702–9.

Selden, Mark. 1993. "The Social Origins and Limits of the Democratic Movement." In *Chinese Democracy and the Crisis of 1989: Chinese and American Reflections,* edited by Roger V. Des Forges, Luo Ning, and Wu Yen-bo, 107–31. Albany: SUNY Press.

Seligman, Adam B. 1992. *The Idea of Civil Society.* New York: Free Press.

Sewell, William H. Jr. 1985. "Ideologies and Social Revolutions: Reflections on the French Case." *Journal of Modern History* 57:57–85.

———. 1996. "The Concept(s) of Culture." Paper presented at a Workshop at the University of Chicago.

Shapiro, Gilbert, and John Markoff. 1998. *Revolutionary Demands: A Content Analysis of the Cahiers de Doleances of 1789.* Stanford, Calif.: Stanford University Press.

Shen Jinguo. 1995. "The Rise and Fall of the World Economic Herald, 1980–1989." *Journalism and Mass Communication Quarterly* 72:642–63.

Shen Tong. 1990. *Almost a Revolution.* New York: Harper Perennial.

Shi Xianmin. 1992. "Beijingshi getihu de fazhan licheng ji leibie fenhua—Beijing xicheng getihu yanjiu" (The development and diversification of the getihu in Beijing—a study of the getihu in Beijing xicheng district). *Zhongguo Shehui Kexue* (Chinese Social Sciences), no. 5:19–38.

Shils, Edward. 1968. "Introduction: Students, Politics, and Universities in India." In *Turmoil and Transition: Higher Education and Student Politics in India,* edited by Philip G. Altbach, 1–13. New York: Basic Books.

Shirk, Susan L. 1982. *Competitive Comrades: Career Incentives and Student Strategies in China.* Berkeley: University of California Press.

———. 1993. *The Political Logic of Economic Reform in China.* Berkeley: University of California Press.

Shu Ming. 1990. "Zhongyu cheli" (Withdrawing from the Square, finally) *Democracy China,* no. 2:22–30.

Shue, Vienne. 1988. *The Reach of the State: Sketches of the Chinese Body Politic.* Stanford, Calif.: Stanford University Press.

Si Chao, ed. 1988. *Shensheng yousi—dangdai zhongguo xinchao qishilu* (Holy concerns—

inspirations from new thinking in contemporary China). 2 vols. Beijing: Zhongyang Minzu Xueyuan Chubanshe.

Sigal, Leon. 1973. *Reporters and Officials.* Lexington, Mass.: D. C. Health.

Simmie, Scott, and Bob Nixon. 1989. *Tiananmen Square.* Vancouver: Douglas & McIntyre.

Skinner, G. William. 1985. "Rural Marketing in China: Revival and Reappraisal." In *Markets and Marketing,* edited by Stuart Plattner, 7–47. Lanham, Md.: University Press of America.

Skocpol, Theda. 1979. *States and Revolutions: A Comparative Analysis of France, Russia, and China.* Cambridge: Cambridge University Press.

———. 1982. "Rentier State and Shi'a Islam in the Iranian Revolution." *Theory and Society* 11:265–83.

———. 1985. "Bringing the State Back In: Strategies of Analysis in Current Research." In *Bringing the State Back In,* edited by Peter Evans, Dietrich Rueschemeyer, Theda Skocpol, 3–37. Cambridge: Cambridge University Press.

———. 1994. *Social Revolutions in the Modern World.* Cambridge: Cambridge University Press.

Smelser, Neil, J. 1962. *Theory of Collective Behavior.* New York: Free Press.

Snow, David A., Louis A. Zurcher, and Sheldon Ekland-Olson. 1980. "Social Networks and Social Movements: A Microstructural Approach to Differential Recruitment." *American Sociological Review* 45:787–801.

Snow, David A., E. Burke Rochford Jr., Steven K. Worden, and Robert D. Benford. 1986. "Frame Alignment Processes, Micromobilization, and Movement Participation." *American Sociological Review* 51:464–81.

Snow, David A., and Robert D. Benford. 1988. "Ideology, Frame Resonance, and Participant Mobilization." *International Social Movement Research* 1:197–217.

———. 1992. "Master Frames and Cycles of Protest." In *Frontiers in Social Movement Theory,* edited by Aldon D. Morris and Carol M. Mueller, 133–55. New Haven: Yale University Press.

Snow, Edgar. 1966. "Comment on the December 9th Movement." *China Quarterly,* no. 26:171–72.

Soley, Lawrence C. 1992. *The News Shapers: The Sources Who Shape the News.* New York: Praeger.

Sommer, Robert. 1967. "Small Group Ecology." *Sociometry* 28:337–48.

———. 1969. *Personal Space: The Behavioral Basis of Design.* Englewood Cliffs, N.J.: Prentice Hall.

Song Li. 1982. "Zhongguo xuesheng geming yundong de laichao" (The wave of the Chinese student revolutionary movement). In *Yaoerjiu yundong huiyilu* (A recollection of the December 9th Movement), edited by Yang Shuxian, Tang Jiming, Xu Keqing, and Wang Donglin, 1–57. Beijing: Renmin Chubanshe.

Song Qiang, Zhang Zangzang, and Qiao Bian. 1996. *Zhongguo keyi shuo bu* (China can say no). Beijing: Zhongguo Gongshang Lianhe Chubanshe.

Spence, Jonathan D. 1990. *The Search for Modern China.* New York: Norton & Company.

Spykman, Nicholas J. 1964. *The Social Theory of Georg Simmel.* New York: Atherton Press.

Steinberg, Marc. W. 1994. "The Dialogue of Struggle." *Social Science History* 18:505–41.

Steinmetz, George, ed. 1999. *State/Culture: State-Formation after the Cultural Turn.* Ithaca, N.Y.: Cornell University Press.

Stepan, Alfred. 1978. *The State and Society: Peru in Comparative Perspective.* Princeton, N.J.: Princeton University Press.

———, ed. 1989. *Democratizing Brazil.* New York: Oxford University Press.

Stinchcombe, Arthur L. 1961. "Agricultural Enterprise and Rural Class Relations." *American Journal of Sociology* 67:165–76.

———. 1975. "Merton's Theory of Social Structure." In *The Idea of Social Structure,* edited by Lewis A. Coser, 11–33. New York: Harcourt Brace Jovanovich.

Stone, Lawrence. 1974. "The Size and Composition of the Oxford Student Body, 1580–1910." In *The University in Society,* vol. 1., edited by Lawrence Stone, 3–110. Princeton, N.J.: Princeton University Press.

Strand, David. 1990. "Protest in Beijing: Civil Society and Public Sphere in China." *Problems of Communism* 34:1–19.

———. 1993. "Civil Society and Public Sphere in Modern Chinese History." In *Chinese Democracy and the Crisis of 1989,* edited by Roger V. Des Forges, Luo Ning, and Wu Yen-bo, 53–68. Albany: State University of New York Press.

Su Xiaokang. 1990. "Huhuan quanminzu fanxing yishi—dianshi xiliepian 'heshang' gouxiang qiantan" (A call for the introspection consciousness of the whole nation —a preliminary discussion on the conception of the TV series *River Elegy*). In *Heshang* (River elegy), edited by Su Xiaokang and Wang Luxiang, 1–6. Taibei: Fengyun Shidai.

Su Xiaokang and Zhang Min. 1987. "Shensheng yousilu—zhongxiaoxue jiaoyu weiji jishi" (Holy concerns—a report on the primary and middle school educational crisis). *Renmin wenxue,* no. 9.

Su Wei. 1992. "Shier xuezhe shang Tiananmen" (Twelve scholars went to Tiananmen Square). *Minzhu zhongguo,* no. 10:81–84.

Sullivan, Lawrence R. 1990. "The Emergence of Civil Society in China, Spring 1989." In *The Chinese People's Movement, Perspectives on Spring 1989,* edited by Tony Saich, 126–44. Armonk, N.Y.: M. E. Sharpe.

Sun Xijun. 1985. "Daxue tong sushe xuesheng renji guanxi jiegou ji xingcheng yuanyin" (The structure and formation of student relations in a university dormitory). *Qingnian yanjiu,* no. 4:30–37.

Swidler, Ann. 1986. "Culture in Action: Symbols and Strategies." *American Sociological Review* 51:273–86.

Szasz, Andrew. 1994. *EcoPopulism: Toxic Waste and the Movement for Environmental Justice.* Minneapolis: University of Minnesota Press.

Szelenyi, Ivan. 1986. "The Prospects and Limits of the East European New Call Project." *Politics and Society* 15:103–14.

Tan, Frank. 1993. "The *People's Daily* and the Epiphany of Press Reform." In *Chinese Democracy and the Crisis of 1989*, ed. Roger V. Des Forges, Luo Ning, and Wu Yen-bo, 277–94. Albany: State University of New York Press.

Tan Gengbing. 1992. "Nongcun xiedou heshiliao" (When could the rural fighting be ended?). *Lilun daobao*, no. 1:37–38.

Tang Wenfang and William L. Parish. 2000. *Urban Life in Reform China.* New York: Cambridge University Press.

Tarrow, Sidney. 1992. "Mentalities, Political Cultures, and Collective Action Frames: Constructing Meanings through Action." In *Frontiers in Social Movement Theory*, edited by Aldon D. Morris and Carol M. Mueller, 174–202. New Haven: Yale University Press.

———. 1994. *Power in Movement.* New York: Cambridge University Press.

———. 1996. "States and Opportunities: The Political Structuring of Social Movements." In *Comparative Perspectives on Social Movements*, edited by Doug McAdam, John D. McCarthy, and Mayer N. Zald, 41–61. New York: Cambridge University Press.

———. 1998. *Power in Movement.* 2d ed. New York: Cambridge University Press.

Teiwes, Frederick C. 1990. *Politics at Mao's Court.* Armonk, N.Y.: Sharpe.

Teiwes, Frederick C., and Warren Sun. 1999. *China's Road to Disaster.* Armonk: M. E. Sharpe.

Terdiman, Richard. 1986. *Discourse/Counter-Discourse: The Theory and Practice of Symbolic Resistance in Nineteenth-Century France.* Ithaca, N.Y.: Cornell University Press.

Tillman, Hoyt Cleveland. 1990. "Yan Fu's Utilitarianism in Chinese Perspective." In *Ideas Across Cultures: Essays on Chinese Thought in Honor of Benjamin I. Schwartz*, edited by Paul A. Cohen and Merle Goldman, 63–84. Cambridge, Mass.: Harvard University Press.

Tilly, Charles. 1976. *The Vendee.* Cambridge, Mass.: Harvard University Press.

———. 1978. *From Mobilization to Revolution.* New York: Random House.

———. 1982. "Britain Creates the Social Movement." In *Social Conflict and the Political Order in Modern Britain*, edited by James E. Cronin and Jonathan Schneer, 21–51. New Brunswick, N.J.: Rutgers University Press.

———. 1986. *The Contentious French: Four Centuries of Popular Struggle.* Cambridge, Mass.: Harvard University Press.

———. 1992. *Coercion, Capital, and European States, A.D. 900–1992.* Cambridge, Mass.: Blackwell.

———. 1994. "Political Memories in Space and Time." In *Remapping Memory: The Politics of Time Space*, edited by Jonathan Boyarin, 241–56. Minneapolis: University of Minnesota Press.

———. 1999. "Epilogue: Now Where?" In *State/Culture: State-Formation after the Cultural Turn*, edited by George Steinmetz, 407–19. Ithaca, N.Y.: Cornell University Press.

————, ed. 1975. *The Formation of National States in Western Europe*. Princeton, N.J.: Princeton University Press.

Tilly, Charles, Louise Tilly, and Richard Tilly. 1975. *The Rebellious Century, 1830–1930*. Cambridge, Mass.: Harvard University Press.

Tilly, Charles, and R. A. Schweitzer. 1982. "How London and its Conflicts Changed Shape: 1758–1834." *Historical Methods* 15:67–77.

Tismaneanu, Vladimir. 1990. *In Search of Civil Society: Independent Peace Movements in the Soviet Bloc*. New York: Routledge.

Tocqueville, Alexis de. 1972. *Democracy in America*. 2 vols. Edited by Phillips Bradley. New York: Knopf.

Triandis, H. C. 1989. "The Self and Social Behavior in Differing Cultural Contexts." *Psychological Review* 96:506–20.

Troyer, Ronald J. 1989. "Chinese Social Organization." In *Social Control in the People's Republic of China*, edited by Ronald J. Troyer, John P. Clark, and Dean G. Rojek, 26–33. New York: Praeger.

Tsou Tang. 1991. "The Tiananmen Tragedy: The State-Society Relationship, Choices, and Mechanisms in Historical Perspective." In *Contemporary Chinese Politics in Historical Perspective*, edited by Brantly Womack, 265–327. Cambridge: Cambridge University Press.

Tuchman, Gaye. 1972. "Objectivity as Strategic Ritual: An Examination of Newsmen's Notions of Objectivity." *American Journal of Sociology* 77:660–79.

Turner, Ralph H. 1969. "The Public Perception of Protest." *American Sociological Review* 34:815–31.

Turner, Ralph H., and Lewis M. Killian. 1987. *Collective Behavior*. Englewood Cliffs, N.J.: Prentice Hall.

Turner Ralph H., and Samuel J. Surace. 1956. "Zoot-Suiters and Mexicans: Symbols in Crowd Behavior." *American Journal of Sociology* 62:14–20.

Unger, Jonathan. 1982. *Education under Mao: Class and Competition in Canton Schools, 1960–1980*. New York: Columbia University Press.

Useem, Bert. 1980. "Solidarity Model, Breakdown Model, and the Boston Antibusing Movement." *American Sociological Review* 45:357–69.

Vaughan, Michalina, and Margaret Scotford Archer. 1971. *Social Conflict and Educational Change in England and France, 1789–1848*. Cambridge: Cambridge University Press.

Vogel, Ezra F. 1989. *One Step Ahead in China: Guangdong under Reform*. Cambridge, Mass.: Harvard University Press.

von Eschen, Donald, Jerome Kirk, and Maurice Pinard. 1971. "The Organizational Substructure of Disorderly Politics." *Social Forces* 49:529–44.

Wachman, Alan M. 1994. *Taiwan: National Identity and Democratization*. Armonk, N.Y.: Sharpe.

Wade, Robert. 1990. *Governing the Market: Economic Theory and the Role of Government in East Asian Industrialization*. Princeton, N.J.: Princeton University Press.

Wagner, Marsha L. 1990. "The Strategies of the Student Democracy Movement in Beijing." In *Tiananmen: China's Struggle for Democracy*, edited by Winston L. Y. Yang and Marsha L. Wagner, 43–80. Baltimore: University of Maryland.

Wakeman, Frederic, Jr. 1993. "The Civil Society and Public Sphere Debate: Western Reflections on Chinese Political Culture." *Modern China* 19:108–38.

Walder, Andrew G. 1986. *Communist Neo-Traditionalism: Work and Authority in Chinese Industry*. Berkeley: University of California Press.

———. 1990. "Economic Reform and Income Distribution in Tianjin, 1976–1986." In *Chinese Society on the Eve of Tiananmen*, edited by Deborah Davis, and Ezra F. Vogel, 135–56. Cambridge: Harvard University Press.

———. 1991a. "Workers and the State: The Reform Era and the Political Crisis of 1989." *China Quarterly*, no. 127:467–92.

———. 1991b. "Popular Protest in the Chinese Democracy Movement of 1989." *UCLA-CSA Working Papers*, no. 6.

Walder, Andrew G., and Gong Xiaoxia. 1993. "Workers in the Tiananmen Protests: The Politics of the Beijing Workers' Autonomous Federation." *The Australian Journal of Chinese Affairs*, no. 29:1–29.

Wang Chaohua. 1992a. "Luelun xuesheng de qunti xingxiang ji yingxiang" (A preliminary discussion of the group image of the students and its impact). *Minzhu zhongguo*, no. 10:75–80.

———. 1992b. "Wo suozhidao de duihuatuan" (What I know about the dialogue delegation). *China Spring*, no. 7:15–17.

———. 1993. "Woyu shier xuezhe shang guangchang" (I went to Tiananmen Square with the twelve scholars). *China News Digest*, no. 12:24–32.

Wang Dianqing et al. 1990. "Dui dangqian shoudu daxuesheng de sixiang zhuangkuang, zouxiang ji jiaoyu duice de yanjiu" (Research on Beijing students' current state of mind, its trends and educational strategies). In *Dui bashi niandai shoudu daxuesheng zongxiang yanjiu* (Longitudinal studies on university students in Beijing during the 1980s), edited by Lixin Cang, 128–37. Beijing: Beijing Shifan Xueyuan Chubanshe.

Wang Fuyi. 1989. "Tieliu dongjin Tiananmen" (Iron wave eastward to Tiananmen). In *Jieyan yiri*, 1:84–91. Beijing: Jiefangjun Wenyi Chubanshe.

Wang Guisheng. 1989. "Guanyu Leifeng de dianxing xiaoying ruohua wenti de sikao" (A reflection on the weakening of the Leifeng spirit). *Dangdai qingnian yanjiu* nos. 7, 8:26–29.

Wang Hongwei. 1989. "Rexue Junhun" (The righteous army spirit). In *Jieyan yiri*, 1:194–97. Beijing: Jiefangjun Wenyi Chubanshe.

Wang Jing. 1996. *High Culture Fever*. Berkeley: University of California Press.

Wang Jintang. 1990. "Xiaoyuan rexianxiang yanjiu" (An analysis of the fever phenomenon on university campuses). *Qingnian gongzuo luntan*, no. 1:15–17.

Wang Meng and Zhao Shilin. 1994. "Huashuo jinri zhongguoren de wenhua xintai" (The cultural mentality of today's Chinese). *Zhongguo qingnian*, no. 3:14–15.

Wang Shaoguang. 1990. "Analyzing the Role of Chinese Workers in the Protest Movement of 1989." In *China: The Crisis of 1989, Origins and Implications*, edited by Roger V. DesForges, Luo Ning, and Wu Yen-bo, 245–57. Buffalo: Council on International Studies and Programs State University of New York at Buffalo. Special Studies, no. 158.

Wang Xiaodong and Qiu Tiancao. 1992. "The Shadow in Passion: A Critique of the Television Series *River Elegy.*" *Chinese Sociology and Anthropology* 24, no. 2:57–62.

Wang Xiaoqiang and Bai Nanfeng. 1986. *Furao de pinkun—zhongguo luohoudiqu de jingji kaocha* (The poverty of the rich—the economic problems of the underdeveloped regions in China). Chengdu: Sichuan Renmin Chubanshe.

Wang Ying, Zhe Xiaoye, and Sun Bingyao. 1993. *Shehui zhongjianceng: gaige yu zhongguo de shetuan zuzhi* (The social middle layer: the reform and the development of associations). Beijing: Zhongguo Fazhan Chubanshe.

Wank, David L. 1995. "Civil Society in Communist China? Private Business and Political Alliance, 1989." In *Civil Society: Theory, History, Comparison*, edited by John A. Hall, 56–59. Cambridge, UK: Polity Press.

Warner, W. Lloyd. 1963. *Yankee City*. New Haven: Yale University Press.

Wasserman, Stanley, and Katherine Faust. 1997. *Social Network Analysis: Methods and Applications*. Cambridge: Cambridge University Press.

Wasserstrom, Jeffrey N. 1991. *Student Protests in Twentieth-century China: The View From Shanghai*. Stanford, Calif.: Stanford University Press.

Wasserstrom, Jeffrey N., and Elizabeth J. Perry. eds. 1992. *Popular Protest and Political Culture in Modern China*. Boulder, Colo.: Westview Press.

Weber, Max. 1978. "The Nature of Social Action." In *Max Weber: Selections in Translation*, edited by W. G. Runciman and E. Mathews, 7–32. Cambridge: Cambridge University Press.

Wei Jingsheng. 1980. "The Fifth Modernization." In *The Fifth Modernization: China's Human Rights Movement, 1978–1979*, 47–69. New York: Human Rights Pub. Group.

Weil, Frederick D., ed. 1996. *Research on Democracy and Society: Extremism, Protest, Social Movements, and Democracy*. Greenwich, Conn.: JAI Press.

Werlen, Benno. 1993. *Society, Action and Space: An Alternative Human Geography*. London: Routledge.

White, Gordon. 1993. *Riding the Tiger: The Politics of Economic Reform in Post-Mao China*. Stanford, Calif.: Stanford University Press.

Whyte, Martin King. 1981. "Distratification and Restratification in China." In *Social Inequality: Comparative and Developmental Approaches*, edited by Gerald D. Berreman, 309–36. New York: Academic Press

———. 1992. "Urban China: A Civil Society in the Making?" In *State and Society in China: The Consequences of Reform*, edited by Arthur Lewis Rosenbaum, 77–101. Boulder, Colo.: Westview Press.

Whyte, Martin King, and William L. Parish. 1984. *Urban Life in Contemporary China*. Chicago: University of Chicago Press.

Wickham-Crowley, Timothy P. 1992. *Guerrillas and Revolution in Latin America: A Comparative Study of Insurgents and Regimes since 1956.* Princeton, N.J.: Princeton University Press.

Williams, Gwyneth I., and Rhys H. Williams. 1995. "'All We Want Is Equality': Rhetorical Framing in the Fathers' Rights Movement." In *Images of Issues: Typifying Contemporary Social Problems,* 2d ed., edited by Joel Best, 191–212. New York: Aldine De Gruyter.

Wilson, James Q. 1973. *Political Organizations.* New York: Basic Books.

Wolfe, Alan. 1977. *The Limits of Legitimacy.* New York: Free Press.

Wong, R. Bin. 1997. *China Transformed: Historical Change and the Limits of European Experience.* Ithaca, N.Y.: Cornell University Press.

World Journal. 1999a. "Changsha shiwei shuji yang baohua bei tingzhi" (The Changsha CCP Secretary Yang Baohua was suspended from his post). April 3.

World Journal. 1999b. "Shenyang xiagang gongren, qingyuan cishu jingren" (An astonishing rate of protest activities by the unemployed workers in Shenyang). April 13.

Worms, Jean-Pierre. 1971. "The Earliest Universities." In *Student Activism: Town and Gown in Historical Perspective,* edited by Alexander DeConde, 72–86. New York: Charles Scribner's Sons.

Wu Daying and Yang Haijiao. 1999. *You zhongguo tese de shehuizhuyi minzhu zhengzhi* (A socialist democracy with Chinese characteristics). Beijing: Shehui Kexue Wenxian Chubanshe.

Wu Dayuan. 1993. "Gaoxiao sixiang zhengzhi gongzuo de kunhuo yu chulu" (Dilemma and solutions of political education in universities). *Shandong Qingnian Guanli Ganbu Xueyuan Xuebao,* no. 2:46–49.

Wu Mouren, Bao Minghui, Ni Peihua, Ni Peimin, and Wang Qingjia, eds. 1989. *Bajiu zhongguo minyun jishi* (Daily accounts on the 1989 democracy movement in China). N.p.

Wu Ren. 1990a. "Wuyue fengbo de qiyuan yu fazhan" (The causes and development of the May incident). *Qingnian yanjiu,* no. 10:1–19.

———. 1990b. "Wuyue fengbo de qiyin yu fazhan; dierbufen: 'fengbo' de quanguocheng (yanjiu ziliao)" (The causes and development of the May incident, II: The whole development of the incident [research materials]). *Qingnian yanjiu,* nos. 11, 12:29–93.

Wu Yan and Zhang Xuehu. 1988. "Guandao xianxiang tanxi" (An analysis of the official corruption phenomenon). *Gongren ribao,* Aug. 24.

Wushitian de huigu yu fansi (Retrospection and rethinking of the fifty days), (Internal circulation only). 1989. Beijing: Gaodeng Jiaoyu Chubanshe.

Xi Bing. 1988. "Kexue yu minzhu jingshen de yang—cong Liu Binyan dao Su Xiaokang" (The development of the spirit of science and democracy—from Liu Binyan to Su Xiaokang). In *Ziyou beiwanglu—Su Xiaokang quanjing baogao wenxueji*

(Free memorandum—a collection of panorama reportage novels by Su Xiaokang), 388–99. Beijing: Zhongguo Shehui Kexue Chubanshe.

Xiang Xiaoji. 1995. "Weile zhongguo shehui zhi gongzheng" (For a fair society in China). *Beijing Spring*, no. 8:71–77.

Xiao Qinfu. 1989. "Diwuci langchao: jingshangre" (The fifth wave: the commercial fever). In *Wuci langchao* (five waves), edited by Xiao Qinfu, 191–261. Beijing: Zhongguo Renmin Daxue Chubanshe.

Xie Li. 1993. "Shenshen xuezi zhengqianmang" (Students were eager to earn money). *Zhongguo qingnian*, no. 3:16–18.

Xiong Yan. 1992. "Xiong Yan caifanglu" (An interview with Xiong Yan) *Press Freedom Guardian*, June 26.

Xu Changhua and Liu Ping. 1985. "Daxuesheng sushe de yanjiu" (Research on student dormitories in universities). *Qingnian yanjiu*, no. 6:26–30.

Xu Deheng. 1987. *Weile minzhu yu kexue* (For science and democracy). Beijing: Zhongguo Qingnian Chubanshe.

Xu Jiatun. 1993. *Xu Jiatun huiyilu* (A memoir of Xu Jiatun). Hong Kong: Xianggang Lianhebao Youxian Gongsi.

Xuanchuan Tongxun. 1988. "Dangqian benshi minqing minyi diaocha fenxi" (Analysis of surveys of current public opinion in Shanghai), (Internal circulation only). No.14:24–27.

Xue Wenxiang. 1989. "Qingnian xinjiao de xianzhuang jiqi yuanyin" (The religious youth, the reality, and its causes). *Dangdai qingnian yanjiu*, nos. 7, 8:17–19.

Xuese de Liming (A Bloody Morning). 1989. Hong Kong: Chi Keung Publishing Co.

Yan Dongyin. 1898. "Qu Dahuitang, genwozou" (Follow me, if you go to the Great Hall of the People). In *Jieyan yiri*, 2:192–200. Beijing: Jiefangjun Wenyi Chubanshe.

Yan Jiaqi. 1992. *Toward a Democratic China: The Intellectual Autobiography of Yan Jiaqi.* Translated by David S. K. Hong and Denis C. Mair. Honolulu: University of Hawaii Press.

Yan Ming. 1989. "Sociology in China: Its Past, Present, and Future." *Chinese Sociology and Anthropology* 22, no. 1:3–29.

Yan Ting and Li Peier. 1989. "Yongzai—Gongren Gansidui" (Bravehearts—The Workers' Dare-to-die Corps). In *Renmin buhui wangji* (People Won't Forget), edited by sixty-four Hong Kong journalists, 131–35. Hong Kong: Hong Kong Journalist Association.

Yang Chung-fang. 1991. "Conformity and Defiance on Tiananmen Square: A Social Psychological Perspective." In *Culture and Politics in China*, edited by Peter Li, Steven Mark, and Marjorie H. Li, 197–224. New Brunswick, N.J.: Transaction Publishers.

Yang Dongping and Chen Ziming. 1984. "Liushi niandai qingnian de guoqu yu xianzai" (The youth of the sixties, its past and present). *Dangdai qingnian yanjiu*, no. 10:6–12.

Yang Guansan. 1989. "The Social Psychological Environment for the 1987 Reform." *Chinese Sociology and Anthropology* 22, no. 2:21–41.

Yang Guansan, Yang Xiaodong, and Xuan Mingdong. 1987. "The Public Response to Price Reform." In *Reform in China: Challenges and Choices: A Summary and Analysis of the CESRRI Survey*, edited by Bruce L. Reynolds, 59–73. New York: Sharpe.

Yang Liwei. 1989. "Youxie yongren danwei tuihui daxuesheng xianxiang dui daxue-sheng de yingxiang" (Some employers returned students to the universities: the phenomenon and its impact on students). *Shehuixue yu shehui diaocha*, no. 2:37–41.

Yang Qingfu. 1989. "Jianku rennai de santiansanye" (Three long days and nights). In *Jieyan yiri*, 1:20–25. Beijing: Jiefangjun Wenyi Chubanshe.

Yang Shangkun. 1990. "Main Points of Yang Shangkun's Speech at the Emergency Enlarged Meeting of the Central Military Commission." In *Beijing Spring, 1989: Confrontation and Conflict*, edited by Michel Oksenberg, Lawrence R. Sullivan, and Marc Lambert, 320–27. Armonk, N.Y.: Sharpe.

Yang Xiong. 1991. "Shinian fengyu zaihuishou—80 niandai daxuesheng redian zhuisu yu sikao" (A glance at the past ten years—rethinking the fevers among the university students of the eighties). *Qingnian tansuo*, no. 6:15–19.

Yang Xiaowei and Cui Shaopeng. 1989. "Dierci langchao: congzhengre" (The second wave: the political career fever). In *Wuci langchao* (Five waves), edited by Xiao Qinfu, 36–97. Beijing: Zhongguo Renmin Daxue Chubanshe.

Yao Yilin. 1987. "Yaoerjiu yundong de huiyi" (A memoir on the December 9th Movement). In *Yaoerjiu yundong* (December 9th Movement), edited by Zhonggong Beijing shiwei dangshi ziliao zhengji weiyuanhui (the party history council of the CCP Beijing Committee), 321–31. Beijing: Zhonggong Dangshi Ziliao Chubanshe.

———. 1989. "Zai zhonggong zhongyang, guowuyuan zhaokai de gebumen fuze-tongzhi huiyishang de jianghua" (A speech at the meeting of leaders of different departments of the communist party central committee and state council). *Xuanchuan tongxun*, no. 13:16–18.

Ye Yonglie. 1988. "Bajin de meng" (The nightmare of Ba Jin). *Xinhua wenzhai*, no. 11:86–94.

Yeh Wen-hsin. 1990. *The Alienated Academy: Culture and Politics in Republican China, 1919–1937*. Cambridge, Mass.: Harvard University Press.

Yu Yingshi. 1992. "Zailun zhongguo xiandai sixiang zhongde jijin yu baoshou—Da Jiang Yihua xiansheng" (Further discussion on radicalism and conservatism in modern Chinese thought—a rejoinder to Mr. Jiang Yihua), *Ershiyi shiji*, no. 4:143–49.

Yuan Mu. 1989. "Guowuyuan fayanren Yuan Mu zai zhongnanhai jizhe zhaodaihui shang de fayan" (The spokesman of the State Council Yuan Mu's speech at a press conference held at Zhongnanhai). In *Bajiu zhongguo minyun jishi* (Daily account on the 1989 Democracy Movement in China), edited by Wu Mouren et al., 736–38. N.p.

Zald, Mayer N. 1996. "Culture, Ideology, and Strategic Framing," In *Comparative Perspectives on Social Movements,* edited by Doug McAdam, John D. McCarthy, and Mayer N. Zald, 261–74. New York: Cambridge University Press.

Zhang Bingsheng and Deng Haiyun. 1989. "Miandui 21 shiji de tiaozhan—Beijing diqu gaodeng yuanxiao qingnian jiaoshi duiwu diaocha" (Facing the challenge of the 21th century—an investigation on young teachers in Beijing's universities). *Guangming Daily,* April 15.

Zhang Boli. 1994a. "Jueshi qianhou" (Around the hunger strike period). *China Spring,* no. 8:57–60.

———. 1994b. "Cong jueshi dao fushi" (Hunger strike, from its beginning to end, I) *China Spring* nos. 3, 4:72–76.

———. 1994c. "Cong jueshi dao fushi" (Hunger strike, from its beginning to end, II) *China Spring,* no. 5:45–48.

———. 1994d. "Cong jueshi dao fushi—baowei Tiananmen guangchang" (Hunger strike, from its beginning to end—defending Tiananmen Square) *China Spring,* no. 6:56–58.

———. 1994e. "Huiyi Tiananmen minzhu daxue" (Recollections of the Tiananmen Square democracy university). *China Spring,* no. 1:84–89.

Zhang Guozuo. 1989. "Fansi chuantong wenhua bixu shishi qiushi—ping 'Heshang' dui lishi de waiqu" (Introspection on tradition must be based on facts—on *River Elegy*'s distortion of history). *Guangming Daily,* Sept. 11.

Zhang Jian and Zhou Yuliang. 1989. *China Education Yearbook: 1948–1984.* Changsha: Hunan Jiaoyu Chubanshe.

Zhang Kun. 1989. "Jiangjun tuoxianji" (Saving the general out of danger). In *Jieyan yiri,* 2:283–95. Beijing: Jiefangjun Wenyi Chubanshe.

Zhang Xibo. 1989. "Womenzai benjin" (Marching forward). In *Jieyan yiri,* 1:167–74. Beijing: Jiefangjun Wenyi Chubanshe.

Zhang Yunhou, Yin Xuli, Hong Qingxiang, and Wang Yunkai. 1979. *Wusi shiqi de shetuan* (Mass organizations during the May 4th era). Beijing: Sanlian Publishing House.

Zhao Dingxin. 1994. "Defensive Regime and Modernization." *Journal of Contemporary China,* no. 7:28–46.

———. 1996. "Foreign Study as a Safety-valve: The Experience of China's University Students Going Abroad in the Eighties." *Higher Education* 31:145–63.

———. 1998. "Ecologies of Social Movements: Student Mobilization During the 1989 Pro-democracy Movement in Beijing." *American Journal of Sociology* 103:1493–529.

Zhao Dingxin and John A. Hall. 1994. "State Power and Patterns of Late Development: Resolving the Crisis of the Sociology of Development." *Sociology* 28:211–29.

Zhao Guangxian. 1989. "Cong lishi de shijiao ping Heshang" (A comment on the *River Elegy* from a historical perspective). *Guangming Daily,* August 23.

Zhao Lumin. 1989. "'7083' budui" ('7083' unit). In *Jieyan yiri*, 2:189–91. Beijing: Jiefangjun Wenyi Chubanshe.

Zhao Qiang, Ge Jing, and Si Yuan. 1990. *Xuerande fengcai* (Red leaves). Hong Kong: Haiyan Chuban Gongsi.

Zhao Suisheng. 1997. "Chinese Intellectuals' Quest for National Greatness and Nationalistic Writing in the 1990s." *China Quarterly*, no. 152:725–45.

Zhao Xiaoqiang. 1989. "Wo suojinglide kaijin yu qingchang" (My personal experiences during the army advancement and Tiananmen Square evacuation). In *Jieyan yiri*, 2:208–15. Beijing: Jiefangjun Wenyi Chubanshe.

Zhao Xinshu and Shen Peilu. 1993. "Some Reasons Why the Party Propaganda Failed This Time." In *Chinese Democracy and the Crisis of 1989*, edited by Roger V. Des Forges, Luo Ning, and Wu Yen-bo, 313–32. Albany: State University of New York Press.

Zhao Xinshu and Xie Yu. 1992. "Western Influence on [People's Republic of China] Chinese Students in the United States." *Comparative Education Review* 36:509–29.

Zhao Yining. 1995. "Zhongguo jingji xunqiu ruanzhaolu" (The Chinese economy seeks a soft landing). *Outlook Weekly*, no. 28:22–23.

Zhao Yuezhi. 1998. *Media, Market and Democracy in China: Between the Party Line and the Bottom Line.* Urbana and Chicago: University of Illinois Press.

Zhao Zixiang. 1986. "Zhongguo shehuixue chongjian lueying" (A short review on the re-establishment process of Chinese sociology). *Xinhua wenzhai*, no. 4:12–15.

Zhao Ziyang. 1990a. "Students' Reasonable Demands to be Met through Democratic, Legal Channels: Zhao." In *Beijing Spring, 1989: Confrontation and Conflict*, edited by Michel Oksenberg, Lawrence R. Sullivan, and Marc Lambert, 254–56. Armonk, N.Y.: Sharpe.

———. 1990b. "Make Further Efforts to Carry Forward the May 4th Spirit in the New Age of Construction and Reform." In *Beijing Spring, 1989: Confrontation and Conflict*, edited by Michel Oksenberg, Lawrence R. Sullivan, and Marc Lambert, 244–51. Armonk, N.Y.: Sharpe.

———. 1994. "Zhao Ziyang zibianshu" (Zhao Ziyang's self-defense). *China Spring*, no. 7:8–14.

Zheng Yi. 1993. *Lishi de yibufen—yongyuan jibuchu de shiyifengxin* (Part of the history—eleven forever undeliverable letters). Taibei: Wanxiang Chuban Gongsi.

Zheng Yongnian. 1999. *Discovering Chinese Nationalism in China.* Cambridge: Cambridge University Press.

Zhonggong Beijing Shiwei Bangongting (The general office of CCP Beijing Committee). 1989. Beijing: Beijing Ribao Chubanshe.

Zhongguo Gaodeng Jiaoyu Daquan (An encyclopedia of Chinese higher education). 1989. Beijing: Gaodeng Jiaoyu Chubanshe.

Zhou, Kate Xiao. 1996. *How the Farmers Changed China: Power of the People.* Boulder, Colo.: Westview Press.

Zhou Xiaochuan and Yang Zhigang. 1992. *Zhongguo caishui tizhi de wenti yu chulu* (The problems and solutions of Chinese finance and taxation system). Tianjin: Tianjin Renmin Chubanshe.

Zhou Xueguang. 1993. "Unorganized Interests and Collective Action in Communist China." *American Sociological Review* 58:54−73.

Zhou Yongjun. 1993. "Liusipai buneng zaida: caifang tiananmen xuesheng lingxiu Zhou Yongjun" (The June 4th cards should no longer be played: an interview with student leader Zhou Yongjun). *China Spring*, no. 4:54−60.

Zhu Ling. 1991. *Rural Reform and Peasant Income in China: The Impact of China's Post-Mao Rural Reforms in Selected Regions.* New York: St. Martin's Press.

Zhu Rongji. 1989. *Jiefang ribao*, May 23, June 9.

Zhu Shuangxi. 1989. "Liangdui liangjin doushiqing" (Twice back, twice forward, our affection for the people). In *Jieyan yiri*, 1:209−12. Beijing: Jiefangjun Wenyi Chubanshe.

Zhu Wentao. 1988. "Lingren shensi de xiaoyuan xinchao" (The worrysome new waves on campuses). *Shehui*, no. 8:8−11.

Zhu Zhonghua. 1982. "Liushisannianqian shanghai xuelian shouchong zujie jishi" (Recollection of a student union-led demonstration in the Shanghai foreign concession). *Tuanjiebao*, July 31.

Zi Chao. 1988. "Youhuan xingbang" (Crisis consciousness stimulates development of a nation). *People's Daily*, Sept. 5.

Zi Ye. 1993. "Renmin ribao: sanshiba xiaoshi de zhengzha." (The last 38 hours of resistance at the *People's Daily*). *China News Digest*, Supplementary, no. 21 (June 28): 1−9.

Zou Jiping and Robert D. Benford. 1995. "Mobilization Processes and the 1989 Chinese Democracy Movement." *The Sociological Quarterly* 36:131−56.

Name Index

Subject Index

DATE DUE
